ALL THAT WAS
PROMISED

OTHER BOOKS BY BLAINE YORGASON

Charlie's Monument

Finding Mercie

One Tattered Angel

Secrets

Spiritual Survival in the Last Days

The Windwalker

ALL THAT WAS
PROMISED

The St. George Temple
and the Unfolding of the Restoration

BLAINE M. YORGASON

Richard A. Schmutz and Douglas D. Alder

DESERET
BOOK

Salt Lake City, Utah

Visit us at DeseretBook.com

Library of Congress Cataloging-in-Publication Data
Yorgason, Blaine M., 1942–   author.
  All that was promised : the St. George Temple and the unfolding of the Restoration / Blaine M. Yorgason, with Richard A. Schmutz and Douglas D. Alder.
      pages cm
  Includes bibliographical references and index.
  ISBN 978-1-60907-367-1 (hardbound : alk. paper)
  ISBN 978-1-62972-299-3 (paperbound)
  1. St. George Temple (Saint George, Utah)—History. I. Schmutz, Richard A., 1925– author. II. Alder, Douglas D., author. III. Title.
  BX8685.S34Y67 2013
  289.3'79248—dc23   2012047360

Printed in the United States of America
Brigham Young University Press, Provo, UT

10 9 8 7 6 5 4 3 2 1

CONTENTS

IN GRATITUDE vii

PROLOGUE 1

Chapter 1
A SACRIFICE OF ALL THINGS, 1859–1861 16

Chapter 2
FIVE YEARS OF STARVATION, 1861–1866 42

Chapter 3
THE WILDERNESS SLOWLY RETREATS, 1866–1871 66

Chapter 4
BRIGHAM YOUNG'S DECISION, 1870–1871 77

Chapter 5
A TEMPLE'S BEGINNINGS, 1871 80

Chapter 6
UNEXPECTED CHALLENGES, 1871–1872 96

Chapter 7
THE WHOLE TERRITORY PITCHES IN, 1873 113

Chapter 8
THE WALLS CLIMB UPWARD, January to November 1874 136

Contents

Chapter 9
THE JOURNAL KEEPER, Winter 1874 152

Chapter 10
TROUBLE ON TRUMBULL, January through March 1875 167

Chapter 11
THE TEMPLE TRAILS, Spring into Summer 1875 183

Chapter 12
THE FONT AND OTHER TRIUMPHS,
July through December 1875 197

Chapter 13
PREPARING TO OPEN, Fall to Winter 1875 217

Chapter 14
A CHANGE IN LEADERSHIP, 1876 230

Chapter 15
PREPARING FOR THE TEMPLE DEDICATION,
November through December 1876 248

Chapter 16
FIRST DEDICATION, 1 January 1877 269

Chapter 17
AN ASTOUNDING DEVELOPMENT, January to 1 March 1877 279

Chapter 18
BRIGHAM YOUNG'S WORK
IS COMPLETED, 2 March to 29 August 1877 291

Chapter 19
FOR WHOM IS THE WORK TO BE DONE? 1877 303

Chapter 20
THE HONEYMOON TRAIL, 1877 and Onward 312

Chapter 21
THE ST. GEORGE TEMPLE, Then and Now 317

Chapter 22
WHY COME TO THE TEMPLE TODAY? 343

Appendix
PIONEERS OF ST. GEORGE, UTAH 349

INDEX 365

IN GRATITUDE

This book is dedicated to the memory of every man, woman, and child who courageously braved the hardships of the desert wilderness in obedience to their prophet and who selflessly gave their all that the St. George Temple might move from fondest dream to sacred reality.

No volume, particularly one that draws from so many personal accounts, is ever compiled without the generous assistance of others. In this case the story of the St. George Temple began with a youthful prophet by the name of Joseph Smith Jr., to whom we and millions of others owe an eternal debt of gratitude on an infinite number of levels, one of which was his worthiness to receive the ministration and sealing keys of Elijah. Then there is Brigham Young, who by the same personal efforts and authority led the newly restored church into the wilderness, and there in the fires of constant adversity forged a cohesive yet earthly kingdom of God. Once he had been called to take the lead in building the first temple in the West, Wilford Woodruff, through personal inspiration and revelation and significant adversity of his own, joined Brigham Young in establishing and codifying all the temple work for both the living and the dead. Such a volume as this could not exist without these three stalwart Church presidents, and we thank them for giving us all this to cherish.

Then came the workers to tiny, primitive, out-of-the-way St. George—the builders and laborers in a physical sense—perhaps as many as two thousand men and women from throughout the Territory of

Utah who accepted calls and came for a winter or for the rest of their lives; it didn't seem to matter to them how long they served, so long as they "wore out their lives" in service. Next came laborers within the finally dedicated temple who had been called to serve the Lord—hundreds and then thousands of men and women who were each called and set apart to administer the sacred ordinances, to record and keep track of the same, to pronounce sealing blessings, and to preside over all the work within the temple as ordinance workers, members of presidencies, matrons, their assistants, recorders, and a host of others. In 2012, more than 2,300 individuals are serving in the St. George Temple, almost all of them volunteers. Our story could never have been told without these wonderfully generous men and women and their families, extending back through the past 140-plus years, and we thank them for their service.

We are grateful also to the numerous men and women who have shared with us personal accounts recorded by their ancestors concerning either their involvement in the settling of St. George and Washington County or in furthering the building of the St. George Temple through the 1870s. While it is not possible to name all the contributors or even to accurately number the men and women who heeded the Lord's call to come and build the temple, to each and every one who so contributed, we express our most sincere and heartfelt appreciation.

In spite of our best efforts, however, we recognize that we have not found the records of every man and woman who gave of themselves in the raising up of the St. George Temple. This saddens us, for not only are we certain that many precious and even sacred experiences concerning life in this desert country and the building of the temple have been missed, but we are just as certain that these experiences were as essential to the building of the temple as any we have recorded here. To those individuals we also express our deepest gratitude—and our sincere hope that in a coming day others will locate and compile those records, and all of us will be treated to the sacred witness of their lives and labor.

We are grateful to Jeanine Vander Bruggen, president of the Daughters of Utah Pioneers McQuarrie Memorial Museum board of directors in St. George, Utah. When Jeanine learned of our effort, she went into the museum's files, copied dozens and dozens of personal accounts by or about Washington County settlers or temple builders and then hand-delivered them to us so we could push forward the work.

Without each of these mostly unpublished accounts, which ultimately numbered in the hundreds, we could never have told the story of the St. George Temple in such a detailed and personal way. In most cases we have retained the spelling and grammar used by the writers of those accounts in order to convey their respective personalities. We have indicated in the notes the occasional departure from that practice.

Finally, we express gratitude to Cory Maxwell, Richard Peterson, Suzanne Brady, and the staff of Deseret Book Company for their time and efforts, which have ultimately turned a sometimes challenging manuscript into something that we hope will bring honor to all who have ever been a part of the glorious work of the St. George Temple, where all that was promised by the prophet Elijah was finally delivered.

PROLOGUE

Central to the restoration of the gospel was the restoration also of temple ordinances and blessings, which were revealed in the first three latter-day temples, in Kirtland, Nauvoo, and St. George. The prophet Elijah restored the keys of the sealing power in Kirtland in 1836. The first baptisms for the dead and the first endowments and sealings for the living took place in Nauvoo in the early 1840s. The first sealings of children to parents and the first endowments for the dead took place in the St. George Temple in 1877.

Brigham Young had urgently wanted to build the Salt Lake Temple because the Saints had been driven out of Nauvoo before he was able to pass the torch of temple work to his successors. So he had designated that temple site on 28 July 1847, just four days after entering the valley, and the Saints started construction in 1853.

After nearly twenty years of on-again, off-again labor, the construction of the Salt Lake Temple was bogged down in a sea of troubles. Brigham could see that he would not live to view the finished temple, yet he held sacred, confidential information and authority in his hands that he could pass along only in a dedicated temple. So he turned his prophetic eye south, toward St. George.

Before we consider the story of the St. George Temple, however, let us remember how Brigham was gifted by the Holy Spirit with Joseph's vision of temple building and temple ordinances, not only receiving the Prophet's vision as his own but developing and enlarging upon it under heaven's guidance. Such a consideration will help explain why Brigham felt driven—and prepared—to complete the St. George Temple during his lifetime.

Rarely have two men been less alike in appearance and tempera-ment yet closer in mind and heart than Joseph Smith and Brigham Young. According to Hugh Nibley: "Brigham Young was the Prophet Joseph's most faithful disciple"[1] and "boundless admirer."[2] "Their teach-ings are one as the minds of the saints and prophets have always been one."[3] When Joseph spoke, Brigham wholeheartedly believed him—and did all in his power to obey the counsel of his Prophet. Throughout his many years as Church president, Brigham never tired of proclaiming Joseph's virtues. Consider, for instance, the following:

"The secret feeling of my heart was . . . that if I could see the face of a Prophet, such as had lived on the earth in former times, a man that had revelations, to whom the heavens were opened, who knew God and his character. . . . I would [be willing to crawl around] the earth on my hands and knees" to see such a man.[4] "When I first heard [Joseph] preach . . . he took heaven, figuratively speaking, and brought it down to earth; and he took the earth, brought it up, and opened up,

---

1. Hugh Nibley, *Nibley on the Timely and the Timeless: Classic Essays of Hugh W. Nibley* (Provo, Utah: Brigham Young University, Religious Studies Center, 1978), vol. 1 in the Religious Studies Monograph series, 234.

2. Hugh Nibley, *Brother Brigham Challenges the Saints* (Salt Lake City: Deseret Book, 1994), 517.

3. Nibley, *Timely and Timeless*, 234.

4. *Journal of Discourses*, 26 vols. (London: Latter-day Saints' Book Depot, 1854–86), 8:228; 4:104.

in plainness and simplicity, the things of God."[5] After that "I had but one prayer, and I offered it all the time, and that was that I might be permitted to hear Joseph speak on doctrine, and see his mind reach out untrammeled to grasp the deep things of God. . . . An angel never watched him closer."[6] "I do not think that a man lived [who] paid more attention to the teachings of Joseph Smith than I did. I studied his words. I learned by them and by the revelations of the Holy Spirit and by visions. I have pondered these things in my heart."[7] "I never did let an opportunity pass of . . . hearing him speak in public or in private, so that I might draw understanding from the fountain from which he spoke, . . . such moments were more precious to me than all the wealth of the world."[8] "Joseph Smith was [the] man called of God to build up his kingdom in the last days, preparatory to the coming of the Son of Man."[9] And how did he do it? By receiving for "the faithful line upon line, precept upon precept."[10] "How came . . . this [Church] organization we now enjoy? It came by revelation . . . step by step."[11]

One of the most significant of these revelations—God's law of eternal progression toward exaltation—came gradually, one step at a time over several years, and ultimately drove each of them more than any other. For Joseph, it was a matter of receiving the information, visitations, and ordinances necessary to enable an individual to become like God. For Brigham, it was finding a way to explain these wondrous

---

5. *Journal of Discourses*, 5:332; Nibley, *Brother Brigham*, 347.

6. Ronald K. Esplin, *The Emergence of Brigham Young and the Twelve to Mormon Leadership, 1830–1841* (Provo, Utah: Brigham Young University, 2006), 49.

7. Brigham Young, St. George stake conference, Sunday, 5 November 1871, as recorded by James G. Bleak, in "Historian Southern Mission Mem. Book, Commencing April 6, 1871," n.p., holograph; photocopy in possession of the authors. See also Box 1, James G. Bleak Papers, Dixie State University Special Collections, St. George, Utah, hereafter cited as Dixie State University Special Collections.

8. *Journal of Discourses*, 12:269–70.

9. *Journal of Discourses*, 1:81–82.

10. Doctrine and Covenants 98:12.

11. *Journal of Discourses*, 9:88–89.

things to even the least knowledgeable of the Saints and implementing them so clearly and certainly that not only a special few but thousands and even millions of the Saints who desired it with all their hearts might actually reach for such lofty heights.

"What are we here for?" Brigham asked his listeners as he sought to prepare them, to guide their minds and hearts toward unlimited spiritual expansion. "To learn to enjoy more, and to increase in knowledge and experience."[12] "We shall never cease to learn, unless we apostatize. . . . Can you understand that?"[13] "God has given us mental and physical powers to be improved,"[14] and "our senses, if properly educated, are channels of endless felicity to us."[15] "Let us not narrow ourselves up, for the world, with all its variety of useful information and its rich hoard of hidden treasure, is before us, and eternity, with all its sparkling intelligence, lofty aspirations, and unspeakable glories, is before us."[16] "And when we have passed into that sphere where Joseph is, there is still another department, and then another, and another, and so on to an eternal progression in exaltation and eternal lives. That is the exaltation I am looking for."[17] And after hearing such simple good sense again and again, most of Brigham's people began to grasp the concept.

It is unclear how soon the doctrine of priesthood ordinances that were essential for exaltation became a part of Joseph's and therefore Brigham's thinking. We do know that the reception of the doctrine followed the Lord's pattern of giving Joseph "line upon line," or moving from "one department to another," as Brigham described it: baptism, confirmation and the gift of the Holy Ghost, sacramental cleansing and

---

12. *Journal of Discourses*, 14:228.

13. *Journal of Discourses*, 3:203.

14. *Journal of Discourses*, 10:231.

15. *Journal of Discourses*, 9:244.

16. *Journal of Discourses*, 8:9.

17. *Journal of Discourses*, 3:375; see also Brigham Young, "Discourse—The Secret of Happiness," address delivered in the Third Ward Meeting House, Salt Lake City, Sunday, 23 June 1874 [1876]; Brigham Young's comments in Nibley, *Timely and Timeless.*

covenanting, priesthood ordinations, and finally, requisite temple ordinances. Each was essential to bring salvation and exaltation within the reach of both the living and the dead.

Whenever the knowledge came, this heaven-tutored understanding filled the minds of both prophets with a shared vision of the need for temples and temple ordinances, as well as for ancient Elijah to come and authorize them. In his initial visit to the young prophet Joseph in 1823, the angel Moroni referred to the coming of Elijah who, Moroni said, would "plant in the hearts of the children the promises made to the fathers, and the hearts of the children should turn to their fathers" (D&C 2:2). During the ensuing annual interviews with his prophet apprentice from 1824 to 1827, Moroni gave Joseph Smith "instructions and intelligence . . . , respecting what the Lord was going to do, and how and in what manner his kingdom was to be conducted in the last days" (JS–H 1:54). In the Articles and Covenants of the Church (D&C 20) presented at the organization of the Church in April 1830, Joseph Smith indicated that the first principles and ordinances of the gospel—faith, repentance, baptism by immersion, and the gift of the Holy Ghost—were necessary and available not only for those in this era but also for "all those from the beginning, even as many as were before he [Christ] came (D&C 20:26), as well as for those who came after,"[18] a promise of future work for the dead.

On 3 August 1831, Joseph Smith dedicated property in Independence, Jackson County, Missouri, as the site of a future temple—the first temple site dedicated in this dispensation. The Prophet understood at least the necessity, if not all the purposes, for temples.

On 27 December 1832, shortly after he met Brigham Young for the first time, Joseph was instructed by revelation to build a house to

---

18. Richard E. Bennett, "Line upon Line, Precept upon Precept: Reflections on the 1877 Commencement of the Performance of Endowments and Sealings for the Dead," *BYU Studies* 44, no. 3 (2005).

the Lord in Kirtland.[19] On 5 June 1833, ground was broken and construction began. Master builder and glazier Brigham Young arrived in Kirtland later that fall and became immediately involved. George A. Smith remembered that "Joseph Smith and Brigham Young worked on [the temple] day after day; also, many others did so. They did not have much fine flour bread to eat. Did not always have molasses to eat with their Johnny cake. Sometimes they had shoes, and sometimes not; sometimes they would have tolerable pants, and sometimes very ragged ones."[20]

Three years later, on the evening of Thursday, 21 January 1836, the First Presidency, Brigham and the Twelve Apostles, and other Church authorities met in the attic story of the Kirtland printing office, where they began the ordinance of washing bodies in pure water,[21] the first ordinance to be administered by Joseph since he had learned the proper modes of baptism, confirmation, administering the sacrament, and priesthood ordination. Brigham was there to participate and to learn. Later in the evening, in the west schoolroom on the upper floor of the unfinished temple, Joseph first administered the ordinance of "anointing."[22] On 27 March a solemn assembly was convened in the temple to dedicate and present it to the Lord for his acceptance. In the evening the Prophet gathered the Twelve and other leaders in the temple, where he gave them instructions concerning both the ordinance of washing of feet and sealing these ordinances by "the spirit of

19. Doctrine and Covenants 88:119–20.

20. George A. Smith, "Remarks at the Ground-breaking of the St. George Temple Site," Sunday, 5 November 1871, Box 1, Bleak Papers.

21. J. Christopher Conkling, *A Joseph Smith Chronology* (Salt Lake City: Deseret Book, 1979), 84–85.

22. Leonard J. Arrington, *Brigham Young: American Moses* (Chicago and Urbana: University of Illinois Press, 1986), 53.

prophecy."[23] It was, therefore, in Kirtland that "the ordinances of washings, anointings, and sealing the anointings, were performed."[24]

On Sunday, 3 April 1836, during another assembly held in the newly dedicated temple, in response to the fervent pleadings of Joseph and Oliver Cowdery, the Savior appeared and accepted the temple as His holy house.[25] Then Moses, Elias, and Elijah appeared in succession to deliver their various keys and authorities. Moses bestowed upon them "the keys of the gathering and the return of the Ten Tribes; Elias . . . the keys of the dispensation of Abraham; and Elijah . . . the keys of redemption and sealing."[26] The appearance of Elijah in the temple fulfilled Moroni's prophecy given years before to the youthful Joseph when the angel declared: "The time has fully come . . . to turn the hearts of the fathers to the children, and the children to the fathers, lest the whole earth be smitten with a curse."[27] Thus Elijah passed to the modern prophet the eternal authority to bring the fulness of this glorious work, even exaltation, to pass, saying, "The keys of this dispensation are committed into your hands."[28]

But that was only the beginning. As the Lord added line upon line to Joseph's understanding of Elijah's work, mission, and authority, the Prophet did his best to share with Brigham and the others in his closest circles all he was learning. "No subject preoccupied the Prophet Joseph Smith more than this one," Truman Madsen wrote. "In his later years he [spoke] at least eight times pleading with the Saints to ponder and pray over this principle."[29] In fact, three times in the last year of his

---

23. Arrington, *Brigham Young*, 53. See also Joseph Smith, *History of The Church of Jesus Christ of Latter-day Saints*, edited by B. H. Roberts, 2d ed. rev., 7 vols. (Salt Lake City: The Church of Jesus Christ of Latter-day Saints, 1932–51), 2:410–28.

24. Bennett, "Line upon Line." See also Smith, *History of the Church*, 2:379–80.

25. Doctrine and Covenants 110:1–10.

26. Arrington, *Brigham Young*, 54.

27. Doctrine and Covenants 110:14–15.

28. Doctrine and Covenants 110:16.

29. Truman G. Madsen, *The Temple: Where Heaven Meets Earth* (Salt Lake City: Deseret Book, 2008), 29.

life, Joseph delivered remarkable sermons pertaining to the glorious connection between temples and the mission and power of Elijah, and Brigham was there to hear and ponder upon each of them.

"How shall God come to the rescue of this generation?" Joseph once asked rhetorically. And then in answer to his own question, he replied, "He will send Elijah."[30] Continuing, he explained, "Elijah was the last prophet that held the keys of this priesthood, and who will, before the last dispensation, restore the authority and delive[r] the Keys of this priesthood in order that all the ordinances may be attended to in righteousness."[31]

Brigham clearly understood why Joseph could hardly stop referring to temples, could hardly keep from endeavoring to help his beloved Saints understand that "the main object [of the gathering] in any age of the world . . . was to build unto the Lord an house whereby he could reveal unto his people the ordinances of his house and glories of his kingdom & teach the people the ways of salvation for there are certain ordinances & principles that when they are taught and practiced, must be done in a place prepared for that purpose."[32] "It is for the same purpose that God gathers together the people in the last days . . . to prepare them for the ordinances & endowment . . . &c."[33] "God decreed before the foundation of the world that th[ose] ordinance[s] should be administered in a house prepared for that purpose."[34] "Also The Order & Ordinances of the Kingdom were instituted by the Priesthood in the council of Heaven before the World was."[35]

---

30. Joseph Smith, *Teachings of the Prophet Joseph Smith*, sel. Joseph Fielding Smith (Salt Lake City: Deseret Book, 1976), 159. See also Madsen, *Temple*, 80.

31. Andrew F. Ehat and Lyndon W. Cook, comps. and eds., *The Words of Joseph Smith* (Provo, Utah: Brigham Young University, Religious Studies Center, 1980), 38, 5 October 1840. See also Ehat and Cook, *Words*, 43, 5 October 1840; 40–41, 5 October 1840.

32. Ehat and Cook, *Words*, 212, 11 June 1843.

33. Ehat and Cook, *Words*, 213, 11 June 1843.

34. Ehat and Cook, *Words*, 213, 11 June 1843.

35. Ehat and Cook, *Words*, 215, 11 June 1843.

In 1839 Brigham was "set apart by [Joseph and the First Presidency] as President of the Twelve."[36] As the blessing concluded, Joseph said to Brigham, "While you live no other man can hold this power that is now conferred upon you."[37]

From that day Brigham held priesthood authority sufficient to lead the Church should something happen to Joseph. But there was still much the Prophet needed to impart before Brigham and the Twelve would be ready for that responsibility. This Joseph accomplished through public discourses as well as in numerous private meetings over the next few years. Of these meetings Brigham later stated, "Here are men sitting around me that sat in the Prophet Joseph's secret councils year after year; I refer to the Twelve Apostles and some others; they heard Joseph say thousands of things that the people have never yet heard."[38]

In these meetings Joseph began to open up to the minds of the apostles what he had earlier termed the mysteries of godliness, at the same time bestowing on them an endowment of power along with additional priesthood keys completing their authority to preside over the Church.[39] Concerning his own experience, Brigham noted in his journal on 4 May 1842 that he, Heber Kimball, and Willard Richards had met with Joseph and Hyrum Smith in the upper room of the Prophet's store. There Joseph "taught the ancient order of things for the first time in these last days, and [I] received my [initial ordinances] and endowments." After a period of instruction, Brigham declared that Joseph "administered to us the first ordinances of the endowment, and gave us instructions on the Priesthood and the new and everlasting covenant."[40]

---

36. "Journal of Wandle Mace," n.d., n.p., typescript, Dixie State University Special Collections.

37. "Journal of Wandle Mace."

38. Nibley, *Brother Brigham*, 313.

39. See Doctrine and Covenants 38:32.

40. Arrington, *Brigham Young*, 102. See also Ehat and Cook, *Words*, 21 January 1844:

Wilford Woodruff added: "Joseph Smith first made known to me the very ordinances which we give to the Latter-day Saints in our endowments. I received my endowments under the direction of Joseph Smith [in the room above his store. He] himself organized every endowment in our Church and revealed the same to the Church, and he tried to receive every key of the Aaronic and Melchisedec priesthoods from the hands of the men who held them while in the flesh, and who hold them in eternity."[41]

As for himself, Joseph recorded that he had been "'instructing them [the Twelve and a few others] in the principles and order of the Priesthood,' communicating priesthood keys 'and all those plans and principles by which any one is enabled to secure the fullness of those blessings which have been prepared for the Church of the Firstborn, and come up and abide in the presence of the Eloheim in the eternal worlds.'"[42]

This endowment, a more complete version of which was ultimately given to Church members in the Nauvoo Temple and later in the Council and Endowment Houses in Salt Lake City, was built upon the foundation of the earlier or initial ordinances administered in Kirtland. The Nauvoo ordinances and instructions, given after Elijah's appearance and therefore under his authority, presented the recipients with even greater spiritual power and understanding.

The "spirit, power & calling of Elijah, is that ye have power to hold the keys of the revelations ordinances, oracles powers & endowments

---

"These ordinances were instituted on 28 September 1843 and in the next five months were conferred on twenty men (and their wives, except for those whose names are asterisked): Hyrum Smith, Brigham Young, Heber C. Kimball, Willard Richards, Newell K. Whitney, William Marks, John Taylor, John Smith, Reynolds Cahoon, Alpheus Cutler, Orson Spencer, Orson Hyde*, Parley P. Pratt*, Wilford Woodruff, George A. Smith, Levi Richards*, Cornelius P. Lott, William W. Phelps, Isaac Morley, and Orson Pratt.*"

41. *Journal of Discourses*, 23:131, 14 May 1882.
42. Richard O. Cowan, *Temples to Dot the Earth* (Salt Lake City: Bookcraft, 1989), 224. See also Wilford Woodruff, *Journal*, 1833–1898, ed. Scott G. Kenney, 9 vols. (Midvale, Utah: Signature, 1983), 2:289, 9 September 1843; 2:161, 20 March 1842.

of the fulness of the Melchizedek Priesthood & of the Kingdom of God on the Earth & to receive, obtain & perform all the ordinances belonging to the Kingdom of God even unto the sealing of the fathers unto the children and the hearts of the children unto the fathers even those who are in heaven.[43] . . . But [how is] . . . this important mission . . . to be fulfilled[?] The keys are to be delivered, the spirit of Elijah is to Come, The gospel [is] to be established[,] the Saints of God gathered[,] Zion built up, & the Saints . . . come up as Saviors on Mount Zion. . . . [How?] by building their temples . . . & going forth & receiving all the ordinances, Baptisms, Confirmations, washings anointings ordinations & sealing powers upon our heads in behalf of all our Progenitors who are dead & redeem them that they may Come forth in the first resurrection & be exalted to thrones of glory with us, [sealing] the Children to the Fathers which fulfils the mission of Elijah."[44]

This message so resonated with Brigham that he expounded upon it at every opportunity.[45] And as his testimony of it increased, so did his understanding. Then, sometime during the winter of 1843–44, Joseph's meetings with Brigham and his trusted associates grew more numerous and more intense. At one point Orson Pratt finally complained, "Why do you give us no rest?" and Joseph replied, "The Spirit urges me."[46]

Orson Hyde stated: "Before I went east on the 4th of April last [1844] we were in council with Joseph almost every day for weeks, says brother Joseph in one of those councils there is something going to happen; I don't know what it is, but the Lord bids me to hasten and give you your endowment before the temple is finished."[47] Added Parley P. Pratt: "This

---

43. Ehat and Cook, *Words*, 329, 21 January 1844.
44. Ehat and Cook, *Words*, 318–19, 10 March 1844.
45. Arrington, *Brigham Young*, 260–61.
46. "Journal of Wandle Mace."
47. Jedediah M. Grant, *A Collection of Facts Relative to the Course Taken by Elder Sidney Rigdon in the States of Ohio, Missouri, Illinois and Pennsylvania* (Philadelphia: Brown, Bicking & Guilbert, 1844), n.p. See also Alexander L. Baugh and Richard Neitzel Holzapfel, "I Roll the Burthen and Responsibility of Leading This Church Off from My Shoulders on to Yours," *BYU Studies* 49, no. 3 (2010): 10.

great and good man was led, before his death, to call the Twelve together . . . and to instruct them in all things pertaining to the kingdom,
ordinances, and government of God. He often observed that he was
laying the foundation, but it would remain for the Twelve to complete
the building. Said he, 'I know not why; but for some reason I am con-
strained to hasten my preparations, and to confer upon the Twelve all
the ordinances, keys, covenants, endowments, and sealing ordinances
of the priesthood, and so set before them a pattern in all things pertaining to the sanctuary [temple] and the endowment therein."[48]

Near the end of March 1844 (the general consensus is that it was
Tuesday, 26 March 1844), Joseph called a final, day-long meeting of
the Twelve, which in the end included just nine of the apostles plus
some others.[49] After opening the morning portion himself with solemn
prayer, Joseph commenced by reviewing his own lifetime of visions, ordinations, and personal suffering. Next he joined with Hyrum to once
again anoint and bless Brigham Young, this time bestowing on him the
fulness of the priesthood, "the keys of the sealing power as conferred in
the last days by the spirit and power of Elijah in order to seal the hearts
of the children to the fathers, lest the whole earth be smitten with a
curse."[50] The Prophet then instructed Brigham to administer the same
ordinance to the eight other members of the Twelve who were present.[51]

The second portion of the meeting took up much of the afternoon,

---

48. *Millennial Star* 5 (1 January 1845): 151.

49. The three missing members of the Quorum of the Twelve were John E. Page,
William Smith, and Lyman Wight. Nor was Sidney Rigdon in attendance.
None of these four received the ordinances; ultimately all four were excommu-
nicated and "faded away" (George A. Smith, in James G. Bleak, "Annals of the
Southern Utah Mission," Book A, 363, typescript, Dixie State University Special
Collections).

50. *Millennial Star* 5 (1 January 1845): 151. Pratt adds: "This last key of the priesthood
is the most sacred of all, and pertains exclusively to the first presidency of the
church, without whose sanction and approval of authority, no sealing blessing shall
be administered pertaining to things of the resurrection and the life to come." See
Bleak, "Annals," Book A, 363.

51. See Bleak, "Annals," Book A, 363.

with Joseph delivering what would turn out to be his last charge or directive to the Twelve. Wilford Woodruff, who lived longer than the others and took numerous opportunities to record his memories, on Friday, 19 March 1897, declared into a graphaphone, or talking machine:

"I bear my testimony that in the early spring of 1844, in Nauvoo, the Prophet Joseph Smith called the Twelve Apostles together and he delivered unto them the ordinances of the Church and Kingdom of God; and all the keys and powers that God had bestowed upon him, he sealed upon our heads, and he told us that we must round up our shoulders and bear off this kingdom, or we would be damned. I am the only man now living in the flesh who heard that testimony from his mouth, and I know that it was true by the power of God manifest to him. At that meeting he stood upon his feet for about three hours and taught us the things of the kingdom. His face was as clear as amber, and he was covered with a power that I had never seen in any man in the flesh before.

"I bear testimony that Joseph Smith was the author of the endowments as received by the Latter-day Saints. I received my own endowments under his hands and direction, and I know they are true principles."[52]

Speaking of his sorrow and fear that he might be slain before that day's work had been accomplished, Joseph reiterated his gratitude to the Lord. He then declared: "You Apostles of the Lamb of God have been chosen to carry out the purposes of the Lord on the earth. Now, I have received, as the Prophet, seer, and revelator, standing at the head of this dispensation, every key, every ordinance, every principle and every priesthood . . . that belongs to the last dispensation and fullness of times . . . by [every] Prophet, Apostle, or Messenger of Life and Salvation. . . . I have sealed all these things upon your heads . . . and now I am free."[53]

---

52. Richard Neitzel Holzapfel and Steven C. Harper, "This Is My Testimony, Spoken by Myself into a Talking Machine," *BYU Studies* 45, no. 2 (2006): 113.

53. Wilford Woodruff, in Conference Report, April 1898, 89. Parley P. Pratt later

"Having done this, [Joseph] rejoiced exceedingly,"[54] saying, "The Lord is about to lay the burden on your shoulders and let me rest awhile; and if they kill me, continued he, the kingdom of God will roll on, as I have now finished the work which was laid upon me, by committing to you all things for the building up of the kingdom according to the heavenly vision, and the pattern shown me from heaven."[55] "You have got all the keys, and all the ordinances and you can confer them upon others, and the host of Satan will not be able to tear down the kingdom, as fast as you will be able to build it up."[56]

Again Joseph reminded Brigham that the endowment for the dead as well as certain sealings, as authorized by these highest keys of sealing power, were to be administered only within properly dedicated temples.[57] Just as Elijah, Moses, and Elias had been required to wait for a dedicated temple in which to deliver their keys and authorities to Joseph, so the dead were being required to await a dedicated temple before receiving by proxy the fulness of their own eternal ordinances.[58] It would be Brigham's responsibility to provide such a holy edifice in which this work could be accomplished. Said Joseph to him: "Brother Brigham, this [endowment ceremony] is not arranged perfectly; however we have done the best we could under the circumstances in which we are placed. I wish you to take this matter in hand: organize and systematize all these ceremonies."[59]

---

explained that these keys "are committed to man for the last time. Their consummation will restore the tribes of Israel and Judah; overthrow all corrupt institutions; usher in the reign of universal peace and knowledge; introduce to the earth her lawful and eternal King, the crucified Nazarene, the resurrected Messiah; banish darkness and death, sorrow, mourning and tears, from the face of our globe; and crown our race with the laurels of victory and eternal life." *Key to the Science of Theology* (Liverpool and London, 1855), 77–78.

54. Woodruff, in Conference Report, April 1898, 89.
55. *Millennial Star* 5 (1 January 1845): 151.
56. Grant, "Collection of Facts."
57. See Woodruff, *Journal*, 2:240, 11 June 1843.
58. See Doctrine and Covenants 110:11–16.
59. Cowan, *Temples to Dot the Earth*, 55.

Brigham never forgot this prophetic injunction.

The Prophet then declared to Brigham in all solemnity: "On your shoulders will [lie] the responsibility of leading this people right for the Lord is going to let me rest awhile."[60]

Three months and one day later, on 27 June 1844, Joseph gave his life in testimony of the divinity of the work God had called him to perform. From that same hour, Brigham Young shouldered the burdens of presidency as he took upon himself the leadership of the Church his beloved Prophet had established in the name of the Lord. Of course, Brigham also received the prophetic mantle, the divinely appointed right to obtain and therefore comprehend and put into practice, for himself as well as for the Saints, every revelation, priesthood, doctrine, ordinance, and key of authority ever held and administered by the Prophet Joseph. These duties and gifts were now his own, and under the guidance of the Holy Spirit he would further enhance them to bless the Saints and lead them toward the eternal destiny that had become as clear to him as ever it had been to Joseph. This destiny would ultimately lead him to build unto the Lord the third temple of the Restoration, making possible at last the great and eternal work for the Saints and for their dead.

---

60. Grant, "Collection of Facts."

Chapter 1

A SACRIFICE OF ALL THINGS

1859–1861

In the spring of 1859, Brigham Young led an expedition into southern Utah, his second, in part to learn why the Saints he had been sending into the area were having such struggles and why so many were abandoning their missions. In addition, he was looking for a site for a "central city in the South," a large arable area not only for a city but for the growing of cotton and other "warm climate" crops such as "flax, hemp, grapes, figs, sweet potatoes [and] fruits of every kind."[1] This site would also need sufficient water to support such a community.

But this was not a new endeavor Brigham was planning, merely a new location. With the exception of some tiny, out-of-the-way communities, Mormon settlements were organized by Church leaders in Salt Lake City, and always had been. Settlers were called to specific locations based upon their skills, aptitudes, and occasionally even their desires, and then sent as "missionaries" to pacify and convert the Native American population, work the soil, and build up homes and communities.

---

1. See Andrew Karl Larson, *I Was Called to Dixie* (Salt Lake City: Deseret News Press, 1961), 17–19.

And so it had happened in the southwest corner of the Territory. Fort Harmony was established on Ash Creek in 1852, and in 1854 an "Iron Mission" was established in Parowan and then Cedar City while even farther south an Indian Mission was established by Jacob Hamblin and his associates on Santa Clara Creek in the semitropical Virgin River Basin. There they built a fort, planted crops, and took up their mission "to live among the natives, learn their language, and teach them the ways of civilization and Christianity."[2]

That winter Hamblin became ill and one of the missionaries, A. P. Hardy, returned to Parowan for "medicine and food." While there, a woman convert from Tennessee gave him a quart of cotton seed with a wish that they would experiment with it. When a planting was made in the spring of 1855, the seedlings grew exceedingly well. In early 1856 these missionaries were joined by their families, and they planted more cotton. To process this larger crop, Zadock K. Judd, a Southerner, "rigged up a gin," and the women wove thirty yards of cloth. Samples were sent to Salt Lake City, reinforcing in the minds of Church leaders that a "cotton industry" could be established in the southern part of the Territory.[3]

Other outlying settlements were soon established over the rim of the Great Basin. In the mid-1850s and during the 1860s, small groups, mostly from Parowan, the "mother colony of southern Utah," settled Toquerville and a half-dozen other locations on the upper Virgin River, near the colorful cliffs of today's Zion National Park.[4] In 1857 two companies of about forty families led by the Adairs and the Covingtons settled farther downstream and named their settlement Washington.

Unfortunately, these early settlements along the river and its

---

2. Juanita Brooks, "The Cotton Mission," *Utah Historical Quarterly* 29 (July 1961): 201–2.

3. Brooks, "Cotton Mission."

4. See Kate B. Carter, comp., *Our Pioneer Heritage* (Salt Lake City: Daughters of Utah Pioneers, 1974), 17:152. These communities ultimately included Pocketville or Virgin City, Grafton, Adventure or Rockville, Shonesburg, and Springdale.

tributaries struggled to achieve viability and soon began to lose population. Intense isolation; droughts alternating with both spring and midsummer flooding from snow-melt or sudden torrential rains, particularly along the volatile Virgin (an impossible-to-control river that washed out every irrigation dam built before 1890); months of heat that often reached 115 degrees and higher;[5] snakes, scorpions, sand-fleas, flies, mosquitoes, and malaria—all caused some to give up in hopeless despair and return north. These conditions were some of President Young's principal concerns during his journey south in 1859.

From Fort Harmony, Brigham and his party crossed over the rim of the Great Basin on what was generously being called a wagon road. This was an extremely rough route that included the nearly impassable Peter's Leap before continuing southeast to Toquerville.[6] Here they

---

5. James G. Bleak, "Historian Southern Mission Mem. Book, Commencing April 6, 1871," n.p., holograph; photocopy in possession of the authors. See also Box 1, James G. Bleak Papers, Dixie State University Special Collections, St. George, Utah. Bleak records the temperature on 16 August 1871 as 119¾ degrees at 4:30 P.M.

6. See Utah State History Markers and Monuments database, "The Roads to Utah's Dixie: The Black Ridge." The Black Ridge between New Harmony and Pintura, north of Toquerville, Utah, was considered the toughest, most discouraging barrier to the colonization of "Utah's Dixie." A deep, rough, lava flow clogged the valley from the base of the towering Hurricane cliffs on the east to the foothills of Pine Valley Mountain on the west. The jolting rocks subjected the pioneer wagons, animals, and human tempers to a terrific strain. There were broken axles, broken wheels and fellies, and broken kingbolts and run-off rims to try the patience of the weary travelers, who were forced to resort to their own ingenuity in making repairs, miles away from any possible relief. Apostle George A. Smith, for whom St. George was named, proclaimed this road to be "the most desperate piece of road that I have ever traveled in my life." Peter's Leap, located two-and-a-half miles north of Pintura, was no doubt the worst part of the route. The road followed an old Indian trail, crossed Leap Creek Canyon, a 165-foot-deep gorge in the lava that was only a hundred feet across, at a point approximately one-and-a-half miles west of where Leap Creek joins Ash Creek. Peter Shirts, a Cedar City pioneer, inspired the name when he was paid $300 by the Washington County Commission to build a road along the old Indian trail on the west edge of the Black Ridge. When asked how wagons would get across the deep canyon that barred the way, he replied facetiously, "We'll leap it!" Thus the 165-foot-deep canyon crossing became "Peter's Leap" and the stream became "Leap Creek." This almost impassable road was used

turned directly south to Washington and then southwest around the southern end of Pine Valley Mountain to Santa Clara.[7]

Though Brigham no doubt knew the residents of Santa Clara and probably visited with all of them during his visit, there was one couple, Billy and Sytha Lay, with whom he would definitely have spent some time. Former members of the group known as the Mississippi Saints, Billy and his brothers-in-law—William Crosby, John Brown, and John Bankhead—had met Brigham Young when they traveled to Nauvoo in 1845, heavily armed, to help defend the Saints while also laboring to finish the Nauvoo Temple.

A year later these same men, in company with a large train of emigrants but not their own families, set out to meet Brigham and the Saints somewhere along the trail to the West. Unfortunately Billy's group got ahead of the main company of Saints and were trying to decide what to do when members of a detachment of the newly formed Mormon Battalion happened upon them, telling them that the Saints had stopped at a place they were calling Winter Quarters and would not be continuing west until the following spring.

Traveling south to Fort Pueblo, Billy and the others helped erect numerous small cabins as well as a large meetinghouse for their group, and then the four brothers-in-law returned to their own families in Mississippi. The next spring, some of their family members were in poor health and unable to emigrate. The men sent west, instead, two of their beloved slaves who had been baptized at the same time as the Crosby family, brothers Hark Lay and Oscar Crosby. Along with Green Flake, another baptized slave, Brigham invited Hark and Oscar to be part of his vanguard expedition to the West. As they neared the Salt Lake

until 1869, when a winding but far less treacherous road was constructed along the east side of Ash Creek.

7. At Santa Clara, Brigham advised the people to move their fort and habitations to higher ground. Had the settlers followed his counsel, they would have avoided the terrible destruction caused by the rains that began in December 1861, leading to terrible flooding in February 1862.

Valley and Brigham grew ill, the three black men and a few others were chosen by Orson Pratt to explore with him the trail ahead—and thus they were part of the very first group to actually enter the Salt Lake Valley.

In 1848, Billy and Sytha and their family, along with the extended Crosby family, arrived in the Valley and were finally introduced to Brigham Young. Hark and Oscar had already built small homes for all of them nine miles southeast of Salt Lake in a place they called Cottonwood, or Mississippiville. At that time all the family slaves were given their freedom. A few years later Billy and Sytha were called to leave the Salt Lake Valley, going with elders Charles C. Rich and Amasa M. Lyman to settle what became San Bernardino, California. In 1857, with the onslaught of the "Utah War," after prospering greatly even without their former slaves and dear friends who had elected to stay in northern Utah, the entire group was called back to Utah. Because they enjoyed the warmer climate, Billy and Sytha and their children turned off to Santa Clara, which became their final home.

In Santa Clara, Brigham must have enjoyed greeting his old friends the Lays, for it had been several years since they had seen one another. But one thing about Billy surely must have troubled the prophet: in spite of all his goodness and devotion to his family and generosity to the Church, from the very beginning, when his wife, her only brother, William Crosby, her mother, Elizabeth Crosby, and all her sisters but one, had been baptized, Billy Lay had steadfastly refused to join the Church.[8]

8. Information for this account has been drawn from Charmaine Lay Kohler, *Southern Grace: A Story of the Mississippi Saints* (Boise, Idaho: Beagle Creek Press, 1995); Robert and Victoria Lay, *Early Pioneers William Harvey Lay, Sytha Crosby Lay, and Their Descendants* (privately published, R. E. Lay, 1995); Sheri Orton, personal research materials concerning the Lay family, St. George Utah; "Mississippi Saints Headed West in 1846," *Church News*, 13 July 1996. Despite not being a member of the Church, Billy (William Harvey) Lay always supported the Saints and defended them to others. He also encouraged his children, all of whom were Church members, by telling them: "If you are going to be a Mormon, be a good one. Not half tugged!" While the St. George Temple was being built,

After tarrying a few days with the Lays, Jacob Hamblin, and the others in Santa Clara, President Young's party followed Santa Clara Creek southeast, moving deeper into desert country until they came to the creek's confluence with the Virgin River and a tiny hamlet called Tonaquint.

From there they continued south down the Virgin a couple of miles to an experimental farm established by Joseph Horne, the Adair brothers, and a few other men President Young had sent south the year before, in 1858. One of these was eighteen-year-old Jacob Peart Jr. Jacob, unmarried, was probably lonely during this farming expedition, his only neighbors besides his fellow laborers being the scorpions, rattlesnakes, and Paiutes. At some point, Jacob and perhaps others discovered on a high cliff on the north side of the Virgin River, about half a mile downstream from its confluence with Santa Clara Creek, a large and quite remarkable likeness of Brigham Young's head in profile, carved by nature into the stone.[9] Having some time on his hands, young Jacob scaled the cliff and, directly in line with Brigham's hopefully approving

---

Billy donated his best wagon and teams for hauling rock and other supplies. When Sytha, who was one of the first women endowed in the St. George Temple, passed away in 1881, Billy grew desperately lonely and more and more worried that he would never see his beloved companion again. In 1885 the aged Jacob Hamblin returned to Santa Clara for a brief visit. He and Billy, whose eldest daughter had married one of Jacob's brothers, no doubt discussed Billy's status, but if they did, nothing seemed to come of it. Later that winter Billy's health began to fail, and as he lay on his deathbed he sent all but his youngest son from the room. "'I must know,' he then breathed. 'Has your mother been sealed to another man?' William assured him she had not. 'Are you sure?' 'Yes, Dad, I am. She only wanted you.' A smile of great joy and relief covered the tired weathered face, as Sytha's 'Billy' closed his eyes for the last time" (Kohler, *Southern Grace*, 72). The date of Billy's passing was 7 March 1886. Billy's temple work, including his sealing to Sytha, was performed in the St. George Temple 14–15 October 1920. Both Billy and Sytha are buried in the Santa Clara cemetery.

9. The naturally hewn visage is best seen when the morning sun of summer casts a shadow defining the face. Interestingly, outside Zion's Bank in downtown St. George is an almost life-size bronze of Brigham Young seated on a bench. The facial profile of the bronze bears a striking resemblance to the naturally carved cliff face—leading some to believe that the sculptor may also have been familiar with the image on the cliff.

gaze and on the same slab of unbroken stone, chiseled into the dark desert varnish a large relief of what is presumably a stylized cotton plant, complete with roots, leaves, and blossoms. When he finished, he scrawled beneath one of the two roots: "I was set [sent] her[e] to rais[e] cotten March 1858 JACOB PEART Jr."[10] Below and several yards to the north he also etched, above his "J. P." initials, his own profile, much smaller than Brigham's but nevertheless facing in the same direction as his prophet.

Near the site of modern Bloomington, Jacob Peart and the Horne company constructed a brush and rock diversion dam in the river; dug ditches; planted peas, corn, potatoes, sugar cane, and cotton; and set out hundreds of peach trees. Returning to Salt Lake at the end of their 1858 harvest season, they brought "with them 575 pounds of cotton (with the seed) and 160 gallons of molasses. They estimated that the cotton cost them $3.40 per pound to produce."[11] Believing that the United States was on the verge of civil war, which would cut off the Saints' supply of cotton, President Young and other Church leaders were elated at the success of the experimental farm and encouraged the settlers to return for another season.

To his satisfaction Brigham found them back on the farm and hard at work in 1859. They had named their farm Heberville after Brigham's friend and counselor Heber C. Kimball. After praising and encouraging them, Brigham told them he felt certain they would enjoy even greater

10. Brooks, "Cotton Mission," 202–21. This mid-nineteenth-century rock carving is easily visible today as one drives north past the Bloomington exit on I-15 just south of the first two exits into St. George, Utah. It is located near the skyline of the cliff to the left (west) of the freeway, and if one looks directly west and upward just as he starts across the freeway bridge over the combined Rio Virgin/Santa Clara Creek, it can be plainly seen. There is an inward jut of the cliff just before the carving, while several feet beneath is a slanted, earth-covered ledge that slopes downward toward the north. This carving is best seen on summer mornings when the sun is illuminating the cliff face. Watch particularly for the giant cotton plant and, a foot or so to the right, the naturally hewn profile of Brigham Young.

11. Juanita Brooks, "St. George, Utah—A Community Portrait," *Symposium on Mormon Culture* (Logan: Utah State University, 1952), 8.

success with their second harvest and that their labor would prove a great blessing to the Saints.[12]

The next day Brigham and his party started back upstream, their intention not only to visit Washington and as many more of the small settlements along the Virgin River as possible but also to continue their search for a large area where they might build up a centrally located city that would become Church headquarters for all settlements below the rim.

Was President Young thinking then of building a temple in the south? Perhaps. Brigham's own record relates that while passing back north through Tonaquint and rounding the end of a steep volcanic ridge, his party entered the bottom of a wide valley that sloped upward to the north and west of the wide river bottoms. Brigham halted his carriage and gazed over the barren, treeless area, and there, on 1 June 1859, his fifty-eighth birthday, he stood up and beheld in vision a future city. In that instant he knew he had located the site he had been looking for. Motioning to his companions to draw near and to follow the sweep of his hand, he spoke these prophetic words: "There will yet be built between these volcanic ridges, a city, with spires, towers, and steeples, with homes containing many inhabitants."[13]

---

12. See Kirk M. Curtis, "History of the St. George Temple" (master's thesis, Brigham Young University, 1964), 6. The same work and toil resulted in even more success in 1859, proving once and for all that cotton, sugar cane, peaches, apricots, and other such crops could be successfully grown in the area. Plans were immediately laid to send more colonists south to aid in growing cotton.

13. James G. Bleak, "Annals of the Southern Utah Mission," Book A, 49, typescript, Dixie State University Special Collections, St. George, Utah, hereafter cited as Dixie State University Special Collections. A variation of this account was recorded by John S. Stucki, who reported that Samuel Knight, one of Jacob Hamblin's missionaries, declared to him that when Brigham started on his way following this visit to Santa Clara: "The road went along the south hills and around the lower point of the big black hill, and when he had traveled a short distance past the black hill so he could see up the valley where the city of St. George and Temple now are, he stopped his team and company all at once; looking over the valley he said, 'I see there a temple and city of about ten thousand inhabitants.'" *Family History Journal of John S. Stucki* (Salt Lake City: Pyramid Press, 1932), 56.

Four short years later, in May 1863, after the new community of St. George had been founded and was growing, Brigham recalled the experience. He told his St. George audience, "Some have asked why this place should have been located [here]. I will tell you: it is the very place I intended the city of St. George to be built upon. When I was on my first visit to the Santa Clara and Tonaquint settlements, I saw in vision this place inhabited by a multitude of people, and large domes were towering up in every direction. I shall yet see this with my natural eyes."[14]

So the question returns: Did President Young's prophetic statement indicate that one day a temple would be built among those "domes," "spires, towers, and steeples"? "Perhaps" is probably as close as can be expected. What is known with certainty is that temples, temple ordinances, and the building and dedicating of a third temple for the Saints were never far from his mind. To be sure, he didn't yet know where that completed temple would be located, in Salt Lake City or some other place. No matter the location, however, Brigham understood clearly not only that a temple was needed by the Saints but that upon his shoulders lay the responsibility to build it.

In Nauvoo, of course, it had seemed a fait accompli. The Nauvoo Temple was less than a year away from completion when Brigham received from Joseph all the priesthood keys, and though there was mounting opposition from a jealous and angry populace, Brigham both hoped and prayed they would have time to perform their baptisms, confirmations, and all the other ordinances for both the living and the dead that Joseph held the keys of authority to perform.

Unfortunately the Prophet and his brother Hyrum had been martyred and the mobs, driven by success and filled with murderous intensity, had given the Saints no more than a few weeks following the

14. Albert E. Miller, *The Immortal Pioneers: Founders of the City of St. George* (Albert E. Miller, 1946), 30.

temple's dedication a year later to abandon their beloved city and the temple that had been constructed at such great sacrifice.

Though he and the other members of the Twelve and the Saints had managed to perform over five thousand endowments and sealings for the living before being driven from Nauvoo, fifteen years later, with the foundation walls of the Salt Lake Temple still buried in the earth due to the 1857 coming of Johnston's army, Brigham knew he was as far as ever from building the Saints' yearned-for temple. Worse, the years of his life were rapidly slipping past. Noticing this, one day two or three years later, "Br. G. A. Smith . . . asked Brother Brigham Young why he was in such a hurry to see the Temple in St. George completed. Prs. B. Young answered, 'What will you do if I die before the Temple is completed[?] [T]he candle is nearly burnt out, and [I] can not last much longer; therefore I want to see this Temple completed before I die, that I can give the Keys [of the Holy Priesthood] to others.'"[15]

It took from Brigham's 1859 journey until 1861 to put into motion the mass movement of Saints needed to establish the city of domes, spires, and steeples he had seen in vision. Following his return north in June, he and the other Church leaders began formulating a plan to create their southern central city and to further strengthen the existing settlements. First, care had to be taken in selecting the needed number of reliable families. The final call listed 309 male names, nearly all heads of families. James G. Bleak (pronounced *Blake*) was one of them. He was called as clerk of the mission. The detailed record he kept forms the most important source for the early history of the mission in general and of St. George in particular. Brother Bleak lists the names of all 309 men, their priesthood, previous homes, and the occupations of most, an impressive forty-four different vocations.[16]

While this planning was going forward, Brigham asked frontiersman

---

15. J. F. Steck to James Wareham, 31 December 1874, as quoted in Jans Christian Anderson Weibye, *Daybooks*, 31 December 1874.

16. Bleak, "Annals," Book A, 56–62.

and fellow Apostle George A. Smith if he, Brigham, might give the new city its name. Elder Smith, who had been involved in the southern colonization ever since he led the mission that settled Parowan, of course assented, whereupon Brigham declared, "We shall name it St. George."[17]

It seems, though, that there is more to this story. According to Smith's descendant George M. Peacock, "Little consideration has been given to [a tragic] event which took place less than a year previous [to this announcement], which deeply involved those who chose the proposed name [and which is why the name is little celebrated]. . . . In 1860 George A. and Bathsheba Smith's . . . 18 year old . . . son and namesake[, George A. Smith Jr.,] . . . was sent on a mission to the Moqui [Hopi] Indians. He was interested in [his mission] and in learning a new language . . . , start[ing] Sept. 4, 1860 . . . in the company and under the direction of Jacob Hamblin and other missionaries. [They] had traveled about seven hundred miles when, on Nov. 2, 1860, the young missionary was killed by [two] Navajo [warriors, one of whom was called Peokon or Peokaan].[18]

"Recorded [for posterity] by Jacob [Hamblin] himself, George [A. Jr.'s] death was far from an accident. He was shot three times with his own revolver, at close range, and then shot with arrows in his upper body. He lived for a short time [in great agony as] the others knew they were trapped and didn't see any easy escape. . . . Young George told the others to leave him and try to escape, but they . . . held him on a mule [and struggled on]. When [the young man] died they wrapped his body in a blanket and tried to seclude it in a depression just off the trail. In the days of the journey back . . . Jacob's mind and feelings were torched

---

17. The abbreviation *St.* was also intended, not only because of British usage with which both George A. and Brigham were familiar from their missions to England—namely, St. George's Cross, St. George's Channel, etc., making the correct spelling of the city's name St. George—but because of the tragic murder of young George A. Smith Jr. the year before.

18. See chapter 5, "A Temple's Beginnings," 86n19.

with the knowledge that he would have to report the death, its manner, and its story, to George's parents and to Brigham Young. . . .

"Attempting to ease the pains encountered by the loss of his friend's son [and] namesake . . . Brigham . . . saw a way to do it by naming the proposed settlement in Southern Utah for his friend . . . and also for his deceased son [who had died] a martyr. . . . Hence the full significance of the appellation, St. George."[19]

By the end of September, the selection of settlers had been made. In the Sunday morning meeting of the October 1861 general conference, George A. Smith stood at the pulpit and read, without advance notice to anyone, the 309 names of those who had been selected. Husbands and wives in the audience were taken by surprise. Some not present heard of it later. But the action itself was no surprise. This was the established way Church leaders commonly extended calls for settlers to establish or build up communities.

But this group was larger than usual, and most had heard of the inhospitable region—a hot, dry, thinly settled land where few would have chosen to settle. However, it didn't matter. A call to be a missionary was something members felt compelled to fulfill, no matter where, when, or what. Neither were they given much time to think about it or to prepare. They were to leave right away. Two apostles, Orson Pratt and Erastus Snow, were assigned to lead them and were given charge over all the settlements of the Cotton Mission.

In November 1861, Brigham added to the list of colonists twenty-nine Swiss families, recent arrivals in the Salt Lake Valley. These were specifically called to bolster Hamblin's colony on the Santa Clara.[20] Though called after the others, the Swiss converts had not yet unpacked their handcarts or settled down, so they were able to leave immediately.

19. George M. Peacock, "Why the Naming of St. George Is Not Recorded," unpublished manuscript, 2012, n.p.; manuscript in possession of the authors.

20. Bleak, "Annals," Book A, 63.

Thus their arrival in Santa Clara preceded by a few days the arrival of the first settlers in St. George.

One of these Swiss immigrants, a brother named George Johann Staheli, was a bugler and cornet player. "When they were in Washington a little town a short distance from S.G., George's cornet fell out of the wagon and was run over. He had it tied to the bow of the wagon to help hold the cover. He felt bad because he knew he would not have money to get another soon and it was his means of support. The company all missed his music."[21]

At this same time Brigham also sent a request to Elder Orson Hyde, in Sanpete County, to call thirty to fifty additional families to the "Southern Mission." Elder Hyde called a group of Scandinavian Saints, who reluctantly accepted, sold their farms and homes, loaded their wagons, and headed south. After scouting out the upstream settlements and finding too little arable land, they turned down the river and came to Washington. Here they received a warm welcome and decided to stay and take their chances in an established community where arable land was plentiful.[22] All these settlement activities were sufficient to cause the territorial legislature, on 3 March 1862, to create Washington County, incorporating "all the portions of the country south of Iron County."[23]

Time would prove the special qualities and talents of many among this group. The survival of St. George and its neighboring communities during the first decade required the ability of dependable leaders and the courageous industry of a faithful people to build settlements and carve out farms. In seventeen short years they would do that and in St.

---

21. LaRae Farnsworth, "Life of George Johann Staheli," n.d., n.p., Daughters of Utah Pioneers McQuarrie Memorial Museum, St. George, Utah; hereafter cited as DUP McQuarrie Memorial Museum.

22. See Andrew Karl Larson, *The Red Hills of November* (Salt Lake City: Deseret News Press, 1957), 39. Andrew Karl Larson was descended from one of these families, as are many others who still live in Washington today.

23. Bleak, "Annals," Book A, 63.

George and Washington also construct a tabernacle, courthouse, cotton mill, and temple. Their remarkable accomplishments attest to their commitment, unity, and character.

The area of the Cotton Mission quite early and quite naturally acquired the appellation "Utah's Dixie." That the use of the term was common by the early 1860s is confirmed in the first stanza of George Hick's song, "Once I Lived in Cottonwood," written in 1864. The stanza reads:

> Once I lived in Cottonwood and owned a little farm,
> But I was called to Dixie, which did me much alarm;
> To raise the cane and cotton, I right away must go;
> But the reason why they called me, I'm sure I do not know.[24]

The plan was for the main body to establish a settlement in the valley that Brigham had seen. But families could choose any of the other small settlements; they all needed reinforcement. Nevertheless, St. George was to be the central city and was to assume the lead role among the mission's towns and villages.

It is worth noting that, physically speaking, those called were in the prime of life. Husbands were typically in their early forties, and wives in their mid-thirties.[25] The venture would also need men with a balance of work skills and professional talents.[26] Thus, among those called to St. George were farmers, vine dressers, blacksmiths, wheelwrights, coopers, millwrights, adobe makers, masons and carpenters, wool carders, tailors,

---

24. All twelve stanzas are found in Larson, *Red Hills*, 69–70.
25. Larry M. Logue, *A Sermon in the Desert: Belief and Behavior in Early St. George* (Urbana: University of Illinois Press, 1947), 5.
26. Juanita Brooks grouped their occupations as listed in Bleak's "Annals." Her list is evidence of the broad cross-section of people being converted to the Church in the United States, Canada, and Europe (at this time principally from Britain and Denmark) and migrating to Utah. It was a challenge for Church leaders, when organizing mission calls, to see that the dozens of settlements being founded had available a balanced cross-section of skills.

weavers, shoemakers, tanners, teachers, musicians, a butcher, a baker, two photographers skilled in daguerreotyping to preserve portraits for posterity,[27] one tobacconist, and one sailor.[28]

Understandably, it was not easy to accept such a call. Most had been in the Salt Lake Valley several years. They had built homes, laid out farms, established businesses, and dwelt in a settled, stable country-side. Meanwhile, word was out that the southern country, as Parley P. Pratt had described, "opens to the view for at least 80 miles" and presents "a wide expanse of chaotic matter . . . huge hills, sandy deserts, cheerless, grassless plains, perpendicular rocks, loose barren clay, dissolving beds of sandstone and various other elements lying in inconceivable confusion—in short a country in ruins, dissolved by the peltings of the storms of ages, or turned inside out, upside down, by terrible convulsions in some former age."[29] Hearing this, as William Fawcett, one of those called, put it, "Some made excuses, some backed out. . . . Some would not sell without sacrifice, others clung to their property or deserted their mission. Some thought they were called for a punishment." Happily, the reluctant were the exception. Most of those called were men and women known to the leaders to be of "sturdy character, courageous, thrifty, obedient, faithful, and honest."[30]

To encourage these settlers, they were assured by Brigham and other leaders that their "mission" to raise cotton was as important as preaching the gospel among the nations. The wives were to go with a

27. An early process of photography using metal plates.

28. "One might question the value of some of these skills in a desert community, but perhaps those who did not contribute to making a living could help make the others' li[ves] worth living by boosting morale. The musicians, the fiddler, the daguerrean, the drum major were among these, while the sailor used his skills to splice the scaffolding at both the tabernacle and the temple." Brooks, "Cotton Mission," 207–8.

29. Quoted in Juanita Brooks, "The Face of the Land," *Utah Historical Quarterly* 29 (July 1961): 196.

30. William Fawcett, "William Fawcett Version of the Dixie Settlement," *Washington County News*, 12 January 1961, in Andrew Karl Larson Papers, Dixie State University Special Collections.

"spirit [of] joy, cheerfulness, and feel a pleasure in going." Erastus Snow wrote, "I feel to go body and spirit with my heart and soul, and I sincerely hope that my brethren will endeavor to do the same."[31]

Because these were the very people who within the next ten years would sacrifice and labor and starve and suffer so thoroughly that they would be deemed ready by Brigham Young to build a holy temple, it seems appropriate to examine their various thoughts upon being "called." For instance, Elisha Averett, coming home "weary" from a hard day's work, hearing the news of his call, "dropped" in his chair and said: "I'll be damned if I'll go." But after a minute he stood up and said, "Well, if we are going to go to Dixie, we had better start to get ready."[32]

Joseph Allen Stout wrote: "I received a letter from my brother stating that him and me were both called to go to the South and raise cotton. Now this was joyful news to me for I was glad to leave that cold country and get where I could raise southern products. But my wife felt bad, for she thought she could not live in a hot climate. . . . I began to try to sell out, but there was so many called at the same time that I could only get one yoke of oxen and a one year old heifer . . . the whole . . . which I left . . . was worth 1200 dollars."[33]

Another, John Pulsipher, was informed by George A. Smith that his name was on the list. "This news was very unexpected to me," he wrote. "I had a good home, was well satisfied, and had plenty to do. But when [Apostle Smith] told me I was selected to go I saw the importance of the mission to sustain Israel in the mountains—we had need of a possession in a warmer climate, and I thot I might as well go as anybody. *Then the Spirit came upon me so that I felt to thank the Lord that I was worthy to go.*"[34]

Charles Pulsipher, John's brother, wrote: "Just in the rush of

---

31. Andrew Karl Larson, *Erastus Snow* (Salt Lake City: University of Utah Press, 1971), 321.

32. Brooks, "Cotton Mission," 206.

33. Curtis, "History," 8.

34. Brooks, "Cotton Mission," 207; emphasis added.

molasses work I received word that I had been called . . . to go to southern Utah or Dixie as it was called, 320 miles, and they wanted word back by messenger if I would be ready to start in four weeks. I sent back word that I would. I hadn't stopped to consider what it would take to get ready and when I looked to see what it would take for an outfit I found that it would take two good wagons and teams to take the family and a year's provisions and I had neither teams nor wagons and I was $400 in debt but I had given my word that I would be ready and I was determined to do all in my power to fill the promise."[35]

Wandle Mace, hearing his name, recorded, "I had not the remotest idea that I would be needed, nor did I feel [the] least inclined to go. But as soon as I heard the call my feelings changed, and I not only felt willing but anxious to respond to the call."[36]

Robert Gardner, co-founder with his brother Archibald of Gardner's Mill and other Salt Lake area milling enterprises, was not at the conference but was told by neighbors a few hours later. "I looked and spit," he wrote, "took off my hat and scratched my head and thought and said, 'all right.' The next day I went up to the City and saw George A. Smith in the Historian's Office. He laughed when I went in and [he] said: 'Don't blame anyone but me. The President told me to get up a list of names suitable for that mission, so I thought of you for one and thought you would be willing to go if called. So I put your name down. But if you don't want to go, step to the President's Office and ask him to take your name off the list and he will do it.' I said; 'I expect he would but I shan't try him. I have come to find out what kind of fitouts [outfits] are wanted and when to go.' He said, 'That is the kind of men we want.'"[37]

On the other hand, John and Margaret Moody were upset at first. John wrote, "I felt as though I could not do it." But he prayed about it. An

---

35. Charles Pulsipher, *Journal* (privately published), 20–21; in possession of Venetta Williams, Santa Clara, Utah.

36. "Journal of Wandle Mace," [144], n.d.

37. "Journal and Diary of Robert Gardner," in Kate B. Carter, comp., *Heart Throbs of the West* (Salt Lake City: Daughters of Utah Pioneers, 1949), 10:311.

answer came in the form of a hymn, running through his mind and convincing him that he "was called by the spirit of God." He added, "those bad feelings began to leave me and soon I was entirely free from them."[38]

A pioneer child, Hannah Bunker Crosby, recorded: "In 1861 father was called to Dixie. I remember the days of preparation . . . before leaving. Mother and my sisters, Emily and Abigail, spent days making crackers. They mixed them and pounded them with a wooden mallet. They dried corn, squash, berries and tomatoes. It was as if we were going into a wilderness expecting to starve. When it was time to go, a big double-bedded government wagon was brought around to the front of the house. It had a bed in each end with a stove in the middle and a chair for mother. It had a ladder down from the door in the center and the kiddies climbed in and out while the wagon was going to walk a while or climb in to get crackers and then [they] got out and walked a while. There were three yoke of oxen. All the relatives and friends mourned and carried on and expected never to see each other again, as though we were going into the wilderness never to return. [Along the way] we camped a few nights in deep snow where men had to shovel snow for a campground and cut trees for a shelter. We landed in Toquerville about the last of November, found a summer climate, cotton still in the pod on the bushes, Indians gathering beans and seeds of all kinds."[39]

So this call was not easy to be happy about, though most willingly sold their possessions (almost always at a financial loss) and went in faith. Charles (Charlie) Walker was one of these. Though a simple workman, he would become an important contributor to Dixie's cultural life. He gives a personal face to much of the history of early St. George. He was called in a second contingent of 250 families in October 1862. He was 29 years old, married, and recorded his experience as follows:

---

38. Logue, *Sermon in the Desert*, 3.
39. Hannah Adelia Bunker Crosby, as quoted in Susan Arrington Madsen, *Growing Up in Zion: True Stories of Young Pioneers Building the Kingdom* (Salt Lake City: Deseret Book, 1996), 81.

"Went to the Bowery. . . . At the close of the meeting 250 men were called to go to the Cotton Country my name is on the list. . . . At night I went to a meeting in the Tabernacle of those that had been called here I learn'd a principle that I shan't forget in awhile it showed to me that obedeance was a great principle in Heaven and on earth. Well here I have worked for the last 7 years thro heat and cold hunger and adverse circumstances and have at last got me a home a Lot with fruit trees just beginning to bear & look pretty. Well I must leave it and go and do the will of my Father in Heaven who ever rules all for the good of them that love and fear him and I pray God to give me Strength to accomplish that which is required of me."[40]

After much effort, Walker sold his home and lot, taking for it $300 worth of wheat, overpriced by his buyer, 2 yoke of oxen, and an "old wagon." Referring to his buyer, he wrote, "I don't think he has done right with me in Selling the wagon at that price . . . but it seems as tho every one that owed me anything were trying to keep it from me I have to sell a great many things almost for nothing as I cannot haul them & many take advantage of my circumstances in putting their price on my articles and on theirs but I am bound to go by the help of the Lord."[41]

And after finally getting packed and ready to pull out, he summarized: "This is the hardest trial I have ever had, and had it not been for the Gospel and those placed over us, I should never have moved a foot to go on such a trip."[42]

On the other hand, Charles Pulsipher "hired other help to run the molasses business and I went to work and built a wagon to fit some irons which I had, bought another running gear of a larger wagon, made the boxes and fitted them for traveling, sold out and paid my debts, got two yoke of cattle for the by-wagon and a fine span of 2½ year old colts

---

40. Charles Lowell Walker, *Diary of Charles Lowell Walker*, edited by A. Karl Larson and Katharine Miles Larson, 2 vols. (Logan: Utah State University Press, 1980), 1:239.

41. Walker, *Diary*, 1:240.

42. Brooks, "Cotton Mission," 206.

but not broke and I was so crowded to get ready that I never got time to hitch them up together to see if they would work until the night before we started. Then I hitched them up and found that I could control them by being very careful and the company came on time, stayed overnight with me and the next morning we put a little stove in the wagon to keep the family of six comfortable for it was getting quite cold weather first of December but we rolled out in good shape, my two brothers teams and my father-in-law, Brother Robbins."[43]

In terms of needed preparations, historian Andrew Karl Larson has written: "Wagons had to be made ready and snug for the rough trip and loaded only with the barest necessities—clothing, bedding, cooking utensils, farming tools, etc. There had to be enough food to last through the winter and spring, for a harvest of small grain could not be expected until midsummer."[44] The challenges of the near three-week-long journey, bouncing and jolting all the way in a wagon with iron-rimmed, wooden wheels, camping out every night in cold, sometimes wet, late fall weather, would be but the beginning of the many character-building experiences that lay ahead.

On their way south, the families traveled in small groups of neighbors and friends until they reached Cedar City, where most arrived by mid-November. Joseph Orton, a bachelor and inexperienced frontiersman, "rigged up a fit-out" of an ox team and an old wagon, the cover of which was a combination of rag carpet and bed-tick. When he stopped for the first night he left the yoke on his oxen so as to be able to distinguish his from the others the next morning. Orton realized this was unnecessarily cruel to the oxen, so each morning from then on he waited until all the others had hitched up their ox teams and then he took the oxen that were left, assuming they were his.[45]

---

43. Pulsipher, *Journal*, 21.
44. Larson, *Erastus Snow*, 325.
45. See Juanita Brooks, "St. George, the City with a Heritage," *Utah Magazine*, August 1936, 13, 18, 38.

Orton may not have been an experienced pioneer and colonizer, but he was always willing to give a try to anything that was asked of him. However, after many misadventures as he tried other occupations (his efforts at farming will be detailed later), Orton was finally advised by Erastus Snow that he had better stick to his shoemaking—a trade at which he was experienced and through which he became a great asset to his new community.[46]

Of his own experience, Robert Gardner recorded: "We started on our mission on the 12 Nov 1861. We traveled to Provo City and there Brother William Lang and wife Ann came up to us and traveled with us the rest of the way. We had a very good time traveling until we came to Round Valley [Scipio, Utah]. There we met with a snow storm right in our face all the way across the valley."[47]

Other than a second snowstorm at Cove Creek [Cove Fort], the Gardner party enjoyed good weather until their arrival in Parowan, where once again Robert met George A. Smith. Elder Smith encouraged Robert to settle in the new city of St. George rather than one of the other communities, and from there to "go and explore for timber and chances of building sawmills."

Gardner goes on: "We then continued on south and soon overtook a great many small companies who started before Brother Lang and I did. They had traveled slowly, many having ox teams. Now we had a chance to camp with companies every night. When we came to the fork of the road [Anderson's Junction] going to either Toquerville or St. George there was a long string of wagons going over the bench to Toquerville, but none on the road to St. George. There was hardly even a track on that road. Brother Lang and I felt a little lost for a minute or two. Then we said; 'we will go where we were told to go and help to make a track.' We have always been glad we did so."[48]

---

46. Larson, *I Was Called to Dixie*, 113.
47. "Journal and Diary of Robert Gardner," in Carter, *Heart Throbs*, 10:36.
48. "Journal and Diary of Robert Gardner," in Carter, *Heart Throbs*, 10:36.

A short distance beyond Anderson's Junction, on the way to present-day Leeds, the Gardners and other migrants to St. George encountered a three-mile stretch of red sand (George Hicks referred to it as the Sandy), so deep and dry that wagon wheels sank near to their hubs, severely testing the remaining endurance of teams and teamsters. Yokes of oxen or teams of mules or horses often had to be doubled up to pull the wagons through. Women, children, and teamsters had to leave their wagons and walk through sand up to their ankles. Further stanzas of George Hicks's poem tell of his encounter with the Black Ridge and then the sand:

> At length I reached the Black Ridge where I broke my wagon down,
> I could not find a carpenter so far from any town;
> So with a clumsy cedar pole I fixed an awkward slide;
> My wagon pulled so heavy then that Betsy could not ride.
>
> While Betsy was a-walking—I told her to take care—
> When all upon a sudden she struck a prickly pear.
> Then she began to blubber out as loud as she could bawl,
> "If I was back in Cottonwood, I would not come at all!"
>
> When we reached the Sandy, we could not move at all,
> For poor old Jim and Bolly began to puff and loll.
> I whipped and swore a little, but could not make the route,
> For myself, the team, and Betsy, were all of us give out.[49]

Halfway through the sands was Grapevine Springs, near present-day Leeds and Silver Reef, a welcome place to rest and make camp. The water was cool and clear though winter forage was scarce. To bring their animals to better grazing would have meant traversing more sand, so most made do until the next day. Robert Gardner wrote, referring to the last day of November:

---

49. Larson, *Erastus Snow*, 326.

"The first night [over the rim] we camped at Grapevine Springs. Now we had heard a great many yarns about the Dixie Country when George A. Smith preached to us at Parowan. . . . Amongst other yarns we heard . . . that the climate changed so fast in a short distance that 30 miles from St. George it was so cold that the people had to wrap up in bed quilts or blankets to keep from freezing. Half a day's journey from there the water left in the sun got warm enough to wash dishes. So this night we camped at Grapevine Springs, this being down in the warm climate, my wife . . . said she was going to test some of these things. So she sat out a cup of water on the wagon wheel to see if it would do to wash the dishes in the morning. When she got up . . . her cup was frozen over with thick ice. She declared that she would not believe any more yarns. However, I explained to her the reason that the water had not gotten hot was because the sun had not shined that night."

After passing Harrisburg, the Gardner party continued toward Washington, and crossing over several sand ridges they topped out on the last ridge and found the town nearly under them "on a nice flat between two ridges." Gardner continues: "Here we found some of our old neighbors who received us and were very kind to us. . . . Robert D. Covington, the Mangums and Adam Richie and others who had been sent on that mission years before. The appearance of these brethren and their wives and children was rather discouraging; nearly all of them had the fever and largo or chills [malaria] as they are called in this country. They had worked hard and had worn out their clothes and had replaced them from the cotton they had raised on their own lots and farms, their women had carded, spun and woven by hand. They had colored it with weeds. The men's shirts and women's and children's dresses and sun bonnets were all made of the same piece of cloth. Their clothes and their faces were all of a color, being blue with the chills. This tried me harder than anything I had seen in my Mormon experience. Thinking that my wives and children, from the nature of the climate, would have to look as sickly as those now surrounding me, I said: 'We will trust in

God and go ahead.' I think this was the first day of December we arrived in Washington Town."[50]

A lava-capped sandstone ridge (today's Foremaster Ridge) some two miles beyond Washington was the party's last challenge. Swamps plus thick groves of black willow and cottonwood trees at the southwest end of the ridge and next to the river made that direction impassable. They had to go up and over the ridge. After a search an opening in the cap-rock was found and with a final effort, they made the climb, crossed the ridge, and descended into the wide, empty valley Brigham had seen. As Robert Gardner put it, "Brother Lang and I joined Elder Snow's party and started over to the place where St. George was to be . . . we came over to what we now call the Old Camp Ground where we found Brothers William Fawcett and Robert Thompson and families camped."[51]

At the Old Camp Ground, where the Dixie State University campus now is, the Gardners and others came upon an area carpeted with wire grass watered from a spring flowing from the east end of what they called the Red Hill. Here they plowed a furrow to channel the water and lined their wagons along both sides. They arrived in early December, and by the end of the year some 250 families had gathered, the number left of the 309 families called, the others either failing to come or having gone up-river to other settlements. Charles Pulsipher recorded simply, "We moved along very well without any serious accident and arrived in St. George on the 24th of December, or rather near where St. George was after located which I helped to survey."[52]

All the new settlers found themselves in an arid, sandy, alkali-filled land of rugged hills, awesome plateaus, and deep canyons carved by the Virgin River and its tributaries. In every way, the migrants found such a country challenging. Water from the Virgin River was so filled

50. "Journal and Diary of Robert Gardner," in Carter, *Heart Throbs*, 10:36–37.
51. "Journal and Diary of Robert Gardner," in Carter, *Heart Throbs*, 10:36–37.
52. Pulsipher, *Journal*, 21.

with minerals that it was virtually undrinkable, even after all the sand and silt had been settled out. Water from nearby springs tasted somewhat better and was usually sufficient for drinking and gardens, though alkali in the soil remained a serious problem. In the first two seasons, seeds did not always sprout and plant growth was often stunted.[53] The bigger problem was controlling the river, which was necessary for irrigating their field crops. Diversion dams of brush and rock were repeatedly washed out. Deep snow accumulating in winter in the mountains, mainly on Pine Valley Mountain to the west and the heights known as Kolob, a part of the Markagunt Plateau (Zion National Park is carved into this plateau) to the east, caused heavy spring runoffs in both Santa Clara Creek and the Virgin River. But a greater threat came from summer thunderstorms. Much of the Markagunt Plateau watershed is "slick rock" country with little vegetation to hold back runoffs from cloudbursts. Coming in July and August, at the height of the growing season, a monsoon-caused flood could wash out a dam in short order. All the energy of the farmers was demanded to repair the dam, clean the sand and mud out of the ditches, and get water back to maturing crops before they parched and died. Some summers a large portion of the crops were lost. Another affliction they faced, mentioned by Robert Gardner, was malaria. Mosquitoes that bred in swamps along the river pestered inhabitants and caused plagues in late summer when physical strength was most needed. Unfortunately, the people were not aware that mosquitoes carried this disease. They blamed it instead on "the night air, the noxious miasma that rose from the swamps."[54] No matter the cause, malaria was a huge problem.

Facing such challenges, Elder Snow's company was the first to move into the empty St. George Valley. Elder Snow had been a steady leader with his people at every turn, every resting place, and every overnight

---

53. Irrigation and fertilization eventually leached the alkali out of the soil, and over time it became very productive.
54. Larson, *I Was Called to Dixie*, 72.

camp on the way south, cajoling and encouraging, though he too had a wife and family, including an infant son, and his own wagons and baggage to care for. Throughout the years ahead, he proved to be a calm leader whom the people learned to trust and respect. Larson says, "Erastus [was never one] to dwell at length on the difficulties he faced. He saw at once the barren nature of the land, but he felt it could be redeemed. . . . He saw the discouragement of those who had been called . . . but never let himself voice disappointment; it was his role to stiffen their backbones and fortify their resolution." Larson further says that "his peers had confidence in . . . his ideas, in his love of people, and in the soundness of his judgment. . . . Never in a hurry, he got things done. Even tempered, understanding, patient, and kindly by nature, he could be stern when the occasion demanded. In him was found a rare combination of the conservatism of the settled East and the newness and liberality of the rugged frontier of the West."[55]

55. Larson, *Erastus Snow*, 318, 327.

Chapter 2

FIVE YEARS OF STARVATION

1861–1866

Despite the daunting appearance and dusty, bone-dry condition of the land around them, December 1861 was spent by Dixie's new citizens laying out the beginnings of a city. They likely had little sense of the difficulties the next five years would bring, nor could they recognize the sanctifying refinement their souls were already experiencing. But Brigham Young seemed to understand, and as the days, weeks, months, and then years crept by, his love for these obedient people grew large.

For them, however, life was both difficult and very busy. Days were spent in scouting the country, holding meetings, and carving out places to live. Evenings provided time for socializing and dancing, as far as their fatigue would permit. In spite of intense hardship and primitive living conditions, these people loved life, and already they were beginning to develop the unified community character that would one day lead to the building of the only pioneer temple in the West.[1]

---

1. The St. George Temple was the only one in the West built without access to a railroad and shipped-in supplies and materials, which is why it is referred to as a pioneer temple. By the times of the construction of the later Utah temples, branch railroad lines reached both Logan and Wales, a coal mining community just a few miles north of Manti in Sanpete County.

Erastus Snow believed in democratic leadership. In his planning meetings every settler felt free to express an opinion. It was a new land, and committees were appointed to explore for resources: water, timber, firewood, and grazing, as well as to lay out and survey the actual town-site. Results were soon reported and further actions taken. The springs rising from the west and east ends of the Red Hill and along its foot were evaluated. The juniper-covered hills lying several miles north of the Red Hill were scouted and possible routes for wagon roads to access this wood were determined.

"George Faucett, who drove one of the first teams into St. George with his father and his sister Hannah Nixon; William and Sophronia Carter, and a few others, arrived November 30, 1861. Their first efforts were to obtain water and then find local building material. George held the reins for his mule team while William Carter guided the same plow with which he [had] plowed the first acre in Salt Lake City, and they plowed a wide, double furrow from north to south across the . . . valley, [into which they diverted] the East Spring stream."[2] It was this ditch that provided accessible water for both people and livestock during their first year in the valley.

A happy discovery was that the ditch ran for some distance across a continuous bed of light gray clay, which they recognized immediately as ideal for the making of adobes.[3] By mid-December a townsite at the northwest end of the valley had been decided on, and Charles Pulsipher and Israel Ivins were assigned to survey it and prepare a plat. The town would have 36 blocks in Plat A, with 8 lots per block.[4] Streets would

---

2. Kate B. Carter, comp., *Our Pioneer Heritage* (Salt Lake City: Daughters of Utah Pioneers, 1974), 1:173.

3. Carter, *Our Pioneer Heritage*, 1:173. Some of these adobes are still to be found in the walls of certain early pioneer homes in the area. See also Albert E. and Mary Ann Cottam Miller, "St. George," in "Histories and Stories," 22–23, manuscript, Dixie State University Archives, 1974, St. George, Utah.

4. All the lots were numbered on the town survey and corresponding numbers were written on slips of paper and placed in a container. Families received their lot based on the number they drew. Quite a bit of trading took place afterward.

be 90 feet wide, including 12 feet for sidewalks. A request for a town charter sent north to the territorial legislature was soon approved and returned. Money was even subscribed for the first community building, to be named the St. George Hall. Amazingly, the new community was named, surveyed, chartered, and had its first public building planned before a single lot was occupied.

For the new citizens of St. George, Christmas that year was a pretty sparse affair. Amelia Jarvis Webb, nine years old at the time, recalled that "Christmas was a sad time for all of us—no toys, candies, cookies, and no resemblance of holiday cheer. We had Christmas dinner of [a] warm bowl of flaxseed meal mush."[5]

Others seem to have had a more enjoyable holiday. "The big Sibley tent owned by Asa Calkins was set up on the adobe yard campgrounds and here [the new settlers] held their first Church meetings; likewise their first social event—the Christmas social and dance. It was a great celebration. The afternoon was warm enough for outdoor sports—wrestling matches, hop-step-and-jump contests for boys and men, foot races for old and young, and a program of singing. The dance started in the early evening. Older folk were to dance inside the tent, and the space around the outside of the tent was cleared for the young people. Oswald Barlow and his orchestra furnished the music for this first dance. . . . [T]he first couple to lead onto the floor after the prayer was . . . Angus M. Cannon and Ann Whitmore."[6]

Fifteen-year-old Jane Thompson Bleak remembers dancing outside the tent. "We accepted this privilege happily and were very decorous. But while we were dancing a lively quadrille, my partner and I moved too close to the ditch which ran between the double row of wagons and tents across the valley. The newly plowed bank gave way and I 'sloshed'

---

5. Amelia Jarvis Webb, "Life Story," 5, n.d., typescript, Daughters of Utah Pioneers McQuarrie Memorial Museum, St. George, Utah.

6. Kate B. Carter, comp., *An Enduring Legacy* (Salt Lake City: Daughters of Utah Pioneers, 1981), 4:359–60. Angus "often told of how lovely Ann was, and how grand they looked dancing that night."

into the water up to well above my ankle, soaking the hem of my rose colored taffeta dress, and almost ruining my dancing slippers of which I was very proud. But we took the incident with a laugh and went on with our dancing, being more careful. It was not long before rain began to fall—just a light, fine shower—gradually getting heavier until the entire dance was closed and people hurried to their various tents and wagons. This marked the beginning of many days of rain."[7]

Throughout January and halfway through February this on-again, off-again rainstorm continued. Again according to young Amelia, "It was a sorry mess. Our wagon covers and tents leaked. All our things; bedding, clothing, fuel (what little we had) got wet and soggy."[8]

As the rains continued the water caused serious flooding. One of those who recorded the event was Charles Pulsipher, who wrote: "President Snow called on my two brothers in connection with me to go out and hunt out a place to keep the stock of the settlement. [We] went up the Saint Clair [Santa Clara] about 20 miles and located for the winter range. It commenced raining the next day . . . and continued for six weeks which made terrible floods down in the lower country, washing away much good land and many houses and one mill belonging to brother J. Hamblin. The flood cut a wide channel down the river and in the night Brother Hamblin was trying to save some of his goods and a large piece of land caved down about 15 or 20 feet into the raging stream. He kept climbing to keep on top and hollered for those above to throw him a rope which [one of the Indians] did and pulled him up the bank before the cave-in was washed away so as to take him downstream. A little delay . . . would have washed him down stream and [he] probably [would] never [have] been heard of any more. During all

---

7. Carter, *Enduring Legacy*, 4:360.
8. Webb, "Life Story," 5.

this cold stormy winter we camped out in a brush shed sleeping in our wagons."[9]

Robert Gardner recorded his take on the storm: "On Christmas day . . . it began to rain and [we] began to dance, and we did dance, and it did rain. . . . The rain continued for three weeks, but we did not dance that long."[10] Besides those in Santa Clara, Washington, and the large St. George encampment, there were a few settlers already at the mouth of Santa Clara Creek where it flowed into the Virgin. Gardner says this spot was known as Seldom Sop, Lick Skillet, Never Sweat, also Tonaquint and Heberville. Though small and known by many names the land there was good and crops were bounteous, the old settlers being James Ritchey, the Adairs, the Mangums, and the Pierces.

Gardner continues: "When the rain storm came . . . a little before it quit it got in a big hurry and let down all at once. It raised the streams of the Virgin and Clara Creek to mighty rivers. They ran away beyond their bounds, and carried away some of the best bottomland. The little settlement on Clara Creek [Tonaquint] was all under water, and the people fled to the hills. The water was several feet deep in their little log houses. We went to their relief and took them our dancing tent for shelter. At the junction of the two streams Great Cottonwood trees came floating down, roots and limbs. It was said that a large anvil came down ahead of the blacksmith shop. A great many pieces of Hamlin's grist mill were carried downstream for four miles. I helped to pick them up. The Virgin instead of being a narrow stream was in many places a quarter of a mile wide."[11]

This flood changed conditions for everyone. The cotton farm at Tonaquint with its small orchard of fruit trees, its garden and crop land, was scooped out entirely and replaced with miles of mud and

9. Charles Pulsipher, *Journal* (privately published), 21; in possession of Venetta Williams, Santa Clara, Utah.
10. Kirk M. Curtis, "History of the St. George Temple" (master's thesis, Brigham Young University, 1964), 12.
11. Curtis, "History," 12.

debris. Harmony Fort above the rim was reduced to a pile of mud; the farms along the upper Virgin were carved away in great slices, until only devastation remained. The Swiss colony at Santa Clara clung to their barren hillside in dugouts, losing only their new ditch, but Jacob Hamblin and the others in Santa Clara lost everything: the fort, the orchards, the molasses mill, and even the small burr flour mill. Gardner continues:

"We were united in everything we did in those days, we had no rich and no poor. Our teams and wagons and what was in them was all we had. We had all things in common, and very common too. Especially in the eating line, for we didn't even have sorgum in those days. We got a pumpkin from an old settler, and thought him an awfully good friend. . . . [When] the rain was finally over, the flood damage estimated, and the city survey completed . . . the men decided that they would draw numbers from a hat to designate their lots, after which they might trade with each other if they cared to, or might later secure additional land. But no one was to move before the day assigned.

"On March 2 the camp was astir long before light. Many families had packed and were ready to move the night before; a few had hoped to be able to boast that they were the first in the valley to reach their location. [George] Jarvis, a former British sailor and ship's captain in the Royal Navy . . . told how he raced his team through the sage, up hill and down dale, tipping over the spring seats and scattering some of his goods. . . . At last he pulled up beside a large mesquite bush . . . on a sand knoll . . . and said, 'Well, we are home. Get out mother.' His wife was an aristocratic young woman from a fine home in England. Looking about, she began to cry; then immediately getting control of herself, she turned to her children and said to them, 'Don't you dare cry. Father says this is home so let's get started.'"[12] They were the first settlers of St. George.

William Carter's young wife, Sophronia, eager for an early garden,

12. Curtis, "History," 12.

had come days before with a grubbing hoe and shovel and cleared a space where their assigned lot was staked, only to learn when they moved in with their wagon that she had grubbed on the wrong side of the stake. She could go down in history as having done the first road-work in the new city.[13]

There were no trees in the valley; its hilly floor was covered with chaparral, creosote bushes, large thorn bushes, and in warmer weather lizards, snakes, scorpions, and many varieties of biting, stinging flies and other noxious insects. But folks were happy to at last have lots in the town where they could settle down and begin building for the future. David H. Cannon wrote in his journal how most must have felt. When he and his wife reached their lot, they got out of their wagon: "[We] knelt [together] in the evening shade behind a large chaparral and thanked the Lord for the land that was ours. We dedicated it to him and asked his blessings upon it and upon our endeavors to make it productive."[14]

Nine-year-old John S. Stucki, pioneering with his Swiss parents in Santa Clara, records that their first order of business in that community was to dig better dugouts in the side of the hill, "covering them with bullrushes and dirt. . . . As we had no team and nothing to get any lumber with, Father split some timber to make a bedstead for him and mother and filled it with straw. For us children he laid a piece of a log on the ground two ways to make a square with the walls of the dugout and then covered the ground with straw without anything to put over the straw, only a traveling mantel of father's to cover us. No pillows, but our clothes. I never have forgotten how the straw cut and pressed into my skin by morning so I would have to pick them out. The two large boxes of clothing and bedding which we had to leave in Florence

---

13. Juanita Brooks, "The Cotton Mission," *Utah Historical Quarterly* 29 (July 1961): 209–10.

14. "They Came in 1861," in Carter, *Our Pioneer Heritage*, 5:22–23.

[Nebraska] before starting to cross the plains would have come in very useful then, as we were almost entirely without bedding and clothing."[15]

To counterbalance the effects of such personal adversity and discomfort, most people strove diligently to help and assist each other. A first necessity was to dig the ditches that would bring water to the lots to supply culinary, livestock, and irrigation needs. Families helped each other clear and level their lots and plant shade and fruit trees and gardens. To keep out wandering livestock, they began fencing their yards with black willow or cottonwood poles entwined with water willows gathered from a broad swath of willow-covered bottomland to the south. The first St. George homes were built of the same material and in the same way, with mud daubed on the outside in an attempt to keep out the wind and dust. During wet weather, these leaky shelters provided only minimal refuge and made life inside miserable.

Erastus Snow, referring to the area's first pioneers, wrote: "They were a long way from stores, shops and other facilities, in a broken country forbidding in all its aspects, which was rocky, sandy, and barren, without roads and where a vast amount of labor and means were necessary to make roads and overcome the natural obstacles of developing the country. All the pioneers were greatly rejoiced at the prospects of help and were ready to throw themselves and all they had at our feet to be used or directed in any way necessary for the good of the communities."[16]

For some, though, conditions were more challenging than others. Young John S. Stucki recalled: "We children had to go without shoes for many years [John was given his first pair of shoes by Jacob Hamblin when he was in his mid-teens]. I never have forgotten the time we got a cow to milk, after a few years of living there without a cow or any milk. As we had no feed we had to turn her out to pick her own living. When

---

15. John S. Stucki, *Family History Journal of John S. Stucki* (Salt Lake City: Pyramid Press, 1932), 60.

16. Erastus Snow, quoted in *Inside St. George*, Fall 2011, 6.

she did not come home I had to go in the coldest of winter weather in my bare feet, and wade the river when it had thick slushy ice floating down it and the ground was also frozen hard. How I would run when I got out of the water to keep my wet feet from freezing to the frozen ground. . . . [In the summer] I often had to go out and herd the cows. . . . The red sand would get so hot during the long, hot summer days, it would nearly blister my bare feet. I would have to run from one bush to another to get my feet in the shade . . . to keep them from getting blistered."[17]

Even in the face of unremitting labor simply to cling to life, many of the settlers were forced to find the time and energy to scour the countryside in order to explore and locate needed resources. Juanita Brooks summarized: "While some men worked at the ditch and dam, others got out lumber, built roads, made adobes, quarried stone, or planted crops. Nor were the women and children idle, for they must assume the garden work, planting, hoeing, and irrigating, and must help according to their strength with every [other] undertaking. Hard as it was, it was not all drudgery. There were quiltings and carpet-rag sewing bees for the women, dances, choir practices, parties and socials. In Zion life should be happy as well as fruitful."[18]

In late February Charles Pulsipher was again sent out with his two brothers "to hunt out a summer range for the stock and as there had been trouble with the Indians and one of them had been killed it seemed a little dangerous to go off 50 or 60 miles into their country but duty required it and we went. Stayed over night with Brother Robison at Pinto. He gave us some information of a place called Shale [Shoal] Creek about 20 miles South West from there so we went on an old trail working the road as we went which was very badly washed out down the descending ground. When we had gone as far as [we] could with our cart we left it and went on foot, found some springs of water. All at once we

17. Stucki, *Family History Journal*, 60.
18. Brooks, "Cotton Mission," 211.

were surprised by 2 Indians. They were very much excited and anxious to find out what we were there for. One of them dodged into the brush and was soon out of sight but not long in returning with quite a crowd with him with their bows and arrows already for us. We had some trouble in talking to them at first but soon got them to understand that we wanted to bring our stock there and wanted them to help us to take care of them. They seemed pleased and showed us the water and grass in the surrounding country [the area of present-day Enterprise] as we decided it would do for our purpose and told them to come over to the other valley and meet us with the stock in fifteen days and help us drive them over which they did and we camped at the first water and made up a good warm supper for all. This act of kindness to them created a friendship that was lasting for in after years when other settlements around us had considerable trouble we never had any with that little band and they would come and tell us if wild bad Indians were around."[19]

Back in St. George a center block of Plat A was set aside as a public square, upon which was quickly built a temporary bowery. Four wards were also organized with a bishop appointed over each; one was set apart as the presiding bishop by Elder Erastus Snow, who in March also convened a general conference for the area.[20] The school that had been organized in the encampment was continued in the developing town, at first in tents and wagon-boxes[21] and then in private dwellings,

---

19. Pulsipher, *Journal*, 21–22.
20. Andrew Karl Larson, *Erastus Snow* (Salt Lake City: University of Utah Press, 1971), 339–40. A presiding bishop at that time had responsibilities similar to those of a stake president today.
21. "One of the early schools consisted of a wagon box set off the running gears onto logs on the ground. . . . The benches were logs split in half with pegs driven in for legs. As progress was made the students moved back a bench, and [Thomas Punter Cottam] remarked, 'Eventually we graduated out of the back of the wagon box,'" William Howard Thompson, ed. and comp., and Parts Written by William Howard Thompson, *Thomas Cottam 1820 and His Wives Ann Howarth 1820 and Caroline Smith 1820, Descendants* (privately published, Thomas Cottam Family Organization, 1987), n.p., typescript excerpt by Lucile Cottam Fish; photocopy courtesy Daughters of Utah Pioneers McQuarrie Memorial Museum, St. George, Utah.

but eventually each ward built its own small schoolhouse. These were simple affairs with a main floor and basement. The basement walls were built of lava rock because it was found to be impervious to alkali corrosion. The upper walls were built with adobe bricks. Meanwhile, church meetings were being held in the bowery, but though it warded off the sun it did little good against the wind and rain. Mail service to and from Cedar City was also established, and thus a new city, with an elected mayor and council, schools, and four Latter-day Saint wards, came into being.

As the spring of 1862 approached, attention had to be given to developing the available farmland. The southeast corner of the valley had some good soil and was best located for bringing water from the river. Land there was cleared and a ditch six feet wide and three feet deep was dug to conduct water from a diversion dam that had been built. The dam had to be built quite a distance upstream from a sandstone promontory, which ended with a high cliff extending to the river. This required that a 900-foot timbered tunnel be dug with pick and shovel through the sandstone in order for the water flowing through the new canal to reach the farmland. This was an arduous and ultimately fruitless task, for as yet the Saints did not know the treachery of this apparently peaceful stream. Due to a shifting river bed, quicksand, and torrential floods that seemed to come just when crops needed water the most, the river was completely unpredictable. Time after time their dams and portions of the canal were washed out by the surging waters, "which greatly discouraged [the settlers], and many of them left to find homes elsewhere." This "contest between the river and the people was waged for almost thirty years, [as] all methods of construction known to divert water into the old Virgin ditch [as it came to be known], were attempted." The river "could be a beastly monster, clawing and gouging away precious land, cattle, trees and bridges and it could be a lifeless river bed bringing drouth to the area. Usually she behaved as a river bearing the name Virgin should, meandering pure and serene along her sandy course, leaving quiet villages and farms undisturbed."[22]

An account from several years later illustrates when the river was not so well behaved. William Atkin III and his brother Joseph owned the large tract that had become Atkinville, on the banks of the river some seven miles south of St. George.[23] "Here [their] children played during happy summer hours under Dixie sun. . . . There were huge marshes on the fifteen acre duck pond filled with beautiful cattail and squawking cranes and birds. The cattails were gathered and dyed to make decorations in the home and to stuff pillows."[24]

There came a day, however, when "it had been thundering and lightning and a storm was brewing on the Markagaunt Plateau, which was the source of [the] heaviest storms [and floods]. The wandering little river [was soon] transformed into a destructive raging torrent which had [already] destroyed dams, ditches, farms, roads and villages. William . . . stood on its banks watching the wall of water hurl itself over his ripe alfalfa fields and saw the tumbling haystacks join the mad parade of pigeon and chicken coops, corral gates, fence posts, currant bushes, melons, cow sheds and willows that came from farther upstream.

"With a single gulp the flood swallowed the duck pond, then gouged great gaps from the irrigation canal that ran along the base of the hill on which he stood. Great chunks of the wheat land were undermined and fell heavily into the roiling stream. It gouged closer to his prize fruit trees: apples, plums, pears and peaches, now bearing fruit.

"'Oh Lord, not my fruit trees,' [William] prayed as the greedy torrent veered toward the orchard and gnawed at the roots of the trees until, one by one, many of the peach, pear, plum and apple trees topped into the turbid water, where struggling and tortured they disappeared

22. Carter, *Our Pioneer Heritage*, 16:413–414.
23. The location of the present-day Sun River retirement community.
24. Carter, *Our Pioneer Heritage*, 16:414–15.

around the bend . . . and became part of the flood's tribute to the Gulf of Lower California.

"That was the breaking point; [William] could bear no more! Tears rolled down his rugged cheeks. He shook his clenched fist savagely at the roaring flood and shouted in a strong [but] quavering voice, 'You may be a virgin to some folks, but to me you're nothing but a raging old whore!'"[25]

By late spring of 1862 it was clear that water would not be supplied to the fields in time for the first season's planting. Except for their irrigated town lots, which would not supply food sufficient for the three communities that now totaled close to 1,200 inhabitants, something else needed to be done for their fields of "lucerne, molasses cane, broom corn, cotton, melons and grapes,"[26] and other foodstuffs they intended raising that first summer. What little remained of the Heberville farm could help, but it couldn't fill the gap.

After much study and prayer Erastus turned his attention to the willow-covered lands along the banks of the lower Santa Clara. He had them surveyed and divided into 2.5-acre lots and parceled them out to any settler who was willing to work one. Joseph Orton, the bachelor shoemaker mentioned earlier, received such a plot. He records: "After grubbing willows and undergrowth from one-half acre of ground, I watered it and planted corn. In course of time returning, [I] replanted

25. Grace Atkin Woodbury and Angus Munn Woodbury, *The Story of Atkinville, a One-Family Village* (Salt Lake City: University of Utah Press, 1957), 1. See also Carter, *Our Pioneer Heritage*, 16:415; photocopy, under the name of Rachel A. Bleak, Daughters of Utah Pioneers McQuarrie Memorial Museum, St. George, Utah. The story told here is a combination of all three accounts.

26. "Valentine Carson, 8 Nov 1831—25 Sep 1898," manuscript, undated typescript, Daughters of Utah Pioneers McQuarrie Memorial Museum, St. George, Utah, 2. Valentine, who stood 6 feet 10 inches tall and was thought by many to be a giant, actually took his wife, Mary Ann, and three young children south in 1858 to labor on the Heberville farm with his uncle Samuel Adair. Their home was a dugout cut into the hillside above the farm. In 1861, prior to the calling of missionaries and the initial settling of St. George, Mary Ann and two daughters passed away, leaving Valentine alone to rear his young son, Samuel Valentine Carson. He married Hannah Waggle in 1863, and together they had eleven children (two of whom also died), making Valentine the father of fourteen.

missing hills and watered it [once more]. Again plodding down, I failed to find my corn patch then or ever afterward, as some unwitting miscreant had cut down a huge cottonwood tree which had hitherto been my unfailing guidepost to its location, consequently as Shakespeare has it 'Love's labor was lost.'"[27] Orton was a wiry man of small stature but with an engaging personality. Besides his shoemaking he had a deep bass voice, and was often called upon to recite poetry or sing the ditties written by Charlie Walker and others.

By degrees and through strenuous efforts by everyone including many in the north, St. George and the surrounding communities were beginning to be built up. By the close of the first farming season, when the initial agricultural work slowed down, people turned to erecting more permanent homes. Most of these usually had two rooms and were built of adobe bricks and lumber, with simple gabled roofs, stone fireplaces, with shed-type lean-to kitchens added on a little later. A few others used the abundant rock found in the nearby hills. Lumber and shingles continued to come from Pine Valley, and the adobe bricks were made in the "adobe yard," usually by those who needed them. Of Sophronia Turnbow Carter, for example, it is recorded "that she mixed the clay [for the adobes, then set them in forms to dry. Once they were dried and ready, she mixed] the mortar, and carried it to her husband, William, in brass water buckets, while he laid up the walls of the house, after he returned from his day's work."

As if that weren't enough, late in the fall when William went back "to Salt Lake City to bring a load of provisions, she plastered the walls, whitewashed them, made the doors and hung the one with a pair of strap hangers she got the blacksmith to make for her; the other with hinges of leather cut from a bootleg. During the absence of her husband

27. Quoted in Andrew Karl Larson, *I Was Called to Dixie* (Salt Lake City: Deseret News Press, 1961), 113–14.

she was [also] confined [to give birth]. The baby was sick two weeks, and dead and buried before her husband returned."[28]

Brigham Young paid his first visit to the new community in September 1862, the end of the settlers' first pitiful harvest. Assessing conditions, he could see that substantial help was needed for the new settlement to survive. After his return to Salt Lake City, two steps were taken: 250 additional families were called in the October conference to provide more manpower, and a sizable works project was proposed. The latter would not only help the town materially but it would also be a morale booster. To initiate the project, Brigham sent a letter to Erastus Snow directing that "a public meeting house" be erected, of sufficient size to seat "at least" 2,000 persons. This would ultimately become the St. George tabernacle. To support its construction, Brigham assigned to St. George all tithes in "labor, livestock, molasses, vegetables and grain" from Cedar City south.[29] A tithing office, yard, and corral were built to handle the donations. Nearly the entire cost of quarrying and preparing the rock, acquiring and hauling lumber and shingles, and the expense of hiring masons, carpenters, painters, and all other workers was paid in commodities.[30]

One family of this second wave of immigrants was that of Thomas and Caroline Smith Cottam, who arrived in St. George with their five children in December 1862. Because Thomas was a builder he immediately erected a small willow house that was described by his son, Thomas Punter Cottam, as follows: "It was a one-room building with a stamped dirt floor, willow-and-mud roof with the tent stretched up for a ceiling, and supplied with light from two [small] windows."[31] This home would do for four years before there was time for adding an addition.

28. Carter, *Our Pioneer Heritage*, 16:174–75.

29. Larson, *I Was Called to Dixie*, 118.

30. Charles Lowell Walker, *Diary of Charles Lowell Walker*, edited by A. Karl Larson and Katharine Miles Larson, 2 vols. (Logan: Utah State University Press, 1980), 1:567–68.

31. Thompson, "Thomas Cottam," 41.

Despite the progress on community infrastructure, failure to harness the river, and the resultant failure to produce sufficient food crops to sustain the people during and after the second summer, left the settlers vulnerable. They could survive the blazing hot sun, Indians that needed placating, grasshopper plagues, alkali-laden soil, malaria that drained the very life from many of them, hordes of rats and other rodents, and swarms of flies and other biting or stinging insects from which they could only escape by submerging themselves in the river or coating their extremities with foul-smelling mud—all these they would somehow endure. But without a sufficient harvest there would be too little food.

In fact, the only St. George crop that flourished in 1863 was cotton, which produced such "a surplus that they hauled 74,000 pounds back to the Mississippi River. . . . There it sold for from $1.40 to $1.90 a pound in trade, the church agent making the charges. . . . The 1864 cotton crop was not so large. They sent 11,000 pounds over the Old Spanish Trail to California and kept in stock 16,000 pounds. The price at home was set at $1.25 per pound. . . . Cotton thus became legal tender to be used for paying bills and making exchanges."[32]

By 1863 the excavation of the tabernacle basement was under way, though it was a slow process. "In facing the task of constructing the Tabernacle, most St. George settlers found that the harsh living conditions they endured made it virtually impossible to 'speedily prosecute the work to completion' as Brigham Young desired."[33] Nevertheless, the first public building in town, the St. George Hall, was completed in November 1863.[34] It was a lava stone building, plastered on the outside,

---

32. Brooks, "Cotton Mission," 211. It was at this point that the decision was made for the Saints to build their own cotton factory on what came to be called the mill stream, near Washington.

33. Brigham Young to Erastus Snow, 1 October 1862, quoted in Michael N. Landon, "A Shrine to the Whole Church, The History of the St. George Tabernacle," *Mormon Historical Studies* 12, no. 1 (Spring 2011): 126.

34. Larson, *Erastus Snow*, 340.

with a main floor and basement. Before the hall was completed, however, on 1 June 1863 the cornerstone of the tabernacle was laid. Due to other pressing necessities, including construction of the large cotton factory that had been made possible by a loan from Brigham Young,[35] construction on the tabernacle was slow at first. In spite of strenuous efforts by many, by 1865 they were still working on the basement, and drought conditions had only worsened.

To help buoy the spirits of the struggling community, for Christmas in 1863 "Thomas Cottam made thirteen dolls of wood with hinges for joints so they could sit down and move their legs and arms. Then he asked a lady who was quite an artist to paint hair, eyes, lips, etc. on them. . . . My mother found one of the dolls by her stocking [that Christmas morning], and in her stocking were a few raisins and several pieces of molasses candy and a slice from an apple. . . . How happy she was! Then [Thomas] let her and a younger brother carry a doll to each little girl in the settlement. Both they and their mothers wept for joy."[36]

Food production was still insufficient to meet the needs of the people from mid-1863 to the harvest of 1865, producing only three-fourths of what was needed. A serious drought that began in 1864 compounded the problem, which continued to worsen in 1865. Wheat and flour transported over the rough wagon roads from the northern settlements was expensive and beyond the ability of most to afford, and they had little to send north or to trade in return.

Erastus Snow visited all the settlements late in the fall of 1864 and found that wheat and flour were in such short supply that they would

---

35. The factory produced both cotton and woolen cloth. But the end of the Civil War in 1865 and then the coming of the railroad to Corinne in 1869 brought low-priced competition from the East and the South, and the need for the factory gradually collapsed. The building currently houses a nursery business.

36. Thompson, "Thomas Cottam," 42, from an account by Lula Romney Clayson. Years later, one of the recipients of these dolls said, "I have loved and cherished that doll for over 50 years. I shall never forget that Christmas morning. We had been told Santa couldn't come so far so it was such a happy surprise to get a doll like that."

not last until another harvest.[37] This meant that as soon as spring broke, people would be coursing through the fields, hillsides, and river banks for whatever "greens" they could find to supplement their diet. Some of the less courageous abandoned the mission. But Erastus was encouraged that in spite of community-wide hunger, most hung on.[38]

An apocryphal tale shared by several, that is also attributed to Elder J. Golden Kimball many years later, has it that George A. Smith quipped to Erastus Snow: "If I had a lot here and one in Hell, I'd sell the one in St. George and live in Hell." Whether or not either man actually made such a quip, there is no doubt that the incredibly challenging living conditions in St. George in the early 1860s would have merited it.

Amelia Jarvis Webb, age 12, whose father, George, was one of the few true volunteers[39] to come south in 1861, wrote that once during the summer of 1864 "I was so hungry that I ate all the green tops from the onions in the garden. Father thought I had let the chickens in and I never told him the truth of the matter."[40]

Ann Prior Jarvis, wife of George Jarvis and Amelia's mother, remembered: "I have seen the tears rolling down the cheeks of my children because of hunger when I had nothing to give them. . . . I expect we would have sold ourselves for flour if anyone would have bought us."[41]

And John S. Stucki, who seemed to have similar thoughts to Sister Jarvis, remembers:

---

37. Larson, *Erastus Snow*, 360.
38. Larson, *Erastus Snow*, 343.
39. Though not officially called, when George Jarvis first heard of the Cotton Mission, he immediately volunteered and with his wife and children became invaluable members of the new community.
40. Amelia Jarvis Webb, "Memories," 6, typescript, Daughters of Utah Pioneers McQuarrie Memorial Museum, St. George, Utah. Amelia, who gave birth to twelve children, was born 3 January 1853 at Garden Place, Poplar, England, and died in St. George 13 August 1908.
41. Carol M. Vincent, "Ann Prior Jarvis, 1829–1913," typescript, Daughters of Utah Pioneers McQuarrie Memorial Museum, St. George, Utah.

"We did not have a thing to eat except pigweeds, cooked in water without anything more nourishing to go with them as we had no cow, no flour and no seasoning of any kind, not even a bit of bread for the little children. When they would cry for some bread, mother would not have any to give, which seemed awfully hard for a mother suffering the pangs of hunger herself. . . . Every day I had to gather the pigweeds. It seemed to me that I could not stand it much longer and live. After we did not have anything else but pigweed for a long time, I was so hungry and weak, although being very small, I asked my father if he would let me go to see if I could not find someone, either in St. George or Washington, that would take me in to feed me for what work I could do, but I could not find anyone in St. George that would accept me that way. Then I went to Washington [where at length I] found a good old Danish couple, by the name of Iverson, that took me in. [Then] I had a good living."[42]

Not satisfied with appeasing his own hunger, however, young John "decided to . . . see if I could find someone that would take my sister, Mary Ann, in. She was about three [and] a half years younger than I. I found a young couple with twin babies that took her in to help with the babies. So she had a better living also. Then I was still very much worried for my parents and the two other little children that they might die of hunger and decided to search the town again to see if I could find anyone that would loan my father some flour. After asking in many houses I found a man that promised to let my father have fifty pounds of flour. It caused the tears to come in [Father's] eyes."[43]

But even those generous efforts did not satisfy the thoughtful boy. He concludes: "I have never forgotten when on a Sunday morning I would [walk] home the eleven or twelve miles, and the good old lady [I stayed with] would give me quite a big bunch of pancakes to take along for my dinner. How I used to rejoice . . . that I could bring those

42. Stucki, *Family History Journal*, 64.
43. Stucki, *Family History Journal*, 65–66.

pancakes to my little brother and sister so they could have a little better dinner . . . and I could eat the pigweeds instead of them [as] I knew how it was to be so awfully hungry."[44]

In addition to the Saints' "greens," small game such as rabbits, ground squirrels, gophers, rodents, and even snakes, all of which the local natives also depended on, were vigorously sought after to assuage the hunger in their pinched bellies. In addition to young John Stucki and his family, many others no doubt felt the lean times as acutely as George Hicks, who lamented:

> *I feel so weak and hungry now, I think I'm really dead;*
> *'Tis seven weeks next Sunday since I have tasted bread.*
> *Of carrot tops and lucern greens we have enough to eat—*
> *But I'd like to change that diet off for buckwheat cakes and meat.*[45]

The situation had become critical. Erastus Snow knew that food-stuffs were absolutely needed from the north. He rushed a plan, asking families to gather whatever each might have that could be sent north to barter for flour and grain. People sent what they could, including things they could ill afford to lose. Many sent farm implements, other tools, and kitchen articles. Some sent their guns, others articles of clothing. They stripped themselves of anything of value that they could spare. The items were collected, identified by contributor, and sent north in wagons to be traded for whatever wheat and flour the articles would bring.[46]

Despite their best efforts, however, it was never enough. Though a few families gave up and went elsewhere, the majority simply tightened their belts or apron strings and plodded onward, certain that one day

---

44. Stucki, *Family History Journal*, 66.
45. Larson, *I Was Called to Dixie*, 123.
46. Larson, *Erastus Snow*, 360–61.

soon their fasting and prayers would be rewarded and they would be blessed with sufficient for their needs.

Nevertheless, even in such extremities, not all was gloom and doom. Dixieites were on the whole a well-educated and cultured people, and it showed in many ways, including their keeping a positive attitude in the midst of intense and unending difficulty. As an example, after filing application, the St. George Library Association won incorporation by act of the territorial legislature in January 1864. In fact, this library was one of the first to be organized in the Territory of Utah by legislative act.[47] A number of the foremost citizens, including Erastus Snow and Orson Pratt, were named to its board of directors.

Besides having a yearning for books, the citizens also expended energy in a variety of other cultural pursuits such as a gardening club, bands and an orchestra, and a dramatic troupe. From wherever they came—the Salt Lake Valley, Nauvoo, or their Eastern or foreign homelands, and no matter how dark the future seemed, culture was an important part of their heritage, and Dixie's citizenry were continually seeking cultural entertainment and enrichment. Besides dancing, choirs and bands were organized at the very start and made music available for every holiday and public occasion. Theatrical productions filled the calendar, presenting nationally current dramas and plays performed by excellent acting and musical talent. A children's choir furnished singing at meetings in the bowery. The 1860s did not yet have the large auditoriums and stages that became available in the 1870s, but from the beginning and even in the toughest years, public entertainment was encouraged by Church leaders and eagerly participated in by all, including local poets, gifted orators, songwriters, good singers, choirs and bands, actors, and people experienced in all aspects of theater. Cultural diversions helped people endure the harshness of pioneer life. For instance, of events on the Fourth of July 1864, Charlie Walker wrote, "Hot and clear Went up to the Liberty pole before sunrise. Played the

---

47. Larson, *I Was Called to Dixie*, 507.

national airs. 9 A.M. playing in the procession of Military &c. Went through the principal streets, thence to the bowery where the citizens had assembled. Music. Declaration of Independence was read. Speeches, toasts, songs, &c made up the entertainment. At night I played Captain O Scuttle in the Farce of Poor Pillicody at the Hall. Came home late."[48]

Charlie's journal also reflects the daily work and side occupations of many. He worked days as a stonemason helping lay up the walls of the tabernacle. Besides this, he was often called upon to prepare the bodies of the dead for burial, and he always filled his numerous and diverse callings in the Church. He also found time to obey Erastus Snow's requests to write poems and songs for most occasions and to take acting parts during the evenings in musicals, dramas, and farces. One of the peoples' favorites, presaging the growing self-confidence and community spirit that emerged out of the hard times of the 1860s, was a ditty Charlie wrote that went as follows:

> *Oh what a desert place was this*
> *When first the Mormons found it.*
> *They said no white man here could live*
> *And Indians prowl'd around it.*
>
> *'Twas said the land it was no good,*
> *And water was no gudder,*
> *And the bare Idea of living here*
> *Was enough to make one shudder.*
>
> *Chorus:*
> *Muskeet, soap root,*
> *Prickly pears, and briars,*
> *St. George ere long will be a place*
> *That every one admires.*

48. Larson, *I Was Called to Dixie*, 262.

Now green Lucern in verdant spots,
Bedecks our thriving City.
Whilst vines and fruit trees grace our lots
And flowretts sweet and pretty.

Where once the grass in single blades,
Grew a mile apart in distance,
It kept the crickets on the go
To pick up their subsistence.

The Sun it is so scorching hot
It makes the water siz, sir.
And the reason why it is so hot
'Tis just because it is, sir.

The [wind] like fury here does blow
That when we plant or sow, sir,
We place our foot upon the seed
And hold it till it grows, sir.[49]

In such ways the families of southern Utah somehow kept up their spirits and scraped by; Erastus and his bishops were always hard pressed to see that none went completely without. Through 1865 the drought continued, with half the expected rainfall, and July and August daily temperatures ranged from 108 to 117 degrees Fahrenheit. George A. Smith, now a counselor to President Brigham Young, lauded the people of Dixie in the October 1865 general conference but also told of their hard times and the need for more people to build up that part of Zion (an additional call did take place but not until 1867). He said: "We have been gratified very much with the efforts and exertions made by our brethren who were sent on missions to our cotton region. . . . They have met with many difficulties. . . . The soil along their streams . . .

---

49. Walker, *Diary*, 1:369.

is composed of such loose material that it is almost impossible to carry a water ditch through it . . . ; dams are washed away . . . , and yet the courage, energy, perseverance, and dilligence of the brethren have not failed. . . . This perseverance, which will eventually bring forth an abundant supply of the needful staples . . . is very commendable."[50]

He went on to add that the Dixie farmers had managed to increase the yield of foodstuffs in 1865, though most were still short of their needs. And yet, he added, "Many vineyards have come into bearing, and extensive new vineyards have been planted. . . . As I [earlier] passed through the [alkali-laden] lots in St. George, I saw their barren aspect. . . . yet men are conquering this soil and making it produce. Nearly three-fourths of all the fruit trees [first] planted in St. George have been unsuccessful, yet the place is [now] looking like the Garden of Eden, showing that perseverance, faith, and energy will conquer everything . . . those brethren . . . are yet struggling . . . but they are not discouraged . . . and [they are] determined to overcome. A people possessed of such great energy . . . are bound to conquer that desert, and not only make it blossom as the rose, but make one of the most delightful regions of the earth."[51] He then asked for additional "skilled men" to take their families and settle in the southern region.

---

50. *Journal of Discourses*, 26 vols. (London: Latter-day Saints' Book Depot, 1854–86), 11:156.
51. *Journal of Discourses*, 11:156–57.

Chapter 3

THE WILDERNESS
SLOWLY RETREATS

1866–1871

George Staheli of Santa Clara, still without his beloved cornet, found life as challenging as did all the others. Each day he "would walk five miles to work, going without breakfast. They would give him his dinner where he worked and he would walk five miles back home each night and go without supper to save food for his children. In the year 1865 the grasshoppers came. In three days they had eaten everything except castor beans and garlic. The next year however, the Saints finally had a good crop, and from then on things seemed to get better. [In 1866] by a stroke of good fortune, John R. Itten, another member of the Swiss Company, received word that he was heir to part of an estate in the old country. And would he, in settlement of the estate, accept a set of ten band instruments valued at $80.00. [He did, and] donated the band instruments to George Staheli and the people of Santa Clara. Once more George was able to play the cornet and teach the other instruments to the people.

"Lack of sheet music was only a temporary handicap, as he was gifted and able to write the music for each instrument. He wrote his own music, some from tunes he knew, and others he composed. He was called Professor Staheli or Trumpeter Staheli. [Now he walked] five miles to St. George to band practice and back again. He also played once a week for a dance in St. George. For his pay he received flour, potatoes, dried fruit, meat, or anything else in the line of food for his family."[1]

Another fairly new southerner, John Peck Chidester, who in 1861 had come south with his wife, Susannah Foy, settled on the millstream in Washington where he spent the first winter living in his wagon box and clearing off his land. In the spring he planted cotton as well as vegetables, hay and grain for his stock, and fruit trees, particularly peach, and grape vines, and over time these did well, water being plentiful in his area. His crops and produce he willingly shared during the lean years, and many were blessed thereby.

John's skills as a carpenter were recognized early, and he was called upon to help build the tithing barn and granary in Washington and the tabernacle in St. George, as well as the school in Washington. "From 1865 through 1868, he was the chief carpenter and superintended the construction of the cotton mill or factory, cutting the timbers and doing the mortise work all with hand tools. By the time the factory became operational, the Chidester girls were old enough that along with their mother they began working there."[2]

In an 1865 report sent to George A. Smith of the First Presidency, Erastus Snow wrote: "The work upon the basement of our meeting-house is substantial and progressing slowly. . . . The chief difficulty [is] the extreme scarcity of breadstuff, especially in St. George and Washington. We thought ourselves hard pressed last year, but it did not compare with the almost universal cry for bread that rings in my ears from early dawn till midnight, and at every corner of the streets. Beef, if

1. LaRae Farnsworth, "Lie of George Johann Staheli," n.d., n.p., Daughters of the Utah Pioneers McQuarrie Memorial Museum, St. George, Utah.
2. Thelma Chidester Anderson, "John Peck Chidester, Pioneer of 1860," 1972, n.p., Daughters of Utah Pioneers McQuarrie Memorial Museum, St. George, Utah.

possible, is scarcer than bread, for the winter has been very hard upon our stock, what little is left.

"I have bought hundreds of bushels of breadstuff, and hauled it down from Beaver and Iron Counties, to feed the families of workmen upon our roads and other public works, without which there must have been much more suffering."[3]

Always Dixieites were kept busy eking out a living in their harsh environment. Besides agriculture, numerous specialized industries were beginning to spring up that brought in additional income or foodstuffs. The first of three such industries, which started out innocently enough but soon evolved into something else, was the growing of grapes for wine. Vines brought in from California grew well in the warm Dixie climate, and the grapes, when pressed, produced an excellent wine that was used for the sacrament and other local needs. One boy, Edward H. Snow, reported, "I had a vine from which I picked enough grapes one year to buy me a pair of shoes from Judge McCoulough, who marketed the grapes in Pioche, Nevada, then a thriving mining camp."[4]

In fact, it didn't take long before most of the juice pressed in Dixie was being crocked or barreled and allowed to ferment, after which it was sold for a truly handsome profit to the Gentiles who occasionally passed through, as well as to the miners from Nevada and, later on, Silver Reef and other Utah mining communities. Because the revelation to Joseph Smith known today as "the Word of Wisdom" had not yet been codified or accepted as a commandment, many of the Saints also took a sip or two.[5] Quickly this practice of occasionally imbibing spread to the young people of the community, particularly the young men. Martha Cragun Cox wrote: "Scarcely a young man could be found that was free of this

---

3. Erastus Snow to George A. Smith, 20 March 1865, in "Correspondence," *Deseret News*, 5 April 1865, quoted in Michael N. Landon, "A Shrine to the Whole Church," *Mormon Historical Studies* 12, no. 1 (Spring 2011): 129–30.

4. Susan Arrington Madsen, *Growing Up in Zion: True Stories of Young Pioneers Building the Kingdom* (Salt Lake City: Deseret Book, 1996), 113.

5. Doctrine and Covenants 89.

vice. For some time, Walter E. Dodge was the [chief] dispenser of the stuff. 'Dodge' became the synonym of wine and wine cellar. . . . There was a crowd of young men who would regularly take their carousal. They literally wore out their lives in drunkenness and exposure."[6]

After being courted by several of these young men and seeking in vain for one who did not imbibe, and sincerely worried about where marriage to one of these might lead her and their future children, Martha prayerfully approached the family of one Mr. Cox, a humble, *sober* polygamist who already had two wives. After getting quite well acquainted with the women and finding she truly loved them and they her, she quietly asked if they thought their husband might be willing to bring her into their family as his third wife. This was done, but not all were pleased. She recorded: "My decision to marry into a plural family tried my family, all of them, and in giving them trial I was sorely tried. . . . The fact was I had asked the Lord to lead me in the right way for my best good and the way to fit me for a place in his kingdom. He had told me how to go and I must follow in the path He dictated, and that's all there was to it."[7] A summary of her published memoirs indicates that she made the right decision. She was loved and happy through her life, her several children grew to revere and respect her as well as the families of her two sister-wives, and as far as can be determined she never had cause to regret her difficult decision.[8]

A second industry that flourished for many years in Dixie, particularly after 1870, was silk making. Among the trees Samuel and Lydia Knight planted on their Santa Clara property shortly after their 1861 arrival were mulberry trees. By the late 1860s, Lydia was growing silkworms and harvesting their cocoons. She was joined in this enterprise by Caroline Jackson, who had planted a mulberry grove on her St.

---

6. Martha Cragun Cox, *Face toward Zion: Pioneer Reminiscences and Journal of Martha Cragun Cox* (privately published, Francis N. Bunker Family Organization and Isaiah Cox Family Organization, Martha Cragun Branch, 1985), 102–3.

7. Cox, *Journal*, 89–90.

8. Cox, *Journal*, 90–269.

George property, and Ann C. Woodberry, who helped keep the industry going for the next twenty-five years.[9]

Finally, because Dixie was first called "The Cotton Mission," and
because the Civil War largely ended the Saints' ability to import cotton
from the South, the success of the early Dixie settlers in the growth and
manufacture of that product for both commerce and personal use is also
worth considering. John Stucki records: "As soon as we could get some
cotton seed we began to raise a little cotton. At first we would pick
cotton from the seed by hand and spin it into yarn. Then a man . . . in
Santa Clara [purchased] a cotton gin. My father and his brother built
a gin house and a water wheel to furnish power to run the cotton gin.
Quite a few people got spinning wheels and other[s] got looms to weave
the yarn into cloth. There was a time when going through town of an
evening, it seemed to me the spinning wheels were humming in nearly
one third of the homes. Before that, people had no money to buy out of
a store and if they could have had money they would not have bought
much . . . as calico was a dollar a yard, and all other goods in like pro-
portion. Some had to make clothes of wagon covers and tent cloth or go
nearly naked. Thus people were [blessed] to make [their own] cloth."[10]

---

9. Kate B. Carter, comp., *Heart Throbs of the West* (Salt Lake City: Daughters of Utah
Pioneers, 1937), 1:11–15. Silkworms when first hatched were very tiny, but from
then on they never stopped eating mulberry leaves, twenty-four hours a day. In six
weeks the worms reached full growth and began spinning a web, which quickly
became a tight cocoon. Before the moth could hatch, the cocoons were soaked
in hot water, which killed the moth and separated the silk filaments to be un-
wound. Usually eight of these filaments were spun on a spinning wheel into a
single thread, and these threads were finally woven into the lovely silk fabric cherished by so many. Hannah Baldwin Crosby, wife of Jesse Crosby, who was called
by Brigham Young to be a lifetime temple ordinance worker in the St. George
Temple, gave room and board to the men who came in the early 1870s to work on
the sacred structure. She meanwhile raised silkworms on shelves in her bedroom,
from which she spun and wove enough cloth to make a white dress and silk stock-
ings to wear to the temple. This dress is presently on display at the Daughters of
Utah Pioneers McQuarrie Memorial Museum in St. George. Hannah labored in
the temple for thirty years, finally stopping the week before her death.

10. John S. Stucki, *Family History Journal of John S. Stucki* (Salt Lake City: Pyramid
Press, 1982), 52–53.

Juanita Brooks observed: "From the first, the people of [Dixie] expected great things; they were always on the edge of something wonderful about to happen. Had not Brother Brigham prophesied that they would build a thriving city? . . . It was the business of the local people to help bring about [this] prediction. As early as 1862 they had dreamed of having clear, cold water, free from sediment and mineral. After the proper business of locating the underground stream by means of a forked peach stick in the hands of a water witch, they sank a well on the public square. It was 172 feet deep and still dry when John Laub arrived in May, 1863, and he worked on it until the end of July. Charles L. Walker, on 21 June 1863, reported: ' . . . the artesian well has been bored to the depth of some 200 feet, but no water issues forth as yet. . . . ' [Unhappily, however deep it got] the well remained a dry hole in the ground . . . [until finally] the people filled up the hole."[11]

In spite of this and other setbacks, including a great plan to build a wharf and warehouse at Call's Landing on the Colorado River in order to facilitate shipping goods and passengers to and from California, but which never shipped a single human being or pound of goods,[12] these hard years did help bond the people and form the character of the community. For "when men [and women] believe with all their hearts that they are called by a prophet of God to do a job, they find that job possible to do. Gradually, with sweat, unceasing toil, and daily yearning towards their Heavenly Father, they accomplished what they set out to do."[13]

To no one's surprise, and many ascribed it to their constant faith and prayers, rainfall improved in 1865 and was even more abundant in 1866. That meant the harvests were also better. Fruit trees, nut trees,

11. Juanita Brooks, "The Cotton Mission," *Utah Historical Quarterly* 29 (July 1961), 219.
12. Brooks, "Cotton Mission," 219.
13. Thelma Chidester Anderson, "John Madison Chidester, Pioneer of 1850," n.d., 7, typescript, Daughters of Utah Pioneers McQuarrie Memorial Museum, St. George, Utah.

and grape vines matured and produced abundant produce for fresh consumption, "bottling," and drying. Almonds especially, along with sun-
dried peaches, apricots, and raisins, were nourishing and tasteful in the
wintertime, and a surplus could be sold to northern co-ops and peddled
by individuals in the towns of central Utah. Molasses from sugar cane
became a valuable product, both for home consumption and trading,
Dixie sorghum becoming highly prized in the northern settlements.
Alkali, the soil nemesis of the first years, through ample use of animal
manure and regular irrigation, was gradually leached and washed out
of the soil. This left fields and gardens in excellent shape to produce
crops. Alfalfa or lucerne for hay was raised more abundantly from 1866
onward, and over time became the most important field crop raised by
Dixie farmers. At the same time, productive gardens on the large city
lots greatly improved diets, food variety, and winter storage.

By all accounts, St. George at the end of the first decade had become an attractive community. Even in 1867 Elder John Taylor was
moved to say, "St. George is the best and most pleasant looking city in
the Territory."[14]

The isolation the community in general had long felt, being so far
removed from Church headquarters and national and world events, was
mitigated not alone by Brigham Young's numerous visits but also by the
completion, on 15 January 1867, of a telegraph line from Salt Lake City.
Its arrival at the St. George Hall where a telegraph office was set up
was reason to celebrate. Charlie Walker wrote: "Communication was
opened . . . immediately and in a little while we were gratified by receiving a dispatch from our beloved President Brigham Young . . . although
hundreds of miles distant."[15]

That same spring the community launched yet another ambitious

14. Juanita Brooks, "Early Buildings," *Utah Historical Quarterly* 29 (July 1961): 245.
15. Charles Lowell Walker, *Diary of Charles Lowell Walker*, edited by A. Karl Larson
    and Katharine Miles Larson, 2 vols. (Logan: Utah State University Press, 1980),
    1:278.

building project—the county courthouse. The same craftsmen who were working on the tabernacle also worked on this building. When completed in 1870, the courthouse had a basement and two upper floors, and was a most impressive building. So, too, would be the tabernacle, the basement of which was finished by the end of June 1868 with the first public meeting held in the unfinished building on 20 March 1869.[16] It would be 1872 before the tower was finished and clocks and bells were installed in its square section, with a clock face on each of the four sides. Even so, Zaidee Walker Miles described what it did for community pride: "The old town had moved forward. . . . They had a clock and a bell. . . . It was grand to have the Clock. . . . We loved it because it gave us prestige. . . . It raised the morale of the people. We went to Church on time, came home on time, opened and closed parties by its time. Our night ramblings were stopped by the pointing hand of the Clock and the clear ringing of the Bell."[17]

With all the grueling labor and the sacrifice of even the basics, often year after year, what was it that set these people apart, that compelled them to stay and keep at it? First and foremost, it was their faith, their religion, the inner core of their belief. Throughout his journal, Charlie Walker expressed this again and again. While still living in the Salt Lake Valley he wrote: "I feel thankful that I'm here and identified with the Saints of the most high God, and when I reflect upon the blessings the Lord has bestowed upon us, his Saints, my heart swells with gratitude, and I feel like praising his holy name all the Day long."[18]

The St. George Stake was officially organized in 1869, with Joseph W. Young, Brigham's eldest son, called as the first stake president. The stake was vast, extending from Shunesburg on the East Fork of the Virgin River, west across Washington County to the settlements on the

---

16. Albert E. Miller, *The Immortal Pioneers: Founders of the City of St. George* (privately published: Albert E. Miller, 1946), 93.

17. Andrew Karl Larson, *I Was Called to Dixie* (Salt Lake City: Deseret New Press, 1961), 574–75.

18. Larson, *I Was Called to Dixie*, 155.

east fringe of Nevada, and south to include Bunkerville and Mesquite. The members of the stake met in both ward and stake meetings. The women's Relief Society performed valuable service; visiting teaching was conducted by the sisters, and a precursor of home teaching, called block teaching, was carried out by the brethren of the priesthood; priesthood bearers administered to the sick while the sisters lovingly cared for and served all who needed them. Baptisms were performed in the Virgin River or in a pond beneath the Red Hill. Priesthood leadership obtained training in doctrine and administration in a school of the prophets, organized in St. George in November 1868 and presided over by Erastus Snow or by Brigham Young when he was in town.

In the mid-twentieth century, Larry Logue, a non-Latter-day Saint sociologist at the University of Oklahoma, published a study of social life in early St. George. He was impressed with the "rhythm" of religious life, of Sunday services, weeknight priesthood and Relief Society meetings, prayer circles for men, Bible classes for women, high council meetings, "ward" (formerly "block") teaching and visiting teaching. The first Thursday of each month was fast day "with its own meeting and offering for the poor."[19] The Mormon ideal of the family and its extension into the community was exemplified by the custom of addressing each other as *brother* and *sister*. Common terms of respect included calling elderly men *father* and elderly women *aunt, auntie,* or *mother*. People settled "intractable quarrels" with Church leaders serving as arbiters or in priesthood councils.[20] In all their meetings speakers taught doctrine, urged unity and repentance, and encouraged personal prayer and scripture reading.

Every settlement was a religious settlement. Folks called to Dixie had been sent as missionaries. Religion was part of everyday life, and moral conviction was put into constant practice. At the same time,

---

19. Larry M. Logue, *A Sermon in the Desert: Belief and Behavior in Early St. George* (Urbana: University of Illinois Press, 1947), 17–18.

20. Logue, *Sermon in the Desert*, 30–31.

civic life and civic government in every Mormon community was an extension of their religious life—a natural extension of Church order. Every man elected or appointed to civil position was also a Church elder, either already holding ecclesiastical office or else in good standing in the community. They practiced what they preached, striving to uphold in community life the moral values taught by the Church.

Another entry by Charlie Walker in his diary reflects this attitude. Commenting on a Sunday talk by Erastus Snow given on 1 July 1866, Walker wrote that the Apostle "showed what kind of men should hold the reins of government in their hands, namely men that would rather die than do an unjust act, and would scorn to cloak wickedness or oppress the innocent and helpless."[21] The Saints expected good governance by their leaders. Community life was the civic face of religious life. "The thought of separation of Church and State never even occurred to them."[22]

By 1871, St. George and its people had come of age. Ten years after its founding, it had matured into a beautiful, livable community. It was surrounded no longer by a forbidding country of desolation but a land of, as a modern resident put it, "'indescribable beauty: wild, primitive, unspoiled, largely unknown, waiting to be enjoyed, waiting to inspire folks and bring them near to their God. [In this place,] it is easy to declare the glory of God, to feel the strength of the hills, to rejoice in the goodness of God, and to sense the order and planning in the Universe.' . . . there might be 'places more spectacular, but few could equal [this one] in serenity and peace.'"[23]

Moreover, building the tabernacle and other significant structures had been good preparation for what lay ahead. The labor required had trained a core of skilled workers and artisans, and had prepared

---

21. Walker, *Diary*, 1:262.

22. Logue, *Sermon in the Desert*, 6.

23. Orval Hafen, *Journal*, as quoted in Bruce C. Hafen, "Pools of Living Water: No Longer a Thirsty Land," *BYU Studies* 51 (2012): 1.

the necessary infrastructure for leadership as well. More important, the undaunted faith of all the people, their courage and determination, their acceptance of mutual cooperation as they labored to fulfill their difficult missions and lives, was more than impressive.[24] After referring to Doctrine and Covenants 133:29, one native son wrote: "Something about digging essentially with your bare hands until you find pools of living water in a barren desert changes you for the better, especially when your motive for digging is to help and cooperate with your neighbors. With irrigation as with everything else they did, [the early Dixie settlers'] very lives depended upon their mutual cooperation. They learned that human interdependence is not a pleasantry but a necessity."[25]

Thus, without hidden intentions or any other desire but to please the Lord by being obedient to their leaders, the Saints of Dixie had readied themselves to receive a greater opportunity, honor, and blessing than any of them could have imagined.

---

24. The 1870 census reveals that the total population of Washington County—all the communities in the area of southwestern Utah—was 3,064. When one considers the relatively small number of males who could be called to the workforce, one sees how imperative it was that all have deep faith to accept another daunting assignment from Church leaders.

25. Hafen, "Pools of Living Water," 1. "And in the barren deserts there shall come forth pools of living water; and the parched ground shall no longer be a thirsty land" (D&C 133:29).

Chapter 4

BRIGHAM YOUNG'S DECISION

1870–1871

In 1864, Brigham Young, who was suffering greatly from arthritis, began spending a week or two each winter in St. George, where he could take advantage of the warmer climate.[1] Besides the weather, there was something else that kept drawing Brigham back with increasing frequency and for longer periods of time. The former builder and glazier had come to truly admire the grit and spirit of Dixie's inhabitants. On Thursday, 9 November 1871, as he dedicated the site for the future temple, he declared to them: "The idea may arise that this is a hard land in which to get a living. Now I am very thankful for the land just as it is. . . . It's a splendid country in which to rear saints."[2] What he was telling them was that he loved them and had come to feel a personal investment in their miracle—the miracle that had gradually transformed Dixie's obedient and courageously stubborn people, as well as the harsh

---

1. See Leonard J. Arrington, *Brigham Young: American Moses* (Chicago and Urbana: University of Illinois Press, 1986), 295.

2. James G. Bleak, "Historian Southern Mission Mem. Book, Commencing April 6, 1871," Thursday, 9 November 1871, n.p., holograph; photocopy in possession of the authors.

desert country of the Virgin River drainage they had come to cherish, into something more noteworthy, even glorious, than anyone, himself included, might have expected. Thus, with great poignancy he also told them: "I have not seen a house or a congregation in the South, but what I have felt a good spirit there; if it was my lot to live here, I could be happy."[3]

Why was the prophet affected so deeply? Because in the midst of abject poverty, unrelenting adversity, often literal starvation, and almost total isolation, these several hundred people had founded and built up a series of communities that by the winter of 1870–71 were comparable to the finest in the entire Territory. To illustrate, in March 1870 Charles R. Savage, a noted Latter-day Saint photographer, traveled south with Brigham's party. He kept a daily record of his observations, a written window through which modern observers can catch glimpses of things as they then were. On 9 March he recorded: "Today we commenced the descent of the rim[;] as we advanced[,] the whole character of the country changes, everything is broken and craggy . . . all around us the earth looks like it had been calcimined [whitewashed], the rocks are a bright red, very few spots of green, everything broken up and desolate looking."

Three days later, in St. George, he was of a completely different mindset: "Spent considerable time in looking through Brother Joseph E. Johnson's garden, where grow figs, pomegranates, almonds, grapes of every kind; everything seems to be growing very luxuriantly; there has been a miraculous amount of labor performed in bringing into cultivation the land around St. George, for on every hand [the] crops out-do any[thing] . . . some shoots of mulberry have been known to grow at the

3. Brigham Young, remarks given at Grafton, Utah, 29 September 1864, in Manuscript History of the Church, 749, Church History Library, The Church of Jesus Christ of Latter-day Saints, Salt Lake City, Utah.

rate of ½ inch to ¾ per diem. Bro. Johnson gave me a fine collection of the finest kinds of European grapes."[4]

After nine incredibly difficult years and "mountains of labor,"[5] not only had the Dixie Saints proven their own obedient and self-sacrificing mettle but their homes and personal properties had been made comfortable and attractive and their community buildings—the St. George Hall, the busily humming cotton factory in Washington, the lovely county courthouse, and the as-yet-unfinished but already stunning St. George tabernacle—were magnificent and well-built. Solid foundations, finely cut stone walls, timbered floors, inner walls and roofs, and even the plaster and finished woodwork all bespoke structural integrity and finely crafted artistry that was not bettered anywhere in the Territory. It was truly remarkable how much the people of Dixie had accomplished, both inwardly and outwardly.

Yes, the large Church-sponsored public works projects had provided them with both work and payment in kind so they might barely survive. Nevertheless, by accepting Brigham's call to uproot their lives and go south to start over, these Dixie Saints had been asked to sacrifice everything, and they had not held back.[6]

4. Kate B. Carter, comp., *Our Pioneer Heritage* (Salt Lake City: Daughters of Utah Pioneers, 1974), 14:41–42.

5. Carter, *Our Pioneer Heritage*, 14:41–42.

6. See *Lectures on Faith* (Salt Lake City: Deseret Book, 1985), 69.

Chapter 5

A TEMPLE'S BEGINNINGS

1871

On 31 January 1871, five weeks after his arrival in St. George, Brigham Young, George A. Smith, and Brigham Young Jr. gathered in a meeting of the St. George school of the prophets held in Erastus Snow's residence, the "Big House."[1] Elder Snow, the stake presidency, members of the high council, and several bishops and their counselors were present. The meeting had addressed normal business when, near the end and "out of the blue," as one who was present described it, Brigham asked, "What [would you think] of building a temple in St. George?"[2] Imagine the astonished looks on the faces of those in attendance. But once the meaning of that question sank in, Erastus Snow shouted, "Glory! Hallelujah!! and all present appeared to share the joy."[3]

---

1. Richard E. Bennett, "Line upon Line, Precept upon Precept: Reflections on the 1877 Commencement of the Performance of Endowments and Sealings for the Dead," *BYU Studies* 44, no. 3 (2005): 54.

2. James G. Bleak, "Annals of the Southern Utah Mission," Book B, 81–82, typescript, Dixie State University Special Collections, St. George, Utah.

3. Caroline S. Addy, "James Godson Bleak, Pioneer Historian of Southern Utah" (master's thesis, Brigham Young University, 1953), 92; photocopy in possession of the authors.

"The brethren unanimously voted in favor of the measure; after which the Council was dismissed with benediction by President Young."[4]

Nine years and one month after the first families had arrived in the St. George Valley, the prophet had challenged them to consider building a temple. And despite circumstances that were still harsh for the settlers, his proposal was met with enthusiasm and joy. Of course the memory of the Nauvoo Temple was still in the minds of many of them, and the very thought of having such a temple right there in their own community was both surprising and thrilling. Neither did they pause to think of the sacrifices it would require or of the meager resources they had with which to build it. There was no second guessing; if the Lord's mortal representative and prophet wanted it, they would do it.

Those in attendance that night had already received the endowment, either in Nauvoo or in the Endowment House in Salt Lake City, and knew the doctrine of necessary eternal ordinances. They, including their young people, were traveling 320 miles or more to the Endowment House in Salt Lake City to receive endowments, to have marriages sealed, or to perform baptisms for their deceased ancestors. The thought of having a temple in St. George, where all these ordinances could be performed all the time, for the living as well as for the dead, filled them with joy.

Brigham and his party returned to Salt Lake City in March and nothing more was heard from Church headquarters until a letter came in April. On the evening of Saturday, 15 April 1871, "locals first heard the news at a meeting of the St. George School of the Prophets" in the St. George Hall.[5] Charles Lowell Walker wrote in his diary: "A letter was read from Br Brigham stating that the time had come that the Saints could build a Temple to the most High in St. George. A

---

4. Addy, "James Godson Bleak," 92.
5. Bennett, "Line upon Line."

thrill of joy seemed to pass over the assembly of Elders present, at the announcement."[6]

According to the meeting's minutes, Brigham directed in his letter that "the building, outside measurement, is 142 ft long by 96 ft wide including the buttresses and 80 ft high to the top of the parapet. It will be built of stone, plastered outside and inside. There will be a tower in the center of one end, and on the extreme corners of the same end right and left of the tower are cylinder staircases. One side of the stairs rests in the cylinder, the other side in a newel in the center of the cylinder. The roof will be built flat and covered with roofing similar to that on the New Tabernacle in this [Salt Lake] City. The building will consist of two stories and a basement. The two main rooms or halls, one over the other, will be 100 ft by 80. The ceilings of these will be arched, resting upon columns and so constructed as to admit of 16 Rooms for council and other purposes, on either stories [story]. The height of the main ceilings in the center is 27 ft—the other ceilings about 9 ft. The basement will contain the font and will be used for ceremonial purposes. This letter is dated Salt Lake City April 5th 1871."[7]

Charlie Walker adds: "Br Brigham and Geo A Smith will be down next October to commence the work and give directions concerning its erection etc."[8]

Brigham's letter moved the priesthood leadership of the St. George Stake and Southern Mission into action. Plans were laid and construction foremen were designated; most had already held those posts in the tabernacle and courthouse construction. Miles Romney was named

---

6. Charles Lowell Walker, "Diary of Charles Lowell Walker," edited by A. Karl Larson and Katharine Miles Larson, 2 vols. (Logan: Utah State University, 1980), 1:329.

7. James G. Bleak, "Historian Southern Mission Mem. Book. Commencing April 6, 1871," 15 April 1871, n.p., holograph; photocopy in possession of the authors. It is interesting that the outside dimensions—the "footprint" of the St. George Temple—are the same as the dimensions and footprint of the Nauvoo Temple. With the exception of the font and two assembly halls, however, the differences in the interiors were numerous.

8. Walker, Diary, 1:329.

construction superintendent; Edward L. Parry, head stonecutter and mason. The architect for the Church, Truman O. Angell, was assigned by Brigham to draw the plans. At the same time, Erastus Snow and other local leaders located a lava quarry on the back side of the ridge west of town[9] and tentatively planned a road to it. A sandstone quarry on the north slope of the Red Hill north of town[10] had furnished stone for the walls of the courthouse and tabernacle and could do the same for the temple. A limestone deposit had been discovered at Middleton by teenager Albert C. Foremaster.[11] The limestone, after being burned in a kiln built by Samuel Judd and his sons and combined with sand from the river, would become mortar for the temple.

When the need for it came, they would scout out a virgin ponderosa pine forest on Mt. Trumbull in northern Arizona, 80 miles southeast of St. George, and there find trees of ample size and number. White and red pine for finish work grew closer by, on Pine Valley Mountain. Meanwhile President Young moved quickly to underwrite the temple project by assigning all tithes from Beaver south, both in cash and in kind, for the building of the temple. It would take that much help and more.

Bishop D. D. McArthur brought up the future temple during his stake conference address on Friday, 5 May 1871. The minutes record that "He rejoiced to hear of the building of a temple in the south, but even this blessing was conditional. If the people felt they did not want a temple it would not be built. If they felt to have a temple, holy to the

---

9. Just west of the site of the recently abandoned St. George airport.

10. As unique as the large stone profile of Brigham Young carved by nature into the cliff above modern Bloomington is a profile of Joseph Smith Jr., or perhaps his death mask, in a small alcove a hundred feet above the western end of the sandstone quarry, if one is looking at the darkened sandstone from the northwest. Glen E. Martin suggests that this stone feature was so prominent that early quarry workers may have chosen the site simply because the Prophet's image was there. No records found by the authors either dispute or support Martin's suggestion.

11. Spencer Truman, "Albert Charles Foremaster, My Grandfather," n.d., n.p., typescript, Daughters of Utah Pioneers McQuarrie Memorial Museum, St. George, Utah.

name of the Lord, then we would have one in which to attend to all the ordinances of the Lord's House."[12]

Though the temple may have been part of numerous discussions that summer and fall, the "Minutes of the Southern Mission" record only three discourses dealing with the temple and baptism for the dead, two by Erastus Snow and one by George A. Smith. Far more often they recorded such mundane issues as the daily and often thrice-daily reading of temperatures. For instance, it listed 119½ degrees in the shade at 3:00 P.M. on 13 July, and 119¾ degrees in the shade at 4:00 P.M. on 16 August. (And there was no such thing as air conditioning!)

There were other difficulties as well. Though the Blackhawk Indian War had ended in the late 1860s, it had led to several fatalities in the southern Utah Territory, both Latter-day Saint and American Indian, that left many with a deep sense of anxiety and concern. Martha Cox wrote frequently of her fear of being out at night and alone, particularly in more sparsely settled areas,[13] while twelve-year-old Isaiah Cox wrote rather pridefully of singlehandedly besting an adult and very determined Paiute would-be thief with a long black buggy whip while he was driving his father's team and wagon toward the cedar forest below Pine Valley Mountain. Afterward he boasted, as any twelve-year-old might, that after he had driven the thief away, he "continued on [his] way and returned the next day with a good load of [fire]wood."[14]

In part to allay such fears and incidents, Erastus Snow sent a party of men under command of John David L. Pearce southeast into the desert country near Warner Valley to erect a small stone fort that came to be called Ft. Pearce.[15] Primarily this small stone fortress was built as

---

12. Bleak, "Historian Southern Mission," Friday, May 5.

13. Martha Cragun Cox, *Face toward Zion: Pioneer Reminiscences and Journal of Martha Cragun Cox* (privately published, Francis N. Bunker Family Organization and Isaiah Cox Family Organization, Martha Cragun Branch, 1985), 69–71.

14. Susan Arrington Madsen, *Growing Up In Zion: True Stories of Young Pioneers Building the Kingdom* (Salt Lake City: Deseret Book, 1996), 66.

15. Spelling of Pearce's name as found in Roberta Blake Barnum, "I Was Called to Dixie," *Inside St. George*, Fall 2011, 7. It is still called Ft. Pearce or, incorrectly, Ft.

a protection for the herd boys who cared for the community livestock kept in Warner Valley,[16] though teamsters traveling to and from Mount Trumbull also made it one of their stops.

In the late summer and fall of 1871, as if an unseen enemy were intentionally seeking to halt construction of the future temple, conflicts with the Indians seemed to flare up again. In part this was due to the passing of Paiute Chief Tutsegavit,[17] who had always been friendly with the Saints and so had kept his people in check. Following his death some members of three bands of the Paiutes—the Clara band, the Beaver Dam band, and the Muddy band—began working together in a major stock-raiding venture. In addition, on 14 August, Martin Sanders was treated with great hostility and felt fortunate to escape with his life after encountering a Paiute raiding party near the Gunlock Fort. That was the day the temperature in St. George was recorded at 119¾ degrees in the shade, which may have contributed to the tension.

The next day, two friendly Indians, Mo-enoch and Railroad George, reported in St. George that the stolen stock was being corralled near the head of Beaver Dam Wash. By that time telegrams were flying up and down the lines, but no one seemed able to reach Erastus Snow, who was traveling back from Salt Lake City. To no one's surprise, the Saints learned a few days later from other friendly Indians that the force behind the theft ring was white—Captain Fenton, a United States Indian agent living on the Muddy River, and a Mr. Patterson, a cattle buyer from Nevada purchasing cattle for the White Pine, Belmont, and Pioche mining districts.

Hardly had that issue been dealt with than a Navajo called Peokon

---

Pierce. Built on the western edge of the vast Warner Valley, the fort overlooks a lovely, tree-filled wash bordered on the north by high stone cliffs and the south by desert. Even today good water is almost always found there.

16. Kate B. Carter, comp., *An Enduring Legacy* (Salt Lake City: Daughters of Utah Pioneers, 1981), 10:266.

17. There are some historical indications that Tutsegavit was a baptized Latter-day Saint, but due to different and often fluid renderings in English of both Paiute and Navajo names, we have been unable to find a record of this ordinance.

(or Peokaan)[18] appeared in Kanab with a force of 79 warriors. The son of the always friendly Navajo chief Spaneshanks and brother to Ira Hatch's Navajo-Paiute wife Sarah Maraboots, Peokon was well known to the Saints as an intractable enemy. Not only did he openly hate his sister and disdain his father, but he had also been one of the two murderers of 18-year-old George A. Smith Jr., who was brutally slain while on his mission to the Hopi in 1860.[19]

In Kanab, Peokon and the Navajos quickly "threw off their friendly mask and demanded 70 horses and 17 beeves [cattle] and other smaller things."[20] Noting that three-fifths of the men of Kanab had just returned from the north in his company and were in an exhausted condition, Erastus called for 50 men from nearby communities to go immediately to Kanab. Next he notified Governor Wood in Salt Lake City of the situation. By the next day and the arrival of the fifty reinforcements plus a few more, Peokon and his band abruptly moderated their demands and sought to do some trading, which was accomplished. Bleak's record says nothing more of this short-lived Navajo "raid" until 20 September, when he noted simply that Nagro, another Navajo chief, had arrived in St. George with his own band, brought there in peace by Brother Ammon Tenney, interpreter,[21] to reestablish friendly relations with the Saints.

Though he was kept apprised of these developments through regular telegraph messages, Brigham seems to have paid them little attention

---

18. Spelling according to James Bleak.

19. See Blaine M. Yorgason, *To Soar with the Eagle* (Salt Lake City: Deseret Book, 1994). Peokon, who in addition to hating the whites also hated his sister Sarah Maraboots, granddaughter of the great Paiute chief Kanosh. He is the same Navajo leader who created so many trials for the Hole-in-the-Rock pioneers after their arrival on the San Juan River in 1880. Thales Haskell finally warned him that if he didn't stop his murderous ways, God would take his life. He didn't, so apparently God did. For further information on this expedition, see Blaine M. Yorgason, vols. 1–3 of the *Hearts Afire* series (*At All Hazards, Fort on the Firing Line,* and *Curly Bill's Gift*; Salt Lake City: Deseret Book, 1997, 1999, 2000).

20. Bleak, "Historian Southern Mission," Sunday, 10 September 1871.

21. See Bleak, "Historian Southern Mission," Wednesday, 20 September 1871.

as he forged ahead with his intention to begin temple construction in the fall. Sometime before October he wrote stake president's counselor Robert Gardner asking him to take some brethren and choose a site for the temple. These men looked at three or four locations but could not agree on which would be best suited for the new building. On Wednesday, 1 November 1871, Charlie Walker recorded: "Freezing a little nights and mornings, pleasant in the daytime. Br Brigham, Geo A Smith, Rob Burton, McDonald, O P Rockwell, Bishop Murdock and some others I do not know came in to night. The President has come to start the Temple, and is expected to stay a while with us."[22]

No doubt there was a stir in the community as people considered the magnitude of the work ahead and perhaps made guesses as to where the temple would be located. No one knew, of course, though word was out that the dedication of the site was planned for the following Monday.

Most likely on Thursday morning, Robert Gardner and his companions led President Young and his group in a caravan to their proposed sites, but none satisfied the prophet. Instead, he invited them to board their buggies or wagons and follow him. He led them southeast to a location on the outskirts of town. Pointing to a vacant block (all the blocks were vacant!) he said, "[Here] is where we will build the temple."

Concerning this event, David Henry Cannon Jr. (son of David H. Cannon, third president of the St. George Temple), reported the ensuing conversation: "But," said Gardner, "Brother Young, this land is boggy. After a storm, and for several months of the year, no one can drive across the land without horses and wagons sinking way down. There is no place to build a foundation."

"We will make a foundation," President Young responded.[23]

Time has shown that the temple site was located midway down a

---

22. Walker, *Diary*, 2:334.
23. David Henry Cannon Jr., "St. George Temple Manuscript," 2, Church History Library, The Church of Jesus Christ of Latter-day Saints, Salt Lake City, Utah.

long talus slope that extends through the town from the Red Hill and over halfway down the valley. A block before the site is reached, the slope levels out, only to fall off again in the next block down from the site. This topography creates the level prominence on which the temple was built. When erected, it would stand out above everything around it. But, as pointed out by Gardner and the others, there was a serious problem with the site that had to be overcome before the temple could be built. Ground water seeping down the slope from the Red Hill hits a below-the-surface limestone formation part way into the chosen block. The formation forces the ground water to the surface creating a spring line and resulting in a bog over the south two-thirds of the block. Gardner and the others tried hard to dissuade Brigham from building there, maintaining that the site would not support a foundation firm enough for a heavy building such as a temple. Brigham's unhesitating response was always, "This site was selected by inspiration and dedicated to the Lord."[24] He insisted against all objections that every obstacle would be overcome.[25]

Brigham reaffirmed this decision in a talk given in a St. George Stake conference in May 1873. He had "diligently sought the Lord," he said, "to know the right location for this Temple," and he received assurance that he had chosen "the right place."[26]

Stake conference convened Friday evening, 3 November 1871, and continued through Saturday and Sunday, with many of the speakers discussing the temple. In his Sunday morning address, President Young motivated his listeners, saying, as before mentioned, that although Dixie is "a desert country," it is "a splendid place to rear Saints,"[27] and

---

24. Brigham demonstrated the same kind of spiritual certainty when he chose the site for the Salt Lake Temple. On 28 July 1847, he "identified a center spot between creeks and [with a wave of his hand] declared to his fellow apostles, 'Here is the 40 acres of temple lot'" (Bennett, "Line upon Line," 48).

25. Kirk M. Curtis, "History of the St. George Temple" (master's thesis, Brigham Young University, 1964), 34.

26. Bleak, "Annals," Book B, 183.

27. Bleak, "Annals," Book B, 128. See also Bleak, "Historian Southern Mission,"

though the people were then "sparse in numbers," he was certain they could succeed in the undertaking. He reiterated that the people in Dixie "were better able to build the Temple than were [they] of Kirtland and Nauvoo." "I was there," he continued. "I knew the circumstances of the Church at the building of the Temple at Kirtland and Nauvoo. And I know the circumstances of the people of St. George. . . . We want to build a temple here and I know we can do this. . . . Where the people set their hearts, there you will find their hands busy to accomplish what the will dictates."[28]

Erastus Snow next read the letters from Joseph Smith to the Saints regarding baptism for the dead as "contained in the covenants,"[29] and then reminded the assembled Saints that a temple in their midst would provide all of them with unlimited opportunities to accomplish the work for their own ancestors.

Of that Sunday session, Charlie Walker wrote, "Went to conference. . . . Pres. E. Snow Spoke on Building a Temple, tithing, etc. . . . [Stake president] Jos. W. Young spoke on temple building and the many blessings we should receive therein. Bro Geo A Spoke on the same subject. Spoke of the poverty [of] the Saints in early days when the Kirtland Temple was built. Bro Brigham dwelt on the same strain. Showed that the People of St. George were better able to build a temple today than the saints were at the time of the building of the Kirtland temple. There was a calm peaceful feeling pervaded the conference."[30] Brigham then "put the proposal to a vote. The support was unanimous.[31] The People with uplifted hands voted to build [a temple] in St George."[32]

Sunday, 20 November 1871. There are slight but interesting differences between these two records of Brigham's talk. Apparently they indicate the editing of James G. Bleak, who made both records.

28. Bleak, "Annals," Book B, 128.

29. See Doctrine and Covenants 127, 128.

30. Walker, *Diary*, 2:335.

31. Bleak, "Annals," Book B, 128.

32. Walker, *Diary*, 2:335.

Monday, 6 November 1871, was initially set for the dedication of the temple site, but it rained that day and the survey had not yet been completed. On Wednesday, 8 November, the survey had been completed and corner stakes were set, placing the temple foundation dead center in Block 27, Platt B, St. George City Survey. The block is 32 rods square containing 6⅔ acres. The building was laid out "east and west, 142 feet [long] outside measurement, including the buttresses, by 96 feet wide, to be 80 feet [high] from the grade of the promenade which is to surround the building to the paraput."[33]

The site dedication took place Thursday, 9 November, Elder Snow's birthday. Charles Walker wrote that the day was "clear, bright and p[l]easant." Some "40 carriages and wagons and a large concourse of People congregated on the southeast corner of the site."[34] George Staheli's band from Santa Clara played for the ceremonies, pouring "forth its strains of melodious harmony, and John M. Macfarlane's excellent St. George Choir was there to sing its sacred anthems"[35] while Brigham Young raised the first shovel full of earth from the site.[36]

President George A. Smith, counselor in the First Presidency, "made remarks appropriate to the occasion." Then, called upon by Brigham, George A. offered the following dedicatory prayer:

"Our Father who art in Heaven, we thank Thee for the privilege of meeting at this time for the purpose of dedicating this piece of ground on which we desire to build a Temple to Thy most Holy name. We Thank Thee, O our Father, for this desert land and that we are permitted to shelter ourselves from the enemies of Thy cause. We thank Thee for restoring the Gospel through Thy servant Joseph Smith and that Thou hast conferred upon him the Holy Priesthood to give to thy

---

33. Bleak, "Annals," Book B, 237–38.
34. Walker, *Diary*, 1:335.
35. LaRae Farnsworth, "Life of George Johann Staheli," n.d., n.p., Daughters of the Utah Pioneers McQuarrie Memorial Museum, St. George, Utah.
36. Andrew Karl Larson, *Erastus Snow* (Salt Lake City: University of Utah Press, 1971), 467.

Church, and that when the Prophet and Patriarch were taken from our midst that Thou didst raise up a wise leader in Thy Servant Brigham.

"We thank Thee that Thy servants have reclaimed this desert ground. We thank Thee for this City. We thank Thee that this piece of ground has been surveyed and chosen as a place on which to build a Temple to thy most holy name, in which we may attend to the ordinances thou hast given for the benefit of the living and the dead. May thy servants be united in building this house, that in it thy laws may be revealed, that the ordinance of marriage may be administered according to the Laws of Heaven, and that the sealings may be according to the laws of Heaven.

"Our Father, we pray thee to look in mercy upon thy Servant Brigham; preserve him from all his enemies; grant that he may live long to minister for Zion; bless his wives and his children and his substance; grant that peace may rest upon him, and success attend all his labors in thy Church. Wilt thou look in mercy upon his Counselors, and bless them with the same blessings in their labors; bless their wives and children and all their interests. Do thou bless thy servant brother Daniel H. Wells, by giving him wisdom and power to attend to the affairs in Salt Lake City; deliver him from all his enemies; and from the bonds now held over him.

"Our Father, bless thy servants the Twelve; endow them with thy Spirit; bless their labors for the good of Israel. We pray thee to bless thy servants the Presidents, and Bishops and the Teachers, and all who officiate in thy name. Our Father do thou avenge the wrongs of thy people upon their enemies, pour out upon them the wrath which thou hast in store for them in thine own due time if they will not repent. Hasten the redemption of the Center Stake of Zion on this land; overrule the discovery of minerals in this land for the good of thy people; put hooks in the jaws of the enemies of Zion, and turn them from their wicked purposes.

"May thy peace be upon the pioneers of this desert, and upon all those who have labored to reclaim the same; may eternal blessings rest upon them and their posterity forever. Yes, bless all thy servants who have done this great work, bless their wives, their children, their substance, and do thou bless them in all their labors.

"We thank thee, O God, for these barren hills, and for the shelter of these rugged rocks and deserts as peaceful dwelling places for thy Saints. Bless this land that it may be sacred as an abode of peace and safety, and happy homes for thy people. Bless this ground on which the Temple is to be erected, that it may be held sacred for this purpose; yea, do thou grant that this Temple ground may never be under the dominion or control of the wicked.

"Our Father, do thou bless our brother Erastus Snow, impart unto him wisdom and power to minister to thy people in this region. Do thou bless the President of this Stake of Zion, and his Counselors, that they may minister for the benefit and blessing of thy people. Bless the Bishops in this land; and do thou bless the people who shall be engaged in building a Temple upon this ground. Grant that the walls of that Temple may be laid in truth, and the top stone laid with shouts of Hosannah to God and the Lamb. Cause that thy power may be in the house; that angels may enter therein and minister to thy servants.

"Bless the Bishop of thy Church in the discharge of all his duties. Bless thy Elders who are abroad preaching thy Gospel. Cause thy power to attend their labors, shield them from the influences of the wicked. Do thou shield all thy servants from the wiles of the wicked. Thou hast known, O Lord, that thy servants have tried to obey thy celestial law of marriage, and that the wicked strive to bring evil upon thy people, and to take away their liberty in this thing. Grant thy protections and blessing to thy people, that they may continue to obey the law.

"Our Father, do Thou bless this land. Cause that it may be fruitful, bringing forth blessings for the sustenance of Thy people. Cause the remnants of Jacob to come to the truth, and the children of Judah to gather to their ancient inheritance, and rebuild Jerusalem. All these blessings, our Father, we feel to ask at thy hand. Hear, O hear our prayer, and grant us our petitions.

"We dedicate this site unto Thee. We dedicate ourselves, our wives and our children and all our sustenance unto Thee and now our Father, with all the faithful, save us in thy glorious kingdom, which we ask in the name of Jesus Christ, Amen."[37]

Following the dedicatory prayer and a choir number, President Young added appropriate comments: "We want a concentration of the labors of the people to build this temple. The idea may arise that this is a hard land to get a living in. I am glad of it. I am thankful. I purpose that the Bishops of this City, Santa Clara and Washington apportion labor among their members to excavate, haul rock, sand, and clay, with Brother Erastus Snow and his help. If the brethren undertake to do this with one heart and with one mind, we shall be blessed exceedingly and prospered. If the people present are one with the First Presidency in this work and will unite, let the brethren and sisters manifest it by the uplifted hand." The response was unanimous.[38] The prophet next instructed the bishops of the wards to "apportion the labor of excavation and transportation of rock, sand, and clay among the people in order that the work might get underway at once."[39]

Then, taking a shovel in his hand, the prophet began the groundbreaking, explaining that the first stone should always be laid at the southeast corner of a building because the first light of day shines upon it when the sun rises in the east.[40] Brigham had evidently been taught by the Prophet Joseph the proper order of laying the cornerstones. This was indicated when he arranged the cornerstones for the Manti Temple. On

---

37. Bleak, "Annals," Book B, 125–28, and Bleak, "Historian Southern Mission." Bleak changed the wording slightly from his Memory Book record, even removing certain sentences as he prepared the "Annals" text; we have combined the two.
38. Bleak, "Annals," Book B, 128.
39. Larson, *Erastus Snow*, 467.
40. Heidi S. Swinton, *Sacred Stone: The Temple at Nauvoo* (American Fork, Utah: Covenant Communications, 2002), 46.

that occasion he said that the first stone is to "be laid at the southeast corner, the point of greatest light, and at high noon there is the most sunlight.[41] All that is to remind us, we would assume, that the temple is indeed a house of light where the heavenly and earthly combine."[42]

Brigham then touched the southeast corner stake with his shovel, saying that under it and "in the foundation will be placed a stone containing sacred records, and immediately over the stake, when the building is completed will be placed another stone containing the records of the temple." Then, taking a shovelful from the east side of the center stake he said: "I now commence by removing this dirt—in the name of Israel's God." The company responded with a loud "Amen." The congregation then sang "The Spirit of God like a Fire Is Burning." Then George A. Smith took a shovelful from the south side of the stake, Erastus Snow from the north side, and Joseph W. Young from the west side. Other dignitaries took turns one by one spading out a shovelful of earth.[43] A ceremonial pick was also used in this effort, made especially for the occasion by blacksmith Samuel Lorenzo Adams, and was afterward "donated by him for preservation as a relic in remembrance of the occasion."[44]

After the groundbreaking, Brigham called on Erastus Snow to speak. Elder Snow reminded everyone that "it had been just 10 years since the people had settled in their valley. At that time Brother Brigham had promised them that the Lord, through His people, would accomplish many things in this land." Many of the promises, Elder

---

41. For the same reason, Brigham Young's office in the Nauvoo Temple was located in the southeast corner room of the attic rooms (Lisle G. Brown, "The Sacred Departments for Temple Work in Nauvoo: The Assembly Room and the Council Chamber," *BYU Studies* 19, no. 3 [Spring 1979]: 668).

42. Truman G. Madsen, *The Temple: Where Heaven Meets Earth* (Salt Lake City: Deseret Book, 2008), 104.

43. Andrew Karl Larson, *I Was Called to Dixie* (Salt Lake City: Deseret News Press, 1961), 580. Joseph Young and John Young were sons of Brigham Young. Both were St. George residents. Joseph became the first president of the St. George Stake when it was created in 1869, but he had ill health and died at the early age of 44 in June 1873. (See Walker, *Diary*, 1:370.)

44. Bleak, "Historian Southern Mission," Thursday, 9 November 1871.

Snow said, "were now fulfilled"; moreover, "he had the faith that all would be fulfilled." He also "prayed the Lord to aid us in building the Temple, and to grant that we may live to see it dedicated, and that our beloved President Brigham may live to officiate at its dedication." He closed with "This is my earnest prayer in the name of Jesus Christ amen." The people gave a hearty "Amen."[45]

Then President Young stood on a chair and instructed the company how to perform the Hosanna Shout. Following their leader, as Walker tells it, each raised his right hand to heaven and "smote" or clapped the left hand, at the same time "exclaiming hosanna! hosanna! To God and the Lamb. Amen! Amen! And Amen!! The congregation was then dismissed by Br. Brigham."[46]

Work on the grounds began immediately. According to Erastus Snow, "At 3 o'clock men and teams were busy digging out the foundation (and) that night I was around the ward getting men to work on the excavation."[47] Ellis M. Sanders plowed the first purl in the excavation of the foundation the afternoon of the same day. "Men with shovels and spades marked the outline; horse-drawn scrapers could be used for the first few feet, but for the most part they must use shovel and wheelbarrow or shovel, windlass, and bucket."[48] The excavations had to be made much larger than the building to accommodate the wide footings and foundations as well as the necessary drains. The first task in building the temple, excavating for the footings and drains and digging out the area for the basement, was under way.

---

45. Larson, *Erastus Snow*, 468.
46. Walker, *Diary*, 2:336.
47. Larson, *Erastus Snow*, 468.
48. Larson, *I Was Called to Dixie*, 580–81.

Chapter 6

UNEXPECTED CHALLENGES

1871–1872

U ntil the work was well under way, not a lot of infrastructure was needed. Nevertheless, certain individuals were immediately se-lected and appointed by Brigham Young to spearhead the work. Some of these were already in St. George, and others were called to go there. Truman O. Angell, who stayed in Salt Lake City, created the design according to the ideas and dimensions his brother-in-law Brigham presented to him. Much of it, including outside dimensions, were the same as the dimensions of the temple in Nauvoo. Miles Romney, an Englishman and master builder, became the general building superinten-dent. Robert Gardner, a Scotsman from the village of Kilsyth who came through Canada, was assigned to be chief lumberman and road-builder. Chief mason Edward L. Parry, who humorously referred to himself as a "home-grown product" was actually born in St. George, Denbighshire, North Wales.[1] Samuel Judd and his sons, converts from England, had

---

1. Leonard J. Arrington, "St. George Tabernacle and Temple: The Builders," lecture given at Dixie State College, St. George, Utah, 21 July 1993, 7; photocopy of type-script in possession of authors. See also Edward L. Parry, "Diary," Brigham Young University Library, Special Collections, Provo, Utah; Albert E. Miller, "The St. George Temple," written for the St. George centennial, 1961.

built the lime kiln in Middleton where the lime for both mortar and plaster would be burned. George Jarvis, a former English sea captain, was responsible to design and build the scaffolding and any other assignments where ropes and knots were used. Archibald McNeil of Scotland took charge of rock quarrying. William Burt headed the plastering and the decoration. David Milne, an artist from Scotland, supervised the painting. Alexander McDonald was the dispenser of commodities from the Tithing Office. And John O. Angus was appointed timekeeper.[2]

A tithing office, yard, and livestock corral had already been built to serve the needs of previous construction projects, including the tabernacle. Now the office and warehouse were both enlarged. The facility was located on the west side of Main Street and 100 South, across the street north of the tabernacle. Donated tithes and contributions would now be brought there from the entire area south of Beaver. Farm products, delivered at harvest, would range from wheat, flour, barley, oats, and corn, to beans, vegetables, and fruits. Milk, cheese, eggs, and similar perishables would be brought in for immediate distribution; livestock would be held in the corral for butchering. Clothing and other personal items would be donated, as well as hay and grain for animal feed, rock salt, and many other items used in daily life; all would need handling and distribution. Scrip could also be exchanged at the cotton factory for cloth, buttons, thread, and needles. During construction of the temple, the tithing office would be one of the busiest places in town. Through it the workforce received its compensation.

Tithing office products would be distributed in exchange for so-called "Tithing Office" (T.O.) scrip issued by the temple construction timekeeper in lieu of money. Some cash, but not much relatively, was also paid out. Workers would receive separate meat tickets which provided a weekly allowance of beef or any other meat if it happened to

---

2. See Ann Leavitt, "The Temple of Our God's Completed: Building the St. George Temple," *Pioneer* 54, no. 4 (2007): 11.

be available. This was not always a satisfactory system, but everyone in town struggled together.

Records were kept in the tithing office and other places to track the cost of building the temple. The exact amount "is difficult if not impossible to [determine] as donated labor, equipment, and supplies for the workers should [also] be figured in the total cost."[3] Nevertheless, an estimate shows the cost to be in excess of $800,000 in 1877 funds—no small sum for pioneer Utah. In addition to the tithes collected in cash and in kind from Beaver south to St. George, the Church, Brigham Young personally, and settlements all over the Territory, helped out.

Following the November 1871 dedication of the temple site, the work of excavating for the basement and footings plus the groundwater drain began immediately and in earnest. Everyone understood that until that preparatory work was completed, construction could not go forward. No one, however, imagined that it would take almost two years of constant labor before the first stones were laid.

After Ellis M. Saunders plowed the first furrow in the excavation, others quickly joined in.[4] Young David H. Cannon Jr. remembered: "While plowing and scraping where the foundation was to be, my horse's leg broke through the ground into a spring of water."[5]

Subsequent digging proved that the limestone formation along the north third of the site was thick enough and hard enough to provide foundation footings. This was also the case for a short distance down the east and west sides. But on most of the east and west sides the ground was completely waterlogged, and the entire soggy bog had to be excavated. That took time. Edward L. Parry wrote: "In digging the greater part we found to be very wet and soft, so much so that it was necessary to dig a frame around the outside within twelve feet of

---

3. Kirk M. Curtis, "History of the St. George Temple" (master's thesis, Brigham Young University, 1964), 58–59.

4. Andrew Karl Larson, *I Was Called to Dixie* (Salt Lake City: Deseret News Press, 1961), 580–81.

5. Curtis, "History," 25.

building a little east of square tower. [In other words, the mud had to be walled off so the digging could continue.] It was so soft in places that a fence pole could be pressed in from twelve to fifteen feet with ease. This caused considerable anxiety as to the best way of making it substantial enough to sustain the enormous weight of the building."[6]

Despite the problems, the excavation work continued. "Because of the muddy site and the decomposed gypsum above it, the trenches for the footings were excavated extra deep and wide at the bottom. They were dug to a depth of 10 to 12 feet and [were] 12 feet wide. Simultaneously, all the material within the 192 x 94 foot interior had to be removed down to the level needed to prepare a basement floor with special footings for the baptismal font and all the supporting columns. This enormous amount of interior material could be partially removed by horse and scraper but most of it had to be taken out by hand, in some places with pick and shovel. The muck was at first toted away by wheelbarrow, then by buckets and windlass. Once out of the hole it all had to be loaded on wagons and hauled from the temple block and unloaded off site. It was hard, grueling labor that consumed week after week and month after month, and so it was not until September 1872, ten months after the site dedication, that Erastus Snow could notify Brigham that the excavation for the basement was complete."[7]

Now came the challenge of preparing footings in those boggy areas that would be firm enough to support the temple's foundation. According to Charlie Walker, Brigham Young also identified the solution to that problem. As he delivered an address in St. George on 15 February 1873, the prophet "spoke of the building of the Temple and the manner of making the foundation, by putting in small volcanic rocks and driving them down with a pile-driver."[8] Immediately this plan was

---

6. Curtis, "History," 34.

7. Larson, *I Was Called to Dixie*, 272.

8. Charles Lowell Walker, *Diary of Charles Lowell Walker*, edited by A. Karl Larson and Katharine Miles Larson, 2 vols. (Logan: Utah State University Press, 1980), 1:361–62.

put into operation as the youth, followed by almost everyone else in town, began gathering chunks of volcanic lava, both large and small, carrying them to the deep excavation and dumping them in.

By this time the lava quarry superintendent Archibald McNeil was assessing the shapes and sizes of the massive lava boulders that had tumbled from the thick black rimrock several hundred feet above what they were calling the quarry.[9] This had been located on the far western side of what was called by the locals the Black Hill, immediately west of the community. Over time these giant columnar boulders of lava had piled up in a small saddle between the huge bluff and a low volcanic hill to the west, and the almost level terrain in the saddle seemed to offer the best location for splitting the boulders into workable-sized slabs and then hauling them back into St. George. Though located by local brethren, the final selection of this quarry site had been made by Brigham, Erastus Snow, and George A. Smith.[10]

Meanwhile, an astonishingly large amount of lava rock was needed to firm up the muddy foundation. According to George A., "It was thought by culling over considerable territory that we could find enough [rock] to build the foundation and carry the building above the dampness of the ground and mineral [to where] the sandstone may be safely used."[11] That was accomplished as everyone pitched in to move the project forward.

While the foundation was being filled in, George A. Smith turned

---

9. According to geologists and local enthusiasts, the high lava flow above the quarry was created during a period of volcanic activity perhaps 200 million years ago, the first of at least two major periods of local volcanism that are evident today. Apparently that earliest flow cooled more slowly than the later flow(s), causing the lava to harden and then crack in massive columnar formations. More recently in geologic time some form of land movement, possibly an earthquake, shook hundreds more of these huge columnar stones loose, tumbling them down the steep bluff until they were accessible to the hammers and drills of the 1870s quarry workers and temple builders.

10. James G. Bleak, "Annals of the Southern Utah Mission," Book B, 443, typescript, Dixie State University Special Collections, St. George, Utah.

11. Zora Smith Jarvis, comp., *Ancestry, Biography, and Family of George A. Smith* (Provo: Brigham Young University Press, 1962), 245.

to his old friend Robert Gardner and asked him to build the needed road to the quarry. Working tirelessly, Gardner and a crew of men he put together went around the south end of the Black Hill on what had once been part of the Old Spanish Trail, and turned north. Perhaps a mile further was a wide sandy draw that headed east and then north-east, climbing to the top of the Black Hill.[12]

Grading a carefully engineered roadway up the eastern side of this draw, the road builders circled to the left or west at the draw's upper end and then leveled the road out as it ran back south along the east side of the higher, lava-topped bluff. Circling west at the southern end of this higher bluff, the road remained almost perfectly level until it headed north again. Then it sloped slightly upward into the aforementioned saddle, crossed the rise, and immediately dropped down into the main area of the quarry.[13] A wide area among the jumbled boulders provided space for a turnaround for the mule teams and wagons; along that turn-around the quarried stones were chained beneath the heavy log wagon-reaches for hauling. Throughout the course of the road up from the bottom and around the second bluff, Gardner's crew had been forced to remove, or level out with loads of sand and rock, thousands of loose chunks and boulders of lava. Many of those smaller boulders, not used for road-base, were hauled back in the evenings to help fill in the boggy temple footings.

Day after day wagonloads of lava stones and rubble were hauled

---

12. The upper portion of this draw, immediately west of the old St. George airport, was for many years used as the town dump.

13. The mile and a half of the upper end of the trail is well marked and easy to hike. A parking area and large sandstone arch atop the airport bluff marks the beginning of the footpath that leads to what is left of the old quarry trail. The portion that circled the head of the draw was eliminated by more recent excavations, but if one looks southwest down the draw, the engineered road, atop a substantial lava base, is clearly evident and the grade is shallow enough for easy hiking down to where it disappears in the sandy bottom of the widening draw. Presumably the teamsters used the shortest route through the sandy bottom until they exited the draw onto what is today called Indian Hills Drive. From there it was an easy pull back around the southern end of the Black Hill and overland to the temple site.

from the Black Ridge and the other lava-topped ridge to the east (called Foremaster Ridge today) and dumped into the massive excavation; so too were dumped bags-full, baskets-full, aprons-full, and every other available container filled with chunks of lava that young and old alike were busy gathering from wherever they happened to be. Gradually the piles of rubble in the bottom of the excavation grew, the ultimate goal being to form a rock-solid footing upon which the temple's foundation could be built.

But how to pound these thousands upon thousands of stones into the seemingly bottomless mud until they formed that footing? And where to find a pile driver such as Brigham had suggested? That would be no simple task. But then someone remembered the cast iron cannon owned by the town militia. Its barrel was filled with lead, encased with thick oak staves held in place by iron bands that were pounded into shape and secured tightly by Samuel L. Adams and other local blacksmiths, and its butt end was used as the pile driver! Thus was created a pile driver weighing between 800 and 1,000 pounds.[14]

But the next problem was how to hoist the pile driver high enough, trip it, and allow it to free-fall onto the stones below. The original Salt Lake and St. George plowman, William Carter, came up with the answer. He devised a 35-foot-tall movable derrick of thick timbers with a system of pulleys at the top that, with a jerk on the rope from one of the men below, tripped the cannon and allowed it to fall freely, even though the chains or ropes running through the pulleys remained connected to the cannon.[15] To make that connection, Carter bolted two iron rings into the wooden staves at the muzzle end of the cannon and hooked them to the ropes running through the pulleys. Mules towed the main rope or chain, hoisting the cannon 30 feet into the air. There it was tripped, and it fell, its crushing weight driving into the mud whatever

14. Curtis, "History," 35.
15. These may have been either rope or chain; they did have chain, and a great deal of rope was used during construction. Though cable appears to have been used on the winch that hauled the trusses, or "bents," to the temple roof three years later, there is no record that it was used in connection with the pile driver.

rock it was aimed to hit.[16] Because the widest end of the cannon pile driver was little more than a foot across, this tedious process had to be repeated over and over again, day after day, thousands upon thousands of times. Only in that manner could the untold tons of fragmented lava rock be pounded into the boggy excavation to form a solid footing. Brigham Young had told them they would know when it was ready for the foundation stones only when the cannon, "when dropped, bounced three times before coming to rest."[17]

Perhaps the best description of how this pile driver worked was penned into a song written by Charlie Walker to commemorate the workers who successfully created the temple footings. Titled "Pounding Rock into the Temple Foundation" and set to the tune of a contemporary song titled "Cork Leg," the lyrics aptly describe the process:

> *Now I pray you be still and all hush your noise,*
> *While I sing about Carter and the pounder and boys.*
> *How the old Hammer climbed and went toward the skies,*
> *And made such a thump that you'd shut both your eyes.*

> *Go ahead now, hold hard, now snatch it again,*
> *Down comes the old gun, the rocks fly like rain;*
> *Now start up that team, we work not in vain,*
> *With a rattle and clatter, and do it again.*

> *Slack up on the South, the North guy make tight,*
> *Take a turn round the post, now be sure you are right;*
> *Now stick in your bars and drive your dogs tight,*
> *Slap dope in the grooves, go ahead, all is right.*

> *Now, right on the frame sat the giant Jimmy Ide,*
> *Like a brave engineer, with a rope by his side,*

16. Curtis, "History," 37.

17. H. Lorenzo Reid, *Dixie of the Desert* (Zion National Park, Utah: Zion Natural History Association, 1964), 235.

"Go ahead, and just raise it," he lustily cried,
"I run this machine and Carter beside!"

I must not forget to mention our Rob,
Who stuck to it faithful and finished the job;
The time it fell down and nearly played hob,
He ne'er made a whimper, not even a sob.

Here's good will to Carter, the pounder and tools,
Here's good will to Gardner, the driver and mules,
Here's good will to the boys, for they've had a hard tug,
Here's good will to us all and the "little brown jug."[18]

A contemporary written account, verified by local historians in-cluding Andrew Karl Larson, explains how this cannon ended up in St. George. Jesse W. Crosby, an early St. George trader, made frequent trips to California. In his journal he wrote that on a trip to San Pedro, he purchased an "iron artillery piece." An American warship had brought it and several others to California to be used in the war with Mexico. After the war these cannon became surplus. Crosby wrote that he brought the unused piece to St. George.[19] There the local militia acquired it and fired it a few times in practice and at celebrations. After its use as a pile driver,

---

18. Larson, *I Was Called to Dixie*, 582.
19. Samuel Wallace Crosby, "Jesse Wentworth Crosby: Mormon Preacher, Pioneer, Man of God," 1977, 75. A popular but incorrect account holds that a brass (not an iron) cannon was abandoned by Napoleon's army upon its retreat from Moscow in Russia. From Moscow it was supposedly taken to Siberia and then to Alaska; from Alaska it somehow was taken to Fort Ross, California. When Sutter bought the fort, not just one but two brass cannon were included in the purchase. Sutter traded them off to Mormon Battalion members who, having been discharged, were on their way to Utah and took temporary employment from him to build the mill-race where gold was eventually discovered. According to this story, these men took the cannon with them to Salt Lake City in 1848. One was reportedly taken to Parowan at the time of its settlement in 1851 and then somehow was transported to St. George in 1861. Juanita Brooks, thinking the story authentic, published it in an article she wrote for the April 1947 issue of *Arizona Highways*. The romantic tale has spread from there, but it is untrue, nevertheless.

the wood staves were removed, the lead drilled or melted out, and eventually the cannon barrel was mounted on display in front of the original St. George Temple Information Bureau. At this writing it can be seen hanging in the annex to the current visitors' center.[20]

Even while the men working the pile driver were accomplishing their herculean task, others were busy constructing a set of drains that would take the water away from the temple. These drains were dug twelve feet outside the foundation excavation, on its west, south, and east sides. They joined in front of the tower, where they formed a single drain that extended due east 327 feet to a point where the water emptied into a wash (now 400 East, known locally as Flood Street). "Each drain is a large tube consisting of black lava and mortar 'in most cases accommodating a man in upright position' for inspection purposes."[21] The drains not only carried away the groundwater from the temple site but also took care of rain water from temple down-spouts and water drained from the font, initiatory washrooms, and, beginning about 1913, indoor toilets.[22] These would be built into the centers of each of the two spiral staircases, beginning on the third level and descending to the basement. An outdoor water tower would also be built next to the temple, and water that was pumped upward by a steam-powered engine in the temple basement would then be gravity-fed into the building's interior, providing running water until after the turn of the century.

Meanwhile, in the summer of 1872 Robert Gardner wrote, "I bought a Steam Saw Mill from Roundy and Berry for $2000.00, and placed it in Grass Valley Canyon and sawed 130,000 feet of lumber, and then sold it to [Ebenezer] Bryce and Samuel Burgess [for] $2500.00. Some time after

20. Larson, *I Was Called to Dixie*, 581–82.
21. Douglas Cox, "History of Robert Gardner, Junior," unpublished manuscript, 272; copy in possession of Richard Schmutz. Cox cites the John T. Woodbury pamphlet used at one time in the temple visitors' center.
22. From 1877 to about 1913, small water closets built into the west wall of the two spiral staircases most likely provided toilet facilities. Clean water was carried in each morning, and waste was removed at night.

that J. W. Young and myself accompanied by James Andrus, Nat Ashby, [&] Oscar Bentley went south to explore for timber for the Temple. We found plenty of timber of good quality seventy [or eighty] miles south at [Mt.] Trumbull near the Colorado River. [Ebenezer] Br[y]ce and [Samuel] Burgess then moved their steam mill to that Pinery in 1872."

Gardner continues: "About that time Brother Snow wished me to come down [from Pine Valley] and superintend the making of [more] roads and [other] outside business, providing homes and work and tools and attend to the general oversight of the workers who were getting material for the Temple. There were over two hundred men coming in from different settlements. I received my pay for this work. The first pay I had received for public service."[23]

Under Gardner's direction a temporary "nine apartment" dormitory was erected on the southeast corner of the temple site to provide housing for many workers. This helped relieve the pressure of too many workers crammed into Erastus Snow's "Big House." In the new dormitory "seven or eight workers" lived in each apartment, one of them serving as company cook.[24] Workers from out of town may also have set up tents near these facilities or on town lots near homes. And many of St. George's permanent residents were already offering rooms for a small fee, usually paid with T.O. scrip by the workers who had little choice but to share these rooms with others.

By late fall another challenge had arisen. The 1872 harvest in Dixie had been smaller than expected, and once again there was danger of real hunger throughout the Virgin River Basin even without the added burden of imported temple laborers. The problem fell into Erastus Snow's lap. In a late January 1873 letter to C. J. Arthur, bishop of the Cedar City Ward, he expressed thanks for the tithing grain that had been sent. But he had to add that it was already used up and asked for as many potatoes as could be sent. He also wanted to know if the

23. Cox, "Robert Gardner," 100–101.
24. Cox, "Robert Gardner," 100–101.

Cedar City Ward would haul them to St. George as a tithe on labor. His letter serves as an example of the cooperative efforts expected of everyone, both in and out of St. George. Members everywhere were called upon to share in the effort of getting the temple built. His letter to Brother Arthur read: "About all our available [work] force of St. George, Washington, and Santa Clara is employed every tenth day on the Temple, besides this the members of the School [of the Prophets] from the settlements turn out every Saturday to work with their hands and teams and much is being paid by these brethren as a Temple offering. I hereby extend to the brethren of Cedar the privilege of donating to the Temple by hauling Tithing potatoes to the place or donating potatoes with or without hauling them all of which will be just as acceptable as though they worked on the Temple ground."[25]

A similar letter was sent a few days later to "the Bishops and Saints of Sanpete Co.," telling them that David H. Cannon of St. George "had been appointed to purchase wheat in Sanpete for the use of those employed on the Temple and Tabernacle." He bade them to help Brother Cannon as best they could to obtain these purchases and "thereby show your goodwill for the prosperity of this Mission and the building of a Temple in this place."[26]

It was at this time that Charles Pulsipher, whose home was then in Hebron (near present-day Enterprise), became involved in an informal but significant meeting. He records: "I had worked [on the Temple] a few days when I attended a meeting in the evening. [A]fter meeting was out there was several standing around the stove [warming up] before starting home. Bp. McArthur said, 'Brother [Erastus] Snow, what are we going to do for provisions to keep these temple hands at work? . . . We have sent for the last load of corn that I have any account of to get.' Brother Snow studied a little and said to him, 'Don't you think considerable could be raised by

---

25. Andrew Karl Larson, *Erastus Snow* (Salt Lake City: University of Utah Press, 1971), 472.

26. Larson, *Erastus Snow*, 472.

free will offerings?' 'Well,' the Bishop said, 'perhaps a little might be got in that way but nothing to what it will take to feed those forty hands and families.' [Brother Snow] turned around to me, putting the question directly to me. 'And what do you think about it, Brother Charles?'

"I was surprised that he should ask me that question. I said, 'About three weeks ago I was up to Cedar City to get my flour for the winter and I found quite a lively interest manifested in regard to the building of a temple and I think that if some thorough arrangement was entered into and persevering missionaries sent out that considerable means could be gathered.' He slapped his hand on my shoulder and said, 'Won't you start out and see what can be done?' I said, 'Why, Brother Snow, I'm not a preacher and not one of the missionaries.' 'Well, we can make you a missionary and you can learn to be a preacher.' 'Well, if you say so of course I will go and do the best I can.' [He said:] 'When you get your pardner of your choice come around and I will see you off.'

"My team was 50 miles away. I went to Brother Israel Ivins and asked him for his team to go with me which was freely turned over. I got Elder H. M. Church to go with me and we drove to President Snow's office the next day and told him we were ready. 'Oh, are you off so soon?' 'Yes sir. We want to go to Washington to have a meeting tonight.' 'Well, I was just starting to a Council Meeting but come in a minute. Brother Ivins, write a few lines as I dictate. "Brothers Pulsipher and Church go with our faith and blessing to gather tithes and offerings for the Temple. Erastus Snow." ' We took the letter of recommendation and started out, feeling very humble and not one word of instruction how to do or keep the accounts but I knew everything should be kept proper account of and show up where it all was so we prepared ourselves with little note books and went from one settlement to the next holding a meeting at every settlement urging the necessity of donating of our means to help along the noble work and as soon as we got a load we would send someone or two to go and take it right down [to St. George] so that the hands might keep at work and thus we kept them a going. We went all through Washington,

Iron, and Beaver Counties, visiting every settlement, gathering offerings from all that we could reach and when we had got through the three counties I found that we had traveled three hundred miles by team and held 22 public meetings and gathered about $8,000 in cash, food goods of all kinds and such things as was needed for the forwarding of the work. . . . [Our accounting plan] we started and they carried it out [with others] all the way through [the completion of the Temple] for they could not see any better way to do business and when we got through we could show up every dollar which was very satisfactory."[27]

Thinking he was finished with his food-gathering mission, Pulsipher returned to his work on the temple. In a short time, however, Elder Snow again sought him out. Pulsipher's account continues: "President Snow said, 'It may be necessary to continue these labors. Where will you be next week?' 'I will be at work on the Temple, I expect.' 'Well, I would like you to go with me and visit the Western Settlements.' [I said,] 'All right.'

"During our last days travel together [through the Western Settlements—Panaca, Pioche, etc.] President Snow said to me, 'I would like you to raise some teams to go up to San Pete and bring in some flour that Brother D[avid] H. Cannon has bought up there for us.' We had a meeting in Pintoe that night and before the close of the meeting I said, 'We want two good teams from here to go up to San Pete and bring in some flour.' When I sat down, President Snow got up and said, 'I hope you will give heed to any call he may make of you for we have appointed him Traveling Agent to do the business [of the Church and Temple] through the different Stakes.' I saw that I was in for it [then,] for I well knew it would take about all of my time to fill that appointment."[28]

But foodstuffs were coming in from other sources as well. In 1870, after a few warring Indians whose identities and motives were never determined had killed brothers Whitmore and McIntyre at Pipe Springs,

---

27. Charles Pulsipher, "A Record of Charles Pulsipher and Family," handwritten document; in possession of Venetta Williams, St. George, Utah.
28. Pulsipher, "Record."

"Anson Parry Winsor was asked by Brigham Young to go to Pipe Springs and . . . take care of the Church herd.[29] He worked to build Winsor Castle at Pipe Springs with his sons Walter, Anson Parry Jr., Alonzo, Frank, and Andrew, and his nephew Abe. Soon after the ground was dedicated for the St. George Temple, Mr. Winsor was asked to drive a herd of Church cattle into St. George . . . to feed the men who were working on the temple. His wife, Emeline Zanetta Winsor, made cheese and butter and sent it monthly into St. George for the temple workers. After 1873 they started to take beef, cheese, and butter into St. George every two weeks as they needed more for the extra temple workers."[30]

Joseph Winsor, who grew up on the ranch, remembered that "in 1873 we started driving thirty head of beef in [to St. George] twice a month. . . . My father [Anson P. Winsor] rode along with us and drove the baggage wagon loaded with butter and cheese made on the ranch. We were milking 100–150 cows during the spring, summer, and fall. All this milk was made into cheese and butter which [we] would pack in little wooden kegs with flour for insulation [until we could haul it] to the temple hands. The cheeses ranged in size from 40 to 80 pounds per cheese. . . . Father took about 13 cheeses each trip. . . . Both beef and dairy cows ran year long on the open range."[31]

Because "grass was so plentiful that good fat beef [could be] supplied every month of the year,"[32] "they continued taking beef, cheese, and butter into St. George every two weeks as they needed more for the extra temple workers."[33]

This system of delivering provisions did much to alleviate the food challenges encountered during the first year and a half of temple

29. Now a national monument, Pipe Springs is located on the Arizona Strip in Arizona, some thirty-five miles southeast of modern-day Hurricane, Utah.

30. Kate B. Carter, comp., *Our Pioneer Heritage* (Salt Lake City: Daughters of Utah Pioneers, 1974), 14:404.

31. Larson, *I Was Called to Dixie*, 240.

32. Larson, *I Was Called to Dixie*, 240.

33. Carter, *Our Pioneer Heritage*, 14:404.

construction. In fact, young Joseph Winsor reported that during one month early in 1875, temple workers—and each winter there were between two and four hundred besides local workers—consumed 30,000 pounds of beef.[34]

Eventually a bakery would also be built on the southeast corner of the temple block.[35] Workers from out of town would obtain bread and other baked goods from it with tithing office script. Joseph Oxborrow and Charles Bennett were put in charge of the bakery. Oxborrow was highly praised for his bread and the huge cakes he baked for holiday celebrations and other occasions honoring the workers.

Another source of supplies for the people of St. George came from the long-distance freighting activities of Jesse Crosby[36] and other freighters, such as David H. Cannon Jr., Easton Kelsey, Alex McDonald, Isaac Hunt, Shadrack Weeks, Elijah Fuller and his son Rivelo, Jim and Tom Pearce, and a man known to history only as "Uncle Wid," perhaps Spencer Wiltbank or Christian Wittwer. These men and certainly others, in addition to their labor on the temple and for their own livelihoods, were called upon to freight into St. George needed supplies and to freight out to the world saleable goods such as cotton, manufactured cotton cloth, sorghum, and Dixie wine. They freighted in all directions, going east until the completion of the transcontinental railroad in 1869 and southwest into San Bernardino and the Wilmington Docks in the Los Angeles area until long after that. There were also continual trips north to wherever the Utah Central railhead happened to be, and then back south to St. George with their yokes of oxen or spans of mules and their loaded wagons. In 1871, on one of these trips to the Wilmington Docks, David H. Cannon Jr. and others of the men named above, along with a young Indian herd-boy named Josh, carried $200 cash raised from among the Dixie Saints as well as $600 in gold coin donated under

---

34. See Larson, *I Was Called to Dixie*, 240.
35. See Cox, "Robert Gardner," 276; copy in possession of Richard Schmutz.
36. Samuel Wallace Crosby, "Jesse Wentworth Crosby."

the spirit of inspiration by Peter Nielson, of Washington.[37] Their mission, given them by stake president David H. Cannon, was to pay for shipping and then freight back to St. George the glass panes for the new St. George tabernacle.

Hannah Elida Baldwin Crosby, Jesse Crosby's wife, was one of many "freighter's widows" left at home for many long and dreary weeks during her husband's freighting expeditions. Yet she was "a resourceful, industrious, stately, dignified person, full of faith and love for the gospel."[38] Besides providing room and board for temple construction workers during those years, she kept busy knitting socks, working old pieces of clothing into quilt blocks or rugs, and taking care of her children. She made each of her children and grandchildren a silk quilt of small silk pieces lined with white muslin. Upon completion of the temple in 1877, Hannah Crosby was appointed a lifetime temple ordinance worker by Brigham Young.[39]

---

37. See Jeffrey R. Holland, "As Doves to Our Windows," *Ensign*, May 2000, 75–77. See also Andrew Karl Larson, *The Red Hills of November* (Salt Lake City: Deseret News Press, 1957), 311–13; Reid Larkin Neilson, "An Ornament to Your City," in *Peter Neilson: A Life of Consecration* (Provo, Utah: Community Press, 1997); Thomas S. Monson, "Tears, Trials, Trust, Testimony," *Ensign*, May 1987, 44.

38. Anna Snow Clements, "Hannah Elida Baldwin Crosby, Wife of Jesse Wentworth Crosby," typescript of original holograph typed by George Cahoon Evans, 1994, page 1, submitted by Nellie Gubler to Daughters of the Utah Pioneers McQuarrie Memorial Museum, St. George, Utah.

39. When Hannah joined the Church in the East, her parents demanded that she never again darken their door. In 1873 while Jesse was on one of his lengthy freighting expeditions, Hannah took a trip east to see her family, not letting them know she was coming. Traveling both by rail and stage, she arrived within a mile of her parents' home. After first visiting with an old childhood friend, she finally reached her mother's door and asked if they might board her for the night before she continued her journey. Her mother said they had just been burned out and were short of bedding, "but you might sleep with one of the girls if you can do no better." They gave her supper, and when she had finished eating, her mother came over and raised her bonnet and asked, "Aren't you one of my girls?" Hannah answered, "Yes, Mother, I am Hannah." Her mother dropped in a chair and cried, the family rushed in, and later her friend came and they all visited most of the night. It was the last time Hannah saw her mother. Clements, "Hannah Elida Baldwin Crosby," 1–4.

Chapter 7

THE WHOLE TERRITORY PITCHES IN

1873

As significant as Pulsipher's and Winsor's efforts were in staving off hunger in St. George, those efforts were not enough. By March 1874, the food shortage had still not been resolved. On 21 March Erastus wrote to Apostle Orson Hyde, who presided over the Sanpete settlements, that "all tithes were exhausted and that the work on the Temple now depended solely on free will offerings until another harvest." What little money they had raised in Dixie was being sent by team to Sanpete to buy and bring back flour and whatever else the people there might be willing to donate.[1]

The shortage persisted into April. The whole town was out of food. In desperation, St. George leaders again dispatched Charles Pulsipher, along with several additional men and teams, to go through the settlements as far north as Sanpete County to acquire supplies. Men went ahead, soliciting in each town. Wagons and their teamsters followed two or three days later, allowing time for people to assemble their donations. Three four-horse teams and three two-horse teams were used to

---

1. Andrew Karl Larson, *Erastus Snow* (Salt Lake City: University of Utah Press, 1971), 473.

haul the donations back to St. George. The supplies came just in time. One of the teamsters, Orson Welcome Huntsman, wrote in his diary: "Arrived home this afternoon finding all well but wanting bread, as the whole town was out of flour, and we had plenty of the good things to eat such as flour, pork and eggs. We donated part of our time and [were] paid out of our loads for the rest of [our] time, therefore we have something to keep body and soul together and was able to do a little on the great work of building the temple at St. George."[2]

The same procedure was used in subsequent years, as Charles Pulsipher's journal amply attests. But food shortages were also sometimes felt in other places in south and central Utah Territory, limiting the ability of those communities to always help with the situation in St. George. Sometimes these situations impacted progress on the temple. In December 1874, George A. Smith had to tell the people that, because of the shortage of grain in the Southern Mission as well as in Millard, Sevier, and Sanpete counties, "some residents of St. George who have been supported by their labors on the temple" would have to be discharged.[3]

Even those accepting "mission calls" to work on the temple were asked to bring their own provisions to at least partly sustain themselves while working. Brigham's logical argument was that, had they remained home, they would consume foodstuffs, so they should bring the equivalent with them, at no loss to their communities. This was practical counsel in time of need! Many single men came; family men also came to "batch it" (live like bachelors), without wives and families.[4]

The need for supplies never let up during the temple's construction, something Church leaders in Salt Lake City were aware of. A letter sent in April 1874 by the Presiding Bishopric—Edward W. Hunter, L. W.

---

2. Orson Welcome Huntsman, "Diary, I," 28–29, typescript, Dixie State University Archives, St. George, Utah.

3. James G. Bleak, "Annals of the Southern Utah Mission," Book B, 362, typescript, Dixie State University Special Collections, St. George, Utah.

4. Bleak, "Annals," Book B, 362.

Hardy, and J. A. Little—to Bishop A. O. Smoot of Provo described the situation:

"We received your grain and Produce report a few days ago of Utah County, the result of prompt and energetic labours of yourself and fellow labourers, with which we were well pleased.

"You will doubtless rejoice with us to learn that the Temple in St. George is progressing very satisfactory, a great many workmen being engaged upon it, and which promises at no distant day to be completed. . . . No mission since the organization of the Church has had so many natural barriers to overcome . . . nor such a lengthy drain on the Faith, Perseverance, Patience and Pockets of the people, as . . . The Dixie Mission; The last and heaviest drain upon their resources is the building of the Temple . . . but their utter inability to complete such a gigantic labour with the means they had at command, necessitated a call for help from their Northern Neighbors, hence we in this City have had the privilege of raising several thousand Dollars through the various wards, for that purpose, and should the members of your County feel desirous [to share] . . . the blessings of that Temple when completed, we hereby extend to all such a cordial invitation to participate; let neither the rich nor the poor be slighted, but everyone in your entire district have a chance to donate something towards the first erected Temple in Utah Territory. . . . When this is first presented to the people many may not be immediately prepared to respond . . . but let all such have a little time to make such turns, as to satisfy their feelings. We are constantly receiving orders for supplies of various kinds to keep the work moving, hence what money you receive, please forward to this office. Those who have no money might wish to turn in some grain. . . . Homemade Cloth or Socks would be very acceptable. . . . Praying God to bless you and all your efforts."[5]

Communities large and small and members well off and poor contributed toward the building of the temple. A complete list of wards

---

5. Kirk M. Curtis, "History of the St. George Temple" (master's thesis, Brigham Young University, 1964), 60–61.

that contributed "seems [not] available." Nevertheless, the names of 49 units that contributed resources were recorded. Not only was money donated but also "flour, grain, stock, sundries, merchandise, home goods, and labor."[6]

It was late in March 1873 before the drains from the temple site were completed and the lava-rock base deemed stable and solid enough to "bounce the cannon three times." It had been a long and arduous task, carried out mostly by St. George workers and workers from other nearby settlements but also with some volunteers from points farther north. Though nothing showed above ground for the nearly 16 months of toil since excavation had begun on 9 November 1871, all the underlying problems had been overcome, just as the prophet had promised.

Constructing the foundation of the new temple was the next big challenge. It too would be constructed of lava rock because—again—it was "impervious to the action of alkali in the soil and groundwater."[7] The foundation stones would be massive slabs "hard as granite and [weighing] 160 pounds per cubic foot,"[8] which amounted to between two and four tons per stone. Each stone measured from 7 to 12 feet long, 3 to 4 feet wide, and 12 to 14 inches thick.

During the entire time that the pounder was being used on the base, quarrymen under the direction of Archibald McNeil were at work in the lava quarry preparing stones for the foundation. McNeil's full-time fellow workmen included Alex Fullerton, Jim Dean, Ephraim Wilson, and Lewis Robbins,[9] and no doubt several more who labored on a part-time basis. Some of these were local while others had come south

6. Curtis, "History," 61–62.

7. Larson, *Erastus Snow*, 471.

8. Hazel Bradshaw, ed., and Washington County Chapter Daughters of Utah Pioneers, *Under Dixie Sun* (Panguitch, Utah: Garfield County News, 1950), 336–43; copy in Daughters of Utah Pioneers McQuarrie Memorial Museum, St. George, Utah.

9. Leonard J. Arrington, "St. George Tabernacle and Temple: The Builders," lecture given at Dixie State College, St. George, Utah, 21 July 1993, 4; photocopy in possession of the authors.

for a season to volunteer their services on the temple project. Quarrying methods included drilling (a two-man job as one held and turned the iron drill while the other swung the heavy mallet or sledge hammer), using "slips and wedges,"[10] and even chipping with smaller iron hammers to remove obtrusive corners and edges. Blasting was never mentioned in the records. The rock was so hard, however, that little of it was changed from the shape it held when freed from whatever boulder it had been a part of. Fitting the stones into place in the temple's foundation would be left to those stonemasons who had been assigned to apply the mortar to the necessary thickness below and between each stone, and then to "lay them up" as level as was possible. The irregularities in size and shape would be made up with mortar.

It was quickly discovered that stones from the quarry were far too heavy to load onto wagons to transport to the temple site. After a little experimentation it was determined that by prying up or using a "sheer-legs" lifting apparatus,[11] one end of a stone could easily be lifted sufficiently to work under it not only lengths of chain or heavy rope but enough sand and small stones to elevate it a few inches above ground level. Once the same thing had been done with the other end, a sturdy wagon was driven over the stone, the ropes or chains beneath the stone were tied securely around thick poles laid lengthwise atop the wagonbed, and once the sand and stones were scraped out from underneath, the stone was left suspended beneath the wagon and ready for hauling. Each stone was then hauled by three teams of mules (for strength and safety, the largest mules in town) from the quarry, down the dugway, back around the south end of the Black Hill, and then on to the temple site, a total of three miles. Master mason Edward Lloyd Parry estimated

---

10. Arrington, "Builders," 4.

11. A sheer-legs was two upright poles with rope at the top tying them together in an upside-down V. Such hoists, with a rope and pulley system secured beneath the apex of the V, could be tipped both forward and back, allowing heavy loads to be lifted by animal power, swung by man-power in either direction to a desired position, and then lowered to where the workers wanted them placed.

that 500 cords, or 64,000 cubic feet, of these stones—some 1,800 wagon trips—were used in laying the temple foundation.

Under the direction of master mason Parry, the first of these quarried stones were laid in the foundation on 10 March 1873. Parry had been so frail as a youth that his stonemason father had apprenticed him to a tailor. "After a few months disgusted with tailoring, Edward returned to his father and grandfather who resignedly put him back to work in his native Welsh village."[12] For the rest of his life Parry laid stonework for dozens of remarkably beautiful structures of every sort.

When the wagons carrying the stones arrived at the temple site, the load was lowered to the ground next to the excavation where it was to be placed. Then it had to be lifted again and set in the foundation. How was this done with hand-operated equipment—especially the first stones that had to be lowered several feet below ground level to the pounded-in excavation? Again the builders accomplished their task with a sheer-legs apparatus. As the foundation and then the walls rose up out of the ground, the several sheer-legs apparatuses rose with it, mounted on the temple walls so the stones and beams could still be hoisted to the desired heights. It was an ingenious system that was used not only to lift stones and mortar but also as an elevator for the workers as the walls rose in height.[13] No doubt these devices were secured to the walls by George Jarvis, a master with ropes and weights. (Later Jarvis would also devise a rope hoist to place the 18,000-pound baptismal font precisely onto the backs of the twelve oxen in the temple basement.) Ultimately 20 tons of rope would be used during temple construction.[14]

At the bottom of the excavation, the first course of lava stones was aligned, three stones wide, to make a 12-foot-wide foundation base. In

12. Arrington, "Builders," 7–8.
13. This description of sheer-legs and its operation was given to the authors by Dr. Elwin Robison, architectural historian and preservation engineer, Kent State University, Kent, Ohio. Sheer-legs can be seen in several old photos of the St. George Temple while it was under construction.
14. Curtis, "History," 156.

that position they were leveled and mortared together, a procedure that continued around the entire base of the temple, and then upward with each succeeding course mortared to the courses below. The manual labor and ingenuity required to accomplish all this work perhaps can no longer be fully appreciated.

One of the local stonemasons who helped lay up the massive foundation was William Atkin, who with his wife, Rachel, and their five children had been called to move to Dixie in the fall of 1868. He and his son, William III, were part of the steady crew of stonemasons who not only laid up the foundations and walls but directed less experienced hands in the same tasks. A third and much younger son, Henry, recalled: "Often it was my duty to carry father's lunch to him while he was working on the temple, and many of us children there on the same errand, loitered about watching the workmen as they pounded the [lava] into the foundation trench, and later as they dressed the great piles of rock slabs and fashioned them into the walls of the first temple built in the west."[15]

Another stonemason who labored on the temple through the entire time of construction was Frederick William Fuhrmeister, or Foremaster. He and his 10-year-old son, Albert, arrived in St. George in 1861 and within a year or so had purchased a house and several lots from Oliver B. Huntington, who was moving back north to Springville. He also bought some farmland around the point of the Black Hill on the Santa Clara Creek, which became known as the Foremaster Bend. He was a master mason; the rock home he built at 350 West 400 South is still standing. It is said that each morning and again after lunch, as he walked from home to the temple site to work, he would pick up a rock and drop it somewhere along his path. By the time the temple

---

15. Reid L. Neilson, *From the Green Hills of England to the Red Hills of Dixie: The Story of William and Rachel Thompson Atkin* (Provo, Utah: Red Rock Publishing, 2000), 79.

was finished he had a fine stone path all the way from his home to the temple.[16]

As the work progressed upward, the foundation was tapered in stages from the 12-foot-wide bottom to a thickness of 3 feet 8 inches at a point 12 feet above ground level, the so-called "water table" height. This brought the erosion-proof black rock to the point above the ground where the smaller, lighter, and more easily quarried sandstone blocks could be used. From that point to the top, the side walls and back or west wall would be 2 feet 8 inches thick. The walls around the spiral staircases and across the east or front of the temple were laid up several inches thicker so they would support the front center tower that would one day be built.

As for the mortar, one day in the mid-1860s, as young Albert Foremaster was riding through the hills west of Middleton, he noticed a ledge of limestone that seemed out of place "on a round knoll [near] . . . the east portal of the water tunnel west of Middleton."[17] This information was passed along to Samuel Judd, who with his sons soon built a lime kiln on the site[18] and began burning lime from the limestone.[19] The lime was mixed with sand from the Virgin River and made

16. Spencer Truman, "Frederick William Fuhrmeister (Foremaster)," n.d., n.p., typescript, Daughters of Utah Pioneers McQuarrie Memorial Museum, St. George, Utah.

17. Spencer Truman, "Albert Charles Foremaster, Grandfather of Spencer Truman," n.d., n.p. typescript, Daughters of Utah Pioneers McQuarrie Memorial Museum, St. George, Utah. See also Kate B. Carter, comp., *Heart Throbs of the West* (Salt Lake City: Daughters of Utah Pioneers, 1941), 3:203, 230–31.

18. The remnants of this kiln were located, probably for the first time in many years, by Stanford S. McConkie in the present-day St. George Tortoise Reserve and can be reached only after approximately a mile of quite strenuous hiking. To more easily see the remnants of the kiln, on Google Earth enter north latitude 3708.272 by west longitude 11333.029, and you will find yourself looking down at the level area directly in front of the old kiln. Location information, including coordinates, was provided by Stanford S. McConkie.

19. An undated description of this process has been left by Lewis Earl Christian, who wrote: "We would haul wagonloads of lime rock to the kiln site [and] stack the kiln full and shut the oven door. A fire would then be kindled in the fire box and kept roaring hot for about 72 hours. This meant someone had to tend the kiln night

into a very durable mortar, which was used on the tabernacle, courthouse, and temple, as well as many homes then being built in the area. Interestingly, as the temple project came to an end, "the supply of limerock was exhausted and there was no other section in the [St. George] valley where good limerock could be found, as it all had too much [additional mineral] formation and would not make lime."[20]

Albert and his uncle Ett Wiltbank not only hauled the burnt lime from Judd's kiln to the temple but also hauled to the temple many of the heavy lava stones from behind the Black Ridge.[21]

Once the actual construction of the foundation had begun, the work went on, day in and day out, summer, winter, fall, and spring. Summers were hot; temperatures in the shade usually hovering around 110 to 115 degrees Fahrenheit in July. Near the end of August 1873, Charlie Walker recorded simply, "Hot."[22] The long days of work in the

and day to keep the fire going. . . . After 72 hours of steady firing, the kiln would be sealed up or 'mudded' in, to allow the lime to finish cooking and the kiln to cool down. When all . . . the heat was gone, the kiln would be opened up. Some of the lime would crumble into powder as soon as the air hit it. Other would stay in chunks. Also, some would be real white, while some would be almost gray. The white lime was used to whitewash walls of dwellings, picket fences, and chicken coops . . . where it served as a cleansing and disinfectant agent. The darker lime was used for plastering and masonry work. . . . The buyers would slack this lime themselves before using [which] meant the adding of water and stirring it until it made a smooth thick mixture which could be applied with a brush. . . . [When slackened] the lime would boil and bubble and heat up as soon as water touched it. With large mud hoes we had to keep stirring this mixture until it was thin and well mixed. If any of it should splash . . . onto our skin it could burn immediately unless we washed it off. If it ever splashed into our eyes, we really suffered. . . . All rock masonry was laid up with this lime to which sand was added . . . at the temple [and tabernacle], the Jacob Hamblin home, and all the black rock walls and . . . foundations were laid up with this kind of mortar." Lewis Earl Christian, "Sandstone, Blackrock, and a Few Other Solid Matters," unpublished manuscript, 47–49; in possession of George Peacock, St. George, Utah.

20. Carter, *Heart Throbs*, 230–31. See also Kate B. Carter, comp., *Chronicles of Courage* (Salt Lake City: Daughters of Utah Pioneers), 1:379.

21. Florence Foremaster, "A Biography of Albert Charles Foremaster, Written by a Daughter," n.d., n.p., typescript; copy in possession of the authors.

22. Walker, *Diary*, 1:376.

summer heat most likely left Walker too tired to do much in the evenings other than take care of chores or carry out his Church duties.

Primitive living conditions contributed much to the difficulty of the work. In St. George, June and August also have many hot days, well over 100 degrees in the shade. At that time there was no shade where the temple workers labored—not at the quarries, not at the temple site! Neither was there cool water, nor any relaxing showers or baths after work. Other than sponge baths or a dip in Dodge's Pond or the tepid waters of the usually shallow Virgin River, the workers simply carried on as best they could. It was the same for the rest of the community's men, women, and children.

The thunderstorm season of late summer always brought strong winds and much dust, but not always rain. Still, on 22 August 1873, Charlie Walker recorded with some relief: "heavy clouds hanging around." Even better, it had rained the night before, "settling the dust and [reviving] the vegitation."[23] Winter days even in the Dixie climate were downright chilly and often blustery, making it uncomfortable to be working outside, whether on the walls or at the quarry, or driving teams over dusty or sometimes wet and muddy roads. Of course fall and spring days were kinder, and everyone appreciated them. But no matter the weather or other circumstances, the laborers did not slack; the temple needed to be built and their faith was strong. They had been called as missionaries, were dedicated to this cause, and they were determined to see it through.

Fortunately, work and the daily routine of life were interrupted from time to time with celebrations. One such was held on Pioneer Day, 24 July 1873. A song written by Charlie Walker, celebrating the temple's divine purpose, was sung by the choir:

> Lo, a temple long expected,
> In St. George shall stand

---

23. Walker, *Diary,* 1:376.

By God's faithful saints erected
Here in Dixie land.

Chorus:
Hallelujah, hallelujah,
Let Hosannas ring,
Heaven shall echo back our praises,
Christ shall reign as king.

Th' noble task we hail with pleasure
Coming from our head,
Brings sa[l]vation, life eternal
For our kindred dead.

Holy and Eternal Father,
Give us strength we pray,
To thy name to build this Temple,
In the latter day.

Oh, how anxious friends are waiting,
Watching every move,
Made by us for their redemption,
With a holy love.

Long they've hoped thro weary ages,
For the present time,
For the everlasting gospel;
With its truths sublime

Lo, the Prison doors are open,
Millions hail the day,
Praying, hoping for Baptism,
In the appointed way.

Glory, glory, Hallelujah!
Let the structure rise,

Rear aloft those noble towers,
Pointing to the skies.

Hell may rage and Satan tremble,
Still that house we'll rear.
Heaven will aid us: angels guard us.
We've no need to fear.[24]

The holiday began with "the usual ceremonies of celebrating the Anniversary of the Pioneers entering the Great Salt Lake Valley." A program followed, featuring speakers, singing, and music by the martial and brass bands. Charlie Walker, one of the speakers, offered a series of toasts, three of which are worth noting:

The Temple Quarrymen

God bless the quarrymen and tools,
And faithful "Ed" with his four mules.

The Hot Weather

The cause of the heat, says a friendly old bummer,
Is the lack of our Snow Storms during the summer.

Pres of the U.S. [Ulysses S. Grant]

Oh, Grant that Grant may never grant,
His grants to us again.
And may the grants He granted us,
Be granted Grant again.[25]

24. Walker, *Diary,* 1:372–73.
25. Walker, *Diary,* 1:374–75. Ulysses S. Grant was adamantly opposed to the Church and polygamy.

Meanwhile, work on the foundation continued. As the foundation walls were built, to provide stability buttresses were laid up and mortared to them. Nine of them were placed to a side, one every 13 feet 8 inches; four were placed on the back wall; four around the radius of each front corner, and two on the front wall beneath the future tower. Each sat on a solid masonry base. The buttresses were 38 inches wide at the base and protruded 48 inches from the wall. As they were laid up they tapered at the center line of the wall to 24 inches in width and were built out some 30 inches from the wall from there up to the parapets.

Even as masons labored to lay the heavy foundation stones, other masons and their helpers moved smaller quarried lava rock to the basement's earthen floor and used them to build sturdy 4-foot-high piers, supported on large lava flagstones placed in the dirt underneath to support the future basement floor. To construct the floor, carpenters placed a network of large beams on the piers and then installed 2x9-inch joists across the beams and placed two layers of 1x6-inch flooring on top of the joists, each board centered exactly over the joint between two boards in the subfloor beneath. This pattern is typical of all the flooring laid down throughout the temple.

The 4-foot clearance between the dirt floor and the finished floor would provide a crawl space that allowed safety inspections of the foundation, and so forth. In the space between piers, water pipes were run, as well as drain pipes from the baptismal font and the lavatories. Good use has since been made of these spaces; they are currently filled with electrical and plumbing installations.

In addition to the piers, masons built up two additional lava rock installations on the dirt floor. In the center of the temple behind the front wall tower base they laid up a 4-foot-high, oval-shaped lava wall complex that would support the future baptismal font. Though the heavy font would rest on the actual stone, floor beams and flooring on which the oxen would stand would also rest on these low walls.

The second interior basement installation consisted of laying up fourteen 4-foot-high lava stone foundations for the support of stone pillars. Each of these pillars would be 14 feet tall—seven in each of two rows along the dirt floor. Large lava flagstones for support were buried beneath. As the stone walls were built up and interior floors installed, stout pillars were also built of cut stone. The pillars were built square in order to be plastered over later and fit unobtrusively into basement walls. The masons installed the pillars at intervals of 12 feet 8 inches, in two rows 20 feet 6 inches out from each side of the foundation walls. As interior construction proceeded, carpenters installed the network of floor joists on top of the pillars for the first main assembly room floor.

Of course this necessitated men to cut and mill the lumber in both Pine and Grass valleys and then for teamsters to haul it into St. George. This was challenging work and often very dangerous. Charles Franklin Foster came to St. George in 1861, both fought and worked with Indians, traveled at least twice to the Missouri River to help emigrants on their way to Utah, and freighted in and out of California numerous times. He wrote: "In 1873 I met with an accident [coming out of Pine Valley], when a heavily loaded wagon, filled with [lumber], tipped over on me, laying me up for a couple of years. I haven't known what good health is since that time."[26] It is noteworthy that Foster lived another sixty-five years, passing away in St. George on 26 January 1936.

Even though volunteer workers were arriving from the north to assist the laborers from St. George, more were needed. In a talk given in the Salt Lake Tabernacle 10 August 1873, George Q. Cannon said that the prophet wanted "a hundred men, supplied with provisions sufficient to last the winter, [to] go down to the southern country, and bestow their labors on building the Temple. . . . We have had a reputation," he said, "of accomplishing everything of this kind that we undertook. But

---

26. Charles Franklin Foster, "Autobiography of Charles F. Foster, As Written by Himself," February 14, 1923, n.d., n.p., typescript; copy in possession of the authors.

let us be faint-hearted and we lose our influence and power both with God and man. All our labors have to be works of faith."[27]

Responses were positive from faithful Saints willing to sacrifice time and means for the cause. A November item in the *Deseret News* noted that "about 50 men from Cache Valley and a number of men from Nephi were on their way south to . . . [work] on the temple."[28] The work was greatly facilitated by such volunteer workers and without doubt could never have been carried through to completion without them. Warm friendships inevitably developed between these brethren from the north and the local southern workers and residents.

Meanwhile, Charles Pulsipher, continuing his mission to gather food and other necessities, wrote: "In [the fall of] 1873 I was in San Pete county visiting the different Wards and I got to Ephraim on Saturday night and had an appointment for 10:00 o'clock next day and that evening I received a telegram from St. George requesting me to send them ten or twelve good stone masons immediately. The next day I read the telegram in meeting and was speaking on the subject and urging the necessity of pushing the work forward as fast as possible while President Young was alive, that he might get the ordinances established and the Temple hands toughly drilled so that all could go on in good order after he had gone and before I was aware of what I was saying I said, 'Come on down and help us build that Temple and we will come up here and help you build one in San Pete,' and when I found what I had said I was surprised for I had never heard of any intention of building [a temple] in San Pete but it was said and I knew it would be done for it wasn't my premeditated sayings so I went right on and never let on that I had said anything out of the common.

"At the close of the meeting they gathered around me and said, 'So we are going to have a Temple up here in San Pete, are we?'

---

27. *Journal of Discourses*, 26 vols. (London: Latter-day Saints' Book Depot, 1854–86), 16:144.
28. Curtis, "History," 47.

"'Yes sir.'

"'Well, when did President Young tell you about it?'

"'He never told me.'

"'And when did you first hear of it?'

"'You heard it as soon as I did.'

"'And do you think it will be so?'

"'Yes, I not only think but I know it will be fulfilled.'

"In about four years I sent up two hands to work on the Manti Temple, thus I filled my promise."[29]

James A. Little, from Kanab, Utah, praised the dedication of these men from the north. In a letter to the *Deseret News Weekly* he avowed that "the motives which actuate these people have but few precedents. There is almost an absence of pecuniary considerations. They are people who have plenty of employment . . . at home. They are actuated by sublime faith . . . such motives do credit to the noble aspirations and large heartedness of any people. . . . [They] certainly deserve credit for a broad philanthropy for which this generation furnishes no parallel."[30]

Workers' wives and families left alone at home also sacrificed, perhaps even more than their absent husbands. When her husband was called to serve, Mary Larsen Ahlstrom of Ephraim in Sanpete County was left at home with four children and was expecting her fifth. She wrote: "Fourteen men were called from Ephraim to go down to St. George to work on the Temple. Peter was one of them. He was away all winter and we got along as best we could."[31] She no doubt faced many challenges, being pregnant and with four young children to care for and outside chores to do during that long winter in Ephraim. No doubt a similar story is behind every married man called to serve in St. George,

---

29. Charles Pulsipher, *Journal* (privately published, n.d.); in possession of Venetta Williams, Santa Clara, Utah.

30. Douglas Cox, "History of Robert Gardner, Junior," unpublished manuscript, 280; copy in possession of Richard Schmutz.

31. Ann Leavitt, "The Temple of Our God's Completed: Building the St. George Temple," *Pioneer* 54, no. 4 (2007): 12.

whether from Sanpete, Utah County, Cache Valley, or any other part of the Territory.

Lars Peter Oveson wrote in his journal that in the fall of 1873, "I was called to go to St. George to work on the Temple as a carpenter, together with a crowd of twelve to fourteen men to work at whatever there was to do. That was my wife's first experience at living alone."[32]

Nor was the journey down and back without peril. Thomas Crowther of Fountain Green in Sanpete County wrote in his journal: "Myself and 10 others were called to spend the winter working on the St. George Temple. . . . We started the 10th of November and had a very rough journey. We were caught in a very severe blizzard. Some had their ears and some their feet frozen. We finally arrived in St. George and spent the winter employed on the Temple. . . . We were released sometime in March, 1874. We returned home feeling well over our labors."[33]

In December 1873, Brigham returned to St. George, bringing with him "General and Mrs. Thomas L. Kane, great and good friends of the Mormons." The Kanes were hosted by Lucy Bigelow Young, Brigham's wife, for the several weeks they spent in St. George, during "which time Kane drew up Brigham Young's will."[34] It was probably also the time when Mrs. Kane organized her notes and perhaps even wrote her memoirs of the journey south with the Prophet, which were later published under the title, *Twelve Mormon Homes, Visited in Succession on a Journey through Utah to Arizona.*[35] Hosting visitors was not unusual for Lucy, who frequently "entertained church and national officials in her St. George home."[36]

During that time the folks in the Southern Mission continued their

---

32. Leavitt, "Building the St. George Temple."
33. Leavitt, "Building the St. George Temple."
34. Arrington, "Builders," 17.
35. Elizabeth Wood Kane, *Twelve Mormon Homes, Visited in Succession on a Journey through Utah to Arizona* (Salt Lake City: University of Utah, Tanner Trust Fund, 1974).
36. Arrington, "Builders," 17.

labors on the temple even as they carried on with their normal rigorous affairs. Local men were donating one day in ten as tithing labor, and many locals were working full time on the temple and taking their pay in tithing scrip. Additionally, tithes and donations in kind, from Beaver in the north to Kanab and Long Valley in the east and Panaca and Pioche in the west, were being contributed by the people of the Mission. Their material donations were sent by wagon to the St. George Tithing Office, which dispensed all collections to the workers.[37] It was a territory-wide effort. Some who still carried Perpetual Emigration Fund debt used their service on the temple to either reduce their debt or pay it off entirely.

Even Christmas of 1873 was a work day. Charles Walker worked on the temple each of the three days before Christmas, and on Christmas Day he was there with "100 men from San Pete . . . some on the walls . . . some on the roads and in the Stone Quarry and others hauling wood, lime, sand all busy pushing the good work along."[38] This continued into January. Even in Dixie, it could be cold outside on winter days. A 7 January 1874 entry by Walker reads: "Rather cold. At work on the Temple." Help had arrived from many towns. "The workmen are getting along very well with the Black Rock [foundation]. There are Bretheren at work on the Temple and in the Quarry from San Pete, Fillmore, Beaver, Kanab, Rockville, Virgin City, Minersville, Panguitch, Cedar Springs [now Holden], Washington, Santa Clara, and St. George, all busy as bees; in fact all the people seem spirited and interested about Building of the Temple."[39]

Of course during construction of the temple the workforce fluctuated. Workers from out of town came mostly in winter when they could leave their farms. Local men, employed in their own occupations, were still expected to donate one work day in ten as tithing. Those

37. Larson, *Erastus Snow*, 473.
38. Walker, *Diary*, 1:379.
39. Walker, *Diary*, 1:381.

who worked more were paid with T. O. scrip issued by the timekeepers. If they were employed full time they were paid half in cash and half in commodities. Charles Walker is an example of a full-time worker who labored wherever he was assigned—for the most part as a stonemason. His first main assignment was on the tabernacle and then on the temple, but at times he worked on roads or projects in other places. For many years this was his main means of supporting his family.

Though the construction workforce was male, temple building was also a community effort. "Everyone contributed as he could. Women did the workers' laundry or they gathered to sew carpet rags for the factory to make up into strips for the hallways when the Temple should be finished. People too poor to give anything else might donate a part of their bagasse [corn and cane stocks salvaged from the harvest] to help feed the oxen that hauled the stone. The teenaged guard who watched over the site through the night donated half his pittance; the Santa Clara Swiss immigrants walked 5 miles to the quarry, worked all day, walked back home, and donated half their wage."[40]

One modern-day laborer's unusual experience illustrates a unique way in which some women helped with the temple construction. He writes: "In the hot summer of 1995 I was asked to install some infra-red transmitters in one of the domed ceilings of the St. George Temple. I was feeling the effects of the intense heat and a miserable summer cold, but to make matters worse the crawl space between the floors was not only hot but very tight and uncomfortable. Besides that, the old rough-sawn trusses were cutting into me and jabbing me with huge slivers as I made my way across them, and I was trying my hardest not to allow the sawdust and plaster from the holes I was cutting in the ceiling to fall and dirty the sacred room below.

"I had finally cut out six of the holes and installed the equipment, and it was time to cut the last hole, located in the center of the high domed ceiling. This hole proved especially difficult because I had to lay

40. Juanita Brooks, "Early Buildings," *Utah Historical Quarterly* 29 (July 1961): 249.

across a very rough beam with sharp splinters that were stabbing into my side with every move I made. At the same time the floor above was so close I was bumping my elbow every time I pulled the keyhole saw back and forth. Because of the heat and cramped situation I twisted painfully onto my side along the splintered timber, and then I carefully sawed out the last piece of old lath and plaster—an oblong cut of about four by eleven inches.

"As it came free in my hand I relaxed and laid my head back on the beam, gasping for air and staring at the removed section of ceiling. What happened then is as vivid today as it was that day. I suddenly found myself inside a one-room cabin such as I had never seen. Across from me on my left was a wall with a fold-down bed, held in place with hemp rope. I saw that it could be folded back up against the wall to make more living space. Directly in front of me was a simple stove with shelving on the wall behind it to hold goods. To my right was a bare wall with a small window made with four panes of irregular glass. In the center of the room were a willow table and two willow chairs that I could tell had also been handmade because the wrappings were quite rough, dried rushes.

"I next noticed two younger adults that I supposed were husband and wife. They were slight people, but for some reason it was the woman's hair that really struck me. It was medium length, but it had the same ruddy red color and sort of kinky little curls or waves that I had seen on many women in Ireland and Scotland. As I stared at her hair there was a knock at the door, and as I watched the sister turn to answer it I noticed the unusual hinges—two straps of cowhide leather fastened so the door swung inward.

"As the sister opened the door I saw two men dressed in black, and I knew they were there on official Church business. I didn't hear any words but I somehow knew the spokesman told the sister they were in need of money or any items these people could give that would help with the building of the Temple. The sister replied sadly that they had nothing else they could give—that they had already given all they had for the building of the Lord's House. Then she seemed to pause and slowly reach up to touch her hair.

"At that instant the heat combined with the pain of lying on the rough timber, seemed to awaken me, and I laid there somehow still transfixed by the ceiling section I had just removed. As I looked more closely, though, I noticed, poking up out of the plaster, a finger-sized swatch of tightly wavy, ruddy red hair—hair that exactly matched the sister's hair I had just seen. Then I knew what she had given the two men! With nothing else left, she had sacrificed her beautiful hair to provide a bonding agent for a little of the Temple's plaster."[41]

As another form of help, local farmers, in addition to their work tithe, loaned teams, wagons, and other equipment for use in hauling rock, lime, sand, coal, lumber, commodities brought from out of town, and for other transportation needs. Non-Mormon Billy Lay was one of these.

For a time Charles Walker was so busy with multiple assignments that his journal entries were few. He was always working but on some days he worked away from the temple. For instance, besides working as a stonemason on the foundation he spent some time helping build "a New Road to the cedars." This would mean a road into the Pine Valley Mountain foothills where wood from Juniper trees[42] could be obtained for winter fires.[43] Everyday life went on.

The laying of the lava stone foundation was finally completed on Saturday, 21 February 1874. That project had taken over eleven months, which meant that two years and three months of steady and laborious work had now passed since dedication of the temple site. In that time

---

41. "Anonymous," n.d., n.p.; copy in possession of the authors. Charles Pulsipher at one time recorded gathering forty bushels of hair, though he did not specify whether it was animal, human, or both.

42. These junipers were called cedar trees by the pioneers, hence Cedar City, Cedar Fort, and so forth.

43. Walker, *Diary*, 1:376–77.

the workers had dug the excavation, pounded in the footing stones, constructed the drainage system, and laid the large foundation stones. Indeed the labor had been hard and time-intensive, but their work had resulted in a foundation durable enough to support the heavy temple.

Walker recorded the achievement: "Today the walls were finished to the required height with the Black Rock, and are now ready to receive the Redrock for which I am not sorry, for we have had a hard time to cut them [the lava stones] and I think they will last through the millennium."[44]

The completion of a stage of building always called for a celebration. That Saturday evening one was held in the basement of the tabernacle. Brigham Young, George A. Smith, and Erastus Snow were present. Walker recorded the festivity, saying that the Church leaders spoke "a few words to those who had worked on the Temple and Blessed those Bretheren who had come from the north to labor in so good a cause. We had a social chat and some singing by the Bretheren and sisters. I sang an original [song], Marching to Dixie. Pies and cakes were handed round and wine [homemade wine was still commonly used in Dixie], all participating in the good feeling which pervaded the assembly. The Bretheren of the north expressed themselves highly pleased [with] the treatment they had received while laboring here."[45]

Edward L. Parry, in a report prepared in March 1874, gave the rock quantities used up to that date: 80 cords of small volcanic rock were pounded into the excavations to make the footings, 150 cords were used in the large drain, and 500 cords of heavy stones were used in the foundation. A cord equals 128 cubic feet, and it may be more impressive to understand in these terms: 10,240 cubic feet of small lava rock was used to make the footings; 19,200 cubic feet of lava stones, mostly small but some large, were used for the drains; and 64,000 cubic feet of the large lava stones were used to build the foundation—a total of 93,440

44. Walker, *Diary*, 1:383.
45. Walker, *Diary*, 1:384.

cubic feet in all.[46] At 160 pounds per cubic foot, the total is 14,950,400 pounds, or 7,475 tons of lava rock that had been gathered, quarried, hauled, and dumped or set in place to form the footings, drains, and foundation of the temple.

The previous summer Charlie Walker had written one last toast, for the temple, which most likely expressed the feelings of all those who had labored so diligently:

> *Our Temple*
>
> *May peace abound within thy walls*
> *And glory round thee shine:*
> *May Zion's workmen, one and all,*
> *Gain blessings at thy shrine.*[47]

The unfinished temple had taken its place in the hearts and minds of these devoted people.

---

46. Bleak, "Annals," Book B, 237–38.
47. Walker, *Diary*, 1:374.

Chapter 8

THE WALLS CLIMB UPWARD

January to November 1874

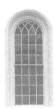

E ver alert to legal ramifications of the anti-polygamy campaign being waged in Washington, D. C., Church leaders in St. George established a trusteeship covering the temple property in January 1874, the month before the lava rock foundation was completed. The trusteeship placed title of the temple lot and all improvements in the hands of three trustees "to hold the title of St. George Temple Block and other property, pursuant to the legal notice which had been given in St. George and vicinity."[1] Three trustees were elected: Robert Gardner, William A. Perkins, and David H. Cannon. They were required to file bonds with the probate court of Washington County "for the faithful performance of their trust." The trusteeship would be concluded at the "will and pleasure" of the trustors, namely, the members of the Church (meaning, in effect, the stake and mission leaders), "in St. George and vicinity," in accordance with the "legal notice" that had been given. A deed to accomplish that when the time came was also prepared.

---

1. "Minutes of a Meeting Held for the Election of Trustees for St. George Temple Grounds and Other Property," Dixie State University Special Collections, St. George, Utah.

This trusteeship would allay any legal interference by individuals or entities against the Church in the course of the temple's construction. What is impressive is the degree of orderliness and legal understanding that existed in the pioneer community. These people were not novices; they were very conversant in civil affairs, attested also in the manner in which the state and locality had moved forward, from the beginning, in the formation of county and local governments with their charters, and by the organization of the court system and early construction of a county courthouse. These developments reflected the high quality and level of education, experience, and sophistication that existed within St. George and the Utah Territory as a whole.

Earlier, on 18 January 1874, Brigham had spoken to the Saints in St. George, urging them to get the temple finished as soon as possible. Those who hadn't yet been endowed needed to be, he said, as did each of their ancestors, so that all would be prepared for the millennial day.[2]

Though hastening the work had been a regular theme, the prophet was growing increasingly anxious for the temple to be completed. It had now been two years and almost three months since groundbreaking, and the workers were just finishing the foundation. Worse, until it was finished there could be no sandstone walls and no work on the interior. In short, the dedication was still years away, and Brigham seems to have been filled with a growing sense of his own mortality.

Nevertheless, "with the rising din over plural marriage and the inevitable squeeze upon the Church by a federal government determined to stop the practice, even if it meant the destruction of the Church, St. George [was becoming] an asylum, Zion's Zion, a place of quiet refuge from the encircling storm."[3]

There and elsewhere, the prophet's thoughts turned more and more

2. George Laub, "George Laub—Utah Pioneer," synopsis of *George Laub Journal* (privately published, n.d.), 2, Sec. III, 12.
3. Richard E. Bennett, "Line upon Line, Precept upon Precept: Reflections on the 1877 Commencement of the Performance of Endowments and Sealings for the Dead," *BYU Studies* 44, no. 3 (2005), 55.

to a particular concept, that "the law of consecration and stewardship [as] outlined by Joseph Smith forty years earlier, was still an attainable goal."[4] Put another way, if the Saints had greater unity in their temporal as well as spiritual affairs, the blessings of the Lord would come upon them with ever greater abundance. "Money, at least the accumulation of such, was never to be the goal; rather, the building of the kingdom of God upon the earth and of serving others selflessly were principles of far greater value."[5] By the Saints dedicating their all to God's service, the Lord would be bound to prosper all aspects of their lives, their challenging agricultural endeavors, their family affairs and community solidarity, even the work on his holy temple. Brigham, like Joseph before him, called this complete unity "the order of Enoch."[6]

On 23 and 24 August 1873, stake president's counselor Robert Gardner had presided over a stake conference where the speakers were assigned by Elder Snow to address the necessity of being united in temporal things and preparing for the order of Enoch. To that end they discussed the need for personal testimony and the necessity of having the Spirit soften their hearts and guide their lives. This appears to have been a preparation for organizing the St. George United Order, the first so organized in the West, which occurred in February 1874.

According to Robert's record, "President Young and George A. Smith spent a good deal of their time in St. George. Being connected with the building of the Temple, I had occasion to call on them very often. One day President Young told me he wanted me to get up a list of the names of the Brethren in St. George who would be willing to go into an organization of a United Order to work together. I did so and in 2 or 3 days I reported ten or twelve names. He said we will start with that many and will call a meeting and organize. So he gave notice of the meeting in the St. George Hall."

4. Bennett, "Line upon Line," 56.
5. Bennett, "Line upon Line," 55–56.
6. Bennett, "Line upon Line," 56.

In that meeting, held 9 February 1874, Brigham explained what he wanted. Robert continues: "He said the Lord wanted the people to be united in their temporal as well as spiritual affairs and that the time had come for them to enter into an Order of this kind."[7] He "declared that the time had come for the people to conform to the revelations to be ONE. To enter into this brotherly, friendly labor has been the responsibility of the saints since the days of Joseph Smith. He also expressed the desire to see the temple construction pushed as rapidly as possible. He chided some brethren for faithlessness in their temple labor assignments. He asked for 100 men to quarry rock or haul sand, clay or lime. He requested that the roof be in place by winter."[8] "Many others added their names to the list in this meeting. He then wished the meeting to nominate a President to preside over the Order in St. George. Bishop William Snow of Pine Valley nominated me to be the President and it was carried unanimously."

Gardner continued: "I think most of the Bishops in the county were elected in a Board to transact the business of the Order. The different fields were organized into working farming companies and a good many mechanical companies were organized."[9]

Gradually the number of temple hands continued to increase; the "old hands" as some of the locals called themselves, pressed ever forward in their labors, and finally, near the end of March, the entire foundation was laid to the water-table and so the project was ready for the sandstone walls to be constructed. The sandstone quarry, which had already supplied the stone for the courthouse and tabernacle, was located in a shallow draw that helped drain a slickrock alcove behind the western

---

7. Douglas Cox, "History of Robert Gardner, Junior," unpublished manuscript, 106; copy in possession of Richard Schmutz.

8. Charles Lowell Walker, *Diary of Charles Lowell Walker*, edited by A. Karl Larson and Katharine Miles Larson, 2 vols. (Logan: Utah State University Press, 1980), 383n15, quoting James G. Bleak, "Annals of the Southern Utah Mission," Book B, 58, typescript, Dixie State University Special Collections, St. George, Utah.

9. Cox, "Robert Gardner," 106.

end of the Red Hill. The quarry, located in the very bottom of the draw, was easily accessible and provided a superior quality of sandstone for construction.

Meanwhile, the indefatigable Charles Pulsipher was still out gathering foodstuffs and other supplies for the workers as well as the local citizens. According to his journal, "In March . . . I started up to Sanpete, got Brother Thomas Terry to go with me and we visited all the main settlements in that Stake where Elder Orson Hyde presided. We had a good time preaching Temple work and building of Temples for about three weeks, gathered up about three hundred sacks of flour, loaded all the teams we could get there and returned again to St. George. We generally formed plenty of friends to stop with over night but we came to a small settlement of only three families and it was nearly night and a stormy night and as the roads were very bad and it was seven miles to the next settlement it was of a necessity that we should stay there and neither of us being acquainted so it fell to Brother Terry's lot to ask for the privelage of staying and he tried two of them but [was] refused so it only left one more. I said, 'Well you have tried two that is your part. Now I will try the other one.'

"I made up my mind that we would stay. I found out the man's name and I urged up the horses and got them on a good trot as we came near the door, jumped out of the wagon and met the man at the door as he came out to see what the excitement was. I reached him my hand and said, 'Good evening Brother Prisby, How are you? We have come to stay overnight with you.' I went to unhitching. 'Where shall we put our horses? We are traveling Missionaries representing the St. George Temple.'

"He answered, 'Right down there to the stable, plenty of feed.'

"We got the people together and had an interesting meeting in the evening and raised about $40.00 of Temple offerings. . . . Before we started out I had got the promise of ten 4 horse teams to come in two weeks. President Snow had gone to [Salt Lake] City to Conference and two of the next Presiding Brethren [in St. George] heard what I was do-ing and they both met [me] and said, 'You are calculating to have ten teams come right after you I hear?'

"'Yes sir.'

"'Well, you have only 113 sacks of flour up there. What are you go-ing to finish up the loads with?'

"'I said, "With flour."'

"'But how do you know you can get the flour?'

"'Because President Snow told me to take them and load them and I have always filled every call that he has made on me and I calculate to fill this one.'

"'If you don't and those teams go up and back without any load who will pay the expense, you or the church?'

"This set me to studying as two of the highest Athorities there at the time had expressed their doubts in regards to my being able to raise that amount. So I . . . instructed half of the teams to come in two weeks and the other five [to] wait until I sent for them but I found that instead of ten I could load fifteen and I telegraphed for the balance to come but they had got to putting in their crops and could not come for another month which brought the flour into St. George after the early harvest had come in . . . and by that failure . . . the Church lost $350.00 and when Brother Snow heard of it he was vexed. . . . Brother Snow said they did not have the faith that you had or they would have let you alone."[10]

On 1 April 1874, the time had arrived for records to be placed in the southeast cornerstone of the temple, a large block of lava that had been hollowed out and prepared to receive them. In Walker's diary we learn the names of the leaders and supervisors present, including Brigham Young, his counselor George A. Smith, and local leaders such

10. Charles Pulsipher, *Journal* (privately published, n.d.); in possession of Venetta Williams, Santa Clara, Utah.

as Erastus Snow, John W. Young, Robert Gardner, A. F. MacDonald, Joseph A. Young, Jacob Hamblin, James G. Bleak, and others.[11]

It was a beautiful "Dixie" day. Walker lyrically praised its beauty. "Spring," he wrote, "with all its vernal beuties is teeming. The fruit trees are out in full bloom; the Lucern is beginning to wave gracefully in the breeze. The air is laden with perfumme and the busy Bees are at work supping the rich nectar of the lovely blossoms while the sweet songsters are warbling songs of praise to him who made all things and pronounced them very good."[12] Everyone was in high spirits for this historical occasion, and everyone welcomed the arrival of spring. After twelve years in their settlement, Dixieites now had beautiful gardens on their large lots; they had planted flowers, fruit and nut trees, and they were growing a remarkable variety of vegetables. With each passing year St. George was becoming more pleasant, attractive, and livable.

Church leaders and others assembled at 11:00 A.M. "to perform the solemn ceremony." Also present were "the men in charge of construction, the workmen, and a large number of others."[13] When the time came, Brigham explained the purpose of the gathering: "to deposit in the place prepared, a box containing records, and some of our publications, in token of our faith, to be here preserved until the Savior comes and then to be subject to His will and pleasure, together with the Temple, for the use of the living and the dead." He then locked the box and placed it in the hollowed out receptacle prepared for it in the cornerstone.[14]

Walker described the wooden box that received the records; also the stone receptacle, hollowed out of the southeast corner foundation stone. The box, he wrote, was "dovetailed, with a pair of brass hinges, [and had] a lock and key." After the last papers were placed in it,

---

11. Walker, *Diary*, 1:386.
12. Walker, *Diary*, 1:386.
13. Bleak, "Annals," Book B, 258–62.
14. Bleak, "Annals," Book B, 258–62.

"Brother Brigham locked it and it was carried up on the wall." At noon he deposited the box "[in] its final resting place in the large stone box. . . . The stone lid was then placed on and cemented by Br Edward Lloyd Parry. And during the day a massive stone block was placed on the top and I think it will stay there safely during the Millennium. I and a number of the workmen witnessed these proceedings and I was truly pleased and much gratified at having the privillege, for now I know how it ought to be done."[15]

Mission historian James G. Bleak listed the items placed in the box, which must have been fairly large. They included copies of the Bible, Book of Mormon, Doctrine and Covenants, hymnbook, Compendium, Catechism, [Orson] Spencer's Letters, *Voice of Warning,* Orson Hyde's Tour of Jerusalem, Three Sermons on Polygamy, Answers to Questions, *Millennial Star* I and XIV, other books and newspapers, and an "Abstract of the History of Southern Utah" by himself.[16] After placement of the records, Brigham Young took off his hat, bowed his head, and offered the dedicatory prayer.[17]

Eleven days later, 11 April 1874, in a circular sent throughout southern Utah encouraging even greater sacrifice and consecration, stake president John W. Young stated in part: "We feel grateful . . . for the work already done in erecting the St. George Temple. We desire to see this work pushed forward with all diligence, so that the earnest desire of the First Presidency may be realized by seeing this Holy House in readiness to have the Ordinances of the Gospel administered therein. It is to the interest of all that the Keys of Salvation now in the possession of but one or two men on the Earth, be bestowed by them upon others before this knowledge pass behind the vail again. This can only be done in a Temple. If these keys are again taken from the Earth because of our tardiness in preparing a place where they can be imparted, how long

---

15. Walker, *Diary,* 1:386.
16. Bleak, "Annals," Book B, 259–62.
17. Bleak, "Annals," Book B, 261–62.

may we have to wait for their restoration? God forbid that negligence in us should so delay this work, as to bring upon us this calamity."[18]

Young's circular had its desired effect, and the local brethren somehow increased their service. Even so, it was not enough. With the lava stone foundation in place, the need for temple hands increased again, driving general Church leaders to call for more and more workers. In May, George A. Smith used both psychology and a little exaggeration to boost St. George as a delightful place to live, whatever the season, and a good place to do volunteer work on a worthy project: "We have got the foundation [of the temple] to the water table, about 18 feet from the ground. . . . The building is in a nice locality and in a very fine climate, where, all winter, and in fact the whole year, there is almost perpetual spring and summer weather; and when the Temple is completed there will be an opportunity to go there and spend a winter and attend to religious ordinances or enjoy yourselves; and if you want to go there through the summer you can eat as delicious fruits as ever grew out of the earth in any country I believe. As far as I have traveled I have never seen anything in the way of fruit that I thought was superior to that which is produced in St. George. We invite one hundred fifty of the brethren to volunteer to go down there this summer to put up this building, and to find themselves while they are doing it. We shall call upon the Bishops, presiding Elders, teachers and others from the various stakes of Zion to take this matter in hand when they reach home, and find brethren . . . who are willing to go . . . so that by Christmas the building may be ready for the roof, [and] we may soon have a font dedicated and the ordinances of the holy Priesthood performed in that place. . . . Our brethren in that vicinity are doing all they can to push

18. John W. Young, "Circular to the Saints of the St. George Stake and Members of the United Order," 11 April 1874, as recorded in Bleak, "Annals," Book B, 277–78.

forward the work, but five or six months help from one hundred or one hundred fifty men is very desirable."[19]

In the meantime the sandstone walls were going up and the need was increasing for timbers and lumber in large quantities to be worked for scaffolding, floor beams, joists, flooring, and studding. Wall stones in large numbers were being quarried, hauled, and hewn, but more carpenters, stonecutters, masons, and mason helpers were needed. Old growth ponderosa pine trees on Mt. Trumbull had to be felled and sawed, and the lumber cured and hauled 80 miles to St. George.[20] More lime had to be burned in Judd's kiln with wagonloads of firewood hauled from the lower slopes of Pine Valley Mountain as well as sand and water hauled from the Virgin River to make mortar. Support and help of all kinds was needed. For President Young and his colleagues in Salt Lake City, it became an even higher priority. All were in a push to move construction along.

Even before the laying up of the sandstone walls had commenced, George Jarvis and his crew, under the superintendence of master carpenter John Chidester of Washington, had erected the first level of scaffolding. This scaffolding was constructed of entire trimmed trees or poles that had been cut on Pine Valley Mountain and hauled by team and wagon the 35 miles to St. George. At the temple site, Jarvis and his crew used heavy rope to lash these poles to the cross-timbers, and upon these were laid the planks cut and milled at Mt. Trumbull upon which the stonemasons stood to do their work.

Jarvis was remarkably skilled with ropes and knew well how to use them in maneuvering heavy weights. In addition to the scaffolding, therefore, they had constructed several sheer-legs that could lift

---

19. *Journal of Discourses*, 26 vols. (London: Latter-day Saints' Book Depot, 1854–86), 17:87–88.

20. It will be noted that differing mileage distances are mentioned by different writers. Robert Gardner thought it was about 70 miles; numerous others, including the Blake brothers, thought it closer to 80. Perhaps these latter were considering the twisting, winding "temple trail" that had been built to follow the easiest course between the hills and over the cliffs, while Gardner was thinking more of the distance "as the crow flies."

the heavy sandstone blocks into place on the growing walls. And as the walls increased in height, Jarvis raised the scaffolding and lashed additional sheer-legs to the scaffolding or walls, enabling the masons to continue upward toward the temple's projected wall height of 80 feet.[21]

At the same time numerous stonecutters and masons were busy cutting and fitting the rock sills, sides, and curved tops of the windows. This involved prodigious labor as well as remarkable skill. Eight arched basement windows were placed in the foundation along the length of each main wall; their sills were set some four feet above the finished basement floor. In the sandstone walls above the foundation were fifty round windows, each placed in an opening 52 inches across that needed curved stones to enclose the 42-inch window frames. There were 58 arched long window openings 15 feet high by 62 inches wide before sills and stone sides and arches were added, and the remainder of the long windows were the same height but somewhat more narrow. In the east and west ends were eight extra-tall windows with openings more than 8 feet wide and some 22 feet high, again with arched tops, each arch made of numerous small cut stones. Additionally, there were six tall outside door openings and 92 inside door openings, most tall and also with arched tops.[22] It is well to remember that each of these openings had to be fitted with smoothed stone sills, straight or curved depending on the window, and all of them needed to be wide enough to cover walls that were at least 2 feet 8 inches thick. By June, Walker could report that "the window sills [are] set in the south and west sides. I am still cutting stones for [them] every day and feel blessed and comforted in laboring thereon. The people are all busy working and find no time for wicked pursuits."[23]

---

21. See Carol M. Vincent, "Ann Prior Jarvis 1823–1913," n.d., n.p.; see also Josephine Jarvis Miles, "St. George Temple," 23 September 1929, n.p., Daughters of Utah Pioneers McQuarrie Memorial Museum, St. George, Utah.

22. Janice Force DeMille, *The St. George Temple: First One Hundred Years* (Hurricane, Utah: Homestead Publishers, 1977), 47.

23. Walker, *Diary,* 1:388.

Meanwhile, the carpenters were using what lumber was available to lay in the temple floors. The basement ceiling height was two feet above the row of arched basement windows. There the masons had placed beam pockets in the stone to receive the butt ends of the first main floor support beams.[24] These notches were placed at intervals of 12 feet 8 inches along each wall to match the square sandstone basement pillars that had been placed at the same intervals along the basement floor. Carpenters could then begin installing the network of heavy beams running from the beam pockets to adjoining pillars and lengthwise from pillar to pillar. On these beams they placed 2x9-inch joists for the main assembly room floor. Next was placed the layer of sub-flooring and flooring, all of 1x4-inch, smooth-cut pine boards, laid lengthwise over the joints of the subfloor beneath. This installation formed the floor of the first main assembly room and, on the bottoms of the joists, wooden lath and plaster formed the ceiling of the basement.

And how were the wooden jams for the sides and arched tops of the doors and windows, as well as the window frames, sashes, and grids produced? While the jams and frames for every door and window in the temple were manufactured locally, the window sashes and grids were manufactured in Salt Lake and shipped by rail and then by wagon to St. George. The glass was manufactured in the East and then shipped by rail to Ogden, transferred to the Utah Central Railroad, and delivered south to York, the rail terminus in Juab County. From there it, too, was freighted by team and wagon to St. George.[25] Window sashes, grids,

---

24. Thomas Weston Welch, "Early Mormon Woodworking at Its Best: A Study of the Craftsmanship in the First Temples in Utah" (master's thesis, Brigham Young University, 1983), 18.

25. E-mail from the Church History Department, Salt Lake City, Utah, 23 April 2012. A distinction must be made between the temple glass and the tabernacle glass. Though there is some disagreement concerning this, the preponderance of local evidence suggests that while the temple glass arrived in St. George in 1875 as described above, the tabernacle glass was manufactured in the East and then shipped around the Horn of South America and up to the Wilmington Docks near San Bernardino; from there it was freighted by wagon across the Mojave Desert to St. George in 1871.

and glass or "lights," therefore, are the only portions of the St. George Temple that were not of local manufacture.

Once the building had been plastered both inside and out, the window and door jams were installed and then sealed. Then carpenters installed the window and door frames, which were then sealed and painted. Meanwhile, the doors as well as the imported sashes and grids were also painted, after which they were hung or installed. With the glass "lights" in place the process was complete, all with such craftsmanship and skill that for more than a hundred forty years the windows and doors have withstood the seasonally harsh St. George weather.

Even as the walls were going up, and despite Charles Pulsipher's constant food-gathering efforts, trying times and looming threats of starvation continued. One close call in the summer of 1874 was reported by Samuel Utley Carter, who had come to St. George in 1861 as a child and who as a young man had been helping with the temple foundation. He was taking his turn caring for the young wheat crop in the Santa Clara fields when seemingly from nowhere a cloud of grasshoppers descended on the large field and began consuming every green thing in their path. Thinking quickly Samuel "herded chickens onto the growing wheat fields to eat up the grasshoppers, and the wheat crop was saved."[26]

By early fall the temple walls had risen to a height of 25 feet above the foundation, but as workers came and went, Church leaders continued to use their sermons to urge ever-increasing numbers to join in the work. For instance, during the October semiannual general conference John Taylor asked if "over 300 men could be found who would go down to St. George this winter, find their own food and work as teamsters, carpenters, stone-cutters, and other callings necessary to forward

---

26. Kate C. Squire, "Samuel Utley Carter's History," 13 January 1955, n.p., Daughters of Utah Pioneers McQuarrie Memorial Museum, St. George, Utah.

the work on the temple."[27] Because of local scarcity, volunteers were always reminded to take "most" of their own provisions.

In the same conference, George A. Smith echoed the theme as he exhorted the Saints to "remember the brethren who are laboring on the Temple at St. George. They have been working all the season, . . . and some of them are destitute of clothing, and other necessaries. Some of the workmen there have labored on the temple from the very beginning, and the walls are now thirty feet high. . . . We have invited the people in every settlement to contribute of their means to continue the work and we have also invited brethren to go down to St. George and labor upon the Temple this winter that the building may be prepared for the roof as soon as possible. . . . When that Temple is finished we can go down there and be baptized for our dead, receive our . . . ordinances and all the blessings pertaining to the Priesthood . . . [but] we do not wish any to go . . . unless they desire to do so, and have got the spirit to go in order that they may assist in forwarding this work. . . . Last winter the masons worked on the walls of the temple all winter, except seven and a half days, when they were prevented by rain. But to all who may have any intention of going there to spend the winter . . . take good warm clothing and thick-soled shoes. Do not [think] you will find summer weather there in the winter season, it is more like pleasant spring weather, and when evening comes, good thick warm clothing is needed."[28]

In a second address, President Smith returned to the subject. Workers from the north, he said, had remained at work on the temple all summer, but they needed shoes and clothing. Three hundred or more men from different parts of the Territory planned to spend the coming winter there. He expected the roof to be in place by the next spring, and "soon" the baptismal font would be placed in the basement. After the temple was completed, he said, many, even those "in feeble

27. *Journal of Discourses,* 17:174.
28. *Journal of Discourses,* 17:163–64.

health," could spend the mild winters there to attend to the ordinances for their dead.[29]

Shortly after conference, however, an unexpected accident at the tabernacle nearly spelled disaster for the project. "On Saturday evening of October 12, 1874 . . . [construction supervisor] Miles Romney . . . while working on the St. George Tabernacle . . . fell from a ladder breaking one of his arms and one of his legs.[30] His injuries were very serious. Indeed . . . his age of 68 years being against him, and he being a heavy bodied man, the shock to his system in addition to the breaking of his bones, must have been very great and much against him. A later dispatch stated that many friends of Miles Romney hoped to hear of his favorable progress and recovery. The last dispatch stated that the patient rested better on Saturday night than on the previous night."

In fact, "through the blessings of the Lord and careful nursing of his beloved wife, Elizabeth, . . . Romney finally recovered sufficiently to resume his activities on the temple and tabernacle."[31]

More workmen came from the north during the fall and winter of 1874–75. On 22 November 1874, Charlie Walker wrote, "I am still laboring on the Temple. There are great number[s] from the north working for the Temple: on the roads, in the [sandstone] quarry, and other Places."[32] The "roads" could have referred to the roads to and from the

---

29. *Journal of Discourses*, 17:258.

30. The tabernacle was still not finished, and Miles Romney was supervising the construction of both the tabernacle and the temple.

31. Gaskell Romney, "Sketch of Miles Romney," typescript, Daughters of Utah Pioneers McQuarrie Memorial Museum, St. George, Utah. See also Verl P. Allman, "Thomas Allman History," n.p., 47; copy in possession of Beth Dillenbeck. These two sources were combined in the above account. The *Deseret News* of 9 May 1877 printed a notice of his death after a short illness which was caused by a fall from a window while working on the St. George tabernacle. The closing paragraph of the obituary reads as follows: "He was a kind father and a steadfast friend, liberal in his views and charitable to all, without fanaticism but firm in his faith. He died as he has lived in faith and fellowship. He leaves a wife, herself ill, seven children, fifty-seven grandchildren, five great-grandchildren and a numerous circle of friends to mourn his departure. He was one of the noblest works of God—An Honest Man."

32. Walker, *Diary*, 1:392.

Mt. Trumbull sawmills being built by Robert Gardner that fall, to a recently discovered bed of coal thirty miles to the east, to the lime kiln at Middleton, or to the sandstone quarry. Walker referred to the latter road a week later: "Pleasant [day]. The Roads are now in good order for hauling Rock to the Temple." Of meeting the following Sunday, he wrote, "A number of the brethren from the North spoke their feelings in regard to the building of the Temple, and for their testimony to the truth of the work in which they were engaged."[33]

Due to the beating it took from many heavily laden wagon trips, the road to the sandstone quarry had need of constant repair. It was the same with all the traveled roads in town and elsewhere. The heavy wagons with their iron-rimmed wheels were constantly eroding the road bed, especially around corners. Dust was common in dry weather and mud when it rained. The most heavily used roads may have been covered over with small stones, or "macadamized," to reduce wear, dust, or mud. A reference to this process was made in a letter sent from St. George by a correspondent calling himself Amram, to the *Deseret News Weekly* in November 1874. Men, he said, were working "in the [red] rock quarry" and at the temple site. "The balance of them worked at turns piking, *macadamizing* and repairing the road from the quarry to the temple."[34]

---

33. Walker, *Diary*, 1:392.

34. Cox, "Robert Gardner," 273, quoting from the letter to *Deseret News Weekly*; emphasis added. The use of an early macadam road-building method was very possible at this date, though neither Walker nor Bleak mentions it. A Wikipedia article tells that dry macadamizing was developed by the Scotsman John Loudon McAdam around 1820. His method used small-sized stones to layer a road. For the bottom six or seven inches of the roadbed, stones no larger than three inches were used. These were not smooth but stones broken off larger pieces with a hammer. The next layer, two inches thick, used hammered stones sized two inches or less. These stones needed to be smaller than the width of the iron rim of the wagon or carriage wheel. Over time, the stones would be ground down and their dust turned to concrete when it was rained on. Whether much distance of roadbed was macadamized in labor-short St. George is not known, but the method was in use in other places and could have been used in St. George, if only partially and on the most used stretches of roadway or corners where the greater damage occurred (see Wikipedia, "Macadamizing").

Chapter 9

THE JOURNAL KEEPER

Winter 1874

O ne of the workers who journeyed south in November 1874 was a young man named George Kirkham Jr. His is an interesting story, and the fine journal he kept of his winter in St. George reveals intriguing details about temple construction and some of the hardships experienced by the workers.[1] He also revealed much about St. George social life and offered unique glimpses of Brigham Young and other local Church leaders. Through it all shines brightly the strength of his testimony.

George was born 11 March 1852 in Surrey, England, to George William and Mary Ann Astington Kirkham. By vocation young George was a master carpenter, though he was also an accomplished oil painter and sketch artist who founded an art school the winter he was in St. George. He and his younger brother Joseph were both talented singers and fiddlers (violinists). While in Dixie they joined the St. George Glee Club, played fiddle for numerous dances in Washington, St. George, and

---

1. George Kirkham, "My Journey to Dixie," in *The Journals of George Kirkham,* ed. Kathy Kirkham Reed (privately published, n.d.), 5–33, typescript; copies in possession of Sheryl Archibald and Richard Kirkham.

Santa Clara, and became very well known throughout the area. During that winter Joseph met, courted, fell in love with, and married a local beauty named Teresa Cragun, younger sister of Martha Cragun Cox, who is renowned even today for her published autobiography. When George, his wife, Mary, who by then was expecting their second child, their year-old son, George Erastus, and his father returned north in the spring, Joseph and Teresa accompanied them, and all of them spent the rest of their lives in Lehi.

After describing in great detail their rather stormy journey south, George and Mary entered a warm and sunny St. George on Thursday, 5 November 1874, having been feasting on handouts of grapes the previous three days. After locating Robert Gardner at the tithing office and receiving permission to stay there until Monday, he and others went and viewed the tabernacle, which was not yet finished. On Sunday, following three days of conference meetings, George and his wife and baby walked to the temple site and strolled around the building. He recorded: "The foundation is built of black rock and the walls are to be of red sandstone. . . . I had many reflections while looking about. I felt to thank God we had the opportunity of coming down to help build up the temple in the sunny south, to the Most High, praise to his most Holy Name. It was very quiet, for there was nobody there but myself and wife and child. I could not help but shed a tear when I thought of the goodness of our Father in Heaven toward us. While we sat upon one of the stones of the temple, we returned thanks. Then we returned to our wagon."[2]

The next morning Robert Gardner directed Kirkham to housing. He wrote: "Well, I obtained a large room in Brother William McCallester's house for the winter. We hauled our things and then went and got a gag of rabbit brush, and some potatoes and meat from the tithing office."[3] This unplastered, mostly unheated room became very

2. Kirkham, *Journal*, 11.
3. Kirkham, *Journal*, 11.

uncomfortable, and, with his own little family in the only bed plus his father and brother on the floor, crowded and often disorderly. Yet to their credit they all made the best of it.

Meanwhile, food-and-supplies gatherer Charles Pulsipher had spent the summer of 1874 organizing the United Order in the tiny communities of Mountain Meadows, Pinto, and Hebron. He writes: "I was appointed Vice President and also foreman of the Mechanic and Building Committee. We worked together very successfully. We built five good houses. My brother, John, was Supt. Of the dairies and brother, Wm, was appointed superintendent of the stock. We raised a good crop of grain, took better care of the stock and made lots of butter and cheese. We settled up in the winter and paid all fair wages so that we came [out] all right but the means did not come in sufficient to keep the Temple work going on as fast as they [wished or hoped] and . . . I was recalled to travel again in company with Brother John L. Smith, George A. Smith's brother. We started out together and were 14 months gathering many offerings and tithes for the Temple. Brother John L., being ordained a patriarch, gave about two hundred patriarchal blessings which I wrote for him."[4]

Late in the fall Brigham Young returned to St. George, staying from November through February. But Walker wrote that "his health is poor, yet he feels well in spirit, and comes down to see us once in [a] while at the Temple, and is very much interested in the erection of the Temple and is using every means in his powe[r] to push the work along."[5]

Despite not feeling well, Brigham must have experienced great satisfaction as he observed the fevered activity of the hundreds of volunteer workers. One wonders, too, how he felt about the personal sacrifices they were making, going back and forth each day between habitations and work, in rough and often too-well-worn clothes, with tired backs,

4. Charles Pulsipher, *Journal* (privately published, n.d.); in possession of Venetta Williams, Santa Clara, Utah.
5. Walker, *Diary*, 1:392.

callused hands, and sometimes bruised and bloodied fingers. No warm showers awaited them. Many must have gone days without lunches. Who saw to drinking water at the work sites? Winter days were "cold and windy," as Walker often remarked; other winter days were no doubt cold and wet. The summer past had been hot, with no shade at the worksites. Every day teams had to be harnessed and unharnessed, curried, fed, and watered. Who furnished these teams? Where were they kept? And who cared for them? Wagons had to be kept in repair, their wheels greased, and work tools had to be sharpened or repaired. Work clothes had to be washed and mended. Many questions could be asked; many situations imagined; many personal stories told—only for the most part these visiting workmen and occasionally their wives were too exhausted to write them. This is our loss even more than theirs. Obviously, the work pace quickened during winter months due to the many volunteers from the north and slowed when the weather was hot with fewer workers, mostly local. But the work went on—always it went on!

George Kirkham, thankfully, was an exception in terms of record keeping, and because he offered such a rich, almost day-by-day view of local goings-on, his journal will be quoted extensively. For instance, on Tuesday 10 November 1874 he recorded that "The weather was cool and cloudy. I was called to work on a private dwelling for Brother Thomas Judd, head clerk in the tithing office for a while, until the lumber arrived at the temple. I went and worked all day with Joseph Judd, who was a fine carpenter, the brother of the other. At night we went and spent the evening at Brother Judd's, and we had a fine time. Wednesday: Weather was clear, we all were well. It was expected that the President [Brigham Young] would be here today. I was told that 12 men had gone to meet him, and at 10 o'clock he arrived. In the afternoon my brother Joseph . . . [shook] hands with him. Thursday: The weather was cloudy and remained so all day. I could see the men at the temple from where I was at work. It was a grand sight. Many of the brethren visited the temple every day and was watching its progress. Friday: After breakfast I went to work. I was told that President Young was very sick. My prayer was he would soon be better. I made some inquires about the President's health, but could not find out how he was. In the evening I spent my time drawing a winter scene for home amusement."[6]

Kirkham's preoccupation with the construction of the temple and the hardships experienced by him, his family, and other citizens of St. George are evident in his journal entries. He continued his writing following a Church meeting on Sunday 15 November 1874: "The . . . speaker was George A. Smith who spoke of the temple. He said that the country was so red that it was expected, and was intended, to plaster the temple white. He said there would be a contrast between the temple and the red soil. He also said that President Young had offered to make offering of the baptism font, of cast iron, which would cost 5000 dollars, as a donation to the temple.[7] Brother Smith spoke at some length and was very encouraging. . . . Tuesday: At night I commenced a drawing school. There were about ten young men who came. . . . We commenced with some simple things and worked along. . . . [Nineteen-year-old] Samuel Jepperson [also in St. George to labor on the Temple], who had some little knowledge of some things . . . wanted to learn the human face and body, which I gave him some lesson[s] in."[8]

"Tuesday November 24: The weather was fine, but muddy underfoot. My wife was busy cooking breakfast over a fire on the hearth, which was very disagreeable. . . . [D]uring the afternoon my wife had a

6. Kirkham, *Journal*, 11.

7. One account of the font's purchase by Brigham Young gives its price as $4,000. When Brigham saw the final product, the story goes, he was so pleased that he offered the foundry an extra $1,000. That George Kirkham recorded in the fall of 1874 that the font "would cost 5000 dollars" seems to indicate the inaccuracy of that story.

8. Kirkham, *Journal*, 12. Jepperson improved sufficiently as an artist that he became known as one of the three "famous Danish artists" in the Church. He and the others, Danquart Weggeland and Carl Christian Anthon (C. C. A.) Christensen, traveled to St. George in 1881 to paint murals in the temple's basement ordinance rooms.

notion to go to a Wild Beast Show, which she did. Wednesday: I went to work, and the men were all [but me] on the temple. I could hear them at work with their stone hammers, tapping, tapping, but could not see them for fog. At night the weather cleared off. Friday: My father went to his work making mortar down at the temple with my brother who worked at the temple with the masons.

"Saturday: The weather was fine but cold and frosty. I went to work. The day turned out warm and clear, like summer. Cords of rock passed our door every day, to the temple. At night I with my brother went into the other part of the house to Brother McCallister's, who owned the house, to play [our violins] for a while. Then I returned to my own apartment and did some writing. I did so by a little lantern which shined very dull. I thought it seemed queer, keeping [an] every-dreary-day sketch of my life. My wife lay asleep on an old bedstead which would hardly keep together. My father sleeps on the floor at the foot of the old bedstead with my brother. We had to put up with a lot of inconvenience, which would have been more happy if we could have had what we needed, leave alone what we would like. But our mission [is] something we were proud of, and with the help of the Lord, we [will] fulfill it and return home with honor."[9]

More and more Kirkham and his younger brother Joseph were becoming involved in the community. Both were of an artistic nature, but George, who was older, extended his efforts to drawing and painting, as well as his fiddling. Meanwhile Joseph, still unmarried, apparently had his eye on a certain local young woman, though George did not yet mention it in his journal.

He continued: "Tuesday Dec 1, 1874: The weather was fine during the middle of the day, but cold morning and evening. The temple walls are now making rapid progress. They were forming the round windows, the 3rd [tier of windows] from the ground. The weather being warm and fine, the men were able to work well at night. I went to my drawing

---

9. Kirkham, *Journal*, 13–14.

school, 10 pupils who were making rapid progress. I spent 3 hours and returned home."[10]

Another who had come to work on the temple that winter was Alexander Spowart Izatt, who on that same day, 1 December, penned home to his wife: "I take much pleasure in writing you a few lines to let you know how I am getting along since I arrived in Saint George on Monday the 23rd of this month, five days sooner than we expected. We made long drives to gain the warm country as soon as possible. We found the climate all we could desire for heat and sunshine. Mornings and nights are quite cool as for the country I can say little for it is nothing but sand and salaratus. Never the less there are some fine beautiful vineyards but the people have had a great deal of labor to make [productive] the little soil they stand upon. There is nothing to encourage people to settle here unless they be Mormons. It can not be compared with the North Country. We cannot see any feed grow here for animals to eat—nothing but salaratus and sage brush. The first question asked us was, is there any [stone]masons along with you[?] and they were glad to learn there were quite a few in our company. We have worked four days on the Temple this week. It is quite a large building being one hundred and forty four feet long and ninety six feet wide. We like the work well and it will be a beautiful building when completed. We are very comfortable put up. We have three rooms, but there is quite a number living in them. Edward Jessop is our cook. H. Adams, H. J. Brown, D. Steel and a dozen more are all living here. There is no time to feel dull here and moreover our cook does not wear petticoats. . . .

"Jane, I hope you are enjoying yourself and that your mind is easy. Asking God to bless you and the family may this be your lot. I will now close hoping you will write when you get this. No more, but remains your husband. Alexander S. Izatt

"Write when you get this soon."[11]

10. Kirkham, *Journal*, 14.
11. Alexander S. Izatt, "Letter," in "A Sketch of the Life of Alexander Spowart Izatt,"

A letter that appeared in the *Salt Lake Herald* on 5 December 1874 from a St. George writer who signed as "J," gives a further sense of "being there" with Brigham and the rest. The writer took a "buggy ride" with George A. Smith. They drove to the temple site, "a nice drive of half a mile south." There they found about 90 men, including carpenters, tenders, and others at work, laying up some 50 tons of rock daily on walls that were then up to the center line of the ground-floor windows. The rock being laid in the main wall, he reports, was "rough dressed" while that used in the window sills, "caps" and at the water table line was smooth dressed. Rock and mortar were hoisted up the walls to the masons with ropes and pulleys and operated by horsepower. The work was well-organized and going smoothly. Timbers for the first floor were also going in "slowly," as the carpenters were not receiving lumber fast enough from the mill at Mt. Trumbull. One force of workers was at Mt. Trumbull and another was building a road some 30 miles east to an "inexhaustible bed of coal" that had been found. George A. next drove "J" to the sandstone quarry where they found approximately 120 men, including stonecutters, fitters, blacksmiths, "and other help" at work on "a quarry front of about a mile, well uncovered and opened and teams were hauling about 50 tons daily of rock cut and prepared to be placed in the wall." He found the quarry an "interesting place to visit. The fine, smooth seam-faces of rock, the sound of the hammer, the thump of the bar, the rattle of drills and click of scores of picks and chisels are music in a business way."[12]

---

n.d., n.p., typescript; in possession of Phillip Jorgensen. Another writer, likely a descendant of Izatt, adds to the bottom of Izatt's letter with at least a hint of frustration regarding what Alexander had sacrificed to work on the temple. "Alexander had a beautiful voice and was often invited out in the community to sing and was well liked. When he finished working in St. George he received $12.00 and a pair of half-soled shoes. When he arrived home his clothes were worn out and his family was in need. He got a little work and received for pay a piece of cloth big enough to make him a coat. Then he obtained two seamless sacks out of which a pair of trousers were made."

12. Kirk M. Curtis, "History of the St. George Temple" (master's thesis, Brigham Young University, 1964), 47–48.

George Kirkham, following a Sunday climb to the "Sugar Loaf" atop the Red Hill and a swing in the cave at its base, continued on Tuesday, 8 December: "I could see a vast difference in the walls of the temple. The work was going fast. I rejoiced to see the weather keep so fine, so we did not have to stop the work on the building. At night myself and brother [Joseph] went to play for a party in the court house. I took my wife with me. We returned a little after midnight."[13]

Another letter from St. George appeared in the *Deseret News* on 10 December 1874. Sent by a correspondent who signed himself "Thistle," he reported that the work was going on rapidly and that some twenty masons were laying up about 50 tons of rock each day. Some "30 cutters and dressers [were] engaged in the quarry and on the ground [at the temple site] preparing the rock for the layers." He noted that twelve wagons were making three or four trips per day hauling the rock to the temple site.[14] Each load reportedly weighed 3,500 pounds.[15] The walls were now about 35 feet above ground level and all were working with determination to perform their tasks.

A month later another correspondent noted something unique in the Latter-day Saint work crews: "The walls of the Temple are being rushed up at a wonderful speed, and all is peace and quiet, little or no intoxication, no police courts and no lawyers."[16] A letter written to the *Deseret News* several months before takes notice of the same moral tone, but again with a unique slant, this time regarding work animals: "Many teams are hauling building materials for the Temple and other buildings, but there is no abuse of animals, no profanity, no boisterous disputes, no angry recriminations. Men and animals perform their

13. Kirkham, *Journal*, 14–15.
14. Curtis, "History," 48, 50.
15. Douglas Cox, "History of Robert Gardner, Junior," unpublished manuscript, 280; copy in possession of Richard Schmutz.
16. Curtis, "History," 50, citing a letter sent to the *Deseret Evening News* in January 1875.

labors with quiet perseverance which seems to say their hearts are in it."[17]

That does not mean there were never any personal "scrapes." For instance, Heber Jones writes: "My great uncle, Patriarch George Miles, told me about Brigham Young's disagreement with Erastus Snow, and how Uncle George's much older half-brother, John Horne Miles, had a fight on the walls of the temple."[18] Concerning the first disagreement, Patriarch Miles continues: "Erastus Snow was so busy with non-paying Church work that in desperation he took food for his families from the Tithing Office. Upset, Brigham Young told him to go work for his livelihood like everyone else. The next time Elder Snow was supposed to be in a meeting, he didn't show up. When Brigham learned he was out laboring in the fields, he went right out and found him. 'What are you doing here?' he asked. 'Why, I'm doing just as you told me—trying to make a living.' So Brigham looked at him and said, 'Now look here, Erastus, you know that we can't get along without you. You know that! So turn this work over to your son, and from now on come to your meetings. Please don't neglect them anymore.'"

As for the second event mentioned by the elderly patriarch, "the fight on the Temple wall was actually on the scaffolding, when one man dropped a hammer which just barely missed my older half-brother, John Horne Miles, who was working below. John, who was hot-headed with a quick temper, looked up and said, 'Drop another one like that and I'll come up there and take it out of you!' The fellow replied, 'You can't come any too soon for me!' So John went up that ladder just like a monkey and they came together and mighty quick they were down on the scaffolding tussling back and forth like two cats, is how George Jarvis put it. George Jarvis finally got them separated, so then John made it

---

17. Quoted in Cox, "Robert Gardner," 275.
18. Heber Jones, "The St. George Temple," talk given at high priests' meeting, 20 March 1977, St. George, Utah, 10, unpublished typescript; in possession of the authors.

right with everyone by asking forgiveness, and they all went back to work."[19]

Meanwhile, George Kirkham was still waiting for lumber from Mt. Trumbull so he could begin carpentry work. For the week of 12 to 19 December, he continued: "Saturday . . . I went to work all day. We always quit work at 4 o'clock on Saturday. At night I went to my drawing school. Monday . . . The weather was fine. I went to work. I didn't feel very well [but] continued to work. At night I went to play for a[nother] party with my brother at the court house. Tuesday . . . Weather looked stormy. Went to work. While we were there, there was a large load of wood brought us [firewood, not lumber for the temple]. We were glad, for we had to get wood where we could, by picking it up here and there. It was sent to us by the church, as we were working for the church. We were very thankful, for we suffered some on account of not having wood to heat our room. The room we lived in was not plastered on the walls or ceiling, and [we were] cold at night. At night I went to my drawing school. Friday . . . The weather was fine but cold. I went to work, and when I returned my wife told me I had been called to be a teacher over the northern brethren who had come to work on the temple. At night I went to play for a party at the court house, for the brethren who worked on the coal road. President Snow and some others were there. Brother Snow thanked the brethren for their labors in that work, and we had a good party. Saturday . . . I went to work, but returned as there was nothing to do for the day [still no lumber]. At night I went to our practice, for we expected to have our concert on the 23rd day of December."[20]

19. From a recorded account by 102-year-old patriarch George Miles of St. George, Utah, to his great-nephew Heber Jones and his wife, Mary LaRee McAllister Jones; recording undated but probably about 1969, the year before Miles's passing. As a young man, John Horne Miles served a mission in England, and when he returned he brought to St. George his mother and his two younger half-brothers, twins George and Arthur Miles. Some of the details here were added during a telephone conversation between Heber Jones and author Blaine M. Yorgason, 16 October 2012.

20. Kirkham, Journal, 15–16.

George A. Smith, who was in St. George at the same time as Kirkham, Izatt, and the others, wrote to his cousin Joseph F. Smith, who was in England. Among other things, he declared:

"The extraordinary expenses incurred in building the temple are beyond the income of that office, as the crops in all the counties composing the Southern District have been light and the tithing is, consequently, small. A large number of men have come from the north, and they are moving the temple work forward rapidly at the present time. A great difficulty is to obtain lumber. Our mills at Mount Trumbull are about [80] miles distant, [55] of which are without water, the great difficulty being to get the lumber hauled [it took seven or eight days to haul a load of lumber to St. George]. Snow is now 18 inches deep at Mount Trumbull, and we are compelled to carry the hay 150 miles to support the cattle that furnish the mills with logs—and grain has to be hauled much further.

"About 100 men are at work in the quarry. The scarcity of money to meet the demands for cash articles is severely felt. . . . The walls of this temple [St. George] are between 30 and 40 feet high, and the work is first-class masonry, every stone being well laid on its natural bed. There is a good deal of spirit manifested by the brethren to push its construction forward. Elder William H. Folsom is now here taking charge of the Architectural Department, and Bishop Nathan Davis of the 17th Ward [Salt Lake City] is here making arrangements for casting the Baptisimal Font and the oxen upon which it is to stand. They are to be of Utah iron, finished with bronze. He has visited the iron works at Iron City and is much pleased with the prospect of Utah being supplied with this indispensable metal from our own mines."[21]

A meeting was held in the tabernacle basement on Christmas Day 1874 for all temple workmen and any of their families who were there.

---

21. *Millennial Star* 7 (5 January 1875): 10. See also Evelyn K. Jones, *Henry Lunt Biography, and History of the Development of Southern Utah and Settling of Colonia Pacheco, Mexico* (privately published, Provo, Utah, 1966), 293–94.

Many local citizens were also present, with George A Smith presiding. After choir singing and temple-themed talks, President Smith spoke of Brigham Young's wish that the building of the temple be hastened so that he "and the Twelve" could "communicate [to others] the keys of knowledge and power which the Prophet Joseph had conferred upon them" at Nauvoo and that could be conferred only in a temple. He recalled being present at Nauvoo when the doctrine of baptism for the dead was introduced. Some "had long records of their dead, for whom they wished to administer. This was seen to be but the beginning of an immense work, and that to administer all the ordinances of the Gospel to the hosts of the dead was no light task." Some had asked "if there could not be some shorter method of administering for so many." The Prophet Joseph in effect replied: "The laws of the Lord are immutable. We must act in perfect compliance with what is revealed to us. We need not expect to do this vast work for the dead in a short time; I expect it will take at least a thousand years." President Smith then asked the St. George audience for a show of hands to indicate their support for the work; "the hands of the assemblage rose as the hands of one man in token that they were willing to use their powers and substance, in building up the Temple and the Kingdom of God on earth."[22] The thousand-year work would soon begin in St. George, and these were the folks who would initiate it!

On Saturday, 26 December 1874, the day after Christmas, George Kirkham wrote a little more regarding the holiday revelry: "The weather was cloudy and cold. I started out for a place called Santa Clara. Some distance, with the St. George Glee Club to give a concert. On our way we passed Adam's Mill. The sun shined very bright. We crossed Cottonwood Creek. We traveled through sand and over rock. We also crossed the volcanic lava bed, which was some 12 miles long. It looked like a stream of rock. I walked over it and picked some of the rock,

---

22. James G. Bleak, "Annals of the Southern Utah Mission," Book B, 364, typescript, Dixie State University Special Collections, St. George, Utah.

and then rode on. We next came to the cotton field, vineyard, and the wheat fields. I also saw a horse feeding in the field which had no tail,[23] which created quite a laugh with the company. The scenery was grand to see. We arrived at Santa Clara and drove to the meeting house and commenced to unload our things. The children came around us like bees. They wanted to know what we would take for [concert] tickets. We told them we would take anything for them. We found ourselves in a quiet little place, most of whom were German [Swiss]. There was a small band there, about 6 or 7 instruments, which came out and played for us. While dinner was being cooked, we went down to look at the Santa Clara River. We saw a large formal garden which had been washed away by the river, which a few years before, a man could jump across. But now we had to stand and look for a cross[ing]. Even some of the houses had been washed away by the high water. We returned and ate a late dinner and then fixed up for our concert. At night we took in for tickets all kinds of pay, such as grapes, molasses and beans. We had a splendid time, after which we went to Brother Starley's [Staheli's?] to supper. After[ward] we went to a next door neighbor to spend an hour or two, and then returned to the meeting house where we intended to sleep all night, as we had our bed clothes with us. Three of us made our bed down on the floor to go to bed. The rest of them commenced their tricks by laying us out of bed and pulling our bed all over the stage floor. We made it again and again, and then one of our 3 put on his clothes, by the name of Thomas Jones, and started for home, some 6 miles. After that, I told the other two brothers of our bed crowd (there was to be 4 sleep in our bed quietly), that we had better give the other boys the slip. And the first chance I got, I put out with one quilt for the first haystack I could find. I ran about one block and a half and got into a haystack. There I laid for some time underneath, and then returned to the meeting house and found the rest asleep. I said hurrah boys, I

---

23. Perhaps the horse's tail had been donated to bind the mortar in the temple walls or possibly the plaster in the home of a local resident.

commenced to torment them by pulling off their bed clothes, but the game ended there and we all had a little sleep. When daylight came we all got up."[24]

Over the next three days Kirkham recorded: "[At work] I could see the [temple] walls halfway up. It was a glorious work, and when I think of it I felt to thank God I could help to do it, and that I lived in the Latter Days when the Lord had set up His Kingdom again for the last time, that all things might be gathered into one as the prophets had predicted from the foundation of the world to the present. I felt thankful for the testimony of Jesus Christ, which I felt to praise the Lord, and whatever my lot is to be, I hoped to be faithful to the Lord. At night I went and played for a party. Wednesday . . . After dinner I saw a wagon loaded with men who had come from Mount [Trumbull]. [We will learn more about this unhappy crew in the next chapter.] When we made inquiry we found there were too many men for the work. At night I spent the evening with my wife and father and brother." And on Thursday, the last day of 1874, he wrote: "The weather was cloudy, it had rained during the night, but not enough to hinder men from going to work. Before I went to work, Bishop Granger of the Third Ward, came to engage us to play for a party on New Years. We went to work all day. At night my brother and myself went to play for a party in the 1st Ward. We had a splendid supper at Bishop Miller's Ward, and then returned to the dance. We stayed until 3 o'clock in the morning, having danced the old year out and the new in."[25]

24. Kirkham, *Journal*, 16–17.
25. Kirkham, *Journal*, 16–17.

Jacob Peart's art (a cotton plant and a self-portrait) carved in the cliff face near Brigham Young's naturally sculpted profile (left center in photo, facing left), above the Virgin River near Bloomington, Utah. This photo has been modified to remove more recent markings and graffiti.

Woman teaching a child to spin cotton, 1860s.

Cotton mill with new upper story, shed, and annex, 1868. Workers with dignitaries in foreground.

Tabernacle under construction, late 1860s.

Paiute wickiup, home of Ta-peats, a Paiute from the vicinity of St. George, Utah. Photo by John K. Hillers, 1873.

Charles Dodge, son of St. George pioneer Walter Dodge, in his vineyard, 1870s.

The Big House, as the St. George home of Erastus Snow was often called, served for many years as the town hotel.

Cannon used as the pile driver of the volcanic black-rock footings of the St. George Temple.

The road that led to the black-rock, or lava-rock, quarry. Photo was taken from near the bottom of the hill.

Lava rock for temple footings and foundation stones was quarried from this site from 1871 to 1874. Note the drill marks in the stone.

The ledge of sandstone that became the quarry for the St. George Temple and other local buildings. Piles of stone rubble litter the draw. The low ledge immediately behind the rubble is what is left of the red-rock quarry. As it happens, the quarry is only a few yards from the fourth green of the Red Hills Golf Course in St. George.

A close view of a portion of the sandstone quarry. Note the drill marks.

Stonecutters near the foundation of the temple, circa 1873. These stones appear to be sandstone from the red-rock quarry. Note the drill marks and square on the stone in the foreground.

Area of Church sawmills on Mt. Trumbull.

Sawmill on Mt. Trumbull, date uncertain. The figure third from left is believed by some to be Robert Gardner.

Hauling timber through the snow on a sled, 1870s. Exact location unknown.

Top of natural switchback trail up the Hurricane Fault, near Diamond Butte on the Arizona Strip. From here the trail wound 30 miles farther to the pinery on Mt. Trumbull.

Sign at the top of Hurricane Fault.

*View westward from
summit of Mt. Trumbull.*

*Iron City coke oven. Originally there were two,
but local residents hauled away the stones of
one for their own building projects.*

Iron City erastra, where sandstone was ground into sand for pig-iron moldings. A mule hitched to the reach turned the grinding stone.

Remains of blast furnace, Iron City, 1870s.

Ox team that hauled the baptismal font to the temple. Some believe the figure at front left is Neal Bladen of Cedar City, who owned one of the three yokes, or teams, of oxen.

Paiute Indian encampment, 1870s. This may have been the 1875 encampment near where George Kirkham lived.

Tithing Office and Bishop's Storehouse, St. George, late 1870s. The community's original Tithing Office had a corral out front and may be the building at right, behind the streetfront structure.

Looking north on Main Street, 1870s.

Temple walls, circa 1874. Note the rubble around the temple. Three men fell from the walls or scaffolding onto this rubble, one from 80 feet up and the others from just a few feet lower, but no one was seriously hurt.

Chapter 10

TROUBLE ON TRUMBULL

January through March 1875

Construction progressed on many fronts during 1875. Workers from northern Utah were present in good numbers. On Monday, January 4, Walker was at work on the wall with over 100 men. Another 100 were at the quarry and "over 40 at Mount Trumbull getting out the lumber." Others were "on the road for the purpose of getting wood, coal, etc."[1] All were working in cold January weather.

One of these workers was Moses Franklin Farnsworth, a man of few words who in 1870 had left St. George to help settle Kanab and who later would have much to do with setting in order the records of the St. George Temple. He wrote: "In 1875 I went to St. George and worked on the Temple and dressed some rocks which were used in the buttresses on the north side, also assisted in laying off 160 city lots around the temple, carrying the chains, etc."[2]

---

1. Charles Lowell Walker, *Diary of Charles Lowell Walker*, edited by A. Karl Larson and Katharine Miles Larson, 2 vols. (Logan: Utah State University Press, 1980), 1:395.
2. Moses Franklin Farnsworth, "A History of My Life," n.d., n.p., typescript; copies in possession of the authors.

An article in the *Deseret Evening News* of 9 January 1875 said that "over 500 men" were working on the temple in St. George. It forecast that the walls would be finished and the roof installed by mid-May. President Young was in town and was visiting the site almost daily. It added that the St. George tabernacle (under construction since 1863 but delayed during the "hard years") would be completely finished within a month. Interestingly, work on the Tabernacle exterior was completed just as work on the temple exterior began; it was the same for the interior, which meant that the skilled workers could move from one job to the other without inconveniencing either project. The article then "toasted" Dixie, reporting that crops "of cotton, grapes, wine and fruit" had been "unusually large" the year past. St. George was "improving" and the country around was "rapidly filling up." Southern Utah was said to be "never more promising than now[, and on] the day before New Year, plows were going in all fields and the buds were swelling."[3] While snow and ice were the order of the day in the north, the timing was appropriate to get in a good word for Utah's Dixie.

George Kirkham, still laboring as a carpenter, creating works of art and teaching others to do the same, as well as playing his fiddle and keeping his journal, began the new year by writing:

"Saturday Jan 2, 1875: The weather was fine. I did not go to work, as I had been up [playing fiddle] the night before. I stayed home all day, drawing a picture of 3 horses heads. At night I went to drawing school. My pupils were getting along well. I spent some happy hours with them. I returned home and I could hear the Indians sing in their camp, as it was only just outside the city. Our place of meeting was close to the outside of the city. The night was very dark. Wednesday: The weather was clear but cold. . . . It was very encouraging to see the rock that is laid up every day on the walls of the temple. I was sorry to hear that one of the men was hurt, but it is not serious thank God. It was my prayer

---

3. Kirk M. Curtis, "History of the St. George Temple" (master's thesis, Brigham Young University, 1964), 50.

that the men might be preserved from accident while working on the temple. At night we had a settling up of our concert we gave at Santa Clara. I got 12 pounds of grapes, 18 pounds of peaches and some little store pay. The boys came to our place to do the business. After some time they left, and after some time we returned to bed. Friday: During the day, I had given to me, by one of the St. George Glee Club, $26.78, for the one night performance, which we gave in the tabernacle on the 23rd of December 1874. It was the largest [cash amount] I ever received for a performance. We took in over 200 dollars [including barter]."[4]

As temple construction continued, Brigham Young and George A. Smith, together or separately, mingled with workers and supervisors, listened to problems, encouraged, and counseled. They did the same with townspeople, at celebrations, evening events, and church. President Young was not always well. He suffered from rheumatism and a throat problem that made speaking difficult.[5] Indeed, for weeks he had been unable to address the people, and by January he felt a deep need to communicate and give counsel and encouragement. Feeling unable to stand before them and deliver an oration, he chose the next best way. In the quiet of his home he wrote out his thoughts and had them read in the tabernacle on Sunday, 10 January 1875. James Bleak copied Brigham's letter into his record.[6] There he offered the explanation that the prophet had not been able to "[address] large assemblies" since his arrival the past November. It is a valuable letter for the insight it gives us into Brigham's thinking and feelings at a critical time in his life. He addressed his letter "To the Saints of St. George and adjacent

---

4. George Kirkham, "My Journey to Dixie," in *The Journals of George Kirkham*, ed. Kathy Kirkham Reed (privately published, n.d.), 18–19, typescript; copies in possession of Sheryl Archibald and Richard Kirkham.

5. There is some evidence that Brigham Young's rheumatism may have been rheumatoid arthritis.

6. James G. Bleak, "Annals of the Southern Utah Mission," Book B, 370–75, typescript, Dixie State University Special Collections, St. George, Utah.

settlements and to those who have come from the North to assist on the St. George Temple."

It is evident in the letter that Brigham sensed that he had not many years left and that nothing was more important to him than to finish and dedicate the temple. He cautioned the workers to be diligent and faithful, for they were involved in a sacred and holy work; he addressed his frustration with the lumbering operation on Mt. Trumbull; he spoke of the specific supplies and equipment he and George A. Smith would soon be shipping from the north; and for the first time in public he mentioned the temple's baptismal font, though George A. and others had been speaking of it for almost two years. He said, "It is our intention also to have a baptismal font brought from the North and have it in its place, and just as soon as the building can be so far finished as to be safe, to dedicate this font and commence baptizing for the dead at the earliest possible day."

President Young also gave much practical advice to the workers from the north as well as those from the area near St. George, and then he wrote at length upon the necessity and blessings that would come from joining and then living according to the United Order.

He concluded his remarks as follows: "You may not understand one fact that is before our eyes: that the Temple in St. George is being built upon the principle of the United Order; and when we cease our selfishness, and our whole interest is for the building of the Kingdom of God on the earth, we can build Temples, and do anything that we want to, with united voice and hands. . . . beloved Saints, we invoke the blessings of Israel's God to rest upon you, and upon all Israel engaged in the building up of His Zion on the earth.

"Your brother in the Gospel, Brigham Young."

Of that Sabbath day, George Kirkham recorded: "Sunday Jan 10, 1875: I went to [art student] Brother Samuel Jepperson's and called [at] the barber shop and got a shave and my hair cut. I ate my dinner at what was called the Big House, where so many of the men boarded who worked on the temple. I returned home and got ready for meeting. My wife and myself went to meeting. We heard a letter read from President Young, which was grand. He said the temple was an excellent offering to the Lord, and said many things that encouraged the Saints. Brother George A. Smith gave some good advice. After meeting we returned home. At night we went to meeting in the First Ward [schoolhouse]. After which, we returned home and my wife wrote a letter to her father and mother, and we retired to bed."[7]

And of the week that followed: "Thursday Jan 14, 1875: I went to work. During the day I saw teams coming in with lumber from Mount Trumble. I had a peculiar thought about the teams. I felt to say God bless them, for they had their labor to perform, which we could not do. I also saw 32 yoke of cattle coming into St. George to go to Mount Trumble to haul lumber for the temple. At night my wife and myself went to hear Brother George A. Smith relate on his trip to Jerusalem, which was very interesting. He had such a beautiful way of relating what he had to say. Friday: The wind blew from the north, cold weather, and was cloudy all day. At night we played for a party in the court house. I sang and danced for them by request."[8]

As the temple walls continued to rise, the process of building the flooring continued on the first main floor level. However, instead of the stone pillars used in the basement, heavy double beams were placed upright on the first and second main floors.[9] They were set in the same pattern and spacing as the stone pillars below them, and served the same purpose: in the first assembly room floor they supported the ceiling and the first mezzanine (now third) floor, and in the second

---

7. Kirkham, *Journal*, 19. Kirkham never did spell Trumbull correctly.

8. Kirkham, *Journal*, 19–20.

9. Ultimately these beams were covered with attractive, hollowed-out, and rounded wood pillars finished in the shape of a quatrefoil, with wooden bases and plaster caps that were added at the end of construction. These pillars are still in use in the temple today and can best be seen in the veil room and fourth floor assembly room.

assembly room floor they supported the ceiling, the second mezzanine (fifth) floor, and the roof.

The floors of each mezzanine were built the same way as the assembly room floors, by placing 2x9-inch joists on the lateral beams, followed by the customary subfloor and floor, both of 1x4-foot pine boards, overlaid. As many as eight rooms were built off each mezzanine hallway and against the north and south temple walls. The partition walls of these rooms were made strong and durable by using 2x14-inch studs secured together with wedged dowels but very few nails. A square tenon cut was made in each end of the stud and "each end [was] placed in a square hole cut into the floor and [into corresponding] ceiling plate boards. . . . Lath were nailed across these studs and plaster applied for a finished wall."[10] In addition, 2x8-inch studs were used to make the inside hallway walls, which were lathed and plastered the same way. Almost no cracking has occurred in these walls over the years. These inside hallway walls separate the mezzanines from the domed 27-foot-high ceilings of the first and second main floors.

Each assembly room floor was originally quite open. Each had the two rows of seven support columns or pillars running the length of the room, and each assembly room had priesthood stands or pulpits at opposite ends of the floor. The stands projected 23 feet into the rooms, leaving some 58 feet of open space between priesthood stands. These rooms were 40 feet wide from pillar row to pillar row. Curtained rooms were also open beyond the pillar rows to the temple side walls on the main floor, though as far as is known, their uses are not mentioned in the records. The pillars with their rounded wood facade, rounded wooden bases and plaster caps, and the beams above covered by decorative plaster of paris molds added attractiveness and grace to the openness of the main rooms. In each outside wall of both assembly rooms

10. Thomas Weston Welch, "Early Mormon Woodworking at its Best; a Study of the Craftsmanship in the First Temples in Utah" (master's thesis, Brigham Young University, 1983), 18.

were eight tall windows. Daylight streaming through the windows created an impressive interior and gave visitors a feeling of awe and reverence. Each assembly room had a 27-foot-high domed ceiling that enhanced the room's aura. These ceilings each bore five large-diameter decorative plaster of paris rosettes, designed for light fixtures to hang from their centers, though no evidence exists that any such fixtures were ever hung. The domed ceilings were painted a very light shade of blue. Lath nailed to curving trusses above, and plastered over, created the dome look.

The full effect of the original interiors of these two main assembly rooms of the temple can be seen and felt in today's fourth floor of the temple or the second main floor assembly room, which remains unchanged since the original construction.

George Kirkham continued his narrative: "Monday Jan 18, 1875: Still raining and very muddy. I went uptown and stayed up most all day painting a vision of a battle field. While there my father came and said there was a young man [who] wanted me. I got up and started home. I found he was from Santa Clara, and wanted us to go and play for a party. We got ready and started. We arrived there safe and met with Brother Stailey [Staheli?], and he was glad to see us. We had a good old duck meal, plenty of sauerkraut. After our supper we went to the dance. There we saw a lot of rude [rough] looking boys and girls dressed in their homemade clothes. We played until 12 o'clock, then they called on me to dismiss the party, which I did. We went to Brother John Hafen's to have something to eat.[11] We stayed there until 3 o'clock [A.M.] when we started for home. It rained a little. We got home by 4 o'clock. I received $2.50 gold for my services. I laid down for awhile, and then got up."

Kirkham continues: "Thursday Jan 21, 1875: I went to work down to the temple. I worked putting in joists for the second floor. In the afternoon I helped to get two of the large stairs in the building. They

---

11. John G. Hafen is the great-grandfather of St. George Temple president Bruce C. Hafen.

were 40 feet long and each weighed about 3500 lbs. While we were busy getting them in, the President [Brigham Young] came along. I shook hands with him. He said he used to wonder how it was to be old, but he knew now as he was getting old fast. While we were at work getting one of those large timbers in through the door, it got a quick start and caught one of the men between it and the door post, which hurt him very badly. The President who was there still stepped up and ordered Brother George A. Smith's carriage, which was close by, to take him up into town where he stayed. He was badly bruised, but was taken care of very soon. At the same time I got my foot sprained and the skin rubbed off two or three places, but nothing serious. At night I hopped into bed.

"Friday Jan 22, 1875: I went to work all day. The scaffold builders raised the last scaffold pole with a large sage brush tied to the top of it."[12]

As the heavy stone walls continued upward without sufficient inner support, they began to lean inward. George Kirkham confirmed this when he recorded: "I was told that the walls were leaning in for the want of timber inside . . . [a]s the buttresses on the outside would press the walls in."[13] It was obvious to both Church architect William Folsom and Miles Romney that the simultaneous building out of the interior, using beams, joists, flooring, and studding for each successive floor, would counter the leaning of the walls and keep them straight and erect. Some carpentry work had indeed been done, but for the work to continue, a steady stream of sized and cured lumber was required. Unfortunately, there had simply been too little lumber cut and hauled from Mt. Trumbull to accomplish this purpose. George A.'s letter to his cousin had alluded to this difficulty, but there is evidence that the problem was deeper than he was letting on and had been going on for a long period of time, and that Charlie Walker and George Kirkham knew nothing about it.

---

12. Kirkham, *Journal*, 19–21.
13. Kirkham, *Journal*, 22–24.

Zora Smith Jarvis wrote that "The getting of the lumber for the Temple had been switched [from Pine Valley Mountain] to the Trumbull area, but had failed for a number of reasons. Eli Whipple, the first director of sawmill operations for the St. George United Order, [had] assumed that responsibility on June 30, 1874."[14] He returned to St. George on 21 November, reporting that the snow was too deep for the animals to graze, so they had moved them five miles from the mill to find feed. This, of course, made hauling the logs impossible, and so the mills had been shut down.

The next evening Whipple and George A. Smith met with Brigham Young to discuss the issue, and then on 11 December a delegation from the United Order met with Brigham and George A. concerning the same thing. On 17 December 1874, Brigham gave instructions regarding the two mills to the leaders of the United Order, and on 19 December he met again with Whipple and a Brother Wilcocks. Believing the issue of the closed mills had been resolved, on 22 December George A. telegraphed Beaver to request some teams with feed to haul lumber for the temple construction. When these teams arrived on Mt. Trumbull in January, the teamsters began hauling back to St. George what lumber had been cut the previous fall. It was these loads coming in that Kirkham reported seeing.

On 26 December 1874, the day after Christmas, a letter from Mt. Trumbull arrived informing Brigham Young that the lumber cutters intended to quit until they received further provisions. According to the letter they wanted coffee, sugar, pepper, pickles, onions, beans, and candle wicking. Frustrated, Brigham responded by return letter that the supplies were not available, and that the men needed "to go home and reflect on their folly."[15] He also reminded them that before they came to work on the temple they had been told that their home wards were

14. Zora Smith Jarvis, comp., *Ancestry, Biography, and Family of George A. Smith* (Provo, Utah: Brigham Young University Press, 1962), 11.

15. Jarvis, *Ancestry*, 11.

to supply their needs. In addition, the St. George Tithing Office had already sent the potatoes, beef, and molasses that the Church had agreed to supply them, which they must have either consumed too quickly or disposed of in some other fashion. Before Brigham Young's letter of chastisement reached them, however, the hands had quit and returned to St. George.[16]

Aware of this situation, Robert Gardner summarized things as follows: "During that time the temple construction was being hurried with all speed. President Brigham Young had sent a large steam saw mill to the Trumbull [timber country] to hurry out the Temple lumber. He turned the mill into the United Order [i.e., the order paid for the mill] and Bryce and Burgess turned their mill (that I had previously sold them) into this Order. Brother [Eli] Whipple was sent to superintend the work, but they had no hay for the teams, and snow fell so deep that many of the men became dissatisfied with the lumber business and stopped. This was very annoying to Brigham Young and George A. Smith."[17]

We find no record of this trouble during the next two weeks, and then Robert Gardner picks up the account: "One day [in late January] I was down at the Temple site when George A. Smith came by in his carriage and called me over to him and told me to get up in his carriage. There he opened his mind to me, concerning the Temple.

"He said, 'You cannot realize how the President is annoyed over this lumber question and how anxious he is to get this Temple completed. He feels he is getting old and is liable to drop off any time and he has [priesthood] keys that he wants to give in that Temple that can only be given in a temple. Likewise Bishop Hunter is very old and he is very anxious to do work in that Temple for his dead before he passes away.'

16. Kirkham, *Journal*, 16–17. These returning lumbermen told George Kirkham on 28 December 1874 that there were too many workers on Mt. Trumbull.

17. Robert Gardner Jr., "Utah Pioneer—1847, Written by Himself at St. George, 29 January 1884," 45; copy in possession of the authors.

He said: 'My own anxiety is great on that subject. I have been thinking ever since that lumber business . . . stopped, where can I put my hand on a man that will go out there, who will not be stopped by trifles, but will get out lumber no matter what it costs so that the Temple may be finished without delay. I cannot get my mind off anyone but you.'

"I said: 'Brother Smith, if I were to study my own feelings, I'd rather go on a mission to China than go out there, but I have nothing to say. If you want me to go there, I will go and do the best I can.' So he said he would talk with the President about it.

"Sometime after that, when the [United] Order Board was in session, Elder [Erastus] Snow nominated me to go to Trumbull and get out what lumber was needed for the Temple. The motion was unanimously carried, but I utterly refused, [and] gave my reason, that I was satisfied that President Young did not want me to get out that lumber, for I knew he had his mind on [Brother] Copeland of Beaver, which was afterwards proven that I was correct.

"After a while President Young and George A. Smith started for Salt Lake [10 February 1875]. Elder Snow and Brother McDonald went to Beaver with them and while there President Young sent for Copeland and tried to get him to go and get out that lumber, but they could not hitch [come to an agreement].[18] Then President Young and his party drove on and while at Cove Creek [Cove Fort; they arrived at 2:10 p.m., 15 February 1875], the first night from Beaver, I received a telegram asking me to go to Trumbull, to use my wisdom and energy to get out that lumber. I would have their blessing and backing, signed by B. Young and George A. Smith.

"I answered, I would go forth. Within a few days after, I went with Brother Whipple and took an inventory of all the property and took possession of both the steam mills, teams and all of the fit outs [outfits]."[19]

---

18. Gardner, "Utah Pioneer—1847," 46.
19. Kirkham, *Journal*, 21–22.

Meanwhile, work on the temple was proceeding as rapidly as possible. George Kirkham recorded: "Thursday Jan 28, 1875: The weather was clear and the sun shining out bright and the birds singing like spring. I did not go to work. I got ready to go to Washington to the [cotton] factory to get some cloth. . . . I went to the store, bought some stamps, envelopes, writing paper, and returned home and wrote a letter to my brother in law. I sent a little drawing of the temple. I afterward posted the letter. . . .

"Friday . . . I was sick . . . with sore eyes . . . [that] were very bad. I could hardly read or write. My wife doctored them up and I went to bed.

"Monday Feb 1, 1875: I went to work all day. . . . I will here state that during the day Brother G. A. Smith wanted to see me regarding the windows arched over before he left to go north. I guess the St. George Temple went up faster than any other ever did."[20]

What Kirkham did not mention, perhaps out of modesty, was that on that day George A. Smith and Miles Romney had appointed him to be head carpenter on the temple. His next entry reveals a meeting with Brigham Young, who "wished to see me about the round window[s]. They should be rounded over before he leaves for the north. The carpenters were doing all they could to forward this part of the work."[21]

In response to what is assumed to be either Brigham's or Miles Romney's request, George immediately made a record of the window count, stating that each long window frame was made with 65 individual pieces of wood cut to fit, and that each round window frame used 74 separate pieces of wood cut to fit, held together with 600 nails. He also reported that each of the 28 quatrefoil-shaped wooden column facades used to cover the upright support beams in the first and second main floor assembly rooms required 352 pieces of wood, cut to fit, in their construction. As for rough construction, he estimated that 400,000 board feet of lumber was used in making the double-layered floors and

---

20. Kirkham, *Journal*, 22.
21. Kirkham, *Journal*, 22; see also Welch, "Early Mormon Woodworking," 23, 27.

circular stairway steps alone. Each circular stairway had 120 steps and the dome stairway had 202 steps.[22]

As he was writing up this report during the evening of 2 February, Kirkham also found time to record in his journal that "while I was writing, my wife was singing 'O Ye Mountains High in the Clear Blue Sky' and so on. I received a letter from my brother James. He was in Sanpete with a theatre company. I was glad to hear from him."[23]

During the next two weeks, Kirkham's time was occupied both with work on the temple and with many distractions that took him from it. In regard to the progress being made on the temple, however, he recorded: "Wednesday Feb 3, all hands were going to work and I went. The carpenters were building a temporary flight of stairs for the President to go up to the first floor, as he could not go upon a ladder. There were five loads of lumber come in [from Mt. Trumbull], and the work was going on beautifully. I was busy framing timber for the floors and otherwise. . . . Thursday . . . I saw President Young go up to the first floor. He looked pretty well. Old Brother George A. Smith went up with our boss, but had to be taken home in a wagon for he was sick. I was told during the day the temple hands had eaten up 30,000 lbs of beef during the month of January. . . . Friday . . . I went to work as usual. While the men were drawing up what they call a center, which was a beam to set in the wall while they form the arch of the windows, it fell.[24] The ropes untied or broke and fell to the ground. It made a scattering, but nobody was hurt. . . . Monday . . . I saw President Young and George A. Smith at the temple during the day. . . . Tuesday I paid 50

22. Kirkham, *Journal*, 22.

23. These arches were made by laying in a semicircle atop a curved wooden frame nine sandstone blocks tapered inward to 8 inches wide by 14 inches deep at their smallest side, with a slight inward curve cut or chipped out at the smallest end. The center, or fifth, stone in this arch was the keystone; the heights of all nine were irregular; and all were held in place by the wooden form until the mortar over and between the stones had dried. The nine mortared stones of each arched window were held in place by the keystone.

24. Kirkham, *Journal*, 22–24.

cents in silver to the temple, although I was working [on it]. Wednesday
. . . We all were well [so] I went to work, during the day I saw President
Young's party leave St. George for Salt Lake City. I watched them until
they were out of sight. Monday Feb 15 . . . The weather was cloudy, but
I went to work. There were 7 loads of lumber that had come in. The
work was going well. Many of the men were talking about going home
when the walls were up. . . . At night I drew a picture of the temple."[25]

The next morning, 16 February, Brigham Young's party left Cove
Fort for the north. Robert Gardner's brief report of his taking over the
Mt. Trumbull lumbering operations on March 2 reads: "I returned to
St. George in a few days and found the masonry work on the temple
was finished and the workers were having a jubilee. As soon as I could,
I started back to Mount Trumbull with 2 cooks, men, and provisions."[26]

Robert makes no mention of which men from St. George composed
his crew of lumbermen, though it seems obvious he would select men
such as Frederick and Benjamin Blake, as well as Ebenezer Bryce and
Harrison Burgess, with whom he had already worked on Pine Valley
Mountain and elsewhere—men whose skills and attitudes he trusted
implicitly.[27] As for the wisdom of taking his wife Mary Ann to assist
him in the lumber business, another of Robert's wives, Celestia, wrote:
"Mary Ann had a special quality of kindness and qualities that linked
the old and new era. Her husband was a pioneer, mill builder, and in-
dustrial leader. Mary Ann stood by his side and shared his hardships.
When Robert went to Trumbull to get out lumber for the St. George
Temple and perform the unusual feat of delivering so much [lumber] in
such a short time, his success was in no small measure due to the fact

---

25. Gardner, "Utah Pioneer—1847," 46. Among those accompanying Gardner were
   his wife Mary Ann and her children, as well as teenager Helen Gubler, who often
   drove the water wagon. This wagon kept the two steam engines at the mills, as
   well as the people, supplied with water from the Nixon Springs spillway.
26. Ebenezer Bryce designed and built the famous Pine Valley Chapel. Bryce Canyon
   National Park is named after him.
27. Jarvis, *Ancestry*, 12.

that Mary Ann went out and cooked for his men. Three good meals each day during that hard work; three short periods each day of relaxation from the sound of saw and ax and the gruff voices of men; three brief periods in the presence of a charming, witty, and encouraging woman had much to do with Robert's outstanding success in his work on the temple."[28]

"Soon I had the mill running," Robert continues. "I fitted the mill out with men and took 6 men with me into the woods; 4 with crosscut saws, and 2 with axes. I took my bills of lumber for the Temple and my ax and measuring pole and selected and marked suitable trees for choppers to cut. When they were cut down, I measured [them for length] and marked them for the men with the crosscut saws."

Evidence gained from Mill Book No. 1 of the Mt. Trumbull Mill Company indicates that Robert had been handed, either as he personally departed from St. George or from teamsters in the weeks and months that followed, lists of specifically cut boards needed at the temple. These lists or "bills of lumber" that he mentioned in his account included each needed board's exact dimensions, including length. Each of these was rough cut at Mt. Trumbull prior to shipping. Thus, on 30 July 1874, the order of teamster William Albert McCullough was filled, which read as follows:

> 5 pic 6 x 12—26 [780 board feet]
> 4 pic 6 x 12—22 [528 board feet]
> 1 6 x 6—22 [66 board feet]
> 1 2 x 6—26 [26 board feet]
> 1 2 x 12—26 [52 board feet]
> 1 4 x 6—18 [36 board feet]
> 1488 @ 2.5c = $37.20

28. Mt. Trumbull Mill Co., Mill Book No. 1, Temple Lumber Delivered July 25, 1874—Dec 20, 1877, Church History Library, The Church of Jesus Christ of Latter-day Saints, Salt Lake City, Folder 5, p. 2; photocopy given to authors by Paul Weaver.

Translating this as well as we are able, we learn that William Albert McCullough, one of many temple teamsters, needed five pieces, or lengths, of lumber, milled or sawed into beams measuring 6x12 inches by 26 feet in length, for a total of 780 linear board feet. With the additional pieces, the total amount of rough-cut lumber on this load would have been 13 large boards, or beams, totaling 1,488 board feet—a heavy load even for three yoke of oxen. With each board foot having a dollar value of 2.5 cents, the total dollar value of that load was $37.50. These records continue page after page, showing, for instance, another bill of lumber carried to Mt. Trumbull by a teamster named Soren Stolensen (whose name may have been dramatically misspelled) that was filled on 16 December 1874, consisting of 4 boards at 6x12x40 and 1 board at 2x6x16; 5 boards for a total of 976 board feet.[29] The attention paid to filling "bills of lumber" provides the modern reader with some idea of the care that was taken and the extent of cooperative labor required to construct this sacred edifice.

---

29. Mt. Trumbull Mill Co., Mill Book No. 1, Temple Lumber Delivered July 25, 1874—Dec 20, 1877, LDS Church Archives, Folder #5, p. 8; photocopy given to authors by Paul Weaver. Though a United States Bureau of Land Management sign on the temple trail above where the trail descends in switchbacks down the Hurricane Fault indicates that lengths of some of the temple timbers were 46 feet, no records found thus far in these mill books indicate anything beyond 42 feet.

Chapter 11

THE TEMPLE TRAILS

Spring into Summer 1875

Robert Gardner was reorganizing and, by his own leadership skills, quiet enthusiasm, and dry humor, jump-starting the lumber operation on Mt. Trumbull. Getting things moving was so desperately needed. Meanwhile, George Kirkham was continuing with his own daily activities, which involved far more than carpenter work on the rising temple. His journal continues:

"Thursday Feb 18, 1875: I went to work, and during the day it rained a little. There were a number of loads of lumber that came in from Mount Trumble. . . . Friday . . . There was lots of lumber come in. During the day we raised the first bent [ceiling truss] in the temple. It was very interesting to see the work rolling on as it is. All seemed to be happy. Tuesday . . . I . . . was working all day on the center tower, 6 ladders from the ground, putting in joists. The wind blew very hard in the afternoon. Part of the day I worked on the second floor [called today the fourth floor assembly room] putting a large bent together. It was very cold all day. . . . I retired early."[1]

---

1. George Kirkham, "My Journey to Dixie," in *The Journals of George Kirkham*, ed.

"Putting a large bent together" would have meant that Kirkham helped lay out, on a pattern most likely drawn in chalk on the floor of the unfinished upper assembly hall, a double layer of 6x12-inch beams of various lengths, with 2x9- to 2x12-inch timbers between them, the latter in a crisscross pattern for stability. Then he and others would have augured or drilled with a brace and bit (a hand drill) from two to four 1⅛–inch holes through every position where the beams and cross timbers intersected, as well as every position where beams were joined at angles with each other. Once these dozens upon dozens of holes, each some 14 inches deep, had been drilled, hand-cut dowels approximately 18 inches in length and slightly wider than 1⅛ inches were pounded completely through; the end that had been pounded was tightened securely with a wedge driven into the end of the dowel. In this manner each "bent," or ceiling truss, was constructed and made firm, after which the entire assemblage, 96 feet long, from two to 14 feet high, and weighing more than a ton, was hoisted with a four-man winch from the second main floor into its position atop the walls, where it helped form the roof.[2] Today the numerous dents in the wood where workers sledge-hammered the bents into position atop the walls remain clearly visible. This was Kirkham's work on 23 February.

The young master carpenter continued: "Saturday Feb 27, 1875: The weather was fine. I stayed home all day to draw some pictures of the temple, as there were so many wanted. I had 6 or 7 to do. I did three of them and then took a walk uptown. I went in and saw the men at work in the large tabernacle, busy plastering. They gave me some specimens of plaster of paris, such as bunches of grapes, brackets, rose sets

Kathy Kirkham Reed (privately published, n.d.), 18–19, 24–25, typescript; copies in possession of Sheryl Archibald and Richard Kirkham.

2. From the fifth floor (mezzanine) of the St. George Temple, one can see the massive, rough-cut beams from which the builders made the temple's seven massive rafters, ceiling trusses, or "bents," as they called them. These very trusses remain in use today, still held tightly together by literally hundreds of long wooden dowels. On the third floor one can also see the doweled 2x12-inch wall timbers laid up criss-crossing each other to form the sturdy mezzanine walls.

[rosettes] and so forth. . . . Monday . . . The weather was very windy [so] I did not go to work. I stayed at home [and] drew 3 pictures of the temple. I wrote, and then went uptown to the paint shop and made a painting of a fishing boat on the sea. . . . At night I went to play for a party in the court house. [Wednesday and] Thursday . . . I went to work as usual. . . . During the day I saw the last stone laid to form the round window. At night . . . the wind blew up and was rough."[3]

Meanwhile, Robert Gardner had arranged the teams and men to haul the downed logs to the two Mt. Trumbull sawmills, built almost side by side about two miles up the road from Nixon Springs. Workers were soon filling the mill yard at Nixon Springs with cut and drying lumber. At that point Gardner organized a lumber hauling company under Isaac C. Haight that was headquartered at Antelope Springs, about "half way to St. George" on what came to be called the Temple Trail.[4]

Apparently there were two distinct branches of this trail, perhaps used in different seasons or by different teamsters. The first wound northward from Mt. Trumbull along the hilly eastern or upper rim of the Hurricane Fault to Antelope Springs, which was at one time a steady water source. Another road from St. George to Antelope Springs had been built in April and May 1874. Robert Gardner also supervised that construction, with labor provided by the United Order. The route was scouted out in early March by a party led by St. George Stake president John W. Young, and work on the road commenced on 26 of April.[5] Forty-five members of the Order, coming from St. George, Santa Clara, Washington, Toquerville, Virgin City, Pine Valley, Harmony, and

3. Kirkham, *Journal*, 24–26.

4. Gardner, "Utah Pioneer—1847," 46. It is not known how long Isaac Haight filled this position, because he was still in hiding from legal officials due to his involvement in the 1857 Mountain Meadows Massacre. His name is not mentioned anywhere else in connection with the lumber-hauling operation.

5. "Journal and Diary of Robert Gardner," in Kate B. Carter, comp., *Heart Throbs of the West* (Salt Lake City: Daughter of Utah Pioneers, 1949), 10:320.

Kanarra (Iron County), worked for twenty days straight, completing it "enough to be passable," though they had only roughed out the dugway.[6] The road crossed the Virgin River southeast of St. George, went through Little Valley to Ft. Pearce,[7] and then up the Ft. Pearce Wash through Warner Valley to the foot of the Hurricane Fault, about three miles south of the present community of Hurricane, Utah. The precipitous cliffs of the Fault represented both a difficult ascent and descent, but the best way was determined and a steep, mile-long dugway was soon built. At the top, the road wound eastward back and forth across the Utah-Arizona border until it reached Antelope Springs.

For the trip to the temple, wagons pulled by three yoke of oxen carried loads considered safe for the descent down either of the two dugways that led from the top of the Hurricane Fault. Truss beams themselves were heavy. All of these were 6 inches wide by 1 foot thick, and some were 40 feet long.[8] Just one of these made a heavy, awkward wagon load. Sometimes two shorter beams made a load, or several that were even smaller. Whatever the load, at either dugway wagon wheels were locked to prevent them from turning, and a heavy log or two were often dragged behind the load to increase resistance. Even then the descent was tricky and dangerous, requiring experienced teamsters. The cross-country route from the bottom of the Fault to St. George was as dry and dusty as it had been on the top, and required water to be carried to the trail, except at Ft. Pearce. After reaching the temple, wagons

---

6. Bleak, "Annals," Book B, 281, 286–87.

7. Ft. Pearce stands today, a lonely little outpost on a hilltop overlooking Ft. Pearce Wash, where water still flows and the trail from Mt. Trumbull once ran. Located a little southeast of today's Washington Fields on the western edge of Warner Valley, there is no roof on the tiny fort, fallen stone walls have been partially rebuilt with rusty twisted rebar, and many of the stones in the walls have names of visitors scratched into them, some recent and others more than a hundred years old. And though it is a silent, lonely, windswept place, it boasts a fine gravel road and parking lot, explanatory signs, picnic tables and hiking trails, and a lingering sense of the dangerous and very real "Old West," whose settlers it was once built to protect.

8. Douglas Cox, "History of Robert Gardner, Junior," unpublished manuscript, 281; copy in possession of Richard Schmutz.

were unloaded and the lumber stacked for use by the carpenters. Men and teams rested a few days, wagon wheels were greased, repairs made, bedrolls aired out, grub stored, water barrels filled, fodder loaded, and another tiresome round trip was begun.

This journey may instead have been taken via the so-called Black Rock Road, which led up the Hurricane Fault and on to Mt. Trumbull by way of Diamond Butte on the Arizona Strip, a few miles north of today's small town of Bundyville. This portion of the trail is marked "Temple Trail" by Bureau of Land Management markers, and a large sign has been placed where the trail drops over the Fault and follows several natural but still precarious switchbacks to the beginning of its own dugway, about halfway down. From there, teamsters rough-locked their wheels, as was done near Antelope Springs, and inched down the precarious route to the desert floor. There is a record of only one accident as teamsters descended this dugway. A heavy load somehow got on top of the three ox teams, and one of the oxen was injured so severely in the headlong rush to the bottom that it was left for dead. A few days later, however, to everyone's surprise, the animal limped slowly into St. George.

At the bottom of the dugway this trail turns north by northwest just east of Diamond Butte, winds roughly 30 miles in that direction, and then passes Ft. Pearce on the southwestern edge of Warner Valley. There it joins the northern trail described above, and continues into St. George. Both these roads to Trumbull and back necessitated a maintenance crew to make repairs and keep them passable.[9] By wagon, either from Mt. Trumbull to St. George or back again, no matter the trail, travel time was about seven days.

Roberta Blake Barnum wrote about the teamster careers of her ancestors Frederick and Benjamin Blake: "Frederick and his brother Benjamin Blake were noted ox team drivers and would bring the lumber

---

9. H. Lorenzo Reid, *Dixie of the Desert* (St. George, Utah: Zion Natural History Association) 1964, 236.

in from the sawmill [on Mt. Trumbull]. . . . The trip [out] was a long and tedious journey of eighty miles. The oxen traveled slowly and there were many miles of desert country with few watering holes. This made it necessary to haul large barrels of water. . . . In the winter the lumber was brought part of the way on sleighs.

"On one occasion when the Blake brothers were taking a load of lumber to St. George, some of the water holes along the way had dried up. They traveled on, finally coming to a small reservoir . . . where the oxen smelled the water and stampeded. So great was their thirst that they ran into the water and were drowned. Frederick almost lost his life trying to save them but was unable to release the oxen from their yoke. He had just paid $500 for this young team of oxen."[10]

The conjoined trails crossed the always treacherous Virgin River, where hidden beds of quicksand nearly cost the lives of Robert and Mary Ann Gardner and their family as they were returning for the last time from Mt. Trumbull. Robert recorded: "I settled up my business and started home for St. George, bringing my wife Mary Ann and her children with me. They had been out with me helping to do the housework. . . . On our [hasty] return to St. George, on the 3rd night out, about 3 in the morning the wagon with my family in it got mired down in the quicksand in the Virgin River. Fortunately, there was a light buggy with us. We had the buggy drive close by [several times] and pick one or two people out of our conveyance [wagon] without making much stop [slowing down] so we all got out. No one hurt but some were scared."[11]

Either branch of the trail was challenging for the same reasons— the recalcitrant Virgin, extremely rough roads, very little fuel for fires, and even less water. The builders of the roads to Trumbull had scraped out catch basins on top of the Fault, called today the Temple Tanks, meant to hold the moisture from the Strip's infrequent and

---

10. Roberta Blake Barnum, "Frederick Blake," n.d., n.p., typescript, Daughters of Utah Pioneers McQuarrie Memorial Museum, St. George, Utah.
11. Gardner, "Utah Pioneer—1847," 46–47.

unpredictable storms. For the most part, as has been pointed out, the teamsters were compelled to carry barrels of water when they left St. George, leaving some along the way for their return trips and using the others to get themselves and their teams to Mt. Trumbull.

With the quickened construction progress that had begun in the spring of 1874 and had continued through the winter and into the spring of 1875, the demand for draft animals and wagons was great and could not be met locally. This was the reason George A. Smith had wired Beaver for additional teams and wagons. Everything that had to be moved anywhere was done by wagons drawn by mules, horses, or oxen. Mules and horses were comparatively fast, oxen laboriously slow. For temple construction, cut sandstone had to be hauled from the quarry, lumber transported from Trumbull, scaffolding poles, white and red pine lumber and lath from Pine and Grass valleys, lime and sand for mortar from Middleton and the river, and coal from mines 30 miles away to the east. Hardware, paint, and other construction supplies were hauled over rough roads from Salt Lake City, as well as machinery, including the steam sawmill Brigham had donated to the St. George United Order for use on Mt. Trumbull and machinery for the cotton mill. Town needs were brought by wagon: foods and supplies from the north and coal and firewood from hills as far away as the future site of Hurricane or south toward the Colorado River. Nothing moved, not even people, without team, cart, carriage, or wagon. Farmers also needed draft animals and wagons for farm work. Huge amounts of fodder, rock salt, and, in the winter, bedding materials, plus corrals, harnesses, and men knowledgeable in animal care were needed for the upkeep of so many large animals.

Demands for draft animals and wagons that could not be met from St. George and nearby towns had to be filled by loan, purchase, or donation from all parts of the territory, as far north as Salt Lake City and beyond. A solicitation addressed to Presiding Bishop A. O. Smoot from A. M. Musser in St. George resulted in donations and purchase of animals and wagons from Brigham City, Willard, Kaysville, and Springville.[12] A letter from Brigham Young to Alex McDonald of the Tithing Office states that some animals and conveyances were loaned and had to be returned or purchased, and Evan F. Greene had loaned the use of 14 yoke of oxen, two ponies, and two logging carts, which now needed to be returned.[13] This sort of thing was actively going on during this period of greatest need. George A. Smith, always anxious to help, loaned his own team to help haul rock during his stay in St. George during the winter of 1874–75.[14]

Robert Gardner continued his narrative: "The distance from Mount Trumbull to St. George was 70 miles.[15] The water nearest to the mills was [at Nixon Springs] 2 miles [away], it took one man [or woman] with a team all the time to haul water to make steam and supply the houses [apparently a makeshift community had been set up]. Milk cows for supplying milk I had located at the spring.[16] Under this arrangement

---

12. Curtis, "History," 41–42.

13. Curtis, "History," 42.

14. Cox, "Robert Gardner," 219.

15. Only Gardner estimated the distance as 70 miles; every other correspondent of which we have record estimated it as 80 miles.

16. There is a large meadow and ranger station near Nixon Springs where Robert's livestock, and perhaps even he and his crews, were housed. The small spring itself is located high on the mountainside to the north. Gardner had the men build a narrow wooden "V" trough to carry the water from the spring down to the meadow where the water wagon was filled. Later, the Blake brothers purchased one of the Church's mills and established a mill on a slope just above this meadow, where today a large sign designates it as the site of the temple mills. Both archaeological and historical research indicate that in this regard the sign is incorrect, and that the Church's two mills were actually established close to each other about two miles up the canyon from Nixon Springs, toward Mount Logan. Their map designation is site AZA; 12; 82; MNA and NA13, 757. Little remains of these mills but barely discernible sawdust pits and the remains of two lava-rock coke kilns, where charcoal was produced for the steam engine's fires. See Roy D. Hunt, "An Historical Sketch of the Mount Trumbull Sawmill Sites" (Arizona, Museum of Northern Arizona Department of Anthropology, Mount Trumbull Area Survey), Appendix V, 177–78. In Kathleen Moffitt and Claudia King, "Archaeological Investigations, Mt. Trumbull Area Survey, Bureau of Land Management, Arizona Strip District," 1975. See also Paul Weaver, "Mt. Trumbull Research Documents." In 2011, Weaver and his son Phillip guided author Blaine M. Yorgason to these

we had a steady stream of lumber running from the standing tree to the Temple causing no hindrance for want of lumber which pleased the Presidency very much. My engagement was for 6 months, it being supposed that it would take about that time to get the lumber for the Temple. But we filled all the bills for [the] Temple and sawed a great deal for customers besides, inside of the 6 months."[17]

Back at the temple site, George Kirkham was getting close to completing his carpentry assignment. On Friday, 4 March, he recorded: "It was a day of rejoicing for us all, for at about 4 o'clock in the afternoon they laid the last rock to the square. I saw them lay it. My brother Joseph helped to lay it to its place. The Brass Band of St. George was up on the building, and as soon as the rock was laid the band struck up. My heart felt full of joy and thanksgiving to the Lord, to be living in such a day, and thankful for the privilege of helping to raise such a beautiful temple. I walked all round the building on the top of the wall, some 80 feet from the ground. There were 2 or 3 hundred people around the building, men, women and children, to witness the scene. When the band commenced to play, the tears flowed down from the eyes for joy unspeakable. After which, Brother McDonald read a telegram from President Young about the temple. He then made a few remarks and then there was some shouting for joy. Then as I was on top of the building, I went down and we all marched up to the town to our

---

sites, as well as along portions of the old Temple Trail as it winds its way toward St. George. All the research documents in this volume that pertain to Mt. Trumbull are courtesy of Paul Weaver.

17. Gardner, "Utah Pioneer—1847," 46. A record book showing all the timber cuts for each day's operation, now in the Church History Library of The Church of Jesus Christ of Latter-day Saints, shows that Robert's lumberjacks cut more than a million board feet for the construction of the temple in that six-month period. Much of this was the timber used in the inside walls and for the roof trusses. Meanwhile, back at Mt. Trumbull, Gardner's crews also cut 300,000 board feet of three grades of lumber for customers who needed it for buildings or fences in the towns of southern Utah. Though most of the lumber for the temple came from Mt. Trumbull, some of it came from Pine Valley Mountain and a single load came from the Buckskin Mountains in the Kaibab Forest. Ten loads also came from Beaver, and the Gardner Mills in Pine Valley cut all the scaffolding poles.

homes, led by the brass band. At night, I played for a party in the court house."[18]

At that party Erastus Snow spoke and the onlookers cheered for the workers. The next morning, a three-hour meeting was held in the tabernacle to further honor these workers. The program interspersed speeches by the leaders with comic items and songs. At this meeting the St. George Stake choir and both the string and brass bands furnished music. After this meeting many of the masons returned to their homes in distant settlements.

George Kirkham gave a slightly different view of this festive meeting. He wrote: "Saturday Mar 5, 1875: The weather was fine. A man came in and told us we were to go to the tabernacle. At about 10 o'clock we went, and such a time we shall never forget as long as we live on earth, and after. We had bread and cheese. The congregation was very large. We had our instruments with us. We played some pieces. [Staheli's] brass band played some pieces also. President Snow called on me to sing. I did so and I had to sing a second song before I took my seat. After which the band played again and bread and cheese was passed around. The wine was carried in water buckets and brass pitchers. There were bushels of tin cups brought in to drink out of. Some of the brethren drank so freely at the wine [that] they became noisy, and some commenced to call out for me to sing. I soon stopped that by rising to my feet and [saying] I did not intend to sing until I was called upon by the brethren on the stand. Brother McDaniel [McDonald?] said that was right and thanked me for doing so. He said he had told the Bishops not to serve any more wine, as there were some of the brethren that could not take a little wine without drinking so much and becoming noisy and disorderly. He said there was only one half of them that drank, yet he said . . . it was all served that they had prepared for the occasion. But all went off well. Brother Snow caused the hearts of the people to rejoice in his remarks. Our meeting dismissed at one o'clock.

18. Kirkham, *Journal*, 26.

From there we all, my wife and brother and myself, went to a wedding party of my brother Joseph, who was married to Teresa Cragun. He was married by Bishop Granger of the Third Ward of St. George, at 6 o'clock. After supper we, my brother and myself, went to play for a party in the court house."[19]

Meanwhile, the need for lumber from Mt. Trumbull continued. The officers of the United Order asked Frederick Blake to replace Robert Gardner and oversee the two Mt. Trumbull sawmills. "He rarely came home during the last four months of sawing lumber for the temple."[20]

By the second week of March, John Chidester and David Mustard, both of whom had been working on the temple from the beginning, along with the other carpenters, were ready for the installation of the roof timbers that were already on the temple site. As mentioned previously, these massive trusses or "bents" had been hoisted beam by beam and board by board to the unfinished fourth main floor where they had been assembled.

Kirkham, now released from his temple assignment, continued: "Friday Mar 11, 1875: In the afternoon I went to the tithing office and settled up. I turned in $91.72 to the St. George Temple. My wife was credited with $40.00 for the work of cooking, and the faithful work she had done during the winter, which had now past. I worked to the amount of 180 dollars. The $91.72 [I donated] was [the cash] I had

---

19. Kirkham, *Journal*, 26.
20. Barnum, "Frederick Blake." While at the sawmill fulfilling this assignment Frederick had a terrible accident, and received severe head injuries. The saw cut into his brain and cut off his ear. The brethren present molded his head back together, gave him a priesthood blessing, and he went right back to work. Later the doctors were able to sew his ear on, but after a time, great pain and the brain damage from his injury made it necessary for him to be sent north to be hospitalized—for seventeen years! Since Frederick never seemed to get better, his third wife, Eliza, divorced him in 1893, marrying William Atkin the next month. After the seventeen years a new, more modern operation was performed, and Frederick became well enough to go home. Eliza, thinking that Frederick would never return to his beloved St. George, retained all of his properties, so Frederick lived the rest of his life in the home of his younger brother Benjamin, dying there on February 4, 1916.

earned playing for parties and otherwise. . . . Friday . . . I saw over one hundred Indians on the way to be baptized. I saw many of the people looking out at the great company of them as they passed by. After breakfast I went up to Mount Hope where the Indians had assembled by a little valley where Brother [Charles R.] Savage, of Salt Lake City, was taking a [photographic] likeness of them, as they squat[ted] on the ground. Then Bishop McArthur called all to order, both Indian and white people. After prayer, Bishop McArthur went down into the water and was followed by one of the Indians. While they stood, Brother Savage took a likeness of them, there in the water. I stood close on the bank and kept an account of them that were baptized. There were 68 females and 66 males, in all, 134 Indians. Such a sight I never saw before in my life. A nation born in a day . . . fulfilling the words of the Prophet [Brigham Young]. . . .

"Saturday . . . I was sitting by our little old stove without any wood, only a few chips to burn. The woman who the house belonged to, who lived in the adjoining room, came in and told us she wanted the room. . . . Well we loaded our things into the wagon and went to Brother Cragun's and stopped there. They were very glad we had come. . . . Tuesday . . . After breakfast we finished loading up our things and then wished all the folks goodbye. We could not help but shed a tear or two when leaving, for the pleasures we had while laboring on the temple, and forming so many acquaintances and friends. We shall never forget our trip to Dixie. At 25 minutes to 12 o'clock, we left St. George for our home in the north. . . . We were happy to think we were on our way home."[21]

---

21. Kirkham, *Journal*, 27–30. In an interesting way, George Kirkham was like ancient Jacob. In December 1872 he had gone to his sweetheart Sara Russon's father in Lehi to ask her hand in marriage. The father replied that such a union was a possibility, but only on the condition that George first marry and begin a family with Sara's older sister, Mary. Apparently George agreed to this, for when he arrived in St. George in the fall of 1874, he was accompanied by Mary and their year-old baby, George Erastus. No mention is made in his journal of his sweetheart and "intended wife" Sara until after his return to Lehi the following April. Upon his

At about this same time, food and other supplies for the temple laborers and others in St. George were again running short. Charles Pulsipher, not yet released from his labors, continued gathering food and supplies wherever possible, though the response was disappointing because crops throughout Beaver and Juab counties, and no doubt other counties in central Utah, had been destroyed by rabbits, creating a scarcity of foodstuff throughout the central and southern part of the Territory.[22]

With George Kirkham gone, William Henry Thompson was named head carpenter. He had charge of lifting and setting in place on the walls the last of the heavy trusses or bents upon which the roof of the temple would rest. The slabs and the ends of these timbers furnished some of the lath for use in constructing the interior walls, the carpenters sawing the lath to make them fit perfectly.

When the last bent was installed on Wednesday, 30 June 1875, another community event took place. James G. Bleak described it:

"At 1:50 P.M., the last Bent of the St. George Temple roof began to rise from the level of the second main floor of the building. The St. George Brass Band under Superintendent John Eardley playing at the time the tune of [Charlie Walker's] 'Temple Song.'"

Despite the fact that he had never fully recovered from his 1874 fall and still had great difficulty breathing, "Miles Romney, Assistant Architect of the building was present, also Norton Jacobs, Superintendent Framer, and Chief Mason Edward L. Parry. Wm. Thompson superintended the raising. George Jarvis [and] the windlass hands [did the hoisting].

---

return, when George reminded Father Russon that the two years were past and he and Sara were still in love, the man refused to allow the marriage, whereupon Sara angrily left her parents' home and moved in with George and Mary. According to Family Search: Family Group Records for George Kirkham, Mary Russon and Sara Russon, George and Sara were sealed in the Endowment House on 14 June 1875. He and Mary had been sealed on 16 December 1872. Ultimately Mary bore seven children, Sara four; printed Family Search Records in possession of the authors.

22. Curtis, "History," 59–60.

"At 1:50. P.M. Josiah G. Hardy drove the first pin to fasten the bent in its place, the band, in the meantime, playing 'Adoration.' At 3:35 P.M., everything pertaining to the bent having been properly secured, the signal was given, 'Let go, all,' and simultaneously the band struck up the tune, 'Old Hundred' and the Stars and Stripes were flung to the breeze by Assistant Architect Miles Romney.

"Many citizens were present to witness this event, among them being Elder Jacob Gates of the General Presidency of Seventies, Patriarch William G. Perkins, bishop[s] McArthur and Milne, and elders Alex. F. McDonald, James W. Nixon, Thomas J. Jones, Jesse W. Crosby, Anson P. Winsor, and Thomas Cottam."[23]

It was a celebratory occasion; after the monumental efforts that had been expended, truly the citizens of St. George were getting anxious to have the temple completed.

---

23. Bleak, "Annals," Book B, 405.

Chapter 12

THE FONT AND OTHER TRIUMPHS

July through December 1875

Sometime prior to February 1873, as Charlie Walker's "Carter and the pounder and boys"[1] were finishing the basalt base upon which the temple foundation would rest, Brigham Young returned to Salt Lake City. Almost immediately he made arrangements to meet with Bishop Nathan Davis concerning a gift he wished to make to the St. George Temple. Serving as bishop of the Seventeenth Ward, Davis owned an iron foundry in Salt Lake City. As they visited, Brigham proposed hiring Davis's firm to cast the baptismal font and 12 oxen for the still-future temple.[2]

Although Davis was a knowledgeable mechanic, he readily admitted that he was not a skilled foundry man. Because of that, his foundry would have trouble with the complex job of making the mold for the oxen. There was, however, a young man in his ward, a recent convert

1. Charles Lowell Walker, *Diary of Charles Lowell Walker*, edited by A. Karl Larson and Katharine Miles Larson, 2 vols. (Logan: Utah State University Press, 1980), 1:362, 395.
2. Margaret M. Cannon, "The St. George Temple Baptismal Font," *Utah Historical Quarterly* (Spring 1995): 152.

newly arrived in the valley, who before coming west had been well-trained as a foundry worker and manager in St. Louis. His name was Amos Howe. Davis and Brigham Young immediately approached Howe for help, which he agreed to give if he could be taken into the company as a partner. The proposal was accepted, and the new company was formed on 1 February 1873.[3]

Howe "was trained in foundry and pattern-making as well as in the profession of engineering. He could calculate stress and tension on what was produced, helping to ensure a suitable product."[4] Howe was also skilled at modeling and carving molds for his castings from wood, around which he formed moist sand casts that would harden to receive the molten iron. After cooling, the casts were broken away, and the various parts of the iron casting were welded together.

Meanwhile, the smelted iron, known as pig iron, had been shipped north to the foundry from the Union Iron Company located in Iron Town, or Iron City, about twenty miles west of Cedar City.[5] The first

---

3. According to a stock certificate issued in the early 1900s, Nathan Davis and Amos Howe established their foundry partnership on 1 February 1873; photocopy in possession of the authors.

4. Charles R. Howe and June Howe Johnson, comps., Howe Family Scrapbook 5; in possession of the Howe family.

5. Old Iron Town, originally Iron City, is located on Pinto Creek about 22 miles west of Cedar City, Utah, five miles south of State Route 56. The settlement was founded in 1868 as a second attempt to mine iron from Iron Mountain after a disappointing yield from the Iron Mission in Cedar City, and the new works were called the Union Iron Company. The 1870 census indicates that 97 people lived on-site in nineteen households. By 1871 there were a post office, a boarding house, a school, a butcher shop, and a general store. By 1875, when the St. George Temple font and oxen were cast in Salt Lake City from the ironwork's pig iron, the Union Iron Company had become the Great Western Iron Company. At its peak, these works consisted of both a large and small furnace with a combined 2,500-pound capacity, a pattern shop, a blacksmith shop, a molding shop, an *erastra* (a device for grinding sand for molds), and two large charcoal kilns. The ironworks produced five to seven tons of pig iron per day, which was shipped throughout Utah as well as into Nevada. Though mining on Iron Mountain continued off and on until the 1980s, due to lack of transportation and long-term effects from the financial panic of 1874, Iron City was abandoned in 1876 and became Utah's first ghost town. Now known as Old Irontown State Park, the ruins are managed by Utah State Parks

step in preparing the iron font and oxen for St. George was for Howe to produce a wooden, life-sized front half of an ox. It is not known how much time was spent on this wooden sculpture, but Amos's granddaughter related that when Brigham Young saw the first patterns for the oxen he chided, "That won't do, Amos."[6] A search was made in both Idaho and Utah for a perfect ox, another task that took several months. But finally, when a suitable model was found, it was brought to the foundry. "There it was corralled and used as a live model" for several weeks. Howe designed the font and oxen and was responsible for the drawings and patterns that were finally used. The new patterns were so successful that Brigham Young exclaimed, "Brother Howe, you have even registered the disposition of the live ox."[7] From that day the work moved forward.

On 17 June 1875 the *Deseret News* published a detailed description of the almost completed font and oxen:

"Castings for the Temple—Today our reporter visited the foundry and machine shops of Messrs. Davis, Howe & Co., 17th ward, where a number of castings for the St. George Temple are being produced.

"Six of the twelve oxen which are to support the baptismal font are completed, and two more are on the way. The animals are life size and modeled in wood from a fine looking, genuine, live ox and the modeler has done his work well, the imitation being excellent, and the castings are trim and neat." Each ox was cast without hooves and with just the front portion of the body, which was to be secured with a long bolt to the frame of the font.

"The [iron] font itself is interesting in form and workmanship. It is oval in shape, 13 feet by 9 feet at the top . . . the bottom weighs about twenty-nine hundred pounds, and the sides about one ton. . . . The

---

and Recreation. (See Wikipedia.com, "Old Iron Town, Utah"; see also Online Utah.com, "History of Irontown, Utah.")

6. Cannon, "Baptismal Font," 153. See also Margaret M. Cannon, interview with Julia Howe Hegstead, Springville, Utah, 22 February 1990.

7. Cannon, interview, 22 February 1990.

whole thing, when placed in position and bronzed, as we understand it is the intention to finish it in that way, will be a splendid piece of work, and it will probably be the only one of its kind in existence."[8]

The writer of the *Deseret News* article also reported of the foundry that "Their facilities for heavy casting are quite extensive," and that the font would "have the appearance of being in one solid piece when finished," with ornamental iron steps leading up to it with a rail and banisters to match.[9]

Late in July 1875 the work was finished, and the half-oxen and un-assembled font were shipped south on the Utah Southern Railroad. At that time the railroad ended at York, which was located somewhere near the Santaquin Hill in northern Juab County. There the various parts were loaded aboard three specially built wagons, each drawn by three teams of oxen.

C. L. Christensen had worked on the temple through the winters of both 1873 and 1874, returning both summers with his wife and infant son to farm in Ephraim, and had remained in Ephraim through the winter of 1874–75 in order to better care for his family. He was, however, called upon to give up much of his 1875 summer to fill a special assignment. In the *Deseret News* of 29 August 1931, he recalled his experiences as one of the crew delivering the [18,000-pound] font from the railroad terminus to St. George:

"Nathan Davis and Bishop Elijah Sheets of Salt Lake came down [to York, Juab County,] and helped us load, and they spared no pains in bolting and timbering so as to make everything safe. My load was the bottom of the font, weighing 2900 lbs., and two oxen, 600 lbs. each. Standing on end, the [font] parts reached the top of the wagon bows. [Bishop Sheets was] an experienced blacksmith, and . . . [he] appointed [me] Captain of the wagon train. [There were] two other men: Andrew

8. Cannon, "Baptismal Font," 154.
9. Cannon, "Baptismal Font," 154.

Sundergaard from Mount Pleasant, and Chris Jensen from Moroni. . . . I had three yoke of oxen and a 3¼ size wagon to draw my load."[10]

According to various family records and traditions, two additional men named Grover and Fife joined the company at Nephi, and Samuel Bennett of Holden was assigned to assist them at some point during the journey.

Christensen continued: "Everywhere along the way we were royally received and entertained."[11] With people relatively isolated in those days, the arrival of the wagon train was a special event in each small town it passed through and provided a welcome respite for the transporters. No one but the local Latter-day Saint bishops were allowed to see what the wagons contained.[12]

"Soldiers traveling to Beaver on foot passed and re-passed the wagon train several times. Because the John D. Lee trial for the Mountain Meadows Massacre was under way in Beaver, the soldiers suspected cannons or other arms were being shipped south and wanted to see what was in the wagons. But the caretakers of the font kept to their instructions and did not let any unauthorized viewers see what they were carrying.

"The weather created a major problem for those transporting the font. With temperatures frequently exceeding 100 degrees Fahrenheit in the shade, some of the oxen pulling the heavy loads nearly died of thirst. Whenever they sensed a stream of water nearby, they tried to stampede to get a drink."[13] To alleviate this problem, as often as practical the group traveled at night. Christensen adds a final note: "The teamsters had plenty of good Dixie wine to keep them cool, and we

---

10. C. L. Christensen, "How the Temple Font Was Taken to St. George," *Deseret News*, 29 August 1931, 8. See also Kate B. Carter, comp., *Heart Throbs of the West* (Salt Lake City: Daughters of Utah Pioneers, 1949), 9:3–5. C. L. Christensen was age 20 when he delivered the font to St. George.

11. Christensen, "Temple Font," 5.

12. Ann Leavitt, "The Temple of Our God's Completed, Building the St. George Temple," *Pioneer* 54, no. 4 (2007): 15.

13. Cannon, "Baptismal Font," 155.

certainly [appreciated] it. We arrived [in St. George] on the 3rd day of August . . . the heat was 119 in the shade."[14]

The stringent rule regarding who might view the cargo must have been relaxed by then. Estella Jackson recorded, "When they arrived in St. George it caused a big excitement and the people from all over town turned out to see the wagons with the font. Although Zaidee Walker [Miles] was a little girl at this time, she well remembers getting up on the wagons and climbing all over the font and oxen.

"As fast as the pieces were unloaded from the wagons they were taken into the Temple basement where they were put in place and bolted and welded together by Mr. Davis from SLC. [As the hoofless oxen were put in place, their hocks—the ankle or heel bone just above the missing hooves—were bolted to the floor.] The Font was assembled on the [basement] floor and welded together, then hoisted into place by man-power with the use of the sailor-type block-and-tackle swung under heavy tripods. The font weighed nine tons and when they had it ready to lift the men were discussing how many mules or oxen would be needed to lift such a heavy weight. George Jarvis, who was in charge of the hoisting [there and throughout the temple], said they could not use either mules or oxen since they would move too unevenly and it must be lifted in place by man-power."[15]

When asked who would help him and how, George asked for four of his British seafaring friends and then explained to President Snow: "With the proper combination of ropes and pulleys, we can do this. I learned all about lifting heavy objects while I worked for Ravenhill and Miller back in England."[16]

14. Carter, *Heart Throbs*, 9:5.

15. Estella Jackson, "History of the Baptismal Font of the St. George Temple," in *The Honeymoon Trail* (privately published, 28 April 1950), n.p.; photocopy in possession of the authors.

16. Mary Miles Kleinman, "Swinging the St. George Temple Baptismal Font into Place," in *Essence of Faith* (Springville, Utah: Art City Publishers, 1973), 243–45; photocopy in possession of the authors.

The four men Jarvis chose—John Horne Miles, Ebenezer and Charles DeFriez, and Thomas Crane—were placed one in each corner of the room. "The manipulation of the ropes was under Jarvis's direction, but because the spectators were also shouting instructions the sailors had difficulty at first hearing his commands. George endured it for several minutes; but seeing it was causing confusion, he finally yelled: 'you landlubbers . . . keep perfectly quiet until we have the font in place!' Silence reigned as everyone watched intently. George Jarvis snapped a few nautical orders and the nine ton font rose slowly and was swung into its place on the oxen without a hitch [and not even a sixteenth of an inch off dead center]."[17]

As previously noted, beneath the font and oxen had been laid a large oval footing or foundation of black lava rock and mortar, the same as for the temple foundation and laid at the same time. The font rested directly upon this massive basalt construction, and the basement floor was then built around it with joists and flooring butted up against the foundation. It was into this floor that the oxen's hooves appear to have been buried.

According to C. L. Christensen, "We did not leave until all the pieces were put in place and bolted together. Apostle Orson Hyde went in and saw the font in place and came out weeping with joy. He thanked God he had lived to see another font in place in a temple of

---

17. Jackson, "History of the Baptismal Font." A somewhat different version of this event was written by Jarvis's daughter, Josephine Jarvis Miles. She wrote: "The font of the Temple was lifted in place on the oxen under his direction. It was fitted together by a man sent from Salt Lake City. Father stationed four sailors, Ebenezer and Charles De Freiz, John Miles and Thomas Crane, one in each corner of the room, and manipulation of the ropes was under his command. There was a crowd of spectators. Some of the 'Land Lubbers' had the temerity to shout instructions. Father endured it for a while, but it was causing confusion, and father was responsible so he ordered every man to shut his mouth and keep it shut until the font was in place. They did so. Then with a few nautical orders to his men, the font weighing 18,000 pounds, rose slowly and was swung onto the oxen without a hitch. Father told me this." George's wife, Ann Prior Jarvis, added: "My husband worked on the temple the entire time and was among the first to get the greatest blessings the Lord has to bestow upon His children."

the Lord. He said this people would never be driven from the Rocky Mountains. I believed him, for I had heard him prophesy before."[18]

Today the font appears to rest upon the backs of these 12 original oxen, four on each side and two at each end, their heads, shoulders, and forelegs appearing to project out from under the font. The twelve oxen stand as a symbol of the twelve tribes of Israel, who are to be gathered together through missionary and temple work. "Consequently, the baptismal font was instituted as a similitude of the grave, and was commanded," according to revelation, "to be in a place underneath where the living are wont to assemble, to show both the living and the dead that all things may have their likeness and that they may accord one with another—that which is earthly conforming to that which is heavenly, as Paul hath declared, 1 Corinthians 15:46, 47, and 48."[19]

"The Baptismal Font with the twelve iron oxen upon which it [seemed to] rest . . . was dedicated temporarily on 11 August 1875, and the first baptisms in the Temple were performed that day—(to initiate people into the United Order)."[20] No baptisms for the dead were performed until 9 January 1877, following the 1 January 1877 partial dedication. It is interesting to consider that it had been thirty-one years since the Saints had left Nauvoo—thirty-one years without a dedicated temple.

With many workers having left St. George in the spring to return to their homes in the north, the remaining masonry work lasted well into the summer of 1875. Charles Walker and others finished it. On Saturday, 31 July, Walker was at work "cutting the Parapett and Buttres rocks."[21] The finish masonry and other work Walker was assigned with others to do continued through summer and into late fall.[22]

---

18. Leavitt, "Building the St. George Temple," 15.
19. See Doctrine and Covenants 128:13.
20. Andrew Karl Larson, *I Was Called to Dixie* (Salt Lake City: Deseret News Press, 1961), 413. See also Walker, *Diary*, 1:413.
21. Larson, *I Was Called to Dixie*, 413.
22. Larson, *I Was Called to Dixie*, 414.

As previously mentioned, the timely arrival of lumber from Mt. Trumbull during the spring of 1875 made possible the construction and installation of the roof timbers, and by 4 July the last stones were being cut to finish laying up the buttresses, cornices, parapets, and battlements at the top of the wall.[23] Following the Fourth of July celebration, the carpenters went to work installing the roof. The roof bents had a low profile or slope, but it was pitched enough for good drainage.

To build the roof, ceiling joists were secured between the bents lengthwise to the temple, and on top of everything two layers of 1x4-inch boards were nailed down—exactly the same as the subfloors and floors had been laid. This construction was then rain-proofed with a tar covering, followed by a composition canvas covering stretched over the fresh tar. Another thick coating of tar was applied to the canvas, which was then covered with a good layer of clean sand that had been hauled up from the river and hoisted to the roof. The sand provided the tar and canvas with protection from the sun.

The interior work was also moving ahead, and work on the temple tower had begun in earnest. The previous January, Erastus Snow and George A. Smith had met with Joseph Schofield, the supervising carpenter prior to Kirkham's appointment, and worked out with him how the tower should be built.[24] The tower's first level was to be a 31-foot, square-framed structure that would be attached to and rest upon the thicker sandstone support walls built up from the basement floor. On top of the square structure, a rather short octagonal tower was erected, bearing two sheet-metal balls with the base of a weather vane running through them.

These metal balls and perhaps the weather vane itself were crafted by Christopher Lister Riding, a "tin man" or "tinsmith" and peddler of

---

23. Albert E. Miller, *The Immortal Pioneers: Founders of the City of St. George* (Albert E. Miller, 1946), 340.
24. Douglas Cox, "History of Robert Gardner, Junior," unpublished manuscript, 281; copy in possession of Richard Schmutz.

sheet-metal wares.[25] Lister came to Cedar City in 1860 and then went on to St. George with the earliest colonists in 1861. Though he was industrious, it wasn't long before he saw that there was not enough business in St. George for his specialty of work, so he secured a little four-wheeled cart and an ox. He loaded the cart with sheet-metal scraps and tools and visited all the northern towns, such as Parowan, Beaver, and Cedar, exchanging his wares for flour, potatoes, butter, cheese, and other goods. Later he secured a horse for his cart and continued his visits until he became a well-known figure throughout the southern part of the state.[26]

Because it was difficult and expensive to ship in sheet metal, Riding made his wares chiefly from discarded metal cans and other metal scraps that people saved for him. The store of wares he then created consisted of buckets, milk pans, tin cups and plates, bread canisters, lamps, canteens, coffee pots, wash boards, and so forth. He was a master workman in every sense of the word, which is attested to by the fact that some of his buckets and pans still exist.[27]

Late in 1875, Riding was asked to craft the two balls that would sit beneath the weather vane atop the tower of the temple. He made them each in two halves running top to bottom, using sheet metal he had gathered and then pounded and soldered or welded into shape. To reinforce these halves he built, or had the carpenters build wooden frames, also in two halves, with specially cut wooden fins radiating outward in a circle with spacers between them top and bottom to ensure that they were solidly in place. Each of these fins was cut vertically on the inner edge and rounded on the outer so that when placed together

---

25. It should be noted that the use of the word *tin* in Lister's trade designations was an archaic term going back to medieval England and its famous Cornish tin mines. Though the epithet was still being used, Lister worked with a more modern material known as sheet metal.

26. "Life of Christopher Lister Riding," n.d., n.p., typescript; in possession of the authors.

27. "Life of Christopher Lister Riding."

the whole formed the wooden framework of the two balls with a 12-inch circular opening running top to bottom through the center of each. Through these openings was placed a 12-inch-thick circular pole approximately 8 to 10 feet long.[28] Once Riding had tacked on his metal covering to complete the balls, soldered them, and then covered both balls with silver paint, he secured them to the upper end of the pole with two iron bands, one above each ball and one beneath. Immediately beneath the lower ball, Riding placed a 24-inch circular metal collar that would carry water away from the opening into the tower below.

Late in 1876, after securing the weathervane to the top of the pole and the collar beneath, the larger and much heavier base was dropped through a hole built into the top of the tower. There, an iron apparatus, built around the pole like a yoke, secured it to the tower. So designed and built, this heavy wooden pole balanced the balls and weather vane against the fiercest winds while allowing the entire apparatus to turn freely, indicating the wind's direction. Thus Christopher Lister Riding had completed his work on the temple—or so he thought!

When the tower's construction was completed, the distance from the ground to the top of the weather vane was 135 feet. Thereafter, the tower's two levels were given a coat of white paint. Unfortunately, architecturally and esthetically this original tower was far too short for the large temple, giving the whole a squatty appearance.

During the previous summer of 1874, Brigham had suggested calling at least 100 single young men to work on the temple. The advantage of this, his nephew, stake president John W. Young, explained in a circular

---

28. An early photo of the temple, held in a private collection at the Harold B. Lee Library, shows the two balls surrounded by a small square of scaffolding, though how Riding or others climbed to that scaffolding is not evident. The perch would have been precarious, no matter the approach. These intricately made balls were destroyed by lightning in 1878. In 1883 Ryding crafted a single replacement ball 30 inches in diameter, as well as the balancing pole and iron collar, which remained atop the temple for more than a hundred years until a new dome and weather vane were installed in the 1990s. Parts of this ball and apparatus exist today but at present are unavailable for viewing.

sent to bishops throughout his stake, was that they could grow used to the hard labor and then remain with the work until its completion rather than being drawn home to waiting families while other, more inexperienced hands took over.[29]

Concerning two young men who received such a call was written: "In 1875 Samuel Bennett and Dave Turner [of Holden] grew bored and made plans to go to Oregon, mostly for adventure, but of course if they could find work they would take it. They had their covered wagon packed with bedding, a few clothes, and good supplies. From the sides of the double-bed wagon box hung their kettles, skillets, fry pans, etc. for cooking their meals over the campfire. On the rack extending from the back of the wagon was a goodly supply of hay and oats for the horses, with nose bags for feeding the grain. This was Sunday [when their preparations were complete] and they were to leave the next morning.

"Samuel's mother tried to persuade them not to go, but as young fellows filled with the spirit of adventure they had made their decision. That afternoon the boys were in [Church] meeting when Bishop David R. Stevens arose and announced, 'We want Samuel Bennett and Dave Turner to go to St. George to work on the Temple.' At the close of the meeting Dave said, 'Well, Bennett, what are you going to do?' Samuel answered, 'I am going to St. George.' Dave was disappointed but after a moment's thought he sided in and said, 'Well, if you're going I'm going too.' So these two young men, together with Murray Fisher and Brother and Sister Niels Tueson of Scipio, rigged up a [second] back action covered wagon with six horses and supplies and [they all] went to St. George to work on the Temple."[30]

At about that same time Charles Pulsipher was again gathering temple offerings. He wrote: "While [we were] in San Pete County

29. James G. Bleak, "Annals of the Southern Utah Mission," Book B, 278, typescript, Dixie State University Special Collections, St. George, Utah.

30. Joan Bennett Jones, *Samuel Bennett Sr., Grandfather of Joan Bennett Jones* (privately published, 1979), 347–51.

Brother Jos. T. Young [Brigham's son] got the surveyor and went up on to the site for the Manti Temple and looked around there for an hour or two and finally got into his bugy and said [to me], 'Father has appointed me to build this Temple but I shall never live to commence it.' He went to his son's home in Manti and died in a few days."

"Shortly thereafter," Pulsipher continued, "Brother John L. [George A. Smith's brother] went with me up onto the Temple site and examined it and found it to be a beautiful location, a location from which you could see all over the valley. I felt pleased that the prediction that I made in '73 was to be fulfilled so soon. There was plenty of fine white rock handy to build with and solid rock foundation to build on."[31]

Of another experience that fall Pulsipher wrote: "I had an appointment for Sunday at 10:00 in a small Ward off from the main road [in Ephraim] and then another for the evening at 7 [in Salina] which was 30 miles apart. I drove from Manti in the morning and reached [Ephraim] about 15 minutes before 10 and when I met the Bishop he said to me, 'Do you understand the Danish language? I see you are an American.'

"'No, I don't understand one word of the Danish language.'

"'Well, we are in a bad fix. Our people came right through [Salt Lake City] and settled here to themselves and have not learned the English language so the only way for us to do is for you to tell what you wish to and I will have to interpret it to them.' So I concluded I would speak about ¾ of an hour and explain all that I could in that time and leave him the same to interpret it to their understanding.

"When I arose I looked at my time and concluded I must stop at 11:00. I commenced speaking and never thought of time any more. I had great liberty but did not understand [t]hat I was saying [anything out of the ordinary]. It [also] seemed to me that I stood about two feet

---

31. Charles Pulsipher, *Journal* (privately published); in possession of Venetta Williams, Santa Clara, Utah.

above them in the air but the floor was on the level, and when I came to an end and thought I had used my portion of the time, I looked and saw that it was 15 minutes to 12:00 o'clock [45 minutes more than he had intended to speak]. I never was so surprised, for I had no idea that I was talking all that time. 'Why,' I said [to the bishop], 'Is it possible I have taken all the time? What shall [we] do, appoint another meeting for you to interpret it?'

"'No. You don't need to, for they understood all right [just as] I did, in the Danish language.'

"So he called out to them and asked if they understood, and they all cried out that they did. It needed no interpreting and as I had to be right off to meet my appointment at Salina, thirty miles away, I did not get a chance to talk [more] with the Bishop about it and never had the opportunity of going there again, but I suppose I must have spoken the Danish language for them to understand it so well, for I know they understood me by the liberal offerings they made just as fast as the clerk could write."[32]

At about this time, Dave Turner from Holden had become one of the teamsters going to and from Mt. Trumbull,[33] while his friend Samuel Bennett worked as a stonecutter on the temple and also assisted in transporting the font and oxen to St. George.[34] But responding to the call to labor on the temple "marked a more sure way for [Samuel's] future life. Many testimonies came to him while [he was] engaged in the glorious work of building this House of the Lord. . . . While he was thus engaged, he met Marta M. Fuhrmeister (Martha M. Foremaster), one of the beautiful daughters of Fredrich W. Fuhrmeister. . . . [After a courtship that lasted well into the following winter] they traveled by team and covered wagon to Salt Lake in bitter cold weather with plenty of snow. Samuel would get [down] and 'buck' the snow in some places

32. Pulsipher, *Journal.*
33. Mt. Trumbull Mill Co., Mill Book # 1, 10, 12, 16, 26, 27.
34. Jones, "Samuel Bennett Sr.," 347–51.

before the horses could venture on. His sister Jane accompanied the young couple. . . . Samuel and Marta were sealed in the Endowment House."[35] They raised a large family, first in St. George and then in Holden, even as they labored to forge a truly eternal union.[36]

Another single man who came to St. George in 1875 was William Brown Jr., "who was twenty years old [when] he was called . . . to go to St. George to work on the temple. . . . He, with other young men from the [Salt Lake] valley left about January fifteenth, 1875 and remained in St. George until the construction of the temple was [complete]. . . . William returned home [without a bride] in 1877."[37]

And a fourth man, who quite possibly came from among the Scandinavian immigrants to Sanpete, was Swen O. Nielson. During his time in St. George he became acquainted with Rachel Violet Atkin, daughter of stonemason William Atkin II and his wife, Rachel. Though there was seven years difference in their ages, the young couple's love blossomed, and the two were married on 14 February 1878, presumably in the completed temple. Rachel Violet was sixteen, Swen was twenty-three.[38]

Late in August 1875, Charles Pulsipher wrote that he and John L. Smith "got word that Brother George A. [Smith] was very sick so we drove down to the city as fast as we could, making 50 miles a day. We

---

35. Jones, "Samuel Bennett Sr.," 351. The young couple made their home in St. George, Utah, where the first three of their children were born. They then moved to Holden, Millard County, Utah, the home of Samuel's parents, where the last eight of their children were born. They lived in Holden for the remaining forty-six years of their lives.

36. As an interesting side note, Samuel and Martha Bennett are the great-grandparents of three of author Blaine M. Yorgason's cousins: Alan Yorgason and his sisters Carol Paxton and Brenda LeCheminant.

37. "William Brown Jr.," n.d., n.p., typescript; in possession of the authors. The book *Temples of the Most High* states that during much of the year 1875 one hundred young men were engaged at the temple in construction work (comp. N. B. Lundwall, rev. ed., Salt Lake City: Bookcraft, 1993).

38. Reid L. Neilson, *From the Green Hills of England to the Red Hills of Dixie: The Story of William and Rachel Thompson Atkin* (Provo, Utah: Red Rock Publishing, 2000), 83.

stayed a few days and he seemed to be a little better so we started out on our Missionary labors again and got part way through San Pete County and got another telegram that he was dead [George A. Smith died on 1 September 1875]. We drove to the terminal of the [rail]road. Brother John L. got on the train and went into the city that night. I drove to Pleasant Grove, left the team with my brother-in-law, H. Beers and went into the City the next day and attended the funeral. I was one of the pall-bearers. I stayed in the city another day and then [Bro. John L. and I again] went on to our Missionary labors."

Sometime late in the fall, Brother Pulsipher recorded another experience—and another witness to him that his work was truly an errand from the Lord.[39] He writes: "I asked Brother Snow at one time about taking offerings from a poor family. 'Yes', he said. 'Accept their offerings and get their names on the Temple records but be sure and leave a blessing with them that they shall be abundantly rewarded in return.'

"I always felt free to do so and many times parties have told me how unexpectedly means had come into their hands to more than make up for what they had donated for the Temple."

For instance, "one morning as I was getting ready to start from Fillmore, Brother Isaac Carling came to me with a dollar bill in his hand and said, 'We have kept this for some time and did not spend it for it would not get what we needed so we have concluded to give it to you for the Temple and trust in your promise that the Lord would open the way for our wants to be supplied.'

"I took it and gave him credit and shook hands with him and said, 'The Lord bless and reward you with many dollars in return.'

"I drove away and thought no more of it. In about a month after I was driving through [Fillmore] in a hurry and I saw someone coming across the square to catch me on foot. I checked up for him to come up and found it was Brother Carling. He said, 'I want to tell you something.'

---

39. Pulsipher did not date this event in his record, so it may have occurred in another year.

"'Well, get right in as I am going your way.'

"So he got in and said, 'Do you remember when you was here last that I gave you a dollar just as you was starting?'

"'Yes, I do.'

"'Well, do you remember what you said to me at the time?'

"'No, I don't know as I do.'

"'Well, I do. You said the Lord bless and reward you with many dollars in return. I want to tell you how soon it was fulfilled. I was going up in town that same afternoon and as I passed a neighbors house he came to the door and said, 'Come in.' So I went to see what he wanted. He said, 'I see that I owe you ten dollars and I want to pay it' and he handed out a ten dollar bill. 'Why brother,' I said, 'That was only a produce deal and I never expected cash on that.' 'Well, it is yours and I feel impressed to give it to you and I guess you need it.' 'Well, yes I do,' so I thanked him for his kindness and went and got all that we really needed at the time. I felt the blessing had been returned to me in a hurry.'"[40]

Another of the long-time residents of St. George who, just as Charlie Walker and David Mustard, worked on the temple from start to finish, was Benjamin Brown Gray. Though Gray was an excellent finish carpenter, he labored wherever he was asked, including doing the rough early carpentry on the temple. Arriving in St. George in 1863, just as many others he and his young wife lived first in a wagon box and then in a dugout, where their first child, a son, was born and then died. His two granddaughters, Bertha Gray Holmes and Myrtle Gray Seegmiller, write that "in the Annals of the Southern Mission, by James G. Bleak, he tells of a meeting held 19 Mar. 1864 called by Erastus Snow for the purpose of inquiring what amount of bread stuff each person had on hand and how many there were in each family. Grandfather reported six in the family and 75 lbs. of bread stuff on hand. . . .

"Grandfather recorded a mayor's deed to lots 4 and 5, block 40,

---

40. Pulsipher, *Journal.*

plat A, St. George City survey on 12 Mar. 1875. . . . [He] was an able tradesman and . . . prospered in his work as a carpenter, [aiding] in all the early building of public buildings and homes."[41]

Another granddaughter, Alyce W. Gray Gubler, remembered: "I played at Grandpa's carpenter bench making dolls with [his wood] shavings for curls. After he'd done such meticulous work from early morning until sunset, he [would] retire to his chair under the big mulberry tree and at his knee I learned my early lessons in English history. He told me the true stories of Henry VIII, Catherine of Aragon, Jane Seymour, Anne Boleyn, Disraeli, and [many others]. . . . [42]

"The cornerstone of the St. George Temple was laid on 1 April 1874 and the dedication took place 6 April 1877. Grandfather worked on the Temple all during its construction, doing much of the fine carpentry and finishing work. His son, Benjamin Franklin Gray, also worked with him and after the completion of the St. George Temple, they went to Manti and worked on that Temple . . . [doing much of] the intricate and beautifully carved woodwork [that was their specialty]."[43]

---

41. Bertha Gray Holmes and Martha Gray Seegmiller, *A Combined History of Our Grandparents, Benjamin Browne Gray and His Wife Jerusha Cecelia Burdick* (privately published, n.d.), 1–5, typescript copy in possession of the authors.

42. Holmes and Seegmiller, *Benjamin Browne Gray* 5–6. Alyce adds: "One of my proudest memories of Grandpa happened like this: [One day] when he came near [a] crowd of pupils [who were standing around], one big boy handed his old Franklin Fifth Reader to Grandpa, [teasing him to read it if he could]. Ordinarily very retiring . . . Grandpa began to [quote], eloquently, masterfully, not the excerpts as published in that reader but the classics in their entirety; Scott's *Lady of the Lake*, Tennyson's *The Idylls of the King*, and etc. One friend, indeed my husband's cousin, never forgot it."

43. Holmes and Seegmiller, *Benjamin Browne Gray* 5, 7–8. In spite of his wonderful accomplishments, Benjamin Browne Gray fell prey to the lure of Dixie wine. His granddaughters' record continues: "Grandfather sank below the level of his higher self when he started drinking. . . . [Unfortunately] Grandfather had the misfortune to be loud and noisy and 'let the whole world know it,' when he became drunk, consequently, [there came a time when] those in authority in the Church in St. George gave him six weeks to quit his drinking or they would excommunicate him. He was unable to do it in that length of time. We are sure we cannot realize how dreadfully painful it is to cope with a drinking problem without proper help. It is a disease that needs psychological and sometimes medical help to combat. Our

By the latter part of 1875 the carpenters were busy building and installing upper floors, partition walls, finishing the spiral stairs and other stairs, with their newel posts, balustrades and railings; also all door frames and doors. They also installed the heavy baseboards to be seen along the temple hallways, especially in the mezzanine floors. Some of these "baseboards" curve around walls such as those in the spiral stair wells. Instead of being made of wood, however, these are made of finely crafted plaster of paris, the same as the curved "moldings" over all the arched interior doorways. The carpenters also built the casings for the round windows and the arched long windows described by George Kirkham. Twin sets of these extra-long and extra-wide windows were placed in the front and rear walls of the temple, their interior arches also made of plaster of paris. It would have taken many hours to build the molds for these beautiful arches, and pouring and then installing the fragile plaster of paris casts would have required extremely delicate handling. These molded arches, set in the thick walls of the tower support complex, are observed best in the northeast end of the third floor mezzanine hallway, but are in other places as well. Unless they are gently tapped with a finger-tip, it is impossible to tell that they are not wood.

The carpenters also built the altars and benches in the endowment rooms and sealing room and alongside the pulpits on both assembly room floors' priesthood stands, and no doubt other benches that were to be used for convocation seating.

This finish carpentry had to be hand-planed and sanded, mostly

church now recognizes this and has a program through the Church Social Service Department to aid Church member alcoholics. [But not back then.] Grandpa was cut off from the Church on 9 Jan. 1886. . . . [His] drinking [also] caused trouble between him and Grandmother and she left him in the early 1880s. . . . [After that he] lived alone in St. George . . . [where,] about a year before he passed away [on 21 October 1913], he [was] rebaptized. He must have been able in time to conquer the drinking habit, [which] really touched our hearts and [made] us proud that he was not bitter, but that he had a true testimony of the gospel and humbled himself to ask for baptism again!"

with tools supplied by the workers. It is said that the only "power" tool available to them early on was a water-powered lathe. "[The] shortage of equipment such as planers, shapers, joiners, and joint cutters, made the consistency in the woodwork unique."[44] When Brigham went back north in February 1875 he promised the people in a letter that he would send back "wood working machinery for planing, mortising, tonguing and grooving, and forming moldings, all this to facilitate the erection of the woodwork of the building"; he would also send "nails,[45] glass, putty, white lead, paints, oil, varnish, brushes and other material needed in the finishing of the building."[46] If some or all of the promised materials and machinery came (it is assumed that it did, though no record of the machinery arrival has been found) they would have helped much in the finish carpentry.

44. Thomas Weston Welch, "Early Mormon Woodworking at Its Best: A Study of the Craftsmanship in the First Temples in Utah" (master's thesis, Brigham Young University, 1983), 12.

45. Nails were a precious item. Except for small square finish carpentry nails such as those used in the windows, most nails used in the temple's lumber construction were square-headed tapered nails made in Utah. They were made of iron and very brittle, breaking off easily and requiring care when driving them into a board (see Welch, "Early Mormon Woodworking," 31).

46. Welch, "Early Mormon Woodworking," 12.

Chapter 13

PREPARING TO OPEN

Fall to Winter 1875

Brigham's ever more pressing need to pass along sacred priesthood keys while he was still alive hastened the construction of the St. George Temple. Despite the fact that everything in St. George but the window sashes, grids, and glass was manufactured locally, certain things were left out or shortcuts found. For example, the interior woodworking is far less ornate than in the three subsequent temples—Logan, Manti, and Salt Lake. Also, as was previously mentioned, a great deal of the interior molding and decorative work, particularly the arched moldings above inner doorways and the stars and quatrefoils below the ceilings in certain of the rooms, was replicated again and again in plaster of paris from one original wood mold.

Nevertheless, the St. George Temple is a stunning example of excellence in early western construction. Thomas Welch says concerning the quality and detail of the woodworking: "The St. George [Temple] workers did not produce a great quantity of interior woodcarving. Their time seems to have been occupied mainly in [constructing doors, door frames,] and window frames, of which they produced 214 separate units. Many of these frames were of [great] complexity and represented hours of hand planing curved surfaces.[1] The greatest emphasis was on the quality of work done. Close examination . . . will reveal a great devotion to detail and a willingness to make every unseen detail [as] perfect as possible. [The finish work in the celestial room] is not what would be expected in a rough frontier town in 1877. The construction shows taste and culture and skill. Woodcarvers and plaster of paris molders were kept busy providing the trim and ceiling decorations . . . the work done is very impressive. . . .

"Quality control was also an obvious concern in the turning of wood pieces. Minute variations can be discerned but only upon the closest examination. The banister spindles of the [original] stairways [such as presently exist on the fourth floor] were all individually done, but varied [little] when examined with calipers."[2]

Securing the right lumber for the finish work was also important. Lumber cut at Mt. Trumbull was ideally suited for rough construction uses, but for interior finishing a "finer grained wood" was needed. This was obtained from Pine Valley where fine-grained pine was harvested. These pines had "a smooth, white grain with few knots." In fact they were "so straight and even grained that later on, some of the logs [were] taken to Salt Lake" and made into "the wooden pipes in the Salt Lake Tabernacle organ."[3]

A wood shop was set up on the temple grounds where the finish

---

1. Though unavailable for viewing, one of these early arched window frames, designed to fit above an interior door, still exists. It was built to fit into a wall 12 inches thick. To make the half-circular frame the carpenters sawed dozens of curved boards of from ¾ to 1 inch thick and 6 inches tall, all cut from larger boards so there was room to create the curve. These individual boards, rarely longer than 15 inches and some a little shorter, were fastened together in a stack that is almost exactly 12 inches thick, fastened side by side and end to end with other cuts of the same width, and held together with short, square iron nails, some of which may have been manufactured locally.
2. Thomas Weston Welch, "Early Mormon Woodworking at Its Best: A Study of the Craftsmanship in the First Temples in Utah" (master's thesis, Brigham Young University, 1983), 31, 33.
3. Welch, "Early Mormon Woodworking," 16.

carpenters could use the fine-grained pine to make "molding trim, doors and door frames, banisters, newel posts, turned banister supports, benches, and the molds for casting plaster of paris decorations."[4] Such craftsmanship was extremely time-consuming. For example, frames for the 116 outside windows had to be cut curved and then fit into the nearly two-feet-thick sandstone walls.[5] The same held true for the two sets of double entry doors and their frames and moldings at the east end of the temple, as well as the other exterior doors.

One of these carpenters, who, like Brigham Young, was a joiner (a workman who constructs and finishes interior woodwork), was a man named George Laub. He started his work on the temple on 6 December 1875. That evening he recorded: "Our Temple is a splendid building and the completion is growing rapid."[6]

Born in Pennsylvania, George was young when his father died, and his penniless mother adopted him out to a carpenter named George Weydler. Weydler was a good man who treated young George as if he were a son and gave him a limited education, later apprenticing him for three years to another carpenter, George Bailey.

While working for Bailey, George joined the Church and moved to Nauvoo, where he became a joiner.[7] After migrating to Salt Lake City and becoming well established, George was called to the Southern

---

4. Welch, "Early Mormon Woodworking," 23.

5. Appreciation for the window structures and glass frames plus the 2½-feet-thick hewn stone openings in which they were set can be gained by visual inspection on any floor in the Temple that gives access to either round or long windows. The stones were hewn on the ground and hoisted up the wall to be mortared into place. The stones for the round windows are remarkable for their size and uniformity. When finished, these hewn stones could be very heavy. A report tells that the sill for the large west window (no longer in existence due to the 1974 remodeling) weighed 3,000 pounds—a ton and a half—and was hoisted and mortared into place on 12 January 1875 (Douglas Cox, "History of Robert Gardner, Junior," unpublished manuscript, 281; copy in possession of Richard Schmutz).

6. George Laub, "George Laub—Utah Pioneer," synopsis of *George Laub Journal* (privately published, n.d.), n.p.; copy available in Daughters of Utah Pioneers McQuarrie Memorial Museum, St. George, Utah.

7. George Laub, *George Laub Journal*, 98, Sec. II.

Mission in "Sept. 1862." His family by then consisted of two wives, Mary J. McGinness and Ann E. Erickson, and their nine children. On 13 May 1863, during his journey south, he wrote: "Lay by Parowan this day. President Young and company returning from 'Dixieland' here spent the day and preached at 4 pm. Now, when Pres. Brigham Young saw me there he spoke to me. . . . I walked along the side of his carriage, at his request . . . to the bishops house where he stopped for the night. Here he told me to go to St. George and tell Br. Snow that he wished me to superintend, or be foreman [over the carpenters and joiners] on the building of the Tabernacle. . . . He said, 'you are also handy enough to build a water wheel or any such work, so when the Tabernacle is ready, send me a letter and I will give you a plan of it'. When I left him he blessed me in the Name of the Lord and bade me peace and prosperity."[8]

On 20 May 1863, the Laubs arrived in "Dixieland." George wrote: "This is a very pleasant situation. Its location is 2 miles north of the mouth of the Virgin and Clary River where the two empty into one common stream. This place is surrounded by high mountains . . . [but] is surely a desert . . . several springs above the city supplies irrigation . . . the land is full of some kind of mineral that obstructs the growth of much vegetation."[9]

The course of his life now set, George spent the next decade farming, building, and using his fine joining skills while working on the tabernacle, courthouse, cotton factory, at least two gristmills, and many private residences in St. George, Pine Valley, Cedar City, and Parowan. He also taught these trades to his eldest sons, George Weydler Laub and John Franklin Laub, and with pride watched them become excellent workers and joiners. "Besides their 2 city lots in St. George where they had a garden, grapes and fruit trees, they farmed land in Santa Clara and raised peas, wheat, corn, alfalfa, cotton, cane and peach trees. They

8. Laub, *Journal*, 99, Sec. II.
9. Laub, *Journal*, 99, Sec. II.

also raised alfalfa in Washington . . . and . . . Homesteaded 60 acres in Diamond Valley."[10]

On 18 January 1874, President Brigham Young again urged the St. George people to get the temple finished as soon as possible so they could get their ordinances done and also the work for the dead and be prepared for the Millennium. George took this to heart but was not given the opportunity to start on the temple until almost two years later—6 December 1875. Thereafter he worked daily, from morning to night, as long as there was adequate light to do so.

On 28 February 1876 he recorded: "This day took a photograph of the Temple. Aaron McDonald, Robert McQuarrie and myself, standing on the parapet . . . I next to the tower, with a white apron, next to Robert McQuarrie with a saw in his hand, then Aaron McDonald.[11] Also, in another where James Booth was photographing, I stand on the outside, one of the 12, with a white apron and a square in my hand." And on 11 December 1876, he was requested to make 80 rods of pipe (presumably wooden) to bring water to the temple. He wrote: "This was a 6 day job."[12]

By the end of 1875 the carpenters had completed a good part of the finish work in the basement, and were working room by room to install door frames and doors, moldings, and the round and arched window frames. As they finished each room the plastering crew followed immediately, bolstered by six plasterers sent to St. George by Presiding Bishop Edward Hunter.[13] In mid-January 1876, a letter sent from St. George appeared in the *Deseret News* stating that the plastering of basement walls was nearing completion. "A strong corps of plasterers was working in the basement to complete the work."[14] These men not only did

10. Laub, *Journal*, 2, Sec. III.
11. Laub, *Journal*, 81, Sec. III.
12. Laub, *Journal*, 81, Sec. III.
13. Cox, "Robert Gardner," 287.
14. Cox, "Robert Gardner," 288.

plastering but they also installed the arched plaster of paris molds over the doors in the thick tower walls.

A large quantity of plaster was needed for this work, which was supplied by the Judd limekiln at Middleton. John Schmutz was there helping make the plaster. He said it "consisted of adding sand to the lime burned by the Judd's in their limekiln at Middleton."[15] In some applications animal and likely even human hair was also added to the mix as a binder. As alluded to earlier in this book, John L. Smith and Charles Pulsipher, on two trips through towns as far north as Holden and Scipio were "gathering means to support the completion of the Temple," and gathered in the process "forty bushels of hair for use in plastering the Temple."[16] According to Walker, plastering the outside walls began about mid-November 1875.[17] By the end of March, David H. Cannon reported to the *Deseret News* that plastering of both the outside walls and the temple interior was "progressing rapidly."[18] In any event, by the onset of 1876, the temple was about to have its rough-cut red sandstone exterior forever covered with a smooth white surface.

Due to the height and size of the building, applying the outside plaster finish was a huge, difficult, and time-consuming job, requiring all the skill and patience that William Burt and his crew could bring to bear. The work started at the top. The battlements, parapet, cornices, and a very short distance down the wall could be coated from the roof. From there down and until scaffolding could be used, the work was done by lowering a worker on a "chair" suspended from the top by rope. An example was Anson Winsor, who "helped whitewash the outside of the building sitting in a hanging chair that hung from the top of the

---

15. Cox, "Robert Gardner," 288.
16. Cox, "Robert Gardner," 286. As mentioned earlier, Pulsipher makes no mention of whether they gathered human or animal hair or some of each kind.
17. Charles Lowell Walker, *Diary of Charles Lowell Walker*, edited by A. Karl Larson and Katharine Miles Larson, 2 vols. (Logan: Utah State University Press, 1980), 1:415.
18. Cox, "Robert Gardner," 288.

Temple by a rope."[19] Winsor, it will be recalled, had earlier helped his
sons supply the temple workers with beef, butter, and cheese from the
Church ranch at Pipe Springs. He had now been called to help finish
the temple. His carpentry and glazing experience enabled him to help
build "the round windows in the upper part, also the window frames
and door frames throughout the temple, some of the doors, and [the]
spiral stairs."[20] From the point where it could be reached from below,
plastering proceeded from atop the scaffolding. By early April 1876 the
outside plastering was completed and a coat of whitewash had been applied, giving the temple its distinctive white finish and making it stand
out in brilliant contrast to the reds, browns, and blacks of the surrounding bluffs.

A near-fatal accident occurred on a cold January day in 1876, not
long after the plastering began. John Burt, son of William Burt, the
man in charge of the plastering, lost his balance and fell from a scaffold
70 feet to the ground. In the fall "his body struck the puglocks bracing
the scaffold." This to some extent broke the fall. Walker saw it all: "He
lay on the ground dead, as we thot. The brethren . . . ["Elders John O.
Angus, Wm. H. Thompson, and Jos. H. Randall at once laid hands
upon his head and administered to him; Bro. Angus being speaker"[21]]
and he showed signs of life. He was taken in the arms of the brethren
to the shanties near the Temple and placed on a bed. His father asked
me to administer to him and anoint him. I did so and promised that
he should live, although after I had made the promise I felt fearfull
of my[s]elf seeing that he looked like a dead man more than anything
else. We all laid our hands upon him and the anointing was sealed by
his Father and He promised the same blessing i.e., of life and recovery.
Then I saw and felt that the Spirit of God had indicted the promises

19. Kate B. Carter, comp., *Our Pioneer Heritage* (Salt Lake City: Daughters of Utah
Pioneers, 1974), 14:404.
20. Carter, *Our Pioneer Heritage*, 14:404.
21. Nels Anderson, *Desert Saints: The Mormon Frontier in Utah* (Chicago: University
of Chicago Press, 1942), 355.

after we had taken our hands off him. He groaned a few times and in a few minutes he spoke a few words. At 4 P.M. we carried him on a cot to the Big House [in town, a mile away], that he might be thoroughly examined by the surgeon and strange to say there was not a Bone broken though he had some severe bruises. In two days after, he sat up and ate his food and with a crutch was able to walk 4 Blocks. How he escaped being smashed to peices is a mystery except that the Angels of God were nigh to him to lighten his fall, and the power of God thro the laying on of hands was manifest in his behalf. All praise and glory be unto God and the Lamb."[22] "By the blessing of the Lord he was back upon his work on the temple in a couple of weeks."[23]

Though many workers were injured during the months and years it took to build the temple, no one was killed. According to research conducted by Jewell Bringhurst,[24] Brigham Young made that promise at the time of the groundbreaking. An observer tells that when he "took the first shovel full of dirt from the place for the foundation . . . [he] stated . . . 'there would not be any person who would lose their lives on any of the works of this Temple.'"[25] Besides the near-fatal fall of John Burt, Thomas Crane fell from the top of the temple but suffered no broken bones. Will Thayne fell 35 feet off the wall and landed on his side across a large timber, but was unhurt. While the lava rocks were being pounded into the foundation, the large derrick that hoisted the cannon to pound the rock fell over and landed on Pete Granger (and perhaps a man known as Rob; see Charlie Walker's song, chapter 6), without causing any significant injury. George Lang's mule team ran away when he

22. Walker, *Diary*, 1:416–17. See also James G. Bleak, "Annals of the Southern Utah Mission," Book B, 42, typescript, Dixie State University Special Collections, St. George, Utah.

23. Anderson, *Desert Saints*, 355.

24. Jewell Bringhurst, "A Brief Sketch of St. George History," 1994, n.p., typescript, Daughters of Utah Pioneers McQuarrie Memorial Museum, St. George, Utah; copy in possession of the authors.

25. Joseph Heinerman, *Temple Manifestations* (Salt Lake City: Joseph Lyon & Associates, 1974), 64.

was hauling one of the large lava rocks from the quarry. He fell from the wagon and had an ear torn off but came out of it otherwise unhurt.[26]

After the interior plastering crew had completed a room, the plaster of paris workers, also under the direction of William Burt, stepped forward to do their jobs. Much of the plaster of paris utilized in the construction of the temple was milled by Samuel Lorenzo Adams, who had come to St. George in 1861. As soon as he had settled his family Adams built a blacksmith shop next door to his home, after which he formed a partnership "with Easton Kelsey in the building of a flour mill for the southern settlements, affording them milling for their wheat," both grown and imported. "To power this mill the west city water supply was diverted from the creek channel by a ditch or canal that ran from the water source along the mountain to the west end of Diagonal Street. Here a building was constructed of red rock, having a basement and two top stories. A fore bay was provided and a flume extended to a penstock, which conveyed the water to a water wheel that transmitted power to the grinding 'burrs' of the mill. Adams, a worker in iron, and Kelsey, a worker in wood, were able, each with his inventive genius, to make all parts of the necessary equipment for milling flour.

"When the County Court House, Tabernacle and Temple were being finished and the need of a machine to crush and roll the fine gypsum needed for the making of the plaster-of-paris decorative ornaments and inside cornices, the inventive skill of Samuel Adams provided the machine which was driven by the water power of the mill."[27]

Plaster of paris is a fine white plaster made from gypsum, pliable when wet yet tough and resilient when dry. Its most decorative forms in the temple are the large rosettes placed in the ceilings of the first and second main assembly rooms, from which interior lighting fixtures

---

26. Heinerman, *Temple Manifestations*, 65.
27. Eleanor McAllister Hall, comp., "Brief Story of the Life of Samuel Lorenzo Adams, 1833–1910," 1970, n.p., typescript; photocopy courtesy Daughters of Utah Pioneers McQuarrie Memorial Museum, St. George, Utah.

were intended to hang, though that never happened. The molds for these rosettes were hand-carved in wood by the finish carpenters. But plaster of paris was used in many other places besides the rosettes and moldings above the arched doorways through the thick tower walls on the main or second and fourth floors as well as on the mezzanine floors. The cornices that decorate the juncture of walls and ceilings in the two main assembly rooms were also made from plaster of paris, as were the two-foot-wide panels below the cornices that feature the two symbols used in the temple's interior construction, the five-pointed star and quatrefoil. In all this, however, it should be noted that the side moldings of all these doors *are* of wood, and each testifies of the hours of hand labor that went into shaping, hand planing, and sanding each one from pieces of soft pine wood.

As the temple was being made ready to open, it was planned that all the ordinances except sealings would be conducted in the basement, which was divided into eleven "rooms." The font room, centered beneath the temple, was the largest and contained the baptismal font. The other rooms, no doubt patterned after the attic story ordinance rooms in the Nauvoo Temple, included canvas-partitioned ordinance "rooms," separate men's and women's rooms for the initial or initiatory ordinances, dressing rooms, lavatories,[28] and a dining room. The basement ceiling was fourteen feet above the floor.

In the basement were also the boiler for heating water, the steam-engine pump, and the pipes through which warm water was pumped to the font and washing baths, while cold water was pumped to the top of the outside water tower. From there gravity carried the water back

---

28. As part of the original temple structure, small water closets were initially built into the outside walls of the circular staircases. Later, flushable lavatories and perhaps even showers were built into the lower levels of the hollow circular centers of the two stairs, the water gravity-fed from the top of the water tower near the northeast corner of the Temple. Tile and drain holes remain as evidence of these early facilities.

down into the temple for wash rooms, perhaps drinking facilities, and whatever other needs the Saints might have had.

Benches for patron seating in these ordinance rooms were arranged in rows, increasing their seating capacity. Examples of the benches are found today behind and alongside the priesthood pulpits on the fourth floor, and in the room behind the east assembly room pulpits. Thomas Welch tells in his study that "The benches [were] curved and shaped from 10 or 12 inch planks, being held together with groove and spline joints. These benches were glued together extremely well. The few places where the benches have cracked are not in the joints."[29] The benches were made of red pine.

The floor above the basement, which Wilford Woodruff called "the next main room over the font"[30] (today's second floor), was primarily an open floor, measuring 99 by 78 feet, with a 27-foot-high domed ceiling. It had partitioned, curtained rooms along its north side. Benches also filled this large main floor, which in the daytime was brilliantly lit as sunshine poured through the tall windows along the south wall.

According to architectural historians, at the east end of this main assembly room, between the tower support walls, were two rooms, one elevated behind the high priesthood pulpits and the other directly below it. It remains uncertain how the lower room was accessed, but the upper room was entered either by side stairs from the main front foyers or from stairs going up either side of the pulpits at the east end of what quickly became the final or celestial room, just as they still do on the second main (fourth) floor, above. These stairs entered the upper room through two narrow doors in the thick wall; they also remain the same.

It is likely these two rooms had a variety of uses during the nineteenth century, including the possibility of storage in the lower room and an office and/or sealing room in the upper, though whether this

---

29. Welch, "Early Mormon Woodworking," 27.
30. Wilford Woodruff, *Journal*, 1833–1898, ed. Scott G. Kenney, 9 vols. (Midvale, Utah: Signature, 1983), 7:311.

was the first sealing room dedicated by Brigham Young Jr. is still undetermined. The room directly above that one, now a dressing area on the third or sealing floor, may also have been the first sealing room, as evidence seems to indicate that it was used early on for sacred purposes.[31] However, starting in the first part of the twentieth century the elevated room off the celestial room was used almost exclusively as the sealing room, while at some point the room below was removed entirely.[32]

One of those who labored in 1876 to finish the temple was Thomas Cottam, who had come to St. George in 1862 with his wife, Caroline Smith Cottam. He made the little dolls mentioned earlier in this volume. After he had a home built he turned his attention to building what was called a "turning shop," located in the southwest corner of his property. His granddaughter Emma Jarvis Cottam McArthur described his shop thus:

"The first recollections I have . . . of the old shop [are of] large double doors which opened onto the sidewalk. Another door was on the east, but a large Z was burned in the double doors. . . . A work bench was along the north wall to the window . . . [and] a large boiler . . . was against the wall on the east, the end against the wall. [Grandfather] used to boil his plaster [of] paris from which he made ornaments for walls and ceilings [such as in the temple]. He got the rock from the West Mountains, had it ground fine [by Samuel Adams], then [he] boiled [it]. When the moisture is boiled out it is ready to use. . . .

"[For chair-making, Brother Cottam] and his sons cut the limbs from the cottonwood trees, hauled them to town, and there they were sawed into usable lengths, ready when seasoned to be split and turned [on his lathe] into backs, legs and rounds for chairs.

"He waded in the sloughs, cut the rushes and dragged them to the

31. At one time it was called the "prayer-circle room" and was most certainly accessed by either of the temple's two spiral staircases.

32. Architectural historians are vague about the uses of these rooms because available sources seem to contradict each other; hence we wait for future discoveries to provide more definitive information.

banks where his boys would help him load them on the wagon so the ox team could haul them to his shop. Over head in the shop was a loft where the rushes were stored. They were tied in bundles and when needed were soaked in water to make them pliable so they could be twisted in order to be neatly woven. [Also] in the shop was a hand-turned lathe. Being a skilled mechanic he made the [chair] frames nicely turned, then wove the seats in, thereby fashioning a very comfortable chair. When the seats wore out he replaced them, making them like new [again]. . . . Besides his private work he did much on the public buildings. He turned many balusters, spindles and posts. . . .

"In this shop he made . . . furniture and over a hundred rush-bottom chairs for the St. George Temple. . . . [In fact,] he and Benjamin (who was called Chairmaker) Blake made all the chairs for the St. George Temple . . . some of which [were] still in use after seventy-five years. There were two styles, one style being [Grandfather's] own [design]. He was very neat in his work."[33]

Thomas's son, Thomas Punter Cottam, who years later became one of the temple's presidents, also worked on the temple, apprenticing to William Burt as a plasterer. The first year, 1876, he worked for 75 cents per day payable in tithing scrip, which was 35 to 40 cents on the dollar. The second year he earned $1.50 per day, and when the temple was dedicated in April 1877, that led to a partnership with his employer and a lifetime career in ornamental plastering. In 1886 he was called to do ornamental plastering work in the Manti Temple, where he served for six months.[34]

---

33. William Howard Thompson, ed. and comp., and Parts Written by William Howard Thompson, with Glenna Cottam Sanderson, "Thomas Cottam and Caroline Smith Cottam," in *Thomas Cottam 1820 and His Wives Ann Howarth 1820 and Caroline Smith 1820, Descendants* (privately published, Thomas Cottam Family Organization, 1987), n.p., chapter typescript by Glenna Cottam Sanderson; photocopy courtesy Daughters of Utah Pioneers McQuarrie Memorial Museum, St. George, Utah.

34. Fern McArthur Hafen, "Thomas Punter Cottam," n.d., n.p., typescript, Daughters of Utah Pioneers McQuarrie Memorial Museum, St. George, Utah.

Chapter 14

A CHANGE IN LEADERSHIP

1876

By early 1876, Miles Romney, assistant temple architect and project superintendent, who had been severely injured in a fall from a ladder almost two years before, was again ailing. His condition was serious enough that he telegraphed Brigham Young to suggest the need for someone to take his place. The catalyst for this suggestion was the need to build the four sets of elaborate pulpits to grace each end of the temple's two main floors, a challenging project that not many were capable of doing. Romney was capable, but simply did not feel well enough to carry the project through.

On 12 April 1876, Brigham Young replied by telegram from Salt Lake City: "Regarding the pulpits, etc., would you like Brother Almond [Allman] to take Charge of the work on the Temple, if so, please inform us."[1]

Miles Romney and Thomas Allman were well acquainted with each other. Both had immigrated from England, though Allman, thirteen years younger, had come to America a year after Romney. Both

---

1. Thomas Allman History, n.d., 49. These telegrams are in possession of the Thomas Allman family; copies in possession of the authors.

were superior carpenters, craftsmen, and artisans; both knew Joseph Smith and Brigham Young personally; both had worked on the Nauvoo Temple; both worked in the public works in Salt Lake City, laboring on the Salt Lake Temple, the Lion House, and the Beehive House; both became famous for their circular staircases (Romney in the St. George tabernacle and Allman later in the Manti Temple); and both had an innate ability to supervise men and oversee large, time-consuming projects. Their only difference was that Romney preferred one architectural style, Allman another—something that apparently bothered Brigham Young very little.

On 19 May another telegram was sent from Brigham Young, who was again in St. George, to Bishop Murdock in Beaver, Utah: "Brother Allman from Provo will arrive Friday P.M. on stage. We Understand stage does not connect. Please send him on so that he Won't have to lay over till Monday."[2]

And so, ever obedient to the prophets, Thomas Allman was on his way to St. George. There he would superintend the finishing of the temple, relieving the ailing Miles Romney of further stress and exhaustion.

It didn't take Allman long to evaluate things and telegraph his report to Brigham Young, who by then was back in Salt Lake City. On 18 June, President Young replied: "Thank you for the good news of the work on the Temple contained in your telegram. Also extend to the workmen our thanks for their faithfulness, the zeal with which they are pushing forward the work."

A month later, on 17 July 1876, an already anxious President Young sent another telegram to Thomas: "To Bro. Allman:—How are things progressing on the Temple? Please report progress."

Thomas Allman responded by telegram the next day: "To Pres. B. Young: The painter is putting first coat priming on font and basement all ready for painting. Bro. Parry building [stone] walls of tank [the

---

2. Thomas Allman History, 49.

cistern beneath the Temple] and at work on one flight of steps—main ceiling is finished and centres up-going to commence side ceilings and move centre scaffold to upper room today—carpentering work is in advance of the plasterers. Have got quite a force on the stand [pulpits] of first main room. Both ranges of columns up in same ready for plaster. Capitals also going on with column and other work in upper room. We have kept the lumber closely cut up but have had sufficient right along. Thos. Allman."[3]

Thomas was not at home on 24 July 1876 when his daughter Jessie May was born in Provo. Nor was he at home two days later when his daughter Emma Jane was married to Samuel Steven Jones. Missing these key events were sacrifices that were part of his temple calling.

On 7 August Thomas sent the following telegram to President Young: "Please send the following articles for Temple to York to meet team now on the way = 1.2 gross 2-inch screws dove-tailed slot no. 14 = 2 gross one-inch screws no. 5 = 2 gross three-fourth-inch screws no. 9, all of National Screw Co. = 24 gross one and one-half inch screw no. 14, Davis Screw Co. = 2 gross one inch screw flat head no. 9, Russell Co. = 2 dozen drilled reversible four-by-four loose-rim butts O.B. Co. = 8 dozen packages of one and half inch brads = 3 doz. New butts best = 4 doz. Sash fasteners = 18 cupboard locks = 32 brass thumb buttons = 4 doz. Small brass bolts three inches long = hundred pounds glue = four hundred fifty pounds zinc white paints = six seven 0.1. Paint brushes first class = six hog hair quill tools assorted sizes. Thomas Allman."[4]

Today we might be hard-pressed to imagine sending such a shopping list to the President of the Church, let alone asking him to fill it. Yet this indicates how fully Brigham was invested in the temple's construction.

Sometime in 1876 Jesse Crosby and others freighted back from the Utah Southern railhead at York, Juab County, numerous supplies for

3. Thomas Allman History, 49.
4. Thomas Allman History, 49.

the nearly finished temple, including the glass panes, window sashes, and grids used in all the temple windows. Perhaps their loads included the supplies Brigham had sent in response to Thomas Allman's telegram.

On 17 September, Thomas sent the following telegram from St. George: "To President Brigham Young—I have to report to you that the mason work on the flights of stone steps east end will be completed next week, the plaster work in basement including cistern room will be completed in a day or two. Stair cases all completed—First main room vestry—sealing room also first tiers of side rooms completed—Upper side rooms/south completed—North side rooms and upper vestry in the course of first coating—The scaffold in the centre of upper main room will be taken down next week—Carpenter work, the columns and stands in upper main room progressing favorably—other work getting along satisfactorily. The tarring and sanding on roof completed—The conducting water pipes from roof are at the bottom of staircases—Preparations making to continue the piping to the tank—Connection has been made from font to engine room—Ought to have a force pump of sufficient capacity to furnish the necessary supply of water, also, one hundred and fifty six feet piping with pump—The plumbing work is progressing—Painter work: Painters have arrived and are busily engaged in vestry—sealing room, large main room and outer courts. The font will be completed next week—Everything is getting along pleasantly and very satisfactorily—Yours very Respectfully, Thomas Allman"[5]

On 25 September 1876, Truman Angell sent Thomas Allman this telegram: "Salt Lake City, Ut. Elder Thomas Allman. Sir:—Your letter of the 19th has just been received. You will make the [fourth floor] East stand, four feet upper platform on floor, three feet the next, two feet the next, one foot the next. The West stand say 3 feet the upper floor, 2 ft 3 ins the next, 1 ft 6 ins the next, and 9 ins to the main floor. You will

---

5. Thomas Allman History, 49.

have to add more width and advance further into the house, that you may bring each seat forward to clear the head: this you can make all right at the top of each seat and back of it as before in the other stands in the Hall below. Respectfully Yours, T. O. Angell G. R.

"P.S. President Young says he will send the letters by the time you need them."[6]

This postcript referred to the fact that Thomas Allman, along with many others, was in St. George serving without pay. Moreover, without an income flowing into his home in Provo the past several months, his large family had used up their store of food and knew not where to obtain more. Thomas finally petitioned Brigham Young for assistance, inasmuch as it had been the prophet who had issued his emergency call. On 15 January 1877, Brigham Young sent the following telegram from St. George: "To. Bp. A. O. Smoot, Provo. Dear Brother: Bros. Allman and Bergh [Berg, of Berg Mortuary, another cabinetmaker from England who was working with Thomas on the temple] have applied to me for the privilege of their families in Provo drawing necessary supplies of provisions. You will please have their need supplied from the Tithing Office and keep a separate a/c of what is paid to them respectively, and we will hereafter give you instructions how to cancel it. Let us know when the Carpet will be ready. We have a team here which we think of sending up to the terminus and in which it may be loaded and brought down. Brigham Young."[7]

Verl Allman, in his *History of Thomas Allman*, quotes four workers whose names are not identified. Yet the quotations give us some idea of the final weeks of frenzied activity before the 1 January 1877 dedication. He wrote: "One of the workers at the Temple recorded the following: 'I could see quite a change while walking through the rooms in the Tower. I came across Brother Thomas Allman, the Superintendent. After talking a little while he then showed me a large amount of stuff

6. Thomas Allman History, 50.
7. Thomas Allman History, 50.

that was ready to be put up. When coming out of the Temple he said he was going to pull down all those board shanties where I live and clear the Temple Block of everything and put up a picket fence around the Temple Block. After chatting a little while he bid me good evening and started for the Big House.'

"From another worker we read: 'Got up early in the morning and went up to Brother Burke and told him that The Boiler had given out. He told me I had better see Brother Allman. . . . I then went Over to Brother Samuel L. Adams and found what I wanted. Brother Adams said he would let Brother Allman have it if Brother Allman could replace it after a while. . . . I then went over to the Big House and found Brother Allman. He then went with me to see Brother Adams and made some arrangement and then helped me to carry it over to the Public Blacksmith to get it straightened out.'

"From another diary we read: 'At two o'clock the whistle blew to assemble at Brother John Angus' office. [They were getting ready to pay tribute to President Brigham Young and his entourage.] . . . Brother Charles Walker was carrying a banner with the inscription "WELCOME BRIGHAM YOUNG, OUR CHIEF BUILDER," and another banner carried by Defritzi [Defriez?] with the inscription "HOLINESS TO THE LORD, Zion Workmen." The first two behind the first banner were Brother Thomas Allman, the Superintendent, and Brother David Milne; the next two Brother Thomas J. Wade and Brother John Angus. . . . We sat down under a bowery on the south side of the Big House about a half hour. We then formed into line and marched out into the street in front of the Court House and the word "Halt" was given and we were dismissed until the President and Company came in sight. Then we fell into line in single file when the President's carriage drove by with his hat in his hand and bowing his head and with a smile on his countenance. The next carriage was Brigham Young Jr., and the third carriage was George Q. Cannon, and Wilford Woodruff with some others. After they had all passed the word was given to fall into double file. The word "Forward March" was then given, keeping time with the beat of the drum as far as John Angus' house when the word "Halt" was given. Then the word was given to fall into line, forward march, down to the Temple, and we were dismissed and returned to our labour. . . . '

"In the diary of a fourth workman we find: 'Tuesday, November 14, 1876. At home, writing, and P.M. at the temple. President Brigham Young, Elder Woodruff, T. O. Angel[l], Thomas Allman, and others present. Wednesday, November 15. Called on President Brigham Young, took the measure of records, so as to have a chest made to hold them in the temple. Thursday, November 16, A.M. Went to the temple, talked with Brother T. Allman. Made arrangements for a record chest to be made. Saturday, December 2, went to the temple with Brother T. Allman and Brother T. O. Angel[l], then took a walk with Brother Raleigh.'"[8]

It is evident that Thomas Allman was not only heavily involved but keenly interested in all facets of the finishing work in and around the temple.

When it was time to begin painting the Temple, the work was done under the supervision of David Milne, a Scottish convert and painter by profession. Milne was called to the Cotton Mission with his wife, Susan, at the 1867 October semiannual general conference and quickly became prominent in town.[9] He built a home and became a captain in the field artillery unit of the St. George militia. In November 1869 he was set apart as bishop of the St. George First Ward, served seven years in that calling, and afterward served a foreign mission. He painted homes in St. George and painted the St. George courthouse, which was completed in 1870. He and his son Alex did most of the painting in the tabernacle,

8. Thomas Allman History, 50.

9. Sean Paulsen, comp., *David Milne: Early Mormon Painter, a Photobiography* (privately published, 1995), 24; copy in Dixie State University Special Collections, St. George, Utah.

where he applied the technique of faux graining. Using this unique staining process he could create on the softwoods of Utah the graining likeness of expensive Eastern hardwoods.[10] He designed and painted the "Holiness to the Lord" crest and the "All-seeing Eye" that can still be seen above the stands on the front wall of the tabernacle.[11] He and his son began painting in the temple, although the records do not allow one to identify their particular work.[12] Though the details are not known, it is clear that Milne had a prominent role in the finish painting in the temple and very likely was in charge of the interior painting even as he had been in the tabernacle.[13] The tradition in the family still living in St. George holds that Milne also painted or helped to paint one or more of the murals in the early basement ordinance rooms.[14]

Andrew Karl Larson writes about the murals, giving credit for their "creation" to the "three famous [Danish] pioneer Utah artists,[15] Dan Weggeland, Carl Christian Anthon Christensen, and Samuel Jepperson [George Kirkham's talented art student],"[16] adding, without documenting his statement, that they "were called to St. George to do

10. Although the "graining" work on the pillars and other places in the tabernacle was removed during an earlier renovation, it was reapplied as part of the most recent renovation and can be seen today.

11. See discussion and photos, Paulsen, *David Milne*, 36–46.

12. Joan Lee, "David Milne, Great Grandfather of Joan Lee," n.d., n.p; photocopy courtesy Daughters of Utah Pioneers McQuarrie Memorial Museum, St. George, Utah.

13. Douglas Cox, "History of Robert Gardner, Junior," unpublished manuscript, 289; copy in possession of Richard Schmutz.

14. See discussion in Paulsen, *David Milne*. Unfortunately, no documentation exists of any murals being painted in 1877.

15. The three were born in Copenhagen, Denmark, and painted murals in the Manti, Logan, and Salt Lake temples, as well as performing work in many other sites. Larson calls Weggeland, and justly so, the "father of Utah art."

16. Though his home was in Provo, it is interesting to speculate where Jepperson went for further art training between 1875 and his return to St. George to paint temple murals in 1881 at the age of 26. Perhaps he went to study under fellow Copenhagen master artists Weggeland and Christensen.

this work."[17] It is interesting also that Terry John O'Brien, citing Larson, says these three painters arrived in St. George in 1881.[18]

Larson, writing prior to 1960, furnished concrete evidence that beautiful murals had been painted in some of the basement rooms. In the course of researching his book, published in 1961, he interviewed "many older residents of the St. George area who well remember particularly the garden scene with its attractive and dazzling display of exotic birds, trees, fruits, foliage, and flowers."[19] Two artists whose names are mentioned in a slightly later time frame are John Fairbanks, who in 1917 painted one of the rooms, and a Brother Pratt, who painted another in 1927. Unfortunately, neither of these murals was preserved during the 1937 renovation.[20]

Following the 1937 remodeling, when the ordinance rooms were removed from the basement and built on what had been called the first main floor, A. F. Everett and Peter W. Kamp were commissioned to paint new murals. Instead of being painted on solid walls, however, these large murals were painted on canvas, which was then hung on the plastered walls of the new rooms. They remained in place until the major 1973–74 remodeling when the rooms were adapted to accommodate the first temple film. At that time the murals were removed, rolled up, and taken to Salt Lake City, where they remained until 1992, when new temple president Elder J. Thomas Fyans requested that they be returned and rehung in the temple's ordinance rooms. Though portions had to

---

17. Andrew Karl Larson, *I Was Called to Dixie* (Salt Lake City: Deseret News Press, 1961), 592.

18. Terry John O'Brien, "A Study of the Effect of Color in the Utah Temple Murals" (master's thesis, Brigham Young University, 1968), 14–15, citing Larson, *I Was Called to Dixie*, 592; however, Larson does not cite that date.

19. Larson, *I Was Called to Dixie*, 592.

20. A portion of an old mural on one of the basement walls, however, did escape destruction—at least for a time. Located behind the elevator going from the basement to the celestial room and beyond, a portion of the painting was hidden behind the elevator until 1999, when workmen chipped it away in order to install a larger elevator.

be cut away to make them fit, the major portion of each mural remains on at least one wall of each ordinance room today—the artistic work of A. F. Averett and Peter W. Kamp.[21]

Because the temple's interior would have become quite warm during the summer months without air circulation, all windows were made to open.[22] There was also no central heating. Within a short time after the temple opened, however, hot water radiators were installed. Information is not available as to numbers or locations where they were placed, but radiators and pipe were purchased for that purpose near the end of 1877. Stoves were also placed in various places throughout the temple. Smoke was vented through chimneys installed up through some of the temple battlements. Several of these were blackened until they were painted over several years ago, and the openings have long since been closed off.

Concerning the finish work of the temple, another tradesman and St. George resident who began his work on the temple in 1875 was William Henry Thompson. He wrote: "Finding nothing to do at my trade in Salt Lake City, I volunteered on the Dixie Mission, and drove one of Orson Pratt's teams into this country, arriving December 3, 1861. At the outbreak of the Indian trouble I was one of those who aided in defending the people from the raids made upon them by the Indians."[23]

Thompson continued: "I was called to work on the St. George Temple in July 1875 by President Brigham Young to take charge of the setting of the heavy timbers including the roof. After that was finished I

---

21. From a conversation with St. George historian Douglas Alder.

22. The round windows were set on swivels that allowed them to be rotated to open and the tall windows in the walls of the first and second assembly room floors could be opened by pushing up from the bottom and pulling down from the top. Presumably some front and back wall windows worked the same way, and basement windows, too. If desired, the double doors opening into the side and rear of the basement and the two sets of large entry doors at the front of the temple could also have been opened. Therefore, air could have circulated into the interior of the temple at all levels.

23. William Henry Thompson, *William Henry Thompson* (privately published, Joseph Lewis Thompson Family Organization, 1976), 84–85, Brigham Young University Special Collections, Provo, Utah; copy in possession of George Peacock.

was appointed to fit up and run the wood working machinery and when the rush of this was over I was requested to put in the steam and water pipes under the basement floor to the font and bathrooms. I fitted up a circular fan as well as a jig saw for cutting circles. I also caused all the ends of timbers that was long enough for lath to be saved from which I cut nearly all the lath[24] used in the Temple. When all the lumber needed to finish the Temple was plained I was ordered to put the boiler in the Temple to be used for heating water in the font and bath tubs."[25]

On Christmas Day Thompson commenced moving the boiler into the temple, which continued until 30 December. At that time "President Young called me out of the temple and asked if we would have all things ready for Monday morning [1 January 1877], the day set for the dedication. I replied I will have all things ready in about two hours. He then said, 'Brother Thompson, I want you to go in there [pointing to the temple] and work for nothing and board yourself and stay until further orders. Will you do it?' I replied that I would go in there as long as I had anything to go on and then you must give something or send me to another place. He smiled and told his teamster to drive on and I went into the temple to fill my mission."[26]

"I . . . labored without pay until I was down to bed rock, my family not having the common necessities of life. [Afterward] I [was hired to work] on through the years as engineer of the Temple, and performing other duties therein as called upon, and on June 15, 1902, I was set apart to assist President D. H. Cannon [in the temple presidency]. On this my seventy-third birthday anniversary, I am on my thirty-seventh

---

24. Thin strips of wood laid side by side on walls and ceilings with approximately ½ inch space between each strip. Over these strips was troweled wet plaster, which not only covered the strips but oozed into the spaces between. Once dry and hardened to the wood, such lath-and-plaster walls or ceilings could last for decades.

25. Thompson, *William Henry Thompson*, 84–85.

26. Thompson, *William Henry Thompson*, 84–85.

year of labor in the St. George Temple."[27] Among other things, during those years Brother Thompson performed 20,350 baptisms for the dead.

As soon as different parts of the temple interior were plastered and received their final coat of paint, cleanup work began. The wood floors were carefully cleaned, then painted, and homemade rag carpets laid down. The Relief Society sisters performed this ongoing work, even while their husbands and sons were engaged on the grounds. One report indicates that a Sister Ivins was directing ladies washing floors and cleaning finished parts.[28]

Relief Societies of the various stakes in the area provided handmade rag carpets for the hallways and homegrown and spun silks for the altar and pulpit fringes. The Provo wool factory supplied about 1,000 square yards of "beautiful light-colored carpet" and the factory in Washington City made the rest. Relief Society sisters also made woven rag carpets for the endowment rooms in the basement.[29]

Considering the many rooms in the temple and their sizes and the extensive wall and floor surfaces, final preparation for the opening would have been a massive job, requiring many hands both male and female. No doubt the citizenry pitched in, young and old. As completion drew near, all were anxious to see the temple finished in its entire splendor, inside and out, and made ready for the 1 January 1877 partial dedication and for the beginning of the long-awaited ordinance work.

Preparation for this activity was soon under way. Sister Ann Catherine Milne, David Milne's wife, participated in all of it: cleaning, carpet making, and ordinance work once the temple opened. In her autobiography she wrote: "The Temple was open for ordinance work

---

27. R. Paul Thompson and Bernice Robinson, comps., "Personal Reminiscences" of William Henry Thompson, n.d., n.p., typescript, Daughters of Utah Pioneers McQuarrie Memorial Museum, St. George, Utah.

28. Cox, "Robert Gardner," 289.

29. Charles Lowell Walker, *Diary of Charles Lowell Walker*, edited by A. Karl Larson and Katharine Miles Larson, 2 vols. (Logan: Utah State University Press, 1980), 1:439.

on Jan. 11, 1877. I was among a group of Sisters whom President Young called upon to do any necessary work which we could do. Such work was upholstering, making carpets, cleaning, etc. Upon completion of this work, one sister asked President Young if we were now released. He said, 'No, you are to continue on as Temple workers as long as you live.'[30] This sister was one of many who served as requested.

As mentioned, Brigham Young, George Q. Cannon, and others arrived from Salt Lake City in early November to assist and oversee preparations for the partial dedication and beginning of ordinance work. On 10 November, Brigham Young, George Q. Cannon, Brigham Young Jr., and Wilford Woodruff inspected the temple "from Baptismal font in the Basement to the top of the roof and it was a glorious sight." They were impressed, and felt the spirit of the nearly finished temple. Wilford Woodruff wrote: "The power of God rested upon us."[31]

The Brethren were also busy supervising preparation of the rooms and facilities for the beginning of ordinance work. During the balance of November, Brigham Young spent time with Wilford Woodruff and Truman O. Angell "preparing [the basement] rooms for the endowment services." In December they were joined by Brigham Young Jr., Alonzo H. Raleigh, and J. D. T. McAllister in "making preparation to start endowment work." They also brought cloth with them with which to make the needed curtains.[32] Thus preparations were being made and ordinance workers trained in all aspects of the holy work for which the temple had been built.

Extensive work on the grounds was under way by late October 1876. The Temple Block was cleared of worker shanties and construction debris, thousands of loads of rich soil were hauled in and spread over the grounds to help the barren block support lawns, trees, and shrubs. The work continued through November and December. Walker reports that

30. Paulsen, *David Milne*, 52–53.
31. Cox, "Robert Gardner," 289.
32. Cox, "Robert Gardner," 289.

on Saturday, 25 November, "about 80 or 90 men [were] working on the Block plowing, scraping, hauling, and grading the ground around the Temple."[33] This volunteer labor was furnished by wards from around the stake, each with a quota, and continued every Saturday until the end of December. Though no trees or shrubs were planted until spring, men were also installing and painting a picket fence placed away from the temple but not around the entire block.[34]

An article appeared in the *Deseret Evening News* on 6 December describing the work being done by "brethren from St. George, Washington, and Santa Clara." Their goal was to grade the Temple Block and make it ready for "planting trees and shrubbery." This original landscaping amply served until 1939 when the grounds were re-landscaped during a Church-wide beautification program, done under the direction "of the stakes of the temple district."[35]

Although the estimate of $800,000 as the cost of building the temple has commonly been cited,[36] the actual cost is probably incalculable, the greater sum of it being in the form of donated materials, wagons, teams, and labor, coming from within the Southern Mission and from throughout the territory. James G. Bleak furnishes in cash amounts the sums that passed through the St. George Stake Tithing Office from 1871 through April 1876:

---

33. Walker, *Diary,* 1:435.
34. Cox, "Robert Gardner," 289.
35. Kirk M. Curtis, "History of the St. George Temple" (master's thesis, Brigham Young University, 1964), 57–58. Four years earlier, in 1935, there had been a major renovation of the interior. The canvas-framed rooms in the basement (creation, garden, and world rooms) were removed, and fixed-wall rooms were built on the main or second floor for them and the veil and celestial rooms. The east main floor priesthood stands or pulpits were also removed at this time.
36. Janice Force DeMille, *The St. George Temple: First 100 Years* (Hurricane, Utah: Homestead Publishers, 1977), 42.

For the year ending Dec. 31, 1871—   2,368.00
　　　　 "　 "　　　　 1872—   3,032.07
　　　　 "　 "　　　　 1873—   32,780.50
　　　　 "　 "　　　　 1874—   108,555.47
　　　　 "　 "　　　　 1875—   123,433.64
And for the first four months of 1876—   35,761.14
Total St. Geo. Books to date: $310,930.85[37]

Bleak also notes that other amounts of cash, such as Brigham's $5,000 donation for the baptismal font and oxen, would "no doubt" have been expended through the Office of the First Presidency and the general tithing offices in Salt Lake City. Post-January finish construction costs, which would have included the celestial room at the east end of the first main floor, and material costs were being incurred during 1877 and for a few years beyond. A report by Wilford Woodruff made as of 31 December 1883, set the cash outlay to that date at $470,394.31.[38] This would have included the cost of rebuilding the lightning-struck tower.

A very early report of the temple's appearance and impact comes from the pen of George Q. Cannon, who came to St. George with Brigham Young and company 1 November 1876 in order to be present at the 1 January 1877 dedication. Of his arrival in the St. George basin, he later wrote: "We were all eager to get a glimpse of the temple as we were crossing the hills, and when we saw it, it stood out in bold relief and in marked contrast with the black and red hills which surround the little valley in which St. George stands. The temple is pure white, and is a massive unique building. It excited peculiar emotions in all the parties to witness once more a temple erected to the Most High God."[39]

Standing on the temple grounds in Logan on 18 May 1877,

37. Bleak, "Annals," Book 1, 438.

38. DeMille, First 100 Years, 42n35.

39. Davis Bitton, George Q. Cannon: A Biography (Salt Lake City: Deseret Book, 1999), 201.

Elder John Taylor made these remarks: "In my visit south to attend Conference, I felt to rejoice exceedingly in seeing the Temple completed at St. [George]. It is a most beautiful building, pure and white as the driven snow, both outside and in. It is elegant in Design, and there is a manifest propriety and adaptability in all its arrangements. The labor and finish exhibit talent and artistic skill of the highest order, and it is chaste, exquisite, appropriate and beautiful in all its appointments. Approaching from the north, with the black basaltic lava mountain frowning on the background, and the grim red sandstone nearer its base, relieved by the beautiful city of St. George, with its shrubbery, its gardens, and orchards, its vines, its trees and flowers, the temple stands as a chaste memorial, a sweet Elysium, a haven of repose, in this beautiful oasis in the desert; and is a proud and lasting monument of its originator and designer, the fidelity of the architect, the skill of the mechanics, and the faith, self-denial, liberality and devotion of the Latter-day Saints.

"When I visited that holy Temple accompanied by my brethren who were with me, we experienced a sacred thrill of joy, and a solemn reverential sensation. As we entered its sacred portals, we felt that we were standing on holy ground, and exclaimed, with one of old, 'Surely this is the House of God, and the gate of heaven.' That is not simply a metaphorical expression, but a reality, for it is in that House . . . that the most sacred ordinances of God are to be performed, which are associated with the interest and happiness of the human family, living and dead. I felt to rejoice in my heart that we had been thus far successful in the building of one temple to the name of our Father and God."[40]

In about 1950, Albert E. Miller wrote: "The beautiful massive rock building, finished in white stucco exterior, surrounded by a great variety of semi tropical plants, stands today like a gem against a background of dark volcanic ridges. It is the first object to meet the eye of all who

---

40. *Journal of Discourses*, 26 vols. (London: Latter-day Saints' Book Depot, 1854–86), 19:22–23.

enter the valley. Seen for hundreds of miles by the aviation flyers by day and by night with the flood lights showing its glorious white surface, it stands a beacon light and guide. It is a monument to the skill, industry and faith of those who pioneered this section of the west and responded to the call of that great leader, Brigham Young, to establish the Dixie Mission."[41]

In 1946, Juanita Brooks wrote: "Almost startling in its whiteness, it seems to transcend and overshadow everything else in the town. It is a thing of permanence and beauty in the midst of the desert, an upward reaching of the spirit, a monument to the glory of God, a classic in community cooperation. . . . The Latter-day Saints have built other temples and will build more, but around none will there be more of the aura of romance, of sacrifice, and of high endeavor than accompanied this, the first in the west. After nearly 70 years it stands [almost] unchanged, still dominating the landscape. As one pilot said, 'From the air it looks like a white gem in a green setting.' It will continue to be a beacon to airplanes, a landmark to tourists, and a holy place to members of the Church."[42]

Eminent historian Andrew Karl Larson wrote: "The Temple draws the eye as to a magnet when one enters the valley. There it stands in calm dignity and cool serenity, undisturbed by the occasional violent expressions of nature or the petty weaknesses of men. Its classic beauty, framed by the foil of gray and vermilion hills flanked by the dark lava runs on opposite borders of the valley, conveys a sense of graceful solidity, a vital sobriety, a rich simplicity, and a restrained grandeur. Unobtrusively it inspires a contentment of mind, a tranquility of spirit, and a feeling that under its shadow one may forget for a moment the troublesome burdens of a strife-torn world. In it one sees the

41. Hazel Bradshaw, ed., and Washington County Chapter Daughters of Utah Pioneers, *Under Dixie Sun* (Panguitch, Utah: Garfield County News, 1950), 343.

42. Juanita Brooks, "St. George, the City with a Heritage," *Utah Magazine*, August 1936, 38.

culmination of the devoted efforts of devout men and women, gifted with a great sensitivity to the qualities that constitute great art. They are gone. But the beauty created by their ideas and their handiwork remains to embody 'the sensible image of the Infinite.'"[43]

Thus the temple has appeared to the eyes of its beholders, from the earliest times to the present, a monument to the faith, imagination, prodigious labor, and sacrifices of those who built it. And ever since, it has served the holy purposes that motivated their sacrifices. H. Lorenzo Reid said it well: "Seldom have men worked with greater devotion. For over [five] years the structure gradually moved toward completion with no word of complaint from workers or donors, but with all hopefully looking forward to the day when the Temple would be completed and they could enter its sacred walls to perform the [sacred] rites for themselves and their kindred dead."[44]

43. Larson, *I Was Called to Dixie*, 592.

44. H. Lorenzo Reid, *Dixie of the Desert* (St. George, Utah: Zion Natural History Association, 1964), 237.

Chapter 15

PREPARING FOR THE TEMPLE DEDICATION

November through December 1876

While Joseph Smith was translating the gold plates, he came upon the following passage: "For behold, thus saith the Lord God: I will give unto the children of men line upon line, precept upon precept, here a little and there a little; and blessed are those who hearken unto my precepts, and lend an ear unto my counsel, for they shall learn wisdom; for unto him that receiveth I will give more; and from them that shall say, We have enough, from them shall be taken away even that which they have."[1]

Though we don't know how quickly the young prophet understood all the messages in this profound verse, we are blessed to understand several things today. First, the Lord intentionally gives us a little bit of knowledge or understanding at a time. Second, He does this out of love and concern for us. Third, he determines by our reaction whether or not we are willing to listen and obey. Fourth, as a reward for listening he gives us more. Fifth, as a protection from too much accountability if we

---

1. 2 Nephi 28:30. See also Isaiah 28:10; Doctrine and Covenants 98:12; 128:21.

decide not to listen, he takes away that which we have. And sixth, this entire divine process allows us to develop wisdom.

So it was with the gospel's restoration. Every blessing or understanding Joseph ever received from the Lord came a little at a time—line upon line; precept upon precept. All Joseph had to do was diligently seek, and as he applied himself to what had already come, more was added to it. Almost from the beginning of his and Joseph's relationship, Brigham recognized this process in his beloved friend, and by the time of Joseph's martyrdom it had become so much a part of Brigham's own nature, his own thinking, that we might say it was almost automatic. Nothing better illustrates this than events in the fall of 1876, when there began a major scramble in St. George on two fronts. The first was to put the physical structure of the temple in order so actual ordinance work could begin, for both the living and the dead. The second was to organize and refine the presentation and administration of the various ordinances and finally commit them to writing. These ordinances, according to Bruce R. McConkie, "are of such a sacred and holy nature that the Lord authorizes their performance only in holy sanctuaries prepared and dedicated for that very purpose. Except in circumstances of great poverty and distress, these ordinances can be performed only in temples, and hence they are commonly called *temple ordinances.*

"Baptism for the dead, an ordinance opening the door to the celestial kingdom to worthy persons not privileged to undergo gospel schooling while in mortality, is a temple ordinance, an ordinance of salvation. All other temple ordinances–washings, anointings, endowments, sealings—pertain to exaltation within the celestial kingdom. Celestial marriage is the gate which puts man on the path leading to the highest of three heavens within the celestial world. (D&C 131:1–4.)

"All of these ordinances of exaltation are performed in the temples for both the living and the dead. Their essential portions have been the same in all dispensations when the fulness of the sealing power has been exercised by the Lord's prophets. (D&C 124:28–41.) They were given in modern times to the Prophet Joseph Smith by revelation."[2]

According to Orson Hyde, the presentation of these ordinances began as Joseph, the Twelve Apostles, and a few trusted others met in regularly called councils. "In one particular Council," Elder Hyde continues, "Joseph seemed somewhat depressed in Spirit, and took the liberty to open his heart to us concerning his presentiments of the future. His own language to us on that occasion, as nearly as we can recollect, was as follows:

"'Brethren, the Lord bids me hasten the work in which we are engaged. He will not suffer that you should wait for your endowment until the Temple is done. Some important scene is near to take place. It may be that my enemies will kill me, and in case they should, and the keys and power which rest on me not be imparted to you, they will be lost from the earth; but if I can only succeed in placing them upon your heads, then let me fall a victim to murderous hands if God will suffer it, and I can go with all pleasure and satisfaction, knowing that my work is done and the foundation laid on which the kingdom of God is to be reared in this dispensation of the fulness of times. Upon the shoulders of the Twelve must the responsibility of leading this Church hence forth rest until you shall appoint others to succeed you. Your enemies cannot kill you all at once, and should any of you be killed, you can lay your hands upon others and fill up your quorum. Thus can this power and these Keys be perpetuated in the Earth.'"[3]

Having made that announcement, Joseph immediately set about carrying it out. First he went to visit at least one of the Nauvoo

---

2. Bruce R. McConkie, *Mormon Doctrine*, 2d ed. (Salt Lake City: Bookcraft, 1966), 779.

3. See Jedediah M. Grant, *A Collection of Facts Relative to the Course Taken by Elder Sidney Rigdon in the States of Ohio, Missouri, Illinois and Pennsylvania* (Philadelphia: Brown, Bicking & Guilbert, 1844), n.p. See also Alexander L. Baugh and Richard Neitzel Holzapfel, "I Roll the Burthen and Responsibility of Leading This Church Off from My Shoulders on to Yours," *BYU Studies* 49, no. 3 (2010): 10.

seamstresses, Elizabeth Warren Allred, wife of one of his bodyguards, James Allred. With fabric he had brought with him the Prophet showed her the pattern of the sacred clothing he had received by revelation, and she immediately agreed to cut and stitch it as instructed.[4]

Once a sufficient number of such items had been sewn, Joseph went on to the next step. Lucius N. Scoville later recalled, "I can testify that on the 3rd day of May, 1842, Joseph Smith the Prophet called upon five or six, viz: Shadrack Roundy, Noah Rogers, Dimmick B. Huntington, Daniel Cairns, and myself (I am not certain but that Hosea Stout was also there) to meet with him . . . in his business office (the upper part of his brick store). He told us that the object he had for us was to go to work and fit up that room preparatory to giving endowments to a few Elders that he might give unto them all the keys of power pertaining to the Aaronic and Melchizedek Priesthoods.

"We therefore went to work making the necessary preparations . . . , [Joseph] being with us and dictating everything."[5] He instructed the men to divide "the main room to represent the various stages in man's eternal progress."[6]

Scoville adds that Joseph "gave us many items that were very interesting to us, which sank with deep weight upon my mind, especially after

---

4. Diary of James T. S. Allred; Letter to Colonel Williams; d.1021/f.92, end of roll #2; July 10, 1844 (from Record of Asena Allred Osborne, Spring City, Utah, 1 August 1951). Taken from history of Eliza Monson, whose great-grandmother was Elizabeth Warren Allred. To that has been added the following summary: "The seamstress hired by Joseph Smith had to cut out the garment three times to get it correct. It indicates the exactness of the pattern to be followed. The minor deviations which she made were not acceptable or approved by the Prophet." Photocopy in possession of the authors.

5. Lucius N. Scoville, "The Higher Ordinances," January [February] 2, 1884, *Deseret News Semi-Weekly*, February 15, 1884, 2; copy in possession of the authors.

6. Richard O. Cowan, *Temples to Dot the Earth* (Salt Lake City: Bookcraft, 1989), 53. See also Dimick B. Huntington, "Oral Reminiscences," Salt Lake City, 12 December 1878; copy in possession of the authors. Huntington wrote: "William Felshaw, Samuel Rolfe, and [myself], Dimick B. Huntington prepared the . . . room in the brick store [upper] chamber for the first endowments. Took some bars of lead to hold up the trees of the garden and a piece of carpet for [a] curtain, Joseph Smith giving directions how to prepare all things."

the temple was finished at Nauvoo, and I had received the ordinances in which I was among the first, as I had been called upon to work in the temple as one of the hands during the winter . . . he told us that we should have the privilege of receiving the whole of the ordinances in due time. The history of Joseph Smith speaks for itself. But I can and do testify that I know of a surety that room was fitted up by his order which we finished in the forenoon of the said 4th of May, 1842."[7] With these preparations completed, "later that same day the first endowments were given."[8]

The day following, Joseph added, "The remainder of the council of yesterday continued their meeting at the same place, and myself and Brother Hyrum [Smith] received in turn from the others, the same that I had communicated to them the day previous."[9]

And so had begun the great work of modern-day temples. It was not, however, a static or unchangeable process. As Richard Cowan has written: "By means of two letters written during the first week of September 1842 the Prophet [Joseph] gave yet further instructions concerning work for the dead. He emphasized the importance of having a recorder present; not only to keep an accurate record, but also to assure that each ordinance is done properly. (D&C 127:6; 128:3.) The Prophet linked this keeping of proper records with the power to bind or loose on earth and have this action recognized in heaven. He indicated that in all ages any ordinance that is performed 'truly and faithfully' by proper authority and properly recorded would be recognized in heaven. (D&C 128:8–9; compare Matthew 16:18–19.) This power to 'bind on earth'

---

7. Scoville, "Higher Ordinances," 2.

8. Cowan, *Temples to Dot the Earth*, 53–54. He adds: "Those receiving these blessings on that day were Hyrum Smith (Associate President and Patriarch to the Church); William Law (Second Counselor in the First Presidency); elders Brigham Young, Heber C. Kimball, and Willard Richards of the Quorum of the Twelve (who would form the new First Presidency just over five years later); Stake President William Marks; Bishops George Miller and Newell K. Whitney; and James Adams (a patriarch and branch president in Springfield, Illinois)."

9. Joseph Smith, *History of The Church of Jesus Christ of Latter-day Saints*, edited by B. H. Roberts, 2d ed. rev., 7 vols. (Salt Lake City: The Church of Jesus Christ of Latter-day Saints, 1932–51), 5:2–3.

and in heaven was associated with the keys which Elijah had restored in 1836. . . . Finally, expanding on the writings of Paul, Joseph Smith declared that 'they (the fathers) without us cannot be made perfect— neither can we without our dead be made perfect.' And that 'their salvation is necessary and essential to our salvation.' This is so because in the celestial kingdom we will be organized as God's family according to the patriarchal order. Hence he taught that there must be 'a welding link of some kind or other between the fathers and the children.' (D&C 128:15, 18.) Vicarious ordinances for the dead, he reiterated, were the means of establishing this link."[10]

From what little was recorded, it seems obvious that Joseph's first administrations of the ceremony were done by lecture only, as no one else had been endowed and trained to assist him. As far as is known, no written text of the 1842 or 1843 procedure exists, nor is there any record of Joseph administering more endowment ordinances prior to his death in 1844.

It took more than a year following Joseph's and Hyrum's martyrdom for the Nauvoo Temple to be sufficiently ready that the attic floor could be dedicated for the performance of temple ceremonies. On 4 December 1845, according to Heber C. Kimball: "About 2 in the afternoon went to the Temple. . . . Soon after P. Pratt, O. Hyde ingaged in putting up canvas and other things to prepare our room. W.W. Phelps brought in some sedars [cedars] to adorn our garden [room]. About sun set Bishop N. K. [Whitney] come in with the Vail, the old one and the new one."[11] The following day Brother Kimball added that his wife, Vilate, and their daughter "Came in for the purpose of Heming" the veil,[12] which was symbolic of the barrier between this life and the next.[13] The day after

10. Cowan, *Temples to Dot the Earth*, 55.
11. Heber C. Kimball Journal, 4 December 1845, in Stanley B. Kimball, ed., *On the Potter's Wheel: The Diaries of Heber C. Kimball* (Salt Lake City: Signature, 1987), 158. We assume "the old one" refers to the veil Joseph used in the room above his store.
12. Kimball, *Potter's Wheel*, 159.
13. Temple veils (also spelled *vail*) are mentioned frequently in both the Old and New

that he added: "The trees set in order in the garden. Sister Elizabeth Ann Whitney came in and sowed on the fringe, going over the top of the canvas running threw the room crost from north to south. . . . Sister Clarisa and Emily Cutler mad[e] a Coten [curtain] going before the Linnen veil"[14] that had been hung previously.

On the following Sunday, 7 December 1845, most of those who had received the ceremony previously met in the temple attic. There Brigham gave them "a view of the Seprate rooms, and the object of them, then pute up the veil and choe [showed] the Order of it. The Brethren and Sisters clothed [at] half past one [and] commenced our meeting at two O'clock"[15] with prayers and supplication to the Heavens that they be allowed time to accomplish the Lord's will in that House.

The members of the Twelve began administering the endowment on Wednesday, 10 December 1845. William Clayton recorded for Heber C. Kimball: "At 3 o clock Sister Mary Ann Young and Vilate Kimball, Elizabeth Ann Whitney, commenced [administering the initial ordinances to] each other being the first in this holy Temple of the Lord."[16] Besides making final adjustments to the room, in a separate room Brigham and Heber C. Kimball administered the same initial blessings to Willard Richards.

Finally, "at 20 minutes to 8 o'clock President Young announced that

Testaments, informing us, for instance, that the veil of the temple that was rent at the time of Christ's crucifixion was hung between the Holy Place and the Holy of Holies (LDS Bible Dictionary, 782). Further references to veils are in Exodus 26:31–35; 36:35; 40:3; Leviticus 16:3; Numbers 18:7; Matthew 27:51; Mark 15:38; Luke 23:45; 1 Corinthians 13:12; 2 Corinthians 3:13–16; Hebrews 6:12–19; 9:2–8; 10:16–25.

14. Kimball, *Potter's Wheel*, 162–63.

15. Kimball, *Potter's Wheel*, 164.

16. William Clayton, *An Intimate Chronicle: The Journals of William Clayton*, ed. George D. Smith (Salt Lake City: Signature, 1991), 203–4. See also James B. Allen and Thomas G. Alexander, eds., *Manchester Mormons: The Journal of William Clayton, 1840–1842* (Salt Lake City: Peregrine Smith, 1974), and James B. Allen, *Trials of Discipleship: The Story of William Clayton, a Mormon* (Urbana: University of Illinois, 1987).

all things were now ready to commence and go through with the ordinances. He said that after we get properly organized and ready to go on without confusion, no person will be permitted to talk, nor walk about in the main rooms, neither would any person be expected to be in the celestial room only those who were necessary to carry on the work. At the same hour he took the chair and appointed P. P. Pratt and John Taylor to assist him in taking those through who were now prepared. . . . These went through all the ordinances until they were passed through the veil, at which time it was half past nine o clock. President Young then called all present into the celestial room where we kneeled down and Amasa Lyman offered up prayers. Some of the brethren and sisters then retired home and the rest continued . . . taking [others] through the whole ordinance until half past 3 o clock in the morning."[17]

It is apparent that Brigham was already changing the way "the story of man's eternal journey" was presented, using the scriptural experiences of Adam and Eve and Satan as examples.[18] In addition to the "instructions that enable participants to make this journey most meaningful, the making of covenants, and the receiving of blessings promised to the obedient" as the recipients moved about "the main room [that had been divided by canvas partitions into various compartments] to represent the various stages in man's eternal progress," previously endowed individuals were now being called upon to take part and even to play certain roles.[19] It must have been obvious to all that this enhanced

17. Clayton, *Intimate Chronicle*, 204.

18. Stanley P. Hirshon, *The Lion of the Lord: A Biography of Brigham Young* (New York: Alfred A. Knopf, 1969), 111.

19. Cowan, *Temples to Dot the Earth*, 53. We can assume that these various rooms represented the world's creation, the Garden of Eden, the fallen or wicked world, the terrestrial or future world of the righteous, and, beyond the temple veil, a final room representing celestial holiness and glory, for that was the pattern in Salt Lake City's Endowment House and later in St. George. See 1 Corinthians 15:40–41, note 40a.

the presentation, for in the days and weeks that followed, additional changes were made and further roles assigned.[20]

At the end of the third day, Friday, 12 December, Clayton recorded: "During the whole of the three days already spent in the [temple], President Young presided and dictated the ordinances and also took an active part in nearly every instance except when entirely overcome by fatigue through his constant labors to forward the work."[21] That intensity of service continued with Brigham and the others who had been called to officiate in the ordinances, so that "during the next eight weeks, nearly 5,600 members (males and females) participated in these ceremonies."[22]

From 1846 until 1877 and the opening of the St. George Temple, the mode of presentation of the ceremonies no doubt evolved even more, at least to fit the circumstances or locations wherein the ordinances were administered—Brigham Young's Salt Lake City office, the Council House, and the Endowment House. But since Joseph had specifically given Brigham the responsibility to "organize and systematize all these ceremonies,"[23] we should not be surprised to learn that President Young did just that, frequently adjusting the process and even the wording to make the flow more coherent and manageable.

From then until now the ordinances have remained essentially as Joseph received and then presented them. What has changed through the years, in certain respects significantly, are the procedures. These, which include some of the dialogue and modes of presentation, developed and were altered according to understanding and circumstances as the spirit of prophecy and revelation dictated.

Based upon occasional brief entries in Wilford Woodruff's journal

---

20. Clayton, *Intimate Chronicle*, 210. Clayton records at least three new roles that were added at this time.

21. Clayton, *Intimate Chronicle*, 209.

22. Lyndon W. Cook, *Revelations of the Prophet Joseph Smith: A Historical and Biographical Commentary of the Doctrine and Covenants* (Salt Lake City: Deseret Book Company, 1981), 251.

23. Cowan, *Temples to Dot the Earth*, 55.

that begin on 25 January 1877, we know that the dramatic or theatri-cal presentation of early portions of the ceremony was continuing in the new St. George Temple. Elder Woodruff noted of his own activi-ties: "Presided in the Temple and Officiated [on the session]."[24] He then listed some of the roles he and others took on that particular day.

Cowan's narrative continues: "While the Saints were struggling to get established in the Rocky Mountains, Church-sponsored activities were limited. Emphasis in temple work was on providing needed ordinances for the living,"[25] with "at least 2,220 endowments for the living administered in the Council House."[26] Meanwhile, work for the dead stopped almost completely following the exodus from Nauvoo. Even with the opening of the Endowment House in 1855, this pattern did not change. Official rec-ords indicate that only thirty-three deceased couples were sealed vicari-ously during the pre-Endowment House period, and no such ordinances at all were performed during the following decade. Similarly, there is a record of only one baptism for the dead in 1855 and of only two in 1857, and of no others during the Saints' first two decades in Utah.

Richard E. Bennett, who has done extensive research into these matters, writes: "Despite the completion of the Salt Lake Council House in December 1850 and later the Salt Lake Endowment House in 1855, and notwithstanding the ongoing efforts at building the Salt Lake Temple, this era [1850–1870] marked a comparative wilderness retreat from temple labors. Economic self-preservation, colonization, missionary work, the gathering, and challenges involved in living the principle of plural marriage—all these and more took priority over temple work."[27]

---

24. Wilford Woodruff, *Journal, 1833–1898*, ed. Scott G. Kenney, 9 vols. (Midvale, Utah: Signature, 1983), 7:324.

25. Cowan, *Temples to Dot the Earth*, 71–72.

26. Richard E. Bennett, "Line upon Line, Precept upon Precept: Reflections on the 1877 Commencement of the Performance of Endowments and Sealings for the Dead," *BYU Studies* 44, no. 3 (2005). 49.

27. Speaking at the cornerstone laying of the Salt Lake Temple in 1853, President Brigham Young said: "There are but few, *very few* of the Elders of Israel now on earth, who know the *meaning* of the word *endowment*. To know, they must

Though Brigham might not have appreciated the word *retreat*, Bennett is correct in his assessment. The myriad challenges of the unsettled American West forced a lengthy hiatus to temple work and temple building. However, this does not mean Brigham had forgotten about or abandoned these doctrines and ceremonies. Better than anyone he knew the responsibility Joseph's last charge had placed upon him. Better than anyone he knew what the Lord expected of the Latter-day Saints in terms of temple building and temple work. And better than anyone Brigham understood the significance of the "keys of the kingdom" that Elijah had restored in Kirtland and that he now held in their fullness; he knew the power in these keys, their blessings, and their incredible potential for uniting the repentant in an unbroken chain of eternal families from the end to the beginning.

Fortunately, he also understood the Lord's law of "line upon line, precept upon precept; here a little and there a little."[28] And though he selected the site of the Salt Lake Temple within days of his 1847 entrance into the valley and yearned to have it built and dedicated, perhaps he sensed that it would be premature to actively motivate his people toward temple work and temple service until they actually had a temple in their midst.

Historian Nels Anderson wrote that Brigham "was a practical and puritanical Vermonter [who] had been a mechanic, a carpenter, and a builder."[29] His Utah sermons certainly reflect this. But his sermons also reflect his unwavering faith not only in the visions, revelations, and the teachings of Joseph Smith, but in the fact that one day the Saints would again dedicate a temple. As an example, Charlie Walker recorded in St.

---

experience; and to experience, a Temple must be built" (*Journal of Discourses*, 26 vols. (London: Latter-day Saints' Book Depot, 1854–86), 2:31; emphasis in original. See also Richard E. Bennett, "Which Is the Wisest Course? The Transformation in Mormon Temple Consciousness, 1870–1893" (paper presented at the Mormon History Association Conference, St. George, Utah, 27 May 2011), 3.

28. Doctrine and Covenants 128:21.

29. Nels Anderson, *Desert Saints: The Mormon Frontier in Utah* (Chicago: University of Chicago Press, 1942), 42.

George on 24 January 1875: "Br Brigham spoke a short time. . . . Spoke encouragingly as to the willingness of the people to go here or there, or to do what was required of them, even more so now than in the days of Joseph Smith. He wished the brethren working on the different departments of the Temple to prosecute the work with diligence. Said he felt to bless the saints and the Zion of our god."[30]

Once such a dedication occurred, then would be the moment when Brigham's preaching would change and Joseph's glorious doctrines concerning work for the dead and eternal exaltation for all, would again take root in the minds and hearts of the people.

As Bennett puts it, "in today's Church, temple attendance and worthiness are synonymous with spiritual rejuvenation and personal obedience." In Brigham's day, by choice hammered into place through overwhelming necessity, the spiritual focus was on more immediate concerns: missionary work, "obedience to the Ten Commandments, the law of tithing, and adherence to celestial [plural] marriage."[31]

This intentional refocusing by Brigham and other Church leaders becomes even more obvious when it is realized that many of the Prophet Joseph's revelations concerning temple work—including Moroni's prophecy to the youthful Joseph concerning the hearts of the fathers and the children being turned toward one another, and the 1836 visit of Elijah and the sealing powers he restored in fulfillment of that prophecy[32]—were events relatively unknown among the Saints until 1876. Only then were they included in the Doctrine and Covenants and canonized by general conference vote in 1880.[33]

Brigham obviously knew of these unpublished revelations, having been present when most of them were revealed to the Prophet Joseph,

---

30. Charles Lowell Walker, *Diary of Charles Lowell Walker*, edited by A. Karl Larson and Katharine Miles Larson, 2 vols. (Logan: Utah State University Press, 1980), 1:397.
31. Bennett, "Wisest Course," 4.
32. See Doctrine and Covenants 2; 110:14–15.
33. See Bennett, "Wisest Course," 8.

having had Joseph both teach and expound upon them in private meetings of the Twelve, and having experienced firsthand the peace and power of their doctrines and ordinances when they were put into practice. Yet Joseph hadn't sermonized on any of them except the purpose and power of Elijah's mission, and even then it may have seemed to most Church members that he was referring to Elijah's mission as if it were still in the future, not behind him in 1836.[34] Following Joseph's example, neither did Brigham delve into such things following their expulsion from Nauvoo, not until 1852 when he believed the Saints were firmly enough established in Utah to begin construction of the Salt Lake Temple. Only then did he agree with Willard Richards to publish section 110 of the Doctrine and Covenants in the *Deseret News* and a year later in the *Millennial Star*.[35]

Despite Brigham's fondest hopes, however, for a host of reasons a dedicated temple continued to elude the Saints. So, despite these two publications, most of the Church members did not fully grasp the significance of temple work or Elijah's life-changing mission. And despite occasional sermons by Brigham and others of the Brethren, neither would they understand for another 24 years, when the St. George Temple was finally nearing completion. Only then, the aged prophet knew, were the people truly ready for such glorious doctrines to be preached and ordinances administered.

As Bennett puts it: "The significance of Section 110 to temple work should not be underestimated. If not on their radarscope before 1876, it virtually lit up Church leadership conversations thereafter, like an overloaded circuit board. It was as if they had discovered a long neglected,

34. For instance, Joseph said: "But [how is] . . . this important mission . . . to be fulfilled[?] The keys *are to be* delivered, the spirit of *Elijah is to Come*" (Andrew F. Ehat and Lyndon W. Cook, comps. and eds., *The Words of Joseph Smith* (Provo, Utah: Brigham Young University, Religious Studies Center, 1980), 318, 21 January 1844; emphasis added. See also Ehat and Cook, *Words*, 43, 5 October 1840; 327–32, 10 March 1844.

35. See Trevor R. Anderson, "Doctrine and Covenants Section 110: From Vision to Canonization" (master's thesis, Brigham Young University, 2010), 12–13, 54–55.

highly effective farm tool or combine to affect a much greater harvest of temple attendance. Said John Taylor in Salt Lake City in October 1877: 'Why a desire to build Temples? What for? That we may administer therein in these ordinances in which we are so greatly interested. You heard through Brother Woodruff how many more administrations there had been for the dead than for the living. This is because Elijah has been here and has delivered the keys that turn the hearts of the children to the fathers and we are beginning to feel after them. Hence we are building a temple here, one in Sanpete, another in Cache Valley, and we have one already built in Saint George. . . . Do we devote our labor and our means? Yes, we do; and it is this spirit which rests upon us that is prompting us to do it, and it will not rest until these things are done.'"[36]

Research by Bennett indicates, in fact, that numerous other revelations or sections were added to the 1876 edition of the Doctrine and Covenants, all of which were canonized by general conference vote in October 1880. "These included not only sections 109 and 110 with their emphasis on Elijah and the Kirtland Temple, but also sections 2, 121–123, 132, and other temple related revelations."[37] He concluded: "In all, 26 sections were added: 2, 13, 77, 85, 87, 108–111, 113–118, 120–123, 125–126, 129–132, and 136."[38]

Whatever the contributing factors may have been, by the late 1860s vicarious ordinances were being performed in increasing numbers under the direction of inspired leaders. For example, Wilford Woodruff recorded in his journal that during 1870 he had personally witnessed

---

36. Journal History of The Church of Jesus Christ of Latter-day Saints, 12 December 1877, Church History Library, Salt Lake City, Utah, hereafter cited as Church History Library.

37. Bennett, "Wisest Course," 7. Bennett adds concerning Trevor Anderson's thesis: "[He] has shown that, although Warren Cowdery preserved this vision in writing, Joseph Smith—for a variety of reasons—never directly referenced it in any of his Nauvoo sermons. Nor did Oliver Cowdery (or more noteworthy, Brigham Young). The first time it was published was in November 1852 in the *Deseret News* by direction of Willard Richards and a year later in the *Millennial Star*."

38. Bennett, "Wisest Course," 8n8.

4,400 baptisms for the dead performed in the Endowment House by elders Joseph F. Smith and Samuel H. B. Smith.[39] In 1872 President Brigham Young declared: "We are now baptizing for the dead, and we are sealing for the dead, and if we had a temple prepared, we should be giving [all other ordinances] for the dead—for our fathers, mothers, grandfathers, grandmothers, uncles, aunts, relatives, friends and old associates." He testified that the Lord was "stirring up the hearts" of many people to search out their pedigrees "and it will continue and run on from father to father, father to father, until they get the genealogy of their forefathers as far as they possibly can."[40]

"Nevertheless, there are some of the sealing ordinances that cannot be administered in the house that we are now using," President Young explained in 1863. "We can only administer in it some of the first ordinances of the Priesthood pertaining to the endowment. There are more advanced ordinances that cannot be administered there."[41] By way of further explanation, Brigham also taught that ordinances designed "to connect the chain of the Holy Priesthood from Father Adam until now, by sealing children to their parents, being sealed for our forefathers, etc., . . . cannot be done without a Temple. . . . Neither will children be sealed to their living parents in any other place than a Temple." In 1865, he therefore urged couples to be endowed before their marriage and to be married or sealed by proper authority; otherwise their children could not be theirs as "heirs to the priesthood." President Young also specified that "no one can receive endowments for another, until a Temple is prepared in which to administer them."[42]

An 1876 circular letter from the First Presidency and the Twelve acknowledged these restrictions but challenged the Saints to overcome

---

39. Woodruff, *Journal*, 6:586.

40. Cowan, *Temples to Dot the Earth*, 72. See also *Journal of Discourses*, 15:138, 24 August 1872.

41. *Journal of Discourses*, 10:254, 6 October 1863.

42. Cowan, *Temples to Dot the Earth*, 72–73. See also *Journal of Discourses*, 16:186–87; Woodruff, *Journal*, 6:232, 13 July 1865.

them: "We feel led to say to the Latter-day Saints throughout these mountains: 'Let us arise and build Temples unto our God at such places as He shall designate, into which we and our children can enter and receive those blessings that He has in store for us.' The First Presidency now called for the construction of two temples [Manti and Logan] in addition to those already under way in Salt Lake City and St. George, and called on ward bishops to provide donated labor for this task."[43]

Cowan added: "With such a small population in the area during the early 1870s, many wondered why a temple was . . . built in St. George [at all]. President John Taylor later pointed out that 'it was found that our Temple in Salt Lake City would take such a long time to build, it was thought best,' to erect another one in southern Utah. In the warmer climate, construction could proceed the year around. Furthermore, President Taylor continued, 'there was a people living here who were more worthy than any others. . . . God inspired President Young to build a Temple here because of the fidelity and self-abnegation of the people.'"[44]

The first individual we know of who was called at Brigham's direction to be a St. George Temple worker, who had to come south from Salt Lake City in order to fulfill his assignment, was John Daniel Thompson McAllister, better known as John or J. D. T. In Salt Lake City he was serving as city fire chief and sergeant at arms in the legislative council, where he was required to attend all council meetings. He was also territorial marshal as well as city marshal (two separate elections), and was a counselor to the bishop of the Eighth Ward. Additionally he had seven wives with families, served two days a week in the Endowment House, and in his "spare time" was foreman of Brigham Young's woolen factory.

In the midst of all that, Brigham Young asked for a Saturday meeting with him. On that day, "September 16, 1876, McAllister called at

43. James R. Clark, comp., *Messages of the First Presidency of The Church of Jesus Christ of Latter-day Saints*, 6 vols. (Salt Lake City: Bookcraft, 1965–75), 2:278–80.

44. Cowan, *Temples to Dot the Earth*, 74. See also *Journal of Discourses*, 23:14, 9 November 1881.

President Brigham Young's [Salt Lake City] office, and President Young called him 'to go to St. George to work in the Temple there.' . . . On Monday, 9 October, John D.T. and his 7th wife, Matilda Christina Nielsen,[45] loaded up the wagon and said good-bye to all and started for St. George. . . . After a journey of twelve days, they arrived in St. George on Saturday, October 21, 1876 at 2:30 p.m. . . . [On Sunday] John and Matilda, in company with Nellie McAllister [John's cousin's wife], Sam Adams, and Nephi Sheets, visited the Temple . . . [and were] taken through it on a tour by John Angus and Wm. Frost. . . . John wrote: 'It is splendid, beautiful, and heavenly.'"[46]

Meanwhile, Wilford Woodruff, accompanying Brigham Young's party, arrived in St. George on 9 November 1876, and after touring the temple the next day with Brigham Young, George Q. Cannon, J. D. T. McAllister, and Brigham Young Jr., recorded in his journal: "I visited the Temple and went through every depart[ment] of it from the Baptismal font in the Basement to the top of the roof and it was a glorious sight. The power of God rested upon us. The Temple is nearly finished and will soon be ready for dedication. The Temple in St. George is 143 feet long, 93 feet wide, 84 feet high to the square and is as white as snow both inside and out and is a Beautiful Contrast with the red appearance of the surrounding country. The Stands at the Melchizedek and Aaronic Priesthoods were Plain but very beautiful. The following are the letters to be placed upon the East Stand:

"P.M.P.H. President of the Melchizedek Priesthood

"P.S.Z. President of the Stake of Zion

---

45. Besides Matilda Christina Nielsen, McAllister was married to first wife, Ellen Handley; second wife, Angeline Sophronia Goforth; third wife, Cornelia Agatha Lenzi; fourth wife, Alvina Mackley; and fifth and sixth wives Ann Davis Hailstone and Margaret Ann Fackander. In St. George he married two additional wives, Ann Eliza Wells (eighth), and Ann Moller (ninth), though his marriage to Ann Moller was an eternal marriage only as they never lived together.

46. Lucile McAllister Weenig, comp., *Biography of John Daniel Thompson McAllister, Utah Pioneer, Second President of the St. George Temple and of the Manti Temple of The Church of Jesus Christ of Latter-day Saints* (privately published, 1980), 50.

"P.H.P.Q. President of the High Priests Quorum

"P.E.Q. President of the Elders Quorum

"Letters upon the west stand are as follows:

"P.A.P. President of the Aaronic Priesthood

"P.P.Q. President of the Priests Quorum

"P.T.Q. President of the Teachers Quorum

"P.D.Q. President of the Deacons Quorum

"The [two] main hall[s] of the Temple [are] 99 feet long 78 feet wide.

"After passing over the House we returned to our abode."[47]

Three days later—a Monday—Brother Woodruff recorded: "I went down to the Temple with Br Angel and looked over the rooms to see how we would [be] organized to prepare for [the ceremonies] . . . I spent the Evening in Company with President Young."[48]

From that day forward, except when he was traveling and speaking in his apostolic calling, Wilford Woodruff was involved in one way or another with the temple. Many evenings he spent with Brigham Young, counseling with him. When he was discussing ordinances and the best mode of administering them he wrote little or nothing about it in his journal. Every other topic, he recorded. For instance, on 11 December 1876, he returned from a short journey to Pine Valley and wrote: "President Young vary poorly with Rheumatic fever. The pain in his feet was so great he Could not hardly touch them to the floor. We administered to him by the laying on of hands. . . . We spent the evening with him."

The next morning: "President Young is some better this Morning. I went to the Temple with B. Young jr., A. H. Raleigh, and T. O. Angel[l] & J. D. T. Mcallister and made still further Arrangements to prepare for [ceremonies]." And the day after that: "I went through the Temple to day to locate the stoves and lengths of pipe. [Ten] stoves was the number decided upon." After staying several days in Leeds for

47. Woodruff, *Journal*, 7:291, 10 November 1876.
48. Woodruff, *Journal*, 7:291, 10 November 1876.

further conference meetings, he added that on 19 December, "I went to the Temple. Aranged about Stoves." The next day, Wednesday, 20 December 1876, "I went to the Temple to make arrangements about the curtains." And during the next three days, "I spent most of the time in the Temple with the Sisters in preparing Carpets &c for the Temple."[49]

J. D. T. McAllister, following a week of sickness himself, on 21 December "assisted at the temple, putting cloth on the frames to tack the screens to which the sisters were sewing." For the next several days he "was very busy helping lay the carpets in the temple and preparing the seats, and getting the temple ready for the opening and dedication on January 1."[50]

Additionally, on Sunday, 24 December, Wilford Woodruff preached in the tabernacle, then attended and spoke at a funeral. And on Christmas Day, he said, "I went to the Temple. [Forty] women were Sewing Carpets and all the men were at work & Josiah Hardy worked at the Buz Saw till 9 o'clock at night to get through so that the Ensign might be moved into the Temple for dedication. Presidet Young rode to the Temple the first time He had been out for three weeks.[51] He has been laid up quite sick with inflamitory Rheumatism in his feet."[52]

And so it went for both men, up to and following the temple's first but only partial dedication on 1 January 1877, directing and helping wherever they could, and laboring over the order of presentation of the temple ordinances.

In preparation for this sacred effort, Brigham, no doubt realizing the need for privacy while meeting with others regarding the sacred temple ceremonies, had directed upon his November arrival that a small office

---

49. Woodruff, *Journal*, 7:297, 21, 22, 23 December 1976.

50. Weenig, *Biography of John Daniel Thompson McAllister*, 52.

51. In his journals Wilford Woodruff almost always abbreviated "President" as "Presidet," and occasionally as "Prest," and we will accept his usages without further corrections or comment. He also occasionally capitalized words we would not capitalize today, and both his writing and spelling indicate a great command of the language but little formal education.

52. Woodruff, *Journal*, 7:296–97, 25 December 1876.

be built "stand[ing] east of his new house."[53] It was mid-November when John Henry Standifird began construction, and the small structure was completed and made ready for furnishings just before Christmas.[54]

With the completion of the temple's basement, main floor assembly room, including pulpits at each end, and a single finished sealing room, Church leaders decided to dedicate those portions so that baptisms and endowments for the dead could begin. According to Charlie Walker, "Brigham Young was very anxious to have the basement and its facilities ready for dedication on New Year's day."[55]

Brigham wasn't alone in his anxiety to see the temple ready for use; almost everyone in the southern country felt the same way, particularly those men and women who had labored so long and so faithfully on the structure. All were anxious to begin performing the labor for which the temple would soon be dedicated. To help this along, Alonzo H. Raleigh, one of Brigham's secretaries or scribes, had brought with him from Salt Lake City the veil from the Nauvoo Temple that had been entrusted to his care when the Nauvoo Temple was abandoned.[56] This was also washed and made ready for use.

Charlie Walker was among those who also worked through Christmas Day. According to him, "sisters" were also "busy sewing

---

53. Amram [pseudonym] to Editor, 15 November 1876, St. George, in "Correspondence," *Deseret News*, 20 December 1876, 746. When the Church took ownership of the Brigham Young winter home, research done by the state had identified this building as a telegraph office, not Young's private office. In 1975, Steven T. Baird identified this as a telegraph office on architectural drawings that he did for the Church. Steven T. Baird, "Plans for Jacob Hamblin home and Brigham Young telegraph office," 1975, MS 11560. More recent research has shown conclusively that the structure was built as Brigham Young's private office.

54. John Henry Standifird, *Diaries*, 1862–1923, 16 Nov. 1876, Church History Library.

55. Walker, *Diary*, 1:439.

56. Alonzo H. Raleigh, Diary, 16 Feb. 1877, Church History Library. Raleigh had been an active worker in the Endowment House "for over twenty five years, & the last half of that time constantly, when there was any Endowments given, which no other Person has done in this generation, the same length of time."

carpet and getting the screen ready."[57] According to Walker's editor, Andrew Karl Larson, the carpets were made of rags from discarded clothing torn in strips and sewed end to end then wound into 6-inch balls. When sufficient numbers of balls had been accumulated, they were then woven into rugs. Larson adds that the "sisters took care to see that the colors were arranged in a pleasing artistic pattern and woven into carpet pieces on homemade looms." He further notes that the preparations were a community effort, citing the example of youthful members of the "Young Ladies Mutual Improvement Association of Virgin City" who were helping make carpets "for the Temple."[58]

Anticipation for the dedication was high and a large crowd was expected to attend the event. Church leaders wanted it to come off without a hitch. Walker was at work, no doubt with many others, on 26 and 27 December. On the night of the 27th he worked until 10 o'clock P.M. and came home "weary and tired."[59] The work continued daily through Saturday, 30 December. That day was "cold and windy." Walker was "at Br Nixon's helping to fix the smoke stack for the Engin at the temple."

Finally the eagerly anticipated day—1 January 1877—arrived. Wilford Woodruff began a 20-page journal entry concerning the dedication with the words: "This is a very important day to the Church and Kingdom of God upon the Earth."[60] And J. D. T. McAllister recorded: "Early morn called on Bro. Woodruff, Raleigh and L. John Nuttall at St. George House. Then went to Pres. Young and engaged Bro. Charles Wilkins to take the large Record Books etc. to the Temple. Went to the Temple at 9 A.M. Prepared for receiving the people."[61]

57. These carpets were for the basement endowment room floors. It's not clear what the "screen" refers to unless it was the white canvas wall partitions.

58. Walker, *Diary*, 1:439n63.

59. Walker, *Diary*, 1:440.

60. Woodruff, *Journal*, 7:303, Monday, 1 January 1877.

61. Weenig, *Biography of John Daniel Thompson McAllister*, 53.

Chapter 16

FIRST DEDICATION

1 January 1877

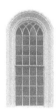

As the Saints began gathering for the New Year's Day dedication, all seemed ready. But then, according to Emma Jarvis Cottam McArthur, "a terrible storm came. It blew over homes, trees and buggies. It blew roofs off [including the barn roof on the block east of the temple]. It was terrible. It was just like the darkness overcoming Joseph Smith before the light came. It was like Satan trying to stop the dedication. People came anyway."[1]

Another witness to the fury of this storm was Rosemary Johnson, who wrote:

"I was almost eight years old, I think, and in the crowd at the [January] Dedication. Some good brother picked me up and put me in the window so I could see & hear, & there was a terrible wind came up and made the windows rattle & I felt sure it was evil spirits trying to get in. No one had ever told me of such things but I was so afraid the glass would not hold them out."[2]

---

1. Thomas Cottam, "Memories of the St. George Temple."
2. Rosemary Johnson Fox Johnson, MSS P 6, Charles Ellis Johnson Collection, L. Tom Perry Special Collections, Harold B. Lee Library, Brigham Young University, Provo,

Toward noon that day, in spite of the blustery weather, the faithful began to assemble in front of the temple. "Prest. Young arrived at 12 noon," recorded J. D. T. McAllister, who continued: "Opened the doors and admitted the Saints into the font room; it became filled, standing room only. Dedication commenced at quarter to one o'clock."[3]

Wilford Woodruff estimated the number of Saints at 2,000, but this is likely an overstatement; the actual count of the crowd leaving via the east doors of the temple, when the day's services were over, was 1,260.[4] With his feet still hurting, Brigham had to be carried from room to room in a chair that had been specially built for the occasion by Thomas Punter Cottam.[5]

Elder Woodruff was invited by Erastus Snow to conduct this first of the three dedicatory prayers that were pronounced that day. "At 30 minutes past 12 o'clock on 1 January 1877, Elder Woodruff stood on the upper step of the [basement] Font and called the attention of the people, and said: 'We are this day blessed with the privilege, that but few, since the days of Adam have ever enjoyed. But few of the sons of Adam have ever had the privilege of entering into a Temple built by the commandment of God in which to administer ordinances both for the living and the dead. We have now assembled to dedicate portions

Utah, n.d., n.p. The quotation was written by Johnson on the back of a photo of the newly finished St. George Temple; information courtesy Tom Wells, photo curator, L. Tom Perry Special Collections. Rosemary Johnson adds: "Bro. Holman told me (years after) that my Father [Joseph Johnson] had asked him to haul 2 or 3 wagon loads of potted plants from our greenhouse for decoration." The Johnson greenhouse was located on the site of the present Ancestor Square in St. George, Utah.

3. Lucile McAllister Weenig, comp., *Biography of John Daniel Thompson McAllister, Utah Pioneer, Second President of the St. George Temple and of the Manti Temple of The Church of Jesus Christ of Latter-day Saints* (privately published, 1980), 53.

4. Hazel Bradshaw, ed., and Washington County Chapter Daughters of Utah Pioneers, *Under Dixie Sun* (Panguitch, Utah: Garfield County News, 1950), 342, 345. Also, Walker states that "about 1,249 were present" (Charles Lowell Walker, *Diary of Charles Lowell Walker*, edited by A. Karl Larson and Katharine Miles Larson, 2 vols. [Logan: Utah State University Press, 1980], 1:443).

5. Janice Force DeMille, *The St. George Temple: First 100 Years* (Hurricane, Utah: Homestead Publishers, 1977), 56.

of this Temple unto God; and I have a request to make of all the Saints who are present and I suppose all who are, profess to be Saints for none others should be here. I realize that this assembly cannot bow the knee in their crowded condition, but you can bow your heads and your hearts unto God; and this I want you to do this day. And when those who offer up prayers in the dedication of this Temple, I want their words repeated in secret by this assembly before the Lord, that our prayers may ascend unto the ears of the Lord of Sabaoth that they may be answered upon our heads. The Saints do not prize, as they should the blessings they enjoy.'

"At the close of these remarks, the following hymn was sung: 'The Spirit of God like a Fire Is Burning,' after which Erastus Snow announced that Elder Wilford Woodruff would offer the dedication prayer."[6]

Brigham Young Jr. recorded: "Bro Wilford Woodruff kneeled near the top of West steps [of the baptismal font], and read a lengthy prayer[;] time[:] 24 minutes. He expressed hope that it would not weaken the faith of any to hear or see him read his prayer from manuscript. All very good and satisfactory."[7]

In part Elder Woodruff's prayer read: "Oh, Our God, we Thy sons and daughters have assembled together in the name of Thy son Jesus Christ, within the walls of this Temple, this day for the purpose of dedicating and consecrating a portion of this house unto the Lord, our God, that it may be holy and acceptable in Thy sight."

From there he mentioned every part of the basement—the foundation, the walls, the windows, the carpeting, the furniture, and especially the font. He praised the timber work, the flooring, the joists, and prayed that they be made holy. He prayed that those who would serve

---

6. James G. Bleak, "Annals of the Southern Utah Mission," Book B, typescript; copy in Dixie State University Special Collections, St. George, Utah, 468.

7. Brigham Young Jr. Diary, 1 Jan. 1877, in Devery S. Anderson, ed., *The Development of LDS Temple Worship* (Salt Lake City: Signature, 2011), 32.

in the temple and all who entered therein would feel God's power and be uplifted. He pled that no unclean thing would be permitted to enter therein.

Elder Woodruff also prayed for the leaders of the Church and the members: "May Thy people accomplish the work whereunto they are ordained, build up the Zion of God, and prepare the earth for the coming of the Son of Man." His conclusion was: "Oh, hear, oh, hear us Lord in these our petitions and answer us from heaven, Thine holy habitation. And we will ascribe all honor, Glory, and thanksgiving unto God and the Lamb both now and forever. Amen and Amen."

Following that first dedicatory prayer, a special song composed by Charles L. Walker, "The Dedication Song," was sung by the congregation. Following the song, the company exited the basement by way of the circular stairs that led to the main assembly room, the first floor above the basement. There they were seated on benches set up that morning by Walker and others. The "main upper room was quite full. Prest [Brigham Young] sat directly in front of the lower east stand on which sat bros Woodruff[,] [Erastus] Snow [,] and myself, and from which bro Snow read his prayer[,] 17 minutes [and] very good."[8] The choir then sang "This House We Dedicate to Thee," after which Erastus Snow offered the dedicatory prayer for this room.

His prayer—with the other prayers offered that day—reflects the devotional feelings of all who attended this partial dedication of the temple: "We implore Thy blessing upon the people and upon this house which we dedicate and consecrate unto the most High. This room especially we hallow unto Thee and beseech Thee to accept it as the offering of Thy people, and sanctify it to their use for sacred and holy purposes and to Thine own glory, it being the principal room on the first floor over the Font and above the basement, together with the adjoining vestry halls, entry ways and outer steps leading up to the same."

Continuing, he said, "We beseech Thee, Holy Father, in the name

8. Anderson, *Development*, 32.

of Thy Son to look down upon Thy servants and people in great mercy and forgive their sins and follies. We thank Thee for Thy care and protection over Thy Servants and handmaidens who have labored to gather the materials sent to build this house and notwithstanding the difficulties and dangers, the accidents and snares, that beset them, the enemy has not had power to slay them nor has limb been broken, nor blood shed upon this building or these grounds consecrated unto Thee. Let Thy choice blessings continue upon Thy people who have labored or contributed to build this house and as much as they have done it in faith, may they and their generations after them and through them, [and] the Fathers before them, enjoy the blessing and exaltations which flow through the ordinances of Thy house and the ministrations of Thy Holy priesthood."

Following Erastus Snow's prayer, the congregation sang "Redeemer of Israel." They then remained seated while Brigham Young, the three apostles who were present, and some 29 local priesthood leaders[9] moved to the tower area at the east end of the first floor and ascended the stairs that led into the sealing room. President Young continued to be carried in his chair.

There they sang "Come, Let Us Anew" and Brigham Young Jr. "delivered or read the dedication prayer,"[10] saying, in part: "We have assembled in this upper room where we anticipate performing the ordinance

---

9. The names of those who went into the sealing room are President Brigham Young, Apostle Wilford Woodruff, Apostle Erastus Snow, Apostle Brigham Young Jr., and elders Alonzo H. Raleigh, John D. T. McAllister, L. John Nuttall, John L. Smith, Anson P. Winsor, Charles H. Wilcken, William Crabtree, Henry Lunt, John M. Macfarlane, Jacob Gates, Truman O. Angell, Alex F. McDonald, David H. Cannon, Charles Smith, Joseph Birch, John O. Angus, Richard Bentley, Jesse N. Smith, Morris Ensign, Christopher J. Arthur, James G. Bleak, Archibald Sullivan, John Lytle, Ira Miles, Dan D. McArthur, David Milne, Henry Eyring, Walter Granger, and Nash Ashby (Evelyn K. Jones, *Henry Lunt Biography, and History of the Development of Southern Utah and Settling of Colonia Pacheco, Mexico* [privately published, Provo, Utah, 1966], 299–300).

10. We are not certain just which room this was, as three possibilities exist, one of which was removed during one of the early remodelings.

of sealing woman to man, children to their parents, and man to his fellow-man, that the bond may reach unto heaven, Thy dwelling place; and when we attain that happy state and rise with the just in the morning of the first resurrection that we may legally claim the relationship of husbands and wives, parents and children, and be crowned sons and daughters of God and joint heirs with Jesus, our elder brother."[11]

Following the dedication of the sealing room the small party returned to the pulpits in the east end of the assembly room. There, President Young, though suffering from rheumatism and having not earlier stood or taken part, "leaning on his cane and one crutch[,] came into the lower M[elchizedek] stand and addressed the saints for some 20 M[inutes.]"[12]

This was a deliberate and powerful sermon. The message Brigham wanted to deliver had obviously been turning in his mind for some time. A writer for the *Womans Exponent* was deeply impressed with President Young's bearing and sincerity and wrote: "The house seemed filled with a heavenly host and the President's face fairly shone with the light of the Holy Ghost."[13] From his own research, historian Andrew Karl Larson described the president's demeanor: "He spoke in the style that bore his trademark: vigorous, and to the point. It may be, too, that the twinges of his affliction made him a bit more sharp and hard tongued than usual. What one senses, as he reads the words that tumbled from his mouth, is a feeling that the president knew that this easily might be the last time he would address so many of the Saints of this mission, and he wanted to get through to them with a warning against the attractions which diverted their attention from the purposes which had brought them to Dixie. . . . He pleaded with them to shoulder their responsibilities to redeem the dead through the temple ordinances."[14]

---

11. Anderson, *Development*, 32.
12. Anderson, *Development*, 32.
13. "St. George Temple: One Hundred Years of Service," *Ensign*, March 1977, 92–94.
14. Andrew Karl Larson, *Erastus Snow* (Salt Lake City: University of Utah Press, 1971), 476.

Thus Brigham spoke his mind and convictions, as well as his disappointments in the behavior of many, his words portraying a good deal of righteous indignation. James G. Bleak recorded the full text of Brigham's speech, though only some portions are included here:

"[If] we were awake to . . . the salvation of the human family, this house would be crowded, as we hope it will be, from Monday morning until Saturday night. This house was built here in this place purposely, where it is warm and pleasant in the winter time, and comfortable to work. . . . What do you suppose the fathers would say if they could speak from the dead? Would they not say, 'We have lain here thousands of years, here in this prison house, waiting for this dispensation to come. Why, if they had the power the very thunders of heaven would be in our ears, if we could but realize the importance of the work we are engaged in. All the angels of heaven are looking at this little handful of people, and stimulating them to the salvation of the human family. So also are the devils in hell looking at this people, too, and trying to overthrow us[,] and the people are still shaking hands with the servants of the devil, instead of sanctifying themselves and calling upon the Lord and doing the work which he commands us . . . to do. . . .

"The spirit was awakened in the people in the north when we gave the word that we should do no more work in the Endowment House—they came to us crying and pleading to be baptized for their dead. What else could they do? They can come here and do the work for their dead, and put these poor prisoners on the ground where they will be free. Do we realize this? As long as we tarry here, we are subject to the world. But now go to, like men and women, and say, we will embrace the truth and enter into the covenants of God and carry them out. Then the bonds are broken, and the hearts of the people are united in the Father. Perhaps, brethren and sisters, you will not get my meaning, but now go to work and let those holes in the ground [silver and gold mines] alone, and let the Gentiles alone, who would destroy us if they had the power. You are running after them, and some of our brethren are putting their wives and daughters into their society, and will go to the devil with them too, if they do not look out. I would not have a dollar on the earth if I had to get it there. It has been the kingdom of God with me. What I have I have got in this kingdom.

"Well, now, some of the Elders are running after these holes in the ground, and I see men before me in this house that have no right to be here. They are as corrupt in their hearts as they can be, and will take them [the Gentiles] by the hand and call them brother! You will go to hell, lots of you, unless you repent. You may think this is plain talk, it is not as plain as you will find by and by. If you ever go to the gates of heaven, Jesus will say he never knew you, [not] While you have been saying your prayers and going to your meetings and are as corrupt in your hearts as men can be. You had better stop now and repent of your sins and sin no more, while there is yet time, and before the doors are closed against you. I want to wake you up, and if I had the power to lift the veil from your eyes and let you see things as they are, you would be astonished. Not but what there are a great majority of the people as good as they know how to be. Now I will say, bless the people, that they may do better, but show some of the Elders of Israel according to their present conduct a dollar on one side and eternal life on the other, and I fear they would choose the dollar. . . . God bless you. Amen."

Then Brigham added a provocative afterthought: "I do not know whether the people are satisfied with the services of the dedication of the Temple or not. We should be satisfied. But I do not mean to, and never expect to be satisfied until the devil is whipped and driven off the face of the earth."[15]

To underscore and make plain that he meant every word, "the Lion of the Lord," as Larson tells it, "raised his heavy hickory cane high above his head and with all his strength brought it down flat on the pulpit. The soft Pinewood yielded to the blow, and to this day the prints

15. Bleak, "Annals," Book B, 483–87.

of the knotted stick still remain [in the wood],[16] a testimony of Brother Brigham's righteous wrath on that momentous day in St. George."[17]

Charles Walker agreed with the prophet. That evening he wrote in his diary: "He smote the stand with his walking stick as he spoke the sentence and made the Room ring again and the marks [dents] are on the stand and will remain there as a testimony of the truth, and the great power by which he spoke."[18]

Erastus Snow followed Brigham with supporting remarks regarding "the folly of the saints in doing things contrary to the counsels of the servants of God."[19] The choir then sang "Glorious Things of Thee Are Spoken, Zion, City of Our God." Brigham Young Jr. offered the closing prayer, and the congregation exited through the large east doors and down the prominent steps. As they exited they were treated once again, as they had been at the groundbreaking, to the melodious strains of the George Staheli Band from Santa Clara, this time blending their instrumental tones as they played from the roof of the temple.[20]

As they retired to their homes amid the Staheli Band's sacred harmonies, the people no doubt talked among themselves and privately pondered this historic moment. Lorenzo Brown, for one, wrote in his

---

16. This pulpit is presently in the care of the Church in Salt Lake City. Some in attendance recalled seeing a stream of fire, or perhaps sparks, come out the end of Brigham's cane, a part of which had been filled with lead to give it more weight and strength to support him. A scorch mark on the pulpit remembered by several, including Eldon McArthur, who refers to it in his "Oral History," no longer seems to exist.

17. Larson, *Erastus Snow*, 477. A variation of this event was recorded by Heber Jarvis, who was in attendance that day. He wrote: "In speaking near the Priesthood stand of the Elders, [Brigham] struck the stand with his knotted cane and said: 'There are men present that have no more right to be here than the devils from hell.' My brother, George Jarvis, was close to the two men he pointed to, and he said they fluttered like wounded ducks" (in N. B. Lundwall, comp., *Temples of the Most High* [Salt Lake City: Bookcraft, 1968], 81–82).

18. Walker, *Diary*, 1:443.

19. Walker, Diary, 1:443.

20. LaRae Farnsworth, "Life of George Johann Staheli," n.d., n.p., Daughters of Utah Pioneers, McQuarrie Memorial Museum, St. George, Utah.

journal the same day: "My heart is filled to overflowing with gratitude to my Father in Heaven for the great privilege of today."[21]

And Jane Blake, daughter of Benjamin ("Chairmaker") Blake and Harriet Hollis Blake, was also in "the large throng who attended the dedicatory services." Of her it has been written: "Well does [Jane] remember what took place on that memorable occasion—the singing, the deep and humble prayers, and the righteous indignation of Brigham Young, who rebuked men for their lack of reverence and left the imprint of his cane across the pulpit from which he was speaking, in emphasizing his statements."[22]

21. "Diary of Lorenzo Brown," n.d., 55, typescript, Dixie State University Special Collections, St. George, Utah.

22. Annie Blake Schmutz, "History," n.d., n.p., 7 February 1942, typescript, Daughters of Utah Pioneers McQuarrie Memorial Museum, St. George, Utah.

The remains of Ft. Pearce, the last stop on the Temple Trail before travelers reached St. George, with Ft. Pearce Wash in the background.

Old Middleton lime kiln, where lime was burned by Samuel Judd and sons for the tabernacle, courthouse, many homes, and the St. George Temple. The lime supply ran out just as the temple was completed. Note the adobe brick lining still standing at the back of the kiln.

View from the limestone-capped ridge where limestone to be burned for mortar and plaster was quarried. The old kiln is about twenty feet below and to the left of this view. The wood to fire the kiln had to be freighted in by wagon and then hand-carried up the steep slope to the kiln.

The last stone is placed on the temple wall, January 1876. Note the two sheer-legs (inverted V-shaped structures on the top front of the temple), one with a rope coming down from it. The rope was pulled by teams of horses or mules to lift cut stones, mortar, and even workers to the top of the temple.

The St. George Temple on a Sunday afternoon. The identities of the well-dressed families are unknown. Note the scaffolding around the top of the tower, securing Christopher Lister Riding as he labored to install the balls and weather vane he had constructed. It is unknown how he climbed to that lofty position.

As above, stuccoing the temple's outside walls from the top down, 1876. Riding's work on the weather vane has been completed and his scaffolding removed. The three men on the parapets during this workday are George Laub (next to the tower), Aaron McDonald (with a saw in his hand), and Robert McQuarrie.

Brigham Young.

Wilford Woodruff, first president of the St. George Temple.

Brigham Young's winter home and office, as seen from the Red Hill, 1880s. In this office Brigham Young, Brigham Young Jr., Wilford Woodruff, and others met almost daily to order, systematize, and record temple ordinances.

Above: 1877 patron name slip.

Left: Temple ready for final dedication, April 1877. Note water tower in the foreground.

David Cannon, seated at center front, and other male temple workers, circa 1902.

Fourteen female temple workers, date uncertain.

William Atkin home, circa 1886. This home was located near the Virgin River, seven miles south of St. George in the present seniors' community of Sun River.

Nisson hay and threshing yard, Washington City, early 1900s. Note the willow fence. Many of the earliest St. George homes were made from such willow walls, daubed with mud for further protection from the elements.

Called by many the "gossip wagon," this wagon was owned and driven by George W. Worthen to pick up sister temple workers, circa 1902.

1880 view of St. George City, looking south from the Red Hill. Both levels of the Black Hill are visible at the right.

A Washington County woman at a loom weaving rag rugs, perhaps for the new temple. Her spinning wheel is also at the ready.

Men hauling rocks for another try at building a dam on the Virgin River, 1880s.

Detail of the old temple tower. Note the two weather vane balls made by Christopher Lister Riding. When the tower was replaced in 1883 by one that was much higher, Riding made only one ball for the weather vane.

Early view of the back of the temple, showing windows that no longer exist due to the addition in 1974 of two stairways and an elevator. Note the exposed sandstone around the parapets and the plastered foundation made to look like sandstone, as well as the single ball under the weather vane.

Parowan Stake temple cottage under construction, 1940s.

Aerial view of temple and community, 1950s. Note the six temple cottages and three rows of new temple apartments.

Aerial view of temple with enlarged annex, 1950s. The Information Bureau, with the old cannon out front, is east (left) of the temple behind the large tree next to the street.

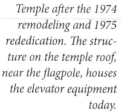

Temple after the 1974 remodeling and 1975 rededication. The structure on the temple roof, near the flagpole, houses the elevator equipment today.

Chapter 17

AN ASTOUNDING DEVELOPMENT

January to 1 March 1877

Another flurry of labor followed the dedication ceremonies as workers scrambled to complete the unfinished portions of the temple, at least sufficiently enough to allow ordinance work to begin. After occupying himself all week recording the dedicatory services in his journal and in a letter to the *Deseret News*, Wilford Woodruff spent Sunday morning in meeting, "giving some instruction on the Endowments," after which he spent the afternoon with Brigham Young and Erastus Snow.

On Monday, 8 January, he "spent the forenoon going through the temple to prepare for [ordinance work] for the dead," and he spent the afternoon writing. The next day, Tuesday, 9 January, he recorded: "This is the day that the first ordinances of the Endowments for the dead was performed in the Temple of God in St. George[.] at 12 o'clock President Brigham Young being present."[1] "We all rejoiced to see him there," wrote John W. Young.[2] "We Commenced to [be] Baptized for the dead," Wilford Woodruff continued. "W. Woodruff baptized the first

---

1. Wilford Woodruff, *Journal, 1833–1898*, ed. Scott G. Kenney, 9 vols. (Midvale, Utah: Signature, 1983), 7:321.
2. John W. Young to W. B. Dougall, telegram, 9 January 1877, Church History

141 persons and Confirmed the first persons President Young laying on hands at the same time. John L. Smith baptized the next 83 persons making 224 baptized on this day. John D. T. Mcallister Confirmed 44, A. H. Raleigh 15, H. W. Bigler 124, Erastus Snow 20. Susie Amelia Young Dunford was the first Baptized & Confirmed by W Woodruff."[3]

Eighty-seven additional baptisms for the dead followed on Wednesday, and on Thursday, 11 January 1877, he recorded: "To day was the first day in which Endowments were given in the Temple at St. George. We gave endowments for 63 for the living and 10 for the dead Total 73. Brigham Young sealed 3 & W Woodruff 29 Couple. 22 Ordained Elders. WW ordained 8 Elders."[4]

James Bleak, historian of the Southern Mission, also recorded: "Endowments for the dead were first administered in St. George Temple. On this day also the first sealing [in the St. George Temple] of woman (dead) to man took place, Apostle Wilford Woodruff doing the sealing. The second sealing for the dead was done by President Brigham Young. The first four sealings of living men and women, this first endowment day in St. George Temple, were done by Apostle Woodruff, and the fifth living sealing was done by President Young.[5] On this date [also]

Library, The Church of Jesus Christ of Latter-day Saints, Salt Lake City, Utah, hereafter cited as Church History Library.

3. Woodruff, *Journal*, 7:321.

4. Woodruff, *Journal*, 7:321.

5. In early 2011, a nineteenth-century "Personal Family Record of Ordinances Performed in the St. George Temple," compiled by a Randall family, was loaned to the St. George Temple presidency by a descendant. On pages 88–89 is recorded, under date of 11 January 1877, two sealings of couples: Joseph Weatherbee Carpenter and Annie Burdett Randall, and Haden Wells Church (Jr.) and Clara Jane Randall. The first couple listed was sealed by Brigham Young, the second by Wilford Woodruff, though the ordinances may have been performed in the opposite order. From the way the sealings were recorded, it is impossible to determine if these were living sealings or proxy sealings for the dead. What we do know is that they were two of the first five sealings in the St. George Temple if they were for the living, or the first sealings if they were for the dead.

one baptism into the United Order, Roseinia Sylvester, took place. Elder Charles L. Walker, baptizer."[6]

Lucy Bigelow Young, Brigham's wife, was called by her husband to serve in the temple not only as an ordinance worker but as the temple's first matron, though we don't know if that was ever her official title. "From the day of her calling she was almost always found in the Temple. . . . When the Manti and Logan temples were dedicated, Lucy went to train ordinance workers and to outline [for them other temple] procedures."[7]

Eighteen days after the dedication, at the age of nineteen years, Jane Blake was married in the St. George Temple. "Many of the young couples, who had awaited this opportunity, were married there during those first weeks. After the Temple ceremony, they had a big family din-ner at the Blake home and in the evening a wedding party, once more dancing in the Blake home, in a large room which had just been added. Many of their friends were there, and it was a happy time."[8]

In the meantime, on 13 January, Brigham Young, John W. Young, Wilford Woodruff, Erastus Snow, and Brigham Young Jr. had issued to all bishops the following statement:

"We herein embody a few instructions which we wish you to *strictly enjoin* upon the brethren and sisters who come to the Temple to officiate for themselves or their friends—. . . The sisters should be provided with two or three white skirts; and the brethren should have their garments to button from the back clear round and up the front; and shirts made to reach down to the knees, or a little below, or one may be pieced to this length for the occasion.

"Before the brethren or sisters go into the Temple to receive

6. James G. Bleak, "Annals of the Southern Utah Mission," Book B, typescript, Dixie State University Special Collections, St. George, Utah, 459.

7. "Sketch of Lucy B. Young in the Temples," *Young Woman's Journal* 4 (April 1893): 299, quoted in Leonard J. Arrington, "St. George Tabernacle and Temple: The Builders," lecture given at Dixie State College, St. George, Utah, 21 July 1993, 17; photocopy of lecture in possession of the authors.

8. Annie Blake Schmutz, "History," n.p., 7 February 1942, typescript, Daughters of Utah Pioneers McQuarrie Memorial Museum, St. George, Utah.

Endowments they must wash themselves all over perfectly clean so as to enter the Temple clean."[9]

At the same time, laboring day after day, Brigham continued deliberating with the brethren, working to perfect the temple ceremonies. Brethren selected for these discussions, though not always all together, included Wilford Woodruff, George Q. Cannon, Alonzo H. Raleigh, L. John Nuttall, Erastus Snow, Brigham Young Jr., James G. Bleak, J. D. T. McAllister, and Evan Melbourne Greene.[10]

On 14 January 1877, Wilford Woodruff recorded: "Spent the evening with Presidet Young. He requested Brigham jr. & W. Woodruff to write out the Ceremony of the Endowment from Beginning to End,"[11] assisted by John D. T. McAllister and L. John Nuttall.[12]

Brigham Jr. recorded on 15 January: "Busy writing with bros [Wilford] W[oodruff] & J[ohn] N[uttall] on ceremonies."[13] And the next night, the 16th: "Spent the evening reading to father what we—Bro Woodruff, Nuttall and myself have written. . . . He made a number of corrections."[14]

On 20, 21, and 22 January, Wilford recorded that he had spent the day in writing and the evening with Brigham Young.[15] He also visited Brigham again on the evening of 24 January.[16] Meanwhile daily drafts

---

9. Devery S. Anderson, ed., *The Development of LDS Temple Worship* (Salt Lake City: Signature, 2011), 34–35; emphasis in original.

10. Documentation isn't always specific concerning the identities of those involved, or the nature of temple matters discussed. Therefore it is difficult to determine if all these men were privy to changes and if matters discussed were more general than specific.

11. Woodruff, *Journal*, 7:322.

12. Woodruff, *Journal*, 7:330–33. As far as is known, the complete temple ceremony had never been recorded; neither had any of the sacred ordinances been committed to paper. Once a dedicated temple repository existed to hold them, such things could properly be committed to writing.

13. Woodruff, *Journal*, 7:35.

14. Woodruff, *Journal*, 7:35.

15. Woodruff, *Journal*, 7:323.

16. Woodruff, *Journal*, 7:323.

were being submitted for Brigham's review and approval. "Engaged all day & evening with Bro Woodruff, McCallister & Nuttall, under the direction of Pres. B. Young," Alonzo H. Raleigh wrote, "in reorganizing Parts of the [ceremonies]."[17]

On 16 February, Brigham visited the temple and "corrected the Parts to some little extent."[18] After reading all pertaining to a particular ordinance or even just a portion of one, it appears that President Young prayerfully considered the ordinance in his mind, trying different words or even approaches until it finally felt right. In this way he directed Woodruff, Nuttall, or others to make changes. These revised procedures would then be reviewed again and again during a second, third, or perhaps even a fifteenth reading, leading either to further revision or final approval.

Wilford Woodruff continued to be involved in the process, recording on 1 February that "Presidet (Young) was present [in the temple] and deliverd a lecture . . . some 30 Minuts."[19] This was prepared by Brigham shortly after he explained to Wilford and others "what the Lecture . . . should portray, and for this purpose [he] appointed a day when he would personally deliver [it]. Elders J. D. T. McAllister and L. John Nuttall prepared writing material, and as the President spoke they took down his words. Elder Nuttall put the same into form and the writing was submitted to President Young on the same evening at his office in residence at St. George. He there made such changes as he deemed proper, and when he finally passed upon it said: This is the Lecture . . . to be observed in the Temple."[20] This lecture replaced whatever lectures had been given by Wilford Woodruff and any of the other

---

17. Alonzo H. Raleigh, Diary, 12 Feb. 1877, Church History Library.

18. Raleigh, Diary, 16 Feb. 1877.

19. Woodruff, *Journal*, 7:325.

20. David John Buerger, *The Mysteries of Godliness: A History of Mormon Temple Worship* (San Francisco: Smith Research Associates, 2002), 110–11. See also L. John Nuttall, "Memoranda, For Presidents W. Woodruff, Geo. Q. Cannon, and Jos. F. Smith," 3 June 1892, Nuttall Papers, Special Collections, Harold B. Lee Library, Brigham Young University, Provo, Utah.

Brethren going as far back as Nauvoo, and would be used in all temples until after the turn of the century.[21]

One gets a sense through Wilford Woodruff's journal entries during this period of Brigham Young's strenuous efforts to perfect all portions of the ceremonies, exactly as the Prophet Joseph had directed him to do. On 9 February, according to one entry, Brigham visited the temple, where he and Woodruff had another discussion. On 10 February, Brigham came again. "And I feel thankful for it," Wilford reported. "The Blessing of God Rested upon the people." After leaving the temple that afternoon, Wilford "spent the evening visiting with Brigham."[22] And even on Sunday, 11 February, "I spent the Evening with President Young."[23] Again on 12 February, Wilford wrote: "I spent the day writing on the Ceremonies & we spent the Evening with President Young reading the Ceremony."[24] He also spent the next evening with Brigham, and on 19 February wrote: "I spent several hours with Presidet Young."[25]

Extant documentation does not specify whether these review sessions took place in Brigham's home or in his next-door office, but it can be surmised that the prophet used the location that provided the greatest privacy. After all, Brigham received callers when at work in his office as well as in his home, so the locations of these sacred evaluation meetings no doubt varied. In early February, however, Alonzo Raleigh did record that he "Visited Pres. B. Young at his Office."[26]

Brigham and the others finished their temple ceremony review at the end of February. "Spent the evening with Presidet Young," Wilford recorded on 25 February,[27] and the next day, which was rainy, he

---

21. Buerger, *Mysteries*, 111–12.
22. Woodruff, *Journal*, 7:326.
23. Woodruff, *Journal*, 7:339.
24. Woodruff, *Journal*, 7:327.
25. Woodruff, *Journal*, 7:328.
26. Raleigh, Diary, 4 Feb. 1877.
27. Woodruff, *Journal*, 7:329.

recorded, "I spent the day at the Temple writing."[28] After two months of intense labor, the procedures for and the writing and recording of the ordinances for the dead were complete, at least for the time being.

It was also in February 1877 that two additional but rather important changes in temple procedure occurred. First, Wilford Woodruff and Lucy B. Young became the first temple ordinance workers to dress entirely in white. On 1 February, President Woodruff recorded in his journal: "W Woodruff Presided. . . . I dressed in pure white Doe skin [a soft cloth fabric, not a deer hide] from head to foot . . . white pants vest & Coat the first Example in any Temple of the Lord in this last dispensation. Sister Lucy B Young also dressed in white."[29]

On 15 February Woodruff recorded the second change, explaining that they used two temple veils instead of just one.[30] This proved so successful that Wilford immediately ordered that a third be made, and it was in place by 3 March.

Meanwhile, Wilford and other leaders involved in working on the temple had also become aware that the canvas-walled ordinance rooms in the basement were not of sufficient size to accommodate the crowds that continued flocking to the temple. No one had anticipated this development. Crowds had streamed through the Nauvoo Temple day and night for approximately two months, but Church leaders knew that had been because the people had understood that mobs were soon to drive them from Nauvoo and their beautiful new temple, and it might be years before they had another opportunity to do temple work.

This was different, and those involved in temple leadership sensed it. Not only were there no vicious mobs to impel them to greater temple activity, but the patrons who attended were coming from farther and farther away, staying in or near St. George for longer periods of time, and spending as much time in the temple as they possibly could,

28. Woodruff, *Journal*, 7:329.
29. Woodruff, *Journal*, 7:325.
30. See Woodruff, *Journal*, 7:325.

laboring constantly to accomplish the glorious work for their own departed ancestors and friends.

After much discussion between Wilford Woodruff, Brigham Young, and the others on how to accommodate the crowds, it was determined to make greater use of the first main assembly room above the basement. To that end the large room was divided into the last two ordinance rooms—terrestrial and celestial. As in the basement, these two rooms were separated by canvas-covered walls, or screens, and the temple veils.

Confirming evidence of this change comes from an account found in the Cannon Family History. George Q. Cannon and his wife were in St. George for the 6 April 1877 final dedication of the temple. His brother David lived in St. George, having arrived with the December 1861 settlers, and had been called with others by Brigham Young to serve as a temple ordinance worker. On Monday, 10 April, George and David were in the temple to do the ordinance work for their deceased father. George was proxy for his father while David officiated for the entire group. George later wrote that he was "extremely satisfied" as the session moved along and more so as they entered the "next to last room." He said, "It was a spacious, high-ceilinged room, oblong in shape, with a simple row of pillars on each side, veils draping the end where the high pulpit stood."[31]

This description fits the east end of the first main floor, placing the room in front of the high priesthood pulpits. The account continues: "As David stepped to the pulpit, in the principle role of the ceremony, and looked down at his brother George Q., who was in the audience officiating for his father, he [David] saw their father standing behind George Q. The father appeared to be standing above the floor, as David

---

31. Beatrice Cannon Evans and Janath Russell Cannon, eds., *Cannon Family Historical Treasury* (George Cannon Family Association, 1967), 318–19; emphasis added; copy in possession of the authors.

could see his figure about to the knees. Hesitating slightly, David proceeded with his part."[32]

Cannon wrote that this "next to the last room" was "finished entirely in white, and always gave one a refreshing feeling of airiness and rest when entering it from the more *ornate* rooms below."[33] The "white" describes the white canvas walls of this room, and the "ornate" rooms below would have reference to the three ordinance rooms still in the basement that had been decorated with live plants and perhaps murals or paintings and other décor.

The Cannon record continues: "As soon as the ceremonies were finished and the congregation dispersed, [David] hurried to find George Q., who by then was dressing in a room below.

"He asked, 'George, did you note anything unusual during the day?'

"George Q. replied, ' . . . our father was with us in every room!'

"The hearts of the Cannon children had turned to their father, and the heart of their father had turned to his children, and these three joined hands and hearts in the launching of the Cannon temple work in this generation."[34]

We have no record of what the Cannons saw in the celestial room that day, or how it was finished. Was it also arranged as a partitioned room, or had its large space (it has since been altered and reduced in size) actually been finished as such rooms are finished today? We don't know. In any event, the two rooms were in use at that time at the front or east end of the first main floor, and were arranged in the same relationship as in the Endowment House in Salt Lake City.[35]

Meanwhile, the three ordinance rooms remaining in the basement had been adapted and enlarged to use the newly available space, and with both male and female initial ordinance rooms and the baptismal

---

32. Evans and Cannon, eds., *Cannon Family*, 319.

33. Evans and Cannon, eds., *Cannon Family*, 319; emphasis added.

34. Evans and Cannon, eds., *Cannon Family*, 319.

35. Lisle G. Brown, "'Temple Pro Tempore': The Salt Lake City Endowment House," *Journal of Mormon History* (Fall 2008): 44–45.

font also in the basement, the temple arrangement was basically set for the next procedural change—one that would alter temple participation forever by establishing what we today refer to as temple worship.

On 23 February, Wilford made this notable journal entry: "I presided in the Temple to day. . . . (While meeting . . . I received a revelation concerning the redemption of my dead.) . . . I spent the Evening with President Young. I [also] wrote 2 letters to Phebe (and sent her the revelation.)"[36]

The next day, 24 February, Brigham visited the temple and spoke at some length with Wilford Woodruff. From what followed, it is apparent that Brigham sustained him in his revelation and encouraged him to proceed with the divine instructions that had been given.

The situation was that "in the early years of the Church, proxy baptisms were performed only for close personal friends or direct-bloodline ancestors, usually no more than four generations back,"[37] which means that only a personal friend, family member, or descendant of the deceased could act as proxy in doing ordinances for that person. Members were also required to be of the same gender as the person for whom ordinances were being performed. Wilford, meanwhile, had been busy for years gathering and compiling an extensive list of his deceased family members for whom little or no proxy work had been done. While he personally could accomplish the work for the deceased males, he had no female family members living anywhere near St. George who could do the work for the females.[38] How to solve this had been the subject of his 23 February prayer and revealed answer.

He recorded: "Ever Since I have been working in this Temple my mind has been Exercised in behalf of the dead, And (I) have felt a great desire to see my dead redeemed before I passed away. A few days ago

---

36. Woodruff, *Journal*, 7:329.
37. Daniel H. Ludlow, *Encyclopedia of Mormonism*, 4 vols. (New York: Macmillan, 1992), 1:96.
38. To show the extent of his dilemma, Woodruff had researched more than a hundred fifty of his female family names.

I went into the Cealing room whare I often go to Pray for I Consider there is no spot on this Earth more acceptable than this Temple . . . with this subject resting upon my mind and I Pray[ed] the Lord to open My way to see my Dead Redeemed. And while I prayed the spirit of the Lord rested upon me and Conveyed the following Testimony to me: 'Let my servant Wilford Call upon the virgins Maidens, Daughters & Mothers in Zion and let them Enter into my /Holy/ Temple on the 1 day of March . . . and there let them receive their . . . [ordinances] for and [in] behalf of the . . . dead . . . [of] my servant Wilford. . . . '

"This was merely a key to me. Light burst upon my understanding. I saw an Eff[ectual] door open to me for the redemption of my dead. And when I saw this I felt like shouting Glory Hallalulah to God and the Lamb.[39]

With Brigham Young's assistance, on 1 March 1877, Wilford's seventieth birthday, a congregation of 154 endowed and temple-worthy sisters from throughout the community gathered in the temple to act as proxies for his deceased female family members. To them he said: "What is gold or silver in Comparison to the redemption of our dead? Nothing. If I Can redeem my dead, and save myself and family I will be satisfied. I feel that when we get into the spirit world we shall see the importance of this days work. . . . Sisters you have the Blessings and Gratitude of my heart."[40]

Twelve days later Woodruff concluded: "By this labor in redeeming our dead by Proxey much Can be accomplished. Our dead can be redeemed. This principle has given me great Joy unspeakable at the thought that I Can live on the earth to behold my Numerous friends redeemed who Are in the spirit world. This principle says to us in loud language that the Lord is Good and Gracious, and that his Mercies Endureth forever."[41]

---

39. Woodruff, *Journal*, 7:332.
40. Woodruff, *Journal*, 7:332.
41. Woodruff, *Journal*, 7:333–34.

And so was instituted a procedural change that allowed any worthy Church member to act as proxy for any deceased person of the same gender, regardless of whether the proxy is a friend or descendant of the deceased. By infinitely expanding the pool of possible proxies, this change made possible a huge expansion and acceleration of ordinance work for the dead,[42] allowing any endowed individual the opportunity of returning to the temple again and again, as often as desired. Today we refer to this as temple worship—returning often to the temples to bless those who have gone before even as we ponder and pray and seek to know the mind and will of our Heavenly Father concerning our own particular needs.

42. In 2012, the First Presidency of The Church of Jesus Christ of Latter-day Saints gave further clarification and emphasis to proxy work, asking people who are doing family history research and temple work not to perform family file ordinances or submit family file names for deceased people not in their own family lines. This did not change the general rule instituted in Wilford Woodruff's time, which still allows any person of the same gender as the deceased to act as a proxy.

Chapter 18

BRIGHAM YOUNG'S WORK IS COMPLETED

2 March to 29 August 1877

On 14 March, a significant event occurred in the life of Brigham Young. Wilford Woodruff recorded that the aging prophet performed the ordinance work for John Sanderson Twiss, "the first time that Presidet Young has Ever [done such work] for any person on Earth."[1] And the next day: "We gave Endts to [many] persons the most we ever gave in one day in that Temple. Presidet Brigham Young spent the [next] day in the Temple [and did the work for] . . . Peirce."[2]

Three times during the following week, Wilford spent the evening with Brigham Young. Though he doesn't mention what they discussed, on 21 March, he wrote: "Presidet Young has been laboring all winter to get up a perfect form of [ordinances] as far as possible. They having been perfected I read them to the Company today."[3]

Though Wilford Woodruff's journal records his own involvement

---

1. The deceased husband of one of Brigham Young's wives.
2. The deceased husband of another of Brigham's wives.
3. Wilford Woodruff, *Journal, 1833–1898*, ed. Scott G. Kenney, 9 vols. (Midvale, Utah: Signature, 1983), 7:340; see also 7:322–23, 325–27, 337, 340–41, January through March 1877.

in "perfecting" the ceremonies, he was no more open regarding details than Brigham Young. Thus we have little specific information regarding the changes that had been made. Two or three things might be considered, however. First, work for the dead, which included ordination for deceased brethren and initial, or initiatory, ordinances for both deceased men and women, as well as certain sealing ordinances for families in a variety of situations both living and dead, had never before been done, at least in this dispensation. One can only imagine the hours it must have taken to work through, first, the wording and the basic ideas of procedure for each and every ordinance and situation they could conceive of, then to prepare a written, word-by-word directive of each ordinance as well as the proper procedures for implementation and recording that would stand the test of time and be used by ordinance workers and recorders in the future.

Fortunately we most likely know the identity of the man who finally made sense of this plethora of work and devised a way of making a proper record of it all, including the day by day ordinances performed—Moses Franklin Farnsworth, of Kanab. In his own journal Farnsworth records:

"On June 9, 1877, I received a call to the St. George Temple by the following letter:

"St. George, June 2, 1877

"Elder Frank Farnsworth

"Kanab, Utah

"Dear Brother:

"Your services are required as a Recorder in the St. George Temple. Come at your earliest convenience. Terms: Put your trust in God, and we will do the best we can for you and your family."

(signed) "Wilford Woodruff."

Brother Farnsworth, who had worked on the temple for a winter as a stone mason and surveyor's assistant, responded promptly, arriving in St. George on 14 June 1877. According to his journal, upon his reporting to the temple he met with Wilford Woodruff, who explained:

"Brother Farnsworth, you may wonder why I called you here. When Pres. Brigham Young went away leaving me to preside over the temple he left me a list of names from which I could call for all the help I needed. Your name was on the list. We have tried recorders, but they soon tire, and it seems a task to get those that will stay. If I was to offer $4.00 or $5.00 a day, I could perhaps get men, but we don't want that class of men. I want men that will throw their whole heart into this work. Our records are crude, our boxes are full of papers piled up, and I want you to take hold of them. Don't work too hard—this is a hot country. When you feel that you need a rest, take it. Work when you want to work and quit when you want to. Now, will you take hold of this work and stay with it?

"The new Recorder replied, 'I will try.'" To appropriately consider the task Brother Farnsworth faced, it would be well to remember that there were no proper record books for recording temple work, no system for keeping track of what was done, and no individual record forms had been adopted for any of it. Farnsworth and his assistants had to create new forms, not only for every ordinance but also forms on which to keep both temporary and permanent temple records. He writes: "We [even] had to do our own ruling and heading. It was an almost Herculean task, but by close application we were enabled to get things into a proper shape. I personally ruled the forms which were adopted, and books made."[4]

By remarkable good fortune the St. George Temple has on loan the small, handwritten, patron name slip for a Mrs. Anne Pringle, b. Middlesex, London, who was baptized by proxy on September 4, 1877, in the St. George Temple; A. P. Winsor, Baptiser. The end of this 1877 ruled slip of paper, which is slightly more than 6 inches long by ¾-inch wide, has been cut off, most likely indicating that the cut-off portion was kept for recording purposes, while the larger portion remained

---

4. Moses Franklin Farnsworth, "Personal Record," n.d., n.p., typescript; copy in possession of the authors.

with the sister who did the work—and ended up back in the St. George Temple 134 years later.

There is little doubt that it was Farnsworth, or those who were assisting him, who developed this inspired idea of using personal patron name slips for each deceased individual, with information repeated on it twice, as the best means of tracking both the person and the ordinance performed.

Even more interesting, today's records show that this particular ordinance was also recorded officially that same day, 4 September 1877, and it remains today the only time both proxy baptism and proxy confirmation for Mrs. Ann [Anne] Pringle were performed and recorded. This record illustrates the inspired effectiveness of the work Brother Farnsworth and the other early temple recorders were called to perform.[5]

Meanwhile, Wilford Woodruff, presiding in the temple by virtue of his apostolic calling though not yet called as temple president, continued to experience his own learning curve. On 22 March 1877 he recorded in his journal: "[I] sealed 11 dead persons to [deceased] John Sanders Twiss Presidet B Young & Sister Twiss as Proxy. I also Adopted two Couple to Presidet B Young. . . . This day was the first time in my life that I Ever heard [of] or performed the Ceremony of Adoption."[6]

---

5. Farnsworth, "Personal Record." As a summary of his first five years labor in the St. George Temple, Farnsworth added the following: "No. days attendance at temple (not including Sabbath days)—1,934; No. baptisms recorded in ink—46,544; No. names called at Font—122,087; No. names indexed—35,925; Pages of minutes—250; No. sealings recorded—24,785; No. adoptions recorded—4,312; No. child to parents recorded—5,821; No. recorded in private records—42,000; My own baptized—15,000; My own endowed—3,000; No. names taken for baptism—150,000; No. letters and postals received & written—3,169. P.S. This does not include penciling which more than exceeds the ink records." Farnsworth continued at his post in the St. George Temple for eleven years, after which he was transferred to Manti, where he continued his labors under the presidency of J. D. T. McAllister. Old age and deteriorating eyesight finally forced him to retire.

6. Woodruff, Journal, 7:340–41. It should be noted that this ordinance, known as the law of adoption, was ended in general conference in 1894 by Wilford Woodruff, then Church President. This ordinance allowed the sealing of one family to

On 30 March, also for the first time in his life, Wilford himself acted as proxy for a deceased man. He spent that evening with the First Presidency and all the Quorum of Twelve save one, meeting in Brigham Young's office next to the prophet's home.

The prophet's health, meanwhile, continued gradually to improve—due in part, some thought, to the St. George climate. Whatever the cause, it was noticeable through his frequent temple appearances, and people were pleased to see it. As for himself, Brigham felt good enough late in the winter to order eight yards of black cloth, from which he wanted a new suit cut and stitched in time for the upcoming general conference, which was to be held in the temple in St. George.

As spring came to St. George with the return of blossoms and leaves to the trees, early blooming flowers, and hungry, darting humming birds, Brigham felt better and better. Not only was he focusing on the needs of the temple and making continual adjustments to specific procedures, but there is little doubt he was also enjoying time with the members of his family residing in St. George—Lucy, her daughters Eudora (Dora), Rhoda, Susa, and Susa's four-year-old daughter, Leah, who loved her grandfather as only a four-year-old can.

Wilford Woodruff, meanwhile, continued in his normal role in the temple until 4 April, by which time most of the general authorities, plus many stake presidents and bishops from the territory, had arrived in St. George for the complete temple dedication. The general membership outside the St. George Stake had been discouraged from attending, it having been noted that capacity was limited in the temple as well as in the community. The next day, 5 April, Woodruff and the Twelve and First Presidency, as part of the first and only general conference

---

another that was not in any way related to the first. From that 1894 meeting onward, President Woodruff directed that all individuals were to be sealed only to their own ancestors and their own posterity, thus establishing the welding link of fathers to children and vice versa as promised by Elijah, quoting Malachi, to Joseph Smith the Prophet. See Boyd K. Packer, *The Holy Temple* (Salt Lake City: Bookcraft, 1980), 190–206.

to be held in St. George, met for a day in the temple, quite possibly in the ornate room behind the east pulpits on the fourth floor.[7] Wilford wrote: "This Stake of Zion was then Organized by appointing J. D. T. McAllister Presidet & Henry Eyring & Br Jones his Councillors. The Priest Teachers & Deacons were [also] organized. I spent the Evening at President Young with the Twelve."[8]

On 6 April 1877, in a solemn assembly gathered together in one of the temple's two main priesthood rooms,[9] the temple was finally dedicated fully. The room was filled to standing room only for the sacred and historic occasion. The Parowan Choir sang the opening hymn: "The Morning Breaks, the Shadows Flee." Normal conference business was conducted; speakers addressed the assembly; and President D.H. Wells, second counselor in the First Presidency, offered the dedicatory prayer.

President Wells mentioned how blessed the Saints had been after gathering in the American West to be able to survive in the desert, build homes, raise crops, and gather the materials of which this temple was composed. "We now dedicate and consecrate it to Thee that it may be holy unto Thee the Lord our God, for sacred and holy purposes." He went on to mention each part of the building: the foundation, the walls, the floors, the baptismal font, each of the five floors and their rooms, the roof and timbers and frames, the steps, the water pipes, chimneys, sewers, doors, windows—the entire building—"from the foundation unto the top thereof, that all may be holy unto the Lord our God."

7. This is the most ornately decorated original room in the St. George Temple, though historians don't know why or exactly what it was used for. Yet it was used for something long enough that when its use was discontinued, part of the floor needed replacing and all of it needed refinishing. One day we hope to understand what the room's purpose was.

8. Woodruff, *Journal*, 7:343.

9. Though no known record exists of which room was used, due to the first main floor being divided in order that part of the endowment ceremonies might be performed there, and also because its lesser Priesthood pulpits may already have been removed for the same purpose, the possibility exists that this Solemn Assembly was held on the second main floor (today's fourth floor).

President Wells then sought blessings for those who served and attended the temple: "We implore Thy blessings upon the various congregations of Thy people who may assemble in this House from time to time, both in their incomings and outgoings and may Thy blessing and Thy Spirit dwell herein and rest upon them for their comfort and edification, and abide richly in their hearts, that they may learn further of Thy ways and walk in Thy paths. . . . We acknowledge Thee and the great deliverance Thou hast wrought out for us, and we pray Thee, O God, in the name of Jesus, to accept of these Thy servants and the people and preserve and keep us in Thy most holy keeping."[10]

That evening in his journal Wilford Woodruff recorded: "The Annual Conference of the Church of Jesus Christ of Latter Day Saints met in the Temple of the Lord at 10 oclok to day. Prayer By D.H. Wells who offered the dedication Prayer. GQ Cannon spoke One Hour and 10 Minuts President Young 10 Minuts. He said all the property that we Could Call our own was our time and talents. The rest belongs to the Lord. Afternoon. Prayer By John Taylor. Joseph F Smith spoke one hour & 10 Minutes, John W Young 10 M."[11]

The next morning, according to the *Deseret News*, Brigham's theme was unity. "Unity of purpose and action, in carrying out the will of our Father, has been my theme all the day long," he declared.[12] Unity of the people with God and each other had empowered the construction of the temple, the tabernacle, the green fields and growing crops. In fact, the whole of civilization in St. George and throughout southern Utah were evidence of the power of unity in both building and bringing the kingdom of heaven to earth. People of one heart and mind laboring side by side, he declared, according to God's will, could "build up Zion."[13]

10. Kirk M. Curtis, "History of the St. George Temple" (master's thesis, Brigham Young University, 1964), 992–96.
11. Woodruff, *Journal*, 7:343.
12. Brigham Young, "Discourse," *Deseret News*, 23 May 1877, 247.
13. *Journal of Discourses*, 26 vols. (London: Latter-day Saints' Book Depot, 1854–86), 8:293.

That idea was central in Brigham's religious thinking. "We have no business here other than to build up and establish the Zion of God," he proclaimed.[14] "The purer the people are the more the Devel will rage, but the less Power the [world] . . . will have to do us injury."[15]

The next evening, 8 April, following the last session of conference, Wilford recorded that Brigham Young "Appointed [him] to take Charge of the Temple and presid[e] over it."[16] The Prophet then gave him a second assignment: "[He] requested me to write all the ordinances of the Church from the first baptism and confirmation through every ordinance of the Church. Geo. Q. Cannon assisted some in this writing, and when I had finished it to the satisfaction of the President, he said to me, 'Now you have before you an ensample to carry on the [work] in all the temples until the coming of the Son of Man.'"[17]

When the Prophet encouraged Woodruff to continue performing eternal marriages, Wilford recorded: "I told [the president] I was not able to . . . do all [of them] as I had injured myself at that labor in the Salt Lake Endowment House."[18] For that reason as well as his apostolic need to travel among the Saints, with the Prophet's approval, Wilford then "Set apart John Daniel Thompson McAllister to officiate . . . in sealing Ordinances."[19] A few days after ordaining David H. Cannon a bishop in the St. George 4th Ward on 18 April, he "set him apart to [administer all the] ordinances in the Temple as He shall be directed by Him who presides over the Temple."[20]

Brigham Young remained in St. George for another week, watching

---

14. Young, "Discourse," 23 May 1877.

15. Woodruff, *Journal*, 7:343–44.

16. Woodruff, *Journal*, 7:345.

17. Wilford Woodruff, "History of the St. George Temple, Its Cost & Dedication and the Labor Thereon," compiled 26 March 1883, in Devery S. Anderson, ed., *The Development of LDS Temple Worship* (Salt Lake City: Signature, 2011), 34.

18. Anderson, *Development*, 34.

19. Woodruff, *Journal*, 7:345.

20. Woodruff, *Journal*, 7:346–47.

as large numbers of people continued to visit the temple and perform ordinances for their deceased loved ones. Obviously pleased with the attendance, he spoke in every meeting held that week. "He was in an ebullient mood and expressed a warm affection for those he addressed. Over the years he had become very close to the people in Dixie and their leaders. He had spent a lot of time mingling with workers and supervisors. He had a genuine feeling for them. He knew them 'individually and collectively as well as he had known any people in the church.' . . . The large congregation was very quiet. [Perhaps] they sensed that this was the final occasion in their earthly existence when they would hear their beloved leader's advice and counsel. His departure from St. George the next day, April sixteenth, marked the last time he would look upon the city, 'between those volcanic ridges' which had become to him a second home."[21]

Between 1861 and 1870 Brigham made at least eight trips from Salt Lake City to St. George and then back again, over rough and sometimes almost impassable roads, each round-trip taking three to four weeks. Beginning at the end of 1870 he also made seven extended visits of two to three months and more, spending much of each winter in his own St. George "winter home"[22] as he kept a close eye on the Saints and the progress being made on the temple.[23]

"I have been with you more than five months," Brigham said during his last evening in St. George. "I have this to say to those present and those of this stake of Zion, you have done an excellent work. This

---

21. Andrew Karl Larson, *Erastus Snow* (Salt Lake City: University of Utah Press, 1971), 477–78.

22. Brigham Young's Winter Home, as it is called, is an official Church historic site, where tours are offered daily. Its address is 67 West 200 North, St. George, Utah. The site comprises the house and small office building that some mistakenly call a telegraph office. The office was built during the last year of Brigham's life, and there is no evidence that a telegraph line was ever installed, either there or in his home, either then or since.

23. See "Chronology and Summary of Brigham Young's Visits to St. George," historic sites files, Church History Library, The Church of Jesus Christ of Latter-day Saints, Salt Lake City, Utah.

temple has sprung up almost as Jonah's gourd.[24] . . . We have done a good and acceptable work the past winter and spring. I am well satisfied with it."[25]

The next morning, 16 April, Brigham left St. George on what would be his final departure. Wilford Woodruff recorded: "President Young & party left at 9:30 for salt lake." Several months later, he added: "This is the last time Prest Brigham Young & W Woodruff Ever met on Earth alive."[26]

On his way north, Brigham stopped in Manti and dedicated a site for the temple that Charles Pulsipher had inadvertently announced at least four years previously. Later in the summer the Prophet traveled to Logan and dedicated a temple site there. The completed Logan Temple would become Utah Territory's second temple in 1884, Manti its third in 1888, and finally the fourth, the Salt Lake Temple, would be completed and dedicated in 1893. But, as much as he might have liked, Brigham Young would not live to see the construction of the Manti and Logan temples even begun, and none but the St. George Temple completed.

Nevertheless, his health remained good through the late summer of 1877, and he was making plans for the future. Then, on Thursday, 23 August, he fell ill with violent cramps. Less than a week later, on 29 August 1877, and despite the efforts of four attending physicians, Brigham Young died of "cholera morbus." In more modern terms, he died of what physicians think was probably a ruptured appendix.[27]

The question might therefore be asked, did President Brigham Young live to fulfill the Prophet Joseph's last charge? Though it had long since stopped being Joseph's charge and had in every sense become

24. See Jonah 4:6–11.

25. James G. Bleak, "Annals of the Southern Utah Mission," 15 April 1877, 1, Dixie State University Archives, St. George, Utah.

26. Woodruff, *Journal*, 7:34.

27. Leonard J. Arrington, *Brigham Young: American Moses* (Chicago and Urbana: University of Illinois Press, 1986), 398–99.

his own, Brigham may not have accomplished all he had hoped and dreamed about lifting and sanctifying the Church while bringing each and every member into the presence of the Lord in and through multiple holy temples. Additionally, the spiritually unifying power of the United Order had proven too challenging for the people and so had already become something less stringent. Nevertheless, perhaps in a coming day it would, along with the other revealed doctrines of the Restoration, have the desired effect that he and his beloved Brother Joseph had always sought—the uplifting and perfecting of the Saints of God.

Meanwhile, he had kept both his quorum and the Church intact after Joseph's death; following death or apostasy within the Twelve, he had kept the ranks of the quorum filled with good and honorable men who had received under his hands the same keys Joseph had once given him; and finally he had led the body of the Saints to the "tops of the mountains,"[28] where despite long years of intense opposition he had finally managed to build unto the Lord a "mountain of the Lord's House."[29] Therein, he knew, the sacred sealing powers of Elijah were at last being used to turn the hearts of the fathers to the children and the children to the fathers so that the whole earth would not be wasted at Christ's coming. And there, in tiny, out-of-the-way St. George, where the Saints of southern Utah had striven through great sacrifice to purify themselves, Zion had at last begun to "be exalted above the hills."[30]

Why there, it might be asked? And today we would answer, because there Brigham Young the prophet had directed the completion and setting in order all the ordinances of the holy temple and committed them to writing. These sacred records, originally kept in the St. George Temple, would set the pattern for administering the ordinances

---

28. Isaiah 2:1; 2 Nephi 12:2.
29. Isaiah 2:1; 2 Nephi 12:2.
30. Isaiah 2:1; 2 Nephi 12:2.

of salvation and exaltation in Logan, Manti, and the Salt Lake Temple after it was dedicated in 1893.

Those things accomplished, Brigham could go to his rest in peace, his beloved St. George Temple having become the first temple of the restoration in which the fullness of ordinance work for both the living and the dead had been performed.[31]

---

31. In the October 1877 semiannual general conference of The Church of Jesus Christ of Latter-day Saints Wilford Woodruff reported that between January 9, 1877, and September 20, 1877, the temple workers had performed 395 live baptisms and 23,989 baptisms for the dead. They had also performed endowments for 424 living males, 520 living females, 4,204 deceased males, and 6,448 deceased females. They had ordained seven deceased brethren to the office of high priest and 4,085 deceased brethren and 264 living brethren to the office of elder. Sealing of 356 families for the living had taken place, as had the sealing of 3,352 females to deceased males. They had sealed 174 children to living parents and 95 to parents already deceased. This is a goodly amount of work for less than six months. See Susan Staker, ed., *Waiting for World's End: The Diaries of Wilford Woodruff* (Salt Lake City: Signature, 1993), 311–12.

Chapter 19

FOR WHOM IS THE WORK
TO BE DONE?

1877

Another significant change to Wilford Woodruff's understanding of temple work came sometime prior to Sunday, 19 August 1877, only a few days before the death of Brigham Young. President Woodruff recorded in his journal: "I spent the evening in preparing a list of the Noted Men of the 17 Century and the 18th including the signers of the declaration of Independence and the Presidents of the United States for Baptism on Tuesday the 21 Aug. 1877."[1] While the historical prominence of those named by President Woodruff has given the following event much recognition, its greater significance is that "this particularly unique group of people, unconnected as they were to any families in the Church,[2] reinforced the doctrine that all the 'worthy dead,' whether

---

1. Wilford Woodruff, *Journal, 1833–1898*, ed. Scott G. Kenney, 9 vols. (Midvale, Utah: Signature, 1983), 7:367.
2. The lone exception of which we are aware was Church member Levi Ward Hancock, who on 29 and 30 May 1877 did the work in the St. George Temple for his direct ancestor John Hancock, whose signature on the Declaration of Independence was by far the most prominent. The work for the other signers was done in August.

family or friend, would be taught the gospel and the ordinances of salvation should be offered to all through proxy work."[3]

Though he did not note it in his journal, President Woodruff said elsewhere that on two of the evenings previous, most likely in the temple room where he often went to pray,[4] he received a glorious vision. In it he was visited by a congregation from the spirit world, many of whom had been prominent in the history of the United States of America. In a discourse given in the Salt Lake Tabernacle on 16 September 1877, President Woodruff described this experience as follows:

"In order that this work may be done, we must have Temples in which to do it; and what I wish to say to you, my brethren and sisters, is that the God of heaven requires us to rise up and build them, that the work of redemption may be hastened. Our reward will meet us when we go behind the vail. . . .

"We have labored in the St. George Temple since January, and we have done all we could there; and the Lord has stirred up our minds, and many things have been revealed to us concerning the dead. President Young has said to us, and it is verily so, if the dead could they would speak in language loud as ten thousand thunders, calling upon

---

3. Richard E. Bennett, "Line upon Line, Precept upon Precept: Reflections on the 1877 Commencement of the Performance of Endowments and Sealings for the Dead," *BYU Studies* 44, no. 3 (2005): 66.

4. Woodruff, *Journal*, 7:331. An alternative account for the location of this vision, which is cherished by descendants of the Thomas and Caroline Cottam family, is described by Lula Romney Clayson. She records: "It was while living in the upstairs of Thomas Cottam's home that the Signers of the Declaration of Independence came to [Wilford Woodruff] three [two] nights in succession, asking that the vicarious work for the dead . . . be done for them" (Lula Romney Clayson, "History of My Grandfather, Thomas Cottam"), as quoted in William Howard Thompson, ed. and comp., and Parts Written by William Howard Thompson, *Thomas Cottam 1820 and His Wives Ann Howarth 1820 and Caroline Smith 1820, Descendants* (privately published, Thomas Cottam Family Organization, 1987), n.p.; photocopy courtesy Daughters of Utah Pioneers McQuarrie Memorial Museum, St. George, Utah. Annie McArthur Jennings, a great-granddaughter of Thomas and Caroline, recalls being told that "during the nights of the vision the family could hear Wilford Woodruff pacing back and forth in the room above them" (Annie McArthur Jennings, personal interview with author, 21 October 2012).

the servants of God to rise and build Temples, magnify their calling and redeem their dead. This doubtless sounds strange to those present who believe not the faith and doctrine of the Latter-day Saints; but when we get to the spirit-world we will find out that all that God has revealed is true. We will find, too, that everything there is reality, and that God has a body, parts and passions, and the erroneous ideas that exist now with regard to him will have passed away. I feel to say little else to the Latter-day Saints, wherever and whenever I have the opportunity of speaking to them, than to call upon them to build these Temples now under way, to hurry them up to completion. The dead will be after you, they will seek after you as they have after us in St. George. They called upon us, knowing that we held the keys and power to redeem them."[5]

The Apostle and temple president then declared:

"I will here say, before closing, that two weeks before I left St. George, the spirits of the dead gathered around me, wanting to know why we did not redeem them. Said they, 'You have had the use of the Endowment House for a number of years, and yet nothing has ever been done for us.[6] We laid the foundation of the government you now enjoy, and we never apostatized from it, but we remained true to it and were faithful to God.' These were the signers of the Declaration of Independence, and they waited on me for two days and two nights. I thought it very singular, that notwithstanding so much work had been done, and yet nothing had been done for them. *The thought never entered my heart, from the fact, I suppose, that heretofore our minds were reaching after our more immediate friends and relatives.* I straightway went into the baptismal font and called upon brother McCallister to baptize me for the signers of the Declaration of Independence, and fifty

---

5. Boyd K. Packer, *The Holy Temple* (Salt Lake City: Bookcraft, 1980), 193–94.

6. Though Woodruff seemed unaware of this, John M. Bernhisel had completed some work for these individuals in August 1876 in the Endowment House in Salt Lake City. See Jennifer Mackley, *Wilford Woodruff's Witness of the Redemption of the Dead.* In a memo from Church History Department, August 2012, it was noted that Bernhisel's work included only baptisms and confirmations, not endowments.

other eminent men, making one hundred in all, including John Wesley, Columbus, and . . . nearly every president of the United States."[7]

"Can you point me to any emperor, king, priest, denomination or power on the face of the whole earth, outside of the Church of Jesus Christ of Latter-day Saints, who has power to go forth and redeem one of their dead? There never was a soul anywhere that could do this until God organized His Church upon the earth.[8] The signers of the Declaration of Independence and the men that laid the foundation of this great American government know full well that there has not been a power on the earth where they could apply to have this principle carried out in their behalf, only the Apostles that held the keys of the kingdom of God in this generation."[9]

President Woodruff concluded, "There is no more glorious principle given to man than the power which you have while holding the Priesthood, to go forth and redeem your fathers, your mothers, your progenitors. . . . Such principles are worthy of contemplation."[10]

On 21 August, once the first day's work for these founding fathers had been completed, Wilford Woodruff recorded: "It was a very interesting day. I felt thankful that we had the privilege and the power to administer for the worthy dead especially for the signers of the declaration of Independence, that inasmuch as they had laid the foundation of our Government that we Could do as much for them as they had done for us.

"Sister Lucy Bigelow Young went forth into the font and was Baptized for Martha Washington and her family and seventy (70) of the Eminent women of the world.[11] I called upon all the Brethren & Sisters

---

7. Quoted in Packer, *Holy Temple*, 193–94; emphasis added.

8. Woodruff, "Remarks Made at the Salt Lake Stake Conference, Sunday, December 12, 1897, by President Wilford Woodruff," *Deseret Evening News* 31, no. 23, 18 December 1897, 9.

9. Woodruff, "Remarks," 18 December 1897, 9.

10. Woodruff, "Remarks," 18 December 1897, 9.

11. Many in the Church seem to have strong feelings about Wilford Woodruff's

who were present to assist in getting Endowments for those that we had been Baptized for to day. . . . There were Baptized in all to day 682."[12]

Three more times President Woodruff publicly referred to this remarkable series of events: during the dedication of the Salt Lake Temple in April 1893, at a stake conference in 1897, and in April 1898, during his last general conference address. At that final time he testified:

"I am going to bear my testimony to this assembly, if I never do it again in my life, that those men who laid the foundation of this American Government and signed the Declaration of Independence were the best spirits the God of Heaven could find on the earth. They were choice spirits, not wicked men. General Washington and all the men that labored for the purpose were inspired of the Lord. Another thing I am going to say here, because I have a right to say it. Every one of those men that signed the Declaration of Independence with General Washington called upon me as an Apostle of the Lord Jesus Christ, in the Temple at St. George two consecutive nights, and demanded at my hands that I should go forth and attend to the ordinances of the house of God for them. Men are here, I believe, that know of this— Brothers J. D. T. McAllister, David H. Cannon and James G. Bleak. Brother McAllister baptized me for all these men, and I then told these

---

"eminent women" and wonder that more is not made of them. In a recent online news article, Seth Adam Smith wrote: "To be clear, Wilford Woodruff's record never states that the eminent women appeared to him. It only states that temple work was done in their behalf" (Seth Adam Smith, "The Eminent Women of the St. George Temple," *Meridian Magazine*, 19 Jan. 2012). Ann Mason, in a comment to the above article, states: "Seth's comment . . . that Wilford Woodruff certainly didn't pull the [womens'] names out of a hat is true. But they did not appear to him either . . . Wilford carefully chose the women from the books written by Evert Duyckinck, *Eminent Men and Women of Europe and America*." Mason adds that instead of worrying whether or not the women appeared along with the men, our focus should instead be "on the real message of Wilford Woodruff's amazing experience and of the role of the living in the redemption of the dead." We agree. Incidentally, according to the research of author Jennifer Mackley, 68 of the names of the Wives/Mothers of Eminent Men for whom the 1877 temple work was done are found in volumes 1 and 2 of Evert Duyckinck's work.

12. This number is the total of baptisms for the dead performed that day, including many family names in addition to Woodruff's eminent men and women.

brethren that it was their duty to go into the Temple and labor until they got endowments for all of them. They did it. Would those spirits have called upon me, as an Elder in Israel, to perform that work if they had not been noble spirits before God? They would not. I bear this testimony because it is true. The spirit of God bore record to myself and the brethren while we were laboring in that way."[13]

Though we have no known corroborating testimony from David H. Cannon, in the biography of John Daniel Thompson McAllister,[14] under date of Tuesday, 21 August 1877, we read: "This day I was baptized for all the dead Presidents of the United States except Martin Van Buren & Jas. Buchanan." McAllister's biographer continues: "The next day, August 22, John 'received [ordinances] for General George Washington and Sister Lucy B. Young received [the same] for Mary Ball, Washington's Mother.' [Then] John 'was ordained a High Priest for Washington.'" On 23 August John recorded that he: "received [ordinances] for Millard Fillmore. Also acted for Augustine Washington and my wife, Ann, for his 1st wife and 2nd, Mary Ball in the sealing."[15] [John] also was ordained a High Priest for Benjamin Franklin, on Thursday, 23 August."[16]

---

13. Wilford Woodruff, Conference Report, 10 Apr. 1898, 89–90.

14. Lucile McAllister Weenig, comp., *Biography of John Daniel Thompson McAllister, Utah Pioneer, Second President of the St. George Temple and of the Manti Temple of The Church of Jesus Christ of Latter-day Saints* (privately published, 1980), 55. McAllister's biographer concludes: "Ann also acted for 'Maria Fackrell, who was sealed to John." Maria Fackrell, according to Mackley, was coincidentally baptized the same day as the eminent women but is not one of the eminent women for whom Wilford Woodruff directed work to be done. Next to her name on the St. George Temple record is the phrase "was in the church" indicating she was a member of the Church before her death. In 1877 it was customary to rebaptize individuals prior to their receiving Temple ordinances, so presumably Maria Fackrell was rebaptized, Lucy B. Young acting as proxy, on August 21—before Ann McAllister acted as proxy for Maria in her sealing to John D. T. McAllister on August 23.

15. Ezra Taft Benson, *The Teachings of Ezra Taft Benson*, 603–4. Only a few couples, including members of George Washington's family and John and Abigail Adams, were sealed in 1877.

16. Weenig, comp., *Biography of John Daniel Thompson McAllister*, 55.

While James Godson Bleak was historian of the Southern Mission and a marvelous record keeper, his only known testimony of Woodruff's visions was given many years after the fact. He said at that time: "I was also present in the St. Geo. Temple and witnessed the appearance of the Spirits of the Signers of the Declaration of Independence and also the Spirits of the Presidents of the U.S. up to that time. And also others, such as Martin Luther and John Wesley (The man that started the Methodist Faith) who came to Wilford Woodruff and demanded that their baptism[s] and endowments be done. Wilford Woodruff was baptized for all of them. While I and Brothers J. D. T. McAllister and David H. Cannon (who were witnesses to the request) were endowed for them."[17]

---

17. Mariel Bleak Spinning, "Family History as Dictated by James G. Bleak to his Great-Granddaughter Mariel Bleak Spinning," n.d., unpublished holograph, copy in possession of Vera Lynn Taggart, Fresno, California. See also Vicki Jo Anderson, *The Other Eminent Men of Wilford Woodruff*, 2d ed. (Cottonwood, Ariz.: Zichron Historical Research Institute and Malta, Idaho: Nelson Book, 1994), 420.

Bleak's statement continues: "These men that we did work for, were choice Spirits, not wicked men. They laid the foundation of this American Gov., and signed the Declaration of Independence. And were the best spirits the God of Heaven could find on the face of the earth to perform this work. Martin Luther and John Wesley helped to release the people from religious bondage that held them during the dark ages. They also prepared the people['s] hearts so they would be ready to receive the restored gospel when the Lord sent it again to men on earth." Wilford Woodruff said, "Would those spirits have came to me and demanded at my hand as an Elder in Israel, that I should go and attend to the saving ordinances in the House of God, for them if they had not been noble spirits before God? They would not. I bear testimony, because it's true. The Spirit of God bore record to myself and these brethren while we were laboring in their behalf."

Unfortunately, based upon the extensive research of Jennifer Mackley, Bleak's statement would have been made sometime after Woodruff's 1898 conference address—since he quotes passages from it—and before Bleak's death in 1918—anywhere from 20 to 40 years after the fact. And because he is dictating to his great-granddaughter who is apparently married, it seems likely to be closer to the 40 years than otherwise. This becomes an issue because his recollections, when compared to Woodruff's several accounts, differ on at least four significant points. First, Bleak is mistaken when he states that, in addition to the Signers, all the US Presidents appeared as well as others such as Martin Luther and John Wesley. Although proxy work was done for all but two deceased U.S. Presidents, according to all four of Woodruff's accounts the only Presidents who appeared to him were George Washington and Signers Thomas Jefferson and John Adams. Second,

We conclude by repeating Wilford Woodruff's feelings the day the baptisms and confirmations of these eminent individuals were completed: "I felt thankful that we had the privilege and the power to administer for the worthy dead especially for the signers of the declaration of Independence, that inasmuch as they had laid the foundation of our Government that we Could do as much for them as they had done for us."[18]

While some have questioned President Woodruff's account on a number of different points, we agree with Woodruff researcher Jennifer Mackley that "his account cannot be taken out of the context of the development of the temple ordinances during the nineteenth century."[19] As with everything else the Lord made known to the leaders of the restored Church, every aspect of temple ordinances and ceremonies came line upon line, precept upon precept, here a little and there a little, exactly as He planned it. And in this case, Wilford's mind was abruptly opened to the fact that the Saints' eternal responsibilities extended far beyond the limits of their own family lines.

We concur with Mackley's conclusion: "It is this role of the living—to search out those for whom they can act as proxies and thus

Martin Luther was not included in the list of Eminent Men and his proxy work was not done at that time. Third, Bleak's statement that Woodruff was baptized for all of them is inaccurate. If he was using Woodruff's 1898 address as his reference, Woodruff's statement that "Brother McAllister baptized me for all these men" refers back to the Signers and not all 121 men. Woodruff was baptized for 54 of the 56 Signers as well as 46 other eminent men and John D. T. McAllister was baptized for 21. Fourth, Bleak's statement that he and the three members of the temple presidency—Woodruff, Cannon, and McAllister—were endowed for all 121 men is inaccurate since more than 70 different men acted as proxies in administering their endowments. And finally, did Bleak actually "witness" one or both appearances of the Signers and George Washington to Wilford Woodruff? And, as he claimed, did McAllister and Cannon also "witness" the visions? Neither Cannon nor McAllister ever hinted that they had, neither did Wilford Woodruff hint at such a thing. As for Bleak's own witness, at this late date we have no way of knowing the facts, but giving a truly fine man the benefit of the doubt, let us accept him at his word while we await the time when we can ask him for ourselves.

18. Woodruff, *Journal*, 7:369.
19. Jennifer Mackley, e-mail to the authors, 11 February 2012.

offer them the opportunity to accept Christ's universal salvation—that makes [Woodruff's] experience in August 1877 an important symbol of temple work. Wilford Woodruff's vision of the redemption of the dead continues to inspire thousands to turn their hearts . . . to their . . . ancestral fathers. . . . As Wilford Woodruff explained to the Saints, it is this work, God's work 'to bring to pass the immortality and eternal life of man' that He asks us to take part in, in holy temples built to His name."[20]

---

20. Moses 1:39. Mackley, *Wilford Woodruff's Witness*. In 1894 Wilford Woodruff, then Church President, announced in general conference new revelation that completely altered two additional temple procedures. In the first he directed that sisters who had been married to nonmember men who were deceased, might thereafter be sealed to them if that was what they wished, once their deceased husbands' temple work had been completed. This ended the long-standing practice of having such sisters sealed to high-ranking Church authorities in order to give them the blessings of sealing. The other change ended the ordinance of adoption. See Packer, *Holy Temple*, 190–206.

Chapter 20

THE HONEYMOON TRAIL

1877 and Onward

As the weeks and months and then years passed, men and women from every direction continued streaming into St. George to participate in the temple's sacred ordinances. Besides coming from Bunkerville, Ivins, Leeds, Rockville, Cedar City, Beaver, Panguitch, Parowan, Salt Lake City, and even Logan and other Cache Valley communities, many patrons came to St. George from even more remote distances. Perhaps the most memorable of these were the folk who followed at least portions of the Honeymoon Trail up from the desert regions of the Southwest. Because there was for many years no temple other than St. George in all the American West or Southwest, all Nevadans and those whose homes were far across the parched and forbidding country of Arizona into New Mexico and even Old Mexico, made their tiresome and perilous way to the temple in St. George. All of these faithful individuals traveled every foot of the way over primitive and rugged wagon roads, including what came to be called the Honeymoon Trail.

During the 1870s while the temple was under construction, certain hardy souls traveled this difficult pathway to St. George with wagonloads of cheese and fruit to feed the temple builders. Once the temple was dedicated, many of these same people used the trail as patrons in order to receive and perform sacred ordinances. There are many legends about the trail, particularly concerning wedding parties that came by team and wagon. Many of those who came considered their time on the trail and in the temple as the spiritual high points of their lives.

The trail, first blazed by Latter-day Saint pathfinders and missionaries to the Indians, men such as Jacob Hamblin, Ira Hatch, and Thales Haskell, began to see actual settlers as early as 1870. These pioneers had been called to establish settlements on the Little Colorado River and beyond. They blazed the way, and soon Latter-day Saint hamlets were springing up along the lower Little Colorado in eastern Arizona. Lot Smith led some of these intrepid colonizers, and though Smith was ultimately killed by Indians, he and the others helped settle Camp Obed, Sunset, Brigham City, and Joseph City, all in Arizona.

It was a constant battle, however, due to "the irascible nature of the Little Colorado . . . [which] could be a raging torrent destroying dams and dykes one day and a useless bed of mud and quicksand the next: 'too thin to plow but too thick to drink.'"[1] One is hard pressed *not* to remember the same description of the ever volatile Virgin River, which remains that way even today.

No matter the challenges of the forbidding landscape, with the dedication of the St. George Temple in 1877 faithful souls who believed in the eternal nature of mankind, began a most difficult undertaking in order that they might participate in sacred binding ordinances. Though branches of the trail originated in numerous areas, including Mesa/Phoenix and the Pima Valley, Snowflake, St. Johns, and western New Mexico, they all somehow merged at Sunset Crossing near modern

---

1. Norma Baldwin Ricketts, ed., *Arizona's Honeymoon Trail and Mormon Wagon Roads* (Mesa, Ariz.: Maricopa East Company, International Society, Daughters of Utah Pioneers [Mesa, Ariz.: Cox Printing Co., 2001], xi, 9. See also Charles S. Peterson, *Take Up Your Mission! Mormon Colonizing along the Little Colorado River, 1870–1900* (Tucson: University of Arizona Press, 1973), 89–90.

Winslow, Arizona. The pathway from there to St. George is the route that became known as the Honeymoon Trail.

Generally heading in a northwesterly direction, the long and winding trail followed the west side of the Little Colorado to Grand Falls, where it crossed to the east side of the river near present-day Cameron, Arizona. From there it left the river and snaked north past the Echo Cliffs and Bitter Springs to Lee's Ferry, where it crossed the Colorado River. Skirting the Vermillion Cliffs, it passed through House Rock Valley and on into Kanab, built just north of the Utah/Arizona border. Pipe Springs was the next stop as the trail wound back into Arizona then passed through Canaan Gap and, now following the Temple Trail that led northwestward from Mt. Trumbull, it dropped down off the Hurricane Fault into Warner Valley and so back into Utah. From there it wound westward past Ft. Pearce and 15 miles further along crossed the Virgin River and entered St. George. "The round trip," writes Dean Garrett, trail historian, "sometimes took as long as six weeks, yet couples embarked on the trip willingly and gladly."[2]

Sources say the very first of the "honeymooners" to make the journey, were Alof Larson, who in 1877 was called with his parents to settle in Arizona, and May Hunt, daughter of Bishop John Hunt, who had come to Arizona earlier with his family. The young people were both living in Snowflake when they apparently met in late 1880, though it may have been earlier. By the spring of 1881 they had decided to be married and so commenced preparations for a fall departure for St. George. By October, after laboring through the spring and summer grading land for the railroad, Alof informed May that he had accumulated teams, a wagon, and sufficient cash necessary to make the longed-for journey. Accompanied by twelve individuals in five wagons, they set out in a drizzling rain. This soon cleared, and for the remainder of the trek they enjoyed fine fall weather. Their traveling companions included Alof's sister Emma, who was accompanied by her future husband

2. H. Dean Garrett, "The Honeymoon Trail," *Ensign*, July 1989, 23.

Jesse N. Smith, stake president of the Snowflake Stake. During the journey to St. George the two young women slept together in one of the wagons, and the men occupied the great outdoors.

Louise Larson Comish, daughter of Alof, wrote of their trip: "A rollicking camp song was composed and sung often, everyone was in high spirits, the miles slipped by without incident or mishap—except that Miss Hunt developed a boil under her arm that Emma poulticed with a strip of bacon, the only thing available, and always she laughed when she applied it. This levity irked Miss May somewhat.

"Twenty days later, the party reached its destination. On 26 October 1881, Alof and May were married in the House of the Lord for time and all eternity by . . . David H. Cannon," acting president of the St. George Temple.

"By December 5th, Mr. and Mrs. Alof Larson were back safely in Snowflake. There was the usual wedding dance held for this popular couple. And Bishop Hunt and his wife had the Larson family in for a dinner party. Then Mons and Ellen returned the compliment by having the Hunts as guests in their home. May records in her journal: 'Father and Mother Larson baked a cake of sugar, eggs and starch on a roller, before a hot fire, or bed of coals, pouring the batter on very slowly as the roller turned and the cake baked. They gave me four inches off the top, which had a nice paper flower in it, which I kept for months.'"[3]

One additional experience is worthy of mention, the account of a woman known only as Grandma Whiting. She says: "I was always so proud of Pa [her husband] because he always had a very good wagon and nice team of horses. When we started out for SG on what was known as the Honeymoon Trail, with about ten other wagons, I was excited because I was about to become a new bride. I had loved Pa since I was about fifteen, but my folks wouldn't let me marry him until I was eighteen.

3. Louise Larson Comish, "Alof Larson, A Biography," 1961, n.p., typescript; copy in possession of the authors.

"There was another young couple who were going to be married also and they rode with us in our wagon. It was so romantic; at night the girls slept in the wagon and the boys slept underneath it on the ground.

"It was a nice trip until we got to the Colorado River. The river had flooded and so they had to float the wagons across. When we finally arrived in St. George and opened out trunks, our beautiful white muslin wedding dresses were rust-colored from the silt of the river. We scrubbed and scrubbed our dresses on washboards with lye soap hoping to get the color out. We scrubbed until we didn't dare scrub them any more for fear we would wear them out! What were we going to do, for we were to be sealed in the temple the next morning?

"That night we knelt by our bed and plead with the Lord to please make our dresses white so that we could wear them in the temple the next morning. Sick at heart we at last fell asleep, and you know, Joycell, when we woke up the next morning, our beautiful wedding dresses were as white as snow!"[4]

One hopes that all the travelers along this trail were so blessed and fared so well.

---

4. "Grandma Whiting," tape recording by Joycell Cooper, photocopy of transcription, Daughters of Utah Pioneers McQuarrie Memorial Museum, St. George, Utah.

Chapter 21

THE ST. GEORGE TEMPLE

Then and Now

Dixie, the 'Cotton Country,'" according to historian Nels Anderson, "was the inland capital of [Brigham Young's] Mormon empire. It was there the first [western] temple was completed. It was there that the United Order was established in 1874. It was there that [he] went in winter to enjoy the milder climate [as well as his family in St. George,] and often his presence served to transfer church headquarters to Dixie during winter months. Also, St. George, with the surrounding area, was the base of [Brigham's] operations for extending the Mormon frontier into Nevada, Arizona, New Mexico, Colorado, and across the border into Mexico. . . .

"The primary objective of Brigham Young's leadership over the church can be stated in simple terms. He would gather the remnants of Israel together; he would move Zion to the Rocky Mountains; he would drill into the Saints the principles of the Gospel laid down by Brother Joseph; he would continue to send missionaries to gather in the chosen from all corners of the earth, and he would build the church so strong that all the legions of hell could not uproot it. Such were the objectives of Joseph Smith. It took a Brigham Young to attain them."[1]

Brigham Young's mortal ministry in The Church of Jesus Christ of Latter-day Saints began with temple building in Kirtland and ended with the dedication of the St. George Temple and the passing on of all the keys and ordinances of the Holy Priesthood. For him, that must have been a satisfying ending.

But then, nothing really ended at all. Brigham had gone ahead, but other prophets followed one after another, as did temples, until now, 135-plus years later, there have been many prophets and numerous temples to dot the earth with more announced or under current construction. And the work in each temple harks back to the frontier village of St. George and the remarkable men and women who, for at least a season of their lives, sacrificed almost everything to bring us this third temple of the Restoration.

Since 1877, the St. George Temple has been part of numerous experiences and events. Yet these, too, are more about the people involved than they are about the sacred structure itself, though the actual building has endured lightning strikes and earthquakes, changes, modifications, updates, and will likely endure more in the coming years.

This chapter, though covering some of the temple's historical highlights since 1877, is more a summary than a complete time line. To illustrate, perhaps we might begin with a powerful strike upon the temple by Nature itself.

In the early morning hours of 16 August 1878, a violent storm hit St. George. A lightning bolt struck the temple tower, destroying the two metal balls and weather vane and setting the wooden tower

---

1. Nels Anderson, *Desert Saints: The Mormon Frontier in Utah* (Chicago: University of Chicago Press, 1942), xviii, 42.

structure ablaze. James G. Bleak reported the incident in a letter to Church President John Taylor and temple president Wilford Woodruff, who was in Salt Lake City at the time:

"You will perceive that the damage is to Dome and tower, consisting of woodwork and lath and plaster work. The main building is all right, except the two upper circular window frames on the S. side of the tower. These are shattered and blackened, though but one light of glass is fractured. Herewith please find enclosed photograph of the St. George Temple, which is sent to aid you in understanding our description. The red ink marks, show the outside damage as far as we can. Shall we repair the damage done or not? Until we hear from you, we shall use a wagon cover, etc., to prevent damage by rain. We greatly recognize the providence of the Almighty in the comparatively slight damage done, in consideration of the severity of the shock. It has not in the least interfered with our ordinance work."[2]

When the letter was written, the full extent of the damage was not yet known, though local leaders thought it was confined to the tower itself. While they awaited instructions they made temporary repairs, including removing what was left of the balls and weather vane. When these items were ultimately replaced, the work was again done by Christopher Riding.

For unexplained reasons, replacing the balls and weather vane and rebuilding the tower was delayed until 1882–83. Until then the full extent of the damage remained unknown, as well as how close the temple had actually come to burning to the ground. That was explained in a letter from John D. T. McAllister to Wilford Woodruff. Written on 30 July 1883, after repair work was under way, this letter read in part:

"We find in repairing the roof, that the hand of the Lord, and nothing else, must have saved the building from being burnt at the time the tower was struck by lightning; for, at a place about 24 feet south, from the

---

2. Kirk M. Curtis, "History of the St. George Temple" (master's thesis, Brigham Young University, 1964), 65.

base of the tower and about 15 inches from the Eastern parapet, one of the workmen found the heel of his boot break through the canvas covering. This led to an examination, and, it was found that one of the roof boards was burst in by the lightning. Close examination showed that . . . the board is missing some 7 x 24 inches [that was burned], but the narrow escape from the fire is manifest in the deeply charred edge of the [remaining] board . . . indicating that the fire must have smouldered for some time, and that too, right in contact with the tar-covered canvas which covers the roof. We acknowledge the preserving care of the Almighty."[3]

The design for the new tower was prepared by William H. Folsom, assistant Church architect, under the direction of Truman O. Angell. Though some prior work was done, reconstruction really began in 1882 when Thomas Allman was sent back to St. George to supervise it. The new tower of the temple was finished late in the winter of 1883.[4] Christopher Lister Riding was reenlisted to replace the two damaged balls with one and to craft a new weather vane. Unfortunately, due to advancing arthritis and other health issues, Riding was unable to climb to the top of the much taller tower to effect the installation. He asked his thirteen-year-old son, John Henry (born 26 May 1870), to climb the tower and install the new equipment atop the dome. John Henry willingly agreed, and over the course of two or three days, he installed the new vane and single ball. They survived the test of time and were not replaced until 1992.[5]

A 3 January 1883 article in the *Deseret News* reported that construction of the new tower was under way, and on 15 February another article said, "The dome on the St. George Temple is undergoing a remodeling,

3. Curtis, "History," 66.
4. See Darrell E. Jones, "The St. George Temple Tower: Evolution of a Design," *Journal of Mormon History* (Spring 2008): 121–26.
5. Phyllis Morley, St. George, Utah. After John Henry Riding's death 15 April 1948, his funeral was held in the St. George Tabernacle, where this account was related over the pulpit. A copy of the record made at the time was given by Morley, a granddaughter of John Henry Riding, to author Blaine M. Yorgason, on 11 May 2013.

but yet it is hardly large enough, considering the size of the building, but is so far ahead of the former that it looks very well as it nears completion."[6]

In confirmation of this assessment, the tower replacement was built 40 feet higher than the original and now measures 175 feet from the ground to the top of the weather vane.

Concerning the ongoing development and proper performance of the temple ordinances, during the administration of John D. T. McAllister, his counselor David H. Cannon had an unusual experience. As related by his granddaughter Josephine Cannon Jones: "One day during a session in the temple the officiator made a mistake in the wording

---

6. Curtis, "History," 67. As Darrell E. Jones found during his research, a completely false story about Brigham Young and the temple tower got started in St. George in an April 1977 article that appeared in the *Color Country Spectrum*. This article was followed by another in the *St. George Magazine* (Jones, "The St. George Temple Tower," 113) that embellished the story, and yet a third with still more innuendo appeared in the same magazine in 1994. The first story undeservedly called the lightning strike Brigham's "revenge" over the supposed refusal of the St. George builders to his request to replace the original somewhat squatty tower during his lifetime. The story originated from a humorous remark made by a Church architectural historian while on a visit to St. George in early 1977. He had just read an 1876 entry in the journal of Brigham Young Jr., which went this way: "One day Brigham Jr. and his father were visiting the nearly completed temple when Brigham remarked to his son that the tower seemed too short for the building." Brigham Jr. merely recorded the comment in his journal. Nothing was publicly said about it at that time nor ever after until a hundred years later. Then a jocular, off-the-cuff remark before friends spread mouth to mouth until, in the course of the first undocumented article, followed by two more, it became accepted fact. Darrell E. Jones researched the matter and published his results in the article cited above, footnote 4. His research turned up no evidence that Brigham Jr.'s journal entry was ever made public prior to the mention of it in St. George in early 1977, nor did any "histories of St. George or Utah's Dixie written before 1977 report Brigham Young's dislike of the short tower or any connection with the subsequent lightning bolt." Jones summarized, saying "in the interests of historical accuracy, let the record show that Brigham Young never publicly expressed displeasure nor did the contemporary Saints believe that Brigham Young sent a lightning bolt to destroy the tower he disliked. Rather, as Bleak reported to Wilford Woodruff, they firmly believed that the 'hand of the Lord' preserved the temple when the tower was struck." The story is a lesson in how easily a snippet of detail dealing with a public figure can gain traction and be embellished into "fact."

of an ordinance and Grandfather stopped him and said, 'it should be . . . ' and repeated the words. [The officiator disagreed, so] they called upon President McAllister and he said he was not sure which wording was correct, so they [Grandfather and the officiator prayed] and after the prayer, Grandfather Cannon said, 'The work must go on and I feel impressed that my wording is correct. Use this wording and I will assume all responsibility.' So the session proceeded as he directed.

"Grandfather knew what a grave thing he had done as the ordinance must be letter perfect. He worried all the rest of the day and that night he prayed earnestly to his Father in Heaven for assurance that what he had done was right. As he lay in his bed thinking about all of this, his bedroom door opened and President Brigham Young walked in. Although President Young had been dead many years, Grandfather said he looked just as natural as he had in life and he knew him immediately. He said to my Grandfather, 'Brother David, the wording of that ordinance should be . . . ,' and he repeated it as Grandfather said it should be. Then he turned and left the room.

"Grandfather lay thinking about this for some time when his bedroom door opened and again President Brigham Young came into his room and repeated exactly what he had said before. A little while later this visitation was repeated for the third time.

"By now it was almost morning and as sleep was far from him, Grandfather decided to get dressed and go over to President McAllister's home and tell him all that had happened. As grandfather reached his own front gate there stood President McAllister. Grandfather said, 'Why, Brother McAllister, I was just coming over to your house to tell you of a great experience I have had tonight.' Then he told him all about it. President McAllister then replied that he had had the same three visits from Brigham Young, and had come to tell Grandfather that his wording in the temple that day was indeed correct."[7]

---

7. Josephine Cannon Jones, conversation with daughter, Gaye Bateman; used by permission.

        ☙   ❧

The time from the mid-1880s until the Manifesto was signed by President Wilford Woodruff in 1890 is generally referred to by Latter-day Saint historians as The Raid. During this time the federal government and its marshals, deputies, and even paid informers waged a continual battle against the Church—both leadership and general membership—over the practice of plural marriage. Some Church leaders were imprisoned for practicing plural marriage, and lay members faced the same fate. Church properties including temples and temple records were threatened with seizure, and hundreds of men, leaders, and lay members alike, were forced into hiding.

Stories of hiding out and near captures abound, including a humorous account of President Wilford Woodruff escaping capture because he was weeding a garden at the Squire home near downtown St. George wearing an oversized "Old Mother Hubbard" dress and bonnet sewn for him by young Sister Emma Squire. She wrote: "Soon after our marriage the president of the Church, Wilford Woodruff, came to live with us. It was the time of the raid, when the Government took the property away from the Mormon people . . . and they were hunting all the men that had plural wives and putting them in jail. . . . We had some neighbors that knew we had someone staying with us, and they were very anxious to [discover] who it was. . . . [So] I made [President Woodruff] a Mother Hubbard dress and sun bonnet and . . . dress[ed] him up . . . and disguise[d] him so he could come [and go]. . . . We called him Grandma Allen so the people wouldn't know."[8]

His beard and craggy facial features hidden by the bonnet's oversized bill, President Woodruff no doubt suppressed smiles of mischievous satisfaction as the hapless deputies searched the home, the orchard,

---

8. Emma Cottam Thompson, "Autobiography," in William Howard Thompson, ed. and comp., and Parts Written by William Howard Thompson, *Thomas Cottam 1820 and His Wives Ann Howarth 1820 and Caroline Smith 1820, Descendants* (privately published, Thomas Cottam Family Organization, 1987), 22.

the vineyard, and the extensive garden in their fruitless quest for the Apostle that they were certain the speechless old lady in their midst had somehow hidden from their view.[9]

One other account, this one concerning hiding up the temple records, also bears repetition. According to Eldon McArthur, "in 1890, when the Temple Presidency decided that they were going to have to keep the temple records away from the government so they could not tell who had been married more than once, my grandfather removed all the records from the temple. His name was Thomas Punter Cottam, and later on he became temple president. Anyway, he built a concrete room in his basement in which to hide them. Remember, he was a plasterer and cement man. . . . So Grandpa built this room down in his basement, and most likely his boys helped him, just like they helped with everything. They built it so well you couldn't tell it was a room. It just looked like part of the basement wall—part of the outside wall. It had no doors in it, no windows, no nothing. Air could go back and forth through it, though, because he had places in his rock foundation that air could come in. So the temple records were cemented up in that hidden room, and they stayed there until 1916 before he moved those records back to the Temple. Twenty-six years! By then Grandpa knew they ought to be [returned to the Temple], because most of the men who knew of their hiding place had died. So he broke down the wall and took the records back to the temple."[10]

9. Thompson, "Autobiography," 22. See also Garth Pickett, telephone interview with the author, 29 May 2012. Garth and Bruce Pickett are great-grandsons of Emma Cottam Thompson. Though these particular experiences obviously occurred several years after the temple's dedication, the Pickett brothers and their friend Ralph Atkin, who was born on the Atkinville farm south of St. George, recall hearing many accounts of Woodruff's narrow escapes during the anti-polygamy Raid of the 1880s.

10. Eldon McArthur, "Oral History," recorded 26 March 2012. He declared: "I'm a grandson of Daniel Duncan McArthur on the McArthur side, and Thomas Punter Cottam on my mother's side. I was born in 1920. I've been asked [by Dr. Wendell Nilson] to say a few words about some of the things that happened in this area." Just a few days after the second of two recorded interviews with Dr. Nilson, Eldon

❧ ❧

Then as now, the temple underwent annual and often semiannual cleaning, and occasionally extra time was taken to do renovations and remodeling. During cleanings the carpets were taken up and either cleaned or replaced, wall cracks and splitting joints and jambs were filled in or repaired, all interior walls were repainted, and all curtains, draperies, doilies, altar covers, veils, chair upholstery, and every other form of fabric was removed and cleaned or replaced. At first this was all accomplished by volunteer labor, but finally professional help began to be used, and soon almost all the cleaning and repair work was done by endowed professionals.

Sometime in the late 1880s or early 1890s, a temple annex was built on the north side of the temple, with a door cut through the temple's north foundation into the basement. This structure surrounded the water tower and was no doubt used to house the boiler, other outdoor equipment, and perhaps housing or office space for a full-time engineer and custodian.

In 1903 there was a temple renovation and a new annex built,[11] which David H. Cannon described in the following letter to Salt Lake City:

"Dear Brethren:

"Yours of 7 May is received in which you ask, 'When do you intend to commence the work of renovation?' In reply [I] will say, we closed the temple on Friday 27 March and on the 28th carpets were taken up, screens were taken down, the work of renovation began in good earnest on Monday 30 March. As a room was whitewashed, the floors and woodwork were scrubbed and cleaned and the carpets put down. . . . On Saturday 25 April the work was pretty well through in the rooms used for

---

McArthur quietly passed away. Interview transcription courtesy Dr. Wendell Nilson, St. George, Utah.

11. It is unknown exactly when the Aaronic Priesthood pulpits were removed from the west end of the Main Floor, though it was long before the Melchizedek Priesthood pulpits were removed from the east end in 1937. As previously mentioned, perhaps they were removed in 1877 when the room was first used for ordinance work.

ordinances. The large assembly room had caused us some trouble, as the ceiling is twenty-seven feet high. Scaffolding was secured and it was thoroughly kalsomined [calcimined]. All the cracks were filled up with gypsum. I can truly say that the rooms never looked as well [as] they do now.

"We invited the sisters of the Relief Society of St. George and adjacent [communities] to come on Saturday 25 April[.] 70 in number came and gave the rooms a thorough sweeping and cleaning. So that on Tuesday 28 April we were ready to reopen. The work in the towers continued which could be done without interruption to us in the ordinance work. The carpenter will be through in the tower tonight. I believe that they have made a good job. The truss work has relieved the pressure of the ceiling joists.

"The plastering and kalcimining [whitewashing] on the inside of the building will be completed in the course of ten days. The outside of the building will consume from 20 to 25 days longer. The work on the outside of the building began yesterday morning. They are making good progress with it.

"Elder Thomas P. Cottam of the Presidency of the St. George Stake has the renovation of the Temple in charge, with Elder Horatio Pickett who has had the repairing of the tower in charge.

"The last time the Temple was renovated, all the water tables and other cut stone about the building was painted, this we will repeat in our renovation. As far as the work has progressed it looks very nice. There has been no person employed in or about the building who have not [been through the Temple].

"I am very pleased with your decision in not closing the Temple . . .

"This will give you an idea of what we are doing and [where] we are at with the renovation.

"Ever desiring the welfare of the Cause of Truth.

"I am your brother in the Gospel.

"David H. Cannon"[12]

---

12. Curtis, "History," 67–68.

Another major renovation occurred in 1917, at which time two marriage rooms were added, one at each end of the celestial room. A fire that occurred late in 1928 would lead to even greater changes. The *Deseret News* reported: "Fire which began in the furnace room at the St. George Temple here at 5:30 o'clock this morning, completely destroyed the annex at a loss of several thousand dollars and threatened the entire structure for two hours.

"David H. Cannon, custodian for many years, had lighted the furnace fire shortly before 5:30 A.M. He came up into the waiting room directly above, and engaged in conversation with Nelson Pearce, temporary night watchman. As they were talking, they smelled smoke and rushed into the furnace room.

"The flames had spread into a pile of cedar wood and coal and were still capable of being brought under control. However, there was no water or hose available, and the two men hastened to sound a general alarm.

"The entire town responded to the call, but by th[en] the flames had gained rapid headway and efforts were centered on saving the furnishings and records in the annex. All the records were carried out of the blazing building and much of the furnishing in the annex.

"The main building was damaged by smoke. Only the walls of the annex remain. In the burned portion, on the south side of the [annex] building, are included the waiting room, assembly room, boiler room, President's Office, and the records room.

"According to President George F. Whitehead, it will be necessary to close the Temple for several weeks."[13]

A lively eyewitness account of the fire was given by Eldon McArthur, who declared: "I was laying in bed, awake but not up. We had a big feather tick, and us boys would snuggle down under it, and it was nice and comfortable. But I was laying there in the middle, about [6]:00 one morning and I heard mother say the temple's on fire. I jumped up, and it was in, I think, the [fall, late November] it could have been. I

---

13. *Deseret News*, 20 November 1928.

was probably 8 or 10 which would have put it in the late 20s. I could see the fire from up there in my room because there was nothing between us and the temple, so I took off. Barefooted, just in my nightshirt. I headed down to the next corner and out, there was an old road that led down through the block, off to what's now the Vernon Worthen Park. There wasn't any houses but the wagon road went down through there and I was running through a skiff of snow, maybe an inch or two, bare-foot, heading for the temple. When I got there, [I could see] the boiler in the room underneath the annex to the temple had blown up, and that's what caused the fire. The only fire department we had was a big spool that had fire hose wrapped around it between two big wheels that were a few feet apart. They had outfits that hooked onto the axle on the outside of these wheels and went forward to where there was a crossbar so that men could get hold of it and drag it by hand. There was no horse involved. It was all by hand and foot to get to a fire. That spool was [kept] up on upper Main street, a block and half above the Tabernacle on the East side of the street. Right there they had a little place where they kept this wheeled hose, back of the old J. C. Penney building. The men came and got ahold of that, they would have brought it down to 100 North, down to the boulevard where they would have hit the bou-levard and come back out to temple street, 200 East, then turned south, and came down the street and I'll bet they was really a honking because they had to be running, dragging that wheel hose. See, the temple is on 400 South so they ran at least 6, 7 blocks with that thing, just getting it down to the temple. But Uncle Jim McArthur, dad's older brother, had already got up on the roof, and he had an axe. He owned a little bakery, and when us kids were going to spend a little money there, he never moved in a hurry. He just waited and waited, moving kind of slow. But up on that roof I never saw anyone move so fast in my life. He cut that roof right through, up one side, over the top, and down the other side, probably thirty feet in each direction. He cut off that whole section of the roof and it fell to the north away from the temple, and that was what saved the temple from catching on fire. I stayed down there and warmed my tootsies around the fire while I watched them put it out."[14]

Meanwhile, the destruction of the annex in 1928 became a primary factor in stimulating Church leaders in Salt Lake City to consider a significant redesign of the St. George Temple. It was time, the Brethren felt, to create a whole new floor plan. Not only would a new annex have to be constructed but, instead of staying with the system of one large room on the main floor divided by curtains or screens, a plan was developed to divide that large area into five permanent rooms. This would be more like the arrangement in the Salt Lake Temple. The decision was finalized, and in 1937 the St. George Temple was closed for a year while it was remodeled. A third annex was also built at that time.

Because the walls of the ordinance rooms were going to be made permanent, artists Joseph A. F. Averett and Peter W. Kemp were commissioned to paint murals for them. Averett was asked to do two rooms and Kemp one. To accomplish this, the artists painted their murals on large canvases, probably off-site.[15] Once completed, they were brought to the temple and carefully hung on the walls of the new rooms.

Edna Rae Gardner Frye writes: "I was born in St. George, Utah, in April 1922. I am the Granddaughter of George Frank Whitehead, who was the 6th President of the St. George Temple. He was called to that position in 1926 and was released in 1937.

"Grandpa and Grandma Whitehead were very kind and loving grandparents. As I recall, there were no temple sessions held on

---

14. McArthur, "Oral History."

15. At the time of the 1973–74 remodeling these canvases were carefully removed from the walls, rolled up, and shipped to Salt Lake City. Their return in the 1990s will be described shortly.

Saturday so Grandpa finished his record-keeping and spent several hours at the Temple on Saturday[s]. Occasionally he let me go with him. . . . One day [he] took me to the top [roof] of the Temple and held me up so I could see all [over] town. There was nothing south of the Temple except the 'Temple Bumps' and tamarack bushes.

"During Grandpa's tenure it was necessary to put in an elevator, so the stairway had to go. Grandpa was a carpenter by trade so he got permission to keep 4 stair rounds and made me a little table so I could play house with my dolls. The legs are the stair rounds with a wooden slab for the top. He painted it green and my great-granddaughters are still using it. What a treasure.

"I also [played on the Temple grounds] where Christian (Cristy) Tschang (a German immigrant) helped with the beautiful grounds. He would let me push the mower (about a foot), pull weeds, and I watched him plant flowers. I could hardly understand him because of his heavy accent. . . .

"Grandpa always went to work early because he would pick up [a few of] the ordinance workers—Brother and Sister Pierce and Brother and Sister Windsor. They were all good friends."[16]

ও ক্ষ

The following account of the 1937 renovation was reported in the *Deseret News:* "An extensive renovation program went forward on the building and grounds improving the equipment and facilities. The building was completely resurfaced. Additions included an elevator within the building. Only one timber had to be removed to make way for the elevator shaft.

"When first completed (1877) the temple had two large assembly rooms with . . . pulpits at each end. The remodeling program of 1937–1938 saw the assembly room on the second [or main] floor remodeled to

16. Edna Rae Gardner Frye, "Temple Memories," n.d., n.p.; copy in possession of the authors.

provide the present spacious rooms for the endowment ceremonies. The large assembly room . . . remains on the third [fourth] floor."[17]

The pulpits were also removed from in front of the main marriage room,[18] and lovely double stairs were built to the two narrow doors, which remain today. A new annex—the fourth—was also built so that patrons could enter on the north side of the temple. There they could change from street clothes into white attire. They would then ascend what came to be called the Grand Stairway to the main floor in the old part of the temple. An elevator was installed near this stairway to aid those who had difficulty with stairs. This new elevator shaft necessitated eliminating the north marriage room immediately off the celestial room and turning the remaining space east of it into a small ante-room.[19]

In addition to all of this, several of the outlying stakes undertook to construct cottages near the temple so that their members, traveling from distant towns, could reside there for a few days while they served in the temple. Each cottage had several rooms. These buildings proved to be very useful. At the same time the temple was undergoing this remodeling, complete landscaping of the temple grounds, as well as the streets surrounding the temple block, was redone.

After completion of the remodeling, President Harold S. Snow announced that baptismal services would be held in the temple on 7 August 1938 and that the temple would open officially for ordinance work on 12 September 1938.

The next major renovation occurred in 1974, but much happened beforehand that brought it to pass. As the St. George Temple moved toward its centennial in 1977, there were several changes that were about to occur. One obvious element that required such change was

---

17. *Deseret News*, 7 August 1938. See also Curtis, "History," 71.
18. Known today as room 5.
19. Today this small room is known by many names, one of which is the Rose Room.

the population growth. Washington County had long been a remote, rural area, but in 1965 it began to grow in population. The 1960 census reported 10,271 people in Washington County. By 1980, there were 26,665; by 1990, some 48,560; by 2000, 96,356; and by 2010, 175,000.

Besides the widespread availability of air conditioning in the 1950s, the most obvious factor in the rapid growth of St. George was the construction of the national Interstate Highway System (I-15), which ended the area's relative isolation. By building the interstate highway through the Virgin River Gorge in 1973, state and national planners allowed St. George to become easily available to trucks, busses, and automobiles. As a result, the community also became available to tourism, merchandising, and construction. Golfing communities and retirement housing were built, and St. George became a destination community, often listed among the nation's most desirable places to live.

Planners at Church headquarters could see this coming as soon as the interstate highway plans were settled regarding the Virgin River Gorge route, which, along with other factors, influenced them to consider expanding the function of the St. George Temple.

In the 1950s, for example, the Church introduced the use of motion pictures in some temples, which helped facilitate temple ordinances for locations serving many languages. Initially, this technology was intended to make it possible to have many small temples in distant lands, with small staffs that served modest-sized groups of patrons. Soon, however, it became evident that the use of films in larger temples would make it possible to conduct multiple sessions simultaneously, meaning that such temples could serve additional patrons and increase the amount of work being done.

In about 1970, the Church architects in Salt Lake City began planning a major overhaul of the St. George Temple based on these and other factors. They decided to replace the existing annex and entrance with a new structure, its footprint much larger than the temple itself at ground level. This annex would also include four new marriage rooms, which would allow marriages to be performed where guests could attend without dressing in white. That was convenient for guests and also reduced pressure on laundry and locker facilities. Other changes included more lockers, an enlarged children's facility, larger office area and clothing rental department, a chapel, and an outside dock facility, and two elevators to the expanded basement, wherein were located a cafeteria along with a laundry and engineering room next to the furnace area. Construction of the entire annex was a significant undertaking. At the same time the parking lot across the street to the north was increased to three times its former size.

The temple was closed for eighteen months while this extensive remodeling took place. While it was under way, a significant but little-known event occurred that bears repeating. While engaged in replacing cracked and broken marble in the old part of the temple, one of the contractors, Art Hopkinson, recalled:

"All the water we used had to be hauled in from a tap, as all the water inside the Temple had been shut off . . . and there was also no power in the building. . . . My son-in-law, Kelly Davis, and I were working late one evening, and we were using a large 500 watt light bulb and hundred foot extension cord.[20] . . . When we ran out of water in our bucket, we decided to call it quits for the day, so we left the empty bucket, gathered up our tools, checked out with the security guard, and went to our hotel room.

"At about 4:00 A.M. I awoke and felt a strong urgency to get back to the temple. Kelly wanted to stop and get some breakfast first, but I told him he would have to wait. At the temple, the same security guard checked us in and said that no one else had been there since we left. As we started up the stairs I could smell smoke, so I started to run. When we got to the top floor we could see that there had been a fire. Apparently we had failed to unplug the light and it had somehow fallen

20. Their written account makes it unclear whether they were working on the fourth or fifth floor.

to the floor. There it had smoldered for a while and then erupted into flames.

"We could see where flames had started up the walls, and the tread on one of the stairs had been burned all the way through. Our empty bucket, which we had left upright, had been turned upside down and the power cord was coiled neatly on top, the light on top of that. In spite of the fact that there had been no available water, the walls, stairs, and old carpeting were all soaking wet, and the fire had been put out. The solemn assembly room was filled with smoke, however, so we opened as many windows as possible, and in 15 minutes the smoke and even the smell were all gone. The guard had not even been aware that there had been a fire . . . [and] a call to the Temple President confirmed that no earthly personage had been in the temple during the night.

"This incident has been a great testimony to me . . . and my son-in-law Kelly . . . that the Lord does watch over and protect His house and in some unknown way . . . [in spite of] our apparent carelessness . . . the . . . Temple was saved from a fiery destruction."[21]

In addition to the designing of a new annex, Church architect Emil Fetzer was assigned by the First Presidency to rethink the whole St. George Temple. The building obviously needed repairs, but perhaps it also needed an interior redesign. Fetzer's report to them was detailed and critical. In his opinion the hundred-year-old temple needed a major renovation. The equipment needed updating, he explained, as did the décor, and the exit options from the rooms on the second floor were inadequate and unsafe in case of an emergency. Each of the three ordinance rooms could seat 120 patrons, but 360 or even 240 individuals

---

21. Art Hopkinson, "My St. George Temple Experience," n.d., n.p.; copy in possession of the authors.

could not all use the spiral staircases if a necessity arose for them to exit quickly.

The 1937 redesign of the temple interior had set up the Salt Lake Temple system of having patrons move through several rooms that represented stages in man's progression. Temple building in the Church since that time had shown that a temple could serve more patrons by combining functions into fewer rooms. Such an arrangement presented Fetzer with a challenge. The rooms needed to be changed so that the temple film could be used in them, but to accomplish that, he needed to find a way to reverse the floor plan so that patrons could enter from the rear and stay in the room for the duration of the film and not move to other rooms. This would allow the film to be shown in the other two rooms simultaneously.

Fetzer left an excellent summary of the whole redesign of the temple. In it he wrote:

"I studied the situation very diligently. I drew dozens of sketch plans of all manner of arrangements, none of which achieved the desired objectives. There seemed to be no logical way that the three rooms could be entered without going through the other rooms.

"One early evening, I was working after normal hours in my Church Architect's offices on the twenty-eighth floor of the Church Office Building. I was troubled in mind and although prayerful about this matter, I had not and could not seem to arrive at a satisfactory plan arrangement for the new Ordinance Rooms for the St. George Temple. I had pursued so many solutions down so many dead end paths. At least I knew many ways that would not work. Finally, with no solution but with the problem firmly in mind, I left my office to go home.

"I drove my car out of the east exit of the underground Church parking terrace onto State Street and turned south. Due to the hour, it was dark and there was very little traffic on the street. When one drives south from the terrace exit but before crossing South Temple, State Street passes under the famous Eagle Gate arch that spans the street. As I was passing under the Eagle Gate, I heard a voice that was clear and distinct but it was not a spoken sound, but rather a transmission of thought into my mind, the message of which was, 'If you move the fire tower stairways out away from the west wall of the Temple, a lobby space will be created.' The import of that thought was immediately recognized and I needed nothing more. An incredibly marvelous, simple, logical and crucial revelation for needed help, had been given to the Church Architect for his work in the functional planning of the Temple and thus for the blessing of those privileged to use the Temple. For this communication to be of utmost benefit, it had been necessary for me to pursue every planning idea that I could possibly consider prior to receiving it. It was a prerequisite to be trained to recognize the significance of the message when it was given and to use it for the maximum benefit. When I was unable to find a solution, I humbly needed this inspiration for the blessing of the House of the Lord.

"Early the next morning, I could not get to my office fast enough. At the drafting table I quickly drew the plan incorporating this wonderful idea that had been given to me. It planned out marvelously. The two stairway fire towers were moved twelve feet out from the west wall of the Temple and a large lobby, the full width of the temple, was thus created next to the back walls of the three Ordinance Rooms. Doorways from the Lobby were provided into each of these rooms. Between the stairways a large modern elevator was incorporated so that all floors could be accessed by stairs and/or elevator.

"The addition on the rear of the Temple was designed to be full height to match exactly with the original Temple design. The back wall of the original Temple was a sheer, flat wall [with just six large windows]. It was just a plain flat surface that had seemingly been prepared for and had been waiting for this new addition. We designed the addition to match in architectural style and details to correspond exactly with the Temple facades including battlements on top of the walls. The new stairways, however, were not circular in shape but rather rectangular for easy and safe use and with comfortable carpeted steps and landings."[22]

The following description of the renovation was found in the *Church News:*

"The renovation involved three areas; addition of a (new) one-level annex to the north side of the temple, an addition to the west side, and extensive remodeling inside the older part of the edifice.

"Included in the north-side annex are . . . lockers for temple patrons, a chapel, offices for the temple presidency [recorder, family file desk, secretarial staff], laundry facilities, and a cafeteria. The west side addition was chiefly constructed for new stairways and elevators, which provide additional access to various rooms of the temple.

"Other changes include new electrical, heating, air conditioning, plumbing, and fire prevention systems; new carpeting, drapes, and furnishings; four new marriage rooms, giving a total of 16, and a new bride's room.

"The large, top-floor solemn assembly room of the temple has remained untouched. On that floor the original wooden beams, which were hauled by ox team in loads that took seven days each to make the journey, remain, and a look through the windows reveals the distortion of the aged glass. . . . The only noticeable change in the top-floor is the addition of a sprinkler system for fire prevention . . . even electric lights are absent.

"The beauty of the temple's [main floor area] has been retained, but the [three] ordinance rooms have been greatly changed. Utilizing [portions of the 1939 murals while being adapted to] the film presentation, [they] now feed into a lovely veil room. From there patrons will proceed through the temple veil and into the Celestial room. These changes will allow twice as much work to be done in the temple as before."[23]

---

22. Emil Fetzer Letter, St. George Temple historical file, Church History Library, The Church of Jesus Christ of Latter-day Saints, Salt Lake City, Utah.
23. *Church News,* 18 October 1975.

Following these renovations, the temple was rededicated in six sessions, beginning on Tuesday, 18 November 1975, and continuing until Wednesday afternoon. President Spencer W. Kimball offered the dedicatory prayer, which was then read by other General Authorities in the following five sessions.

શ ∞

Today, as patrons and visitors approach the temple near the city center of St. George, either in the daytime or at night, they see a dignified, gleaming-white, five-story structure in the middle of a square city block, surrounded by handsome gardens and trees. The temple is located in a residential neighborhood about four blocks outside the city's business district but still in the block plan area with wide streets laid out by the original pioneers.

The site, chosen by Brigham Young in 1871, was then outside the settled town but has proven to be both convenient to local temple patrons and easily located by visitors from outside the area. The building is on a slight hill and can be seen from a distance, from the north and south entrances into the town and from the surrounding hills.

The temple is bordered by Church-owned properties on all sides that have prevented any tall structures from obstructing the view. A large parking lot is on the north block; the St. George East Stake Center and its two parking lots occupy the east block. Fifty-one apartments for temple patrons are on the adjacent block to the south, and the temple president's home is on the west. Thus the temple is in a peaceful place, appropriate to its sacred character.

On the southeast corner of the temple block is a visitors' center, smaller but otherwise similar to the one at Temple Square in Salt Lake City. Both of them have a large white statue of Christ, the *Christus*, copied from the original in Denmark by Bertel Thorvaldsen. The St. George *Christus* is in a circular room with large glass windows so it may be viewed from the outside as well as the inside.

The visitors' center was dedicated on Saturday, 30 October 1993, by Elder Joseph B. Wirthlin of the Quorum of the Twelve Apostles. Initially fifteen couples were called as full-time missionaries to serve there and in the nearby historic sites. Soon sister missionaries were also called to serve as guides. An annex was added to the building that was close to the tourist entrance to the square, making it easier to enter the center. That annex houses historic artifacts, including the cast-iron cannon that was used to pound in the temple footings during the early 1870s. The visitors' center has become an integral part of the St. George Temple experience and the community. Its art and displays draw local residents as well as thousands of tourists.

In 1990 a temple was completed and dedicated in Las Vegas, an area that had been in the St. George Temple District. At that time eighteen of the forty stakes in the St. George Temple District were transferred to the Las Vegas Temple District, though nearby Nevada stakes in Bunkerville, Mesquite, Ely, Panaca, Caliente, and Pioche remained in the St. George district. The result was that the next year (1991) there were 200,000 fewer ordinances performed in the St. George Temple.

Nevertheless, the steady population growth in the St. George District caused new stakes to be organized, and by 2008 the number of ordinances had reached a level beyond the 1990 division total. By 2012 the St. George Temple District contained 46 stakes.

On 2 September 1992, at 4:30 A.M., an earthquake occurred in Washington County, Utah. Its epicenter was in the Washington Fields where the Hurricane Fault is located. It was initially registered at 5.9

on the Richter scale but was later upgraded to 6.5. Major damage was caused to several hillside homes in nearby Springdale.

As a result of this earthquake, the temple required some repairing but was generally left intact. "On the east side the engineers determined that there had been gradual sinking over the decades. The firm they hired propped up the foundation ¾ of an inch and filled in the space with sand and cement. Seventy-six young men, returned missionaries from Rexburg, Idaho; Provo, Utah; Salt Lake City and St. George, Utah, were hired to carry buckets of mixed concrete into the basement to be used in that project. The engineers installed steel piers, which were placed on the foundation rock to support the building. Jerry Evans crawled all over the roof and much of the building. There were problems in the tower and other supports on the roof. He noted that when the stucco was renewed in 1947, the building had been wrapped in steel mesh. He felt that this mesh casing had served to help keep the [temple] surface intact during the earthquake."[24]

Today, temple patrons, particularly visitors from distant places, come to the temple and marvel at how the building has weathered the challenges for over 135 years. Some know the story of how tens of thousands of small lava rocks were pounded into the ground by the old iron cannon to stabilize the wet site. They might also know that huge blocks of lava stone were laid on this base to serve as the footing and foundation, twelve feet wide at the base and tapering upward to three-and-a-half-feet wide where the two-and-a-half-foot-thick red sandstone walls begin. They probably do not realize that these careful preparations, made long ago in the 1870s—including the 18 months taken to drain the area and pound in the footings—paid off over a century later when the 1992 earthquake tested the huge structure, which was built entirely without steel reinforcement.

Numerous seismic studies have since been done, and the results evidence that the foundations are stable. Seismic instruments continue to

---

24. Dennis Stout, interview with Douglas Alder, December 2008.

monitor the stability of the foundations and walls and ensure the safety of temple patrons.

A massive amount of labor, not always visible but vitally important, is performed by the maintenance and engineering staff of the St. George Temple. Such work includes constant maintenance on the grounds: monitoring the health of large trees, planting flowers each season, watering and mowing lawns, trimming shrubbery, and so forth. Cleaning the temple and doing the laundry, preparing food in the cafeteria, conducting office work, answering the phones, painting both the exterior and interior of the building, replacing carpets and repairing furniture, keeping records and maintaining computers, and cleaning the inside of the building every night, are the regular agenda. The list could go on and on, as it has for nearly a century and a half. Consistently and without fanfare, this vital work is performed by both employees and volunteers, so that when patrons and ordinance workers arrive each morning, the sacred work can proceed without interruption.

A second replacement of the temple dome (the first having occurred in 1883 after a lightning strike) occurred in 1992. The temple was closed between 25 June and 23 August so a new roof and dome could be installed. Normal weathering and additional lightning strikes caused the wood supporting the roof and in the dome to need replacement. The roof work proceeded almost without notice, but the dome was another matter.

The old ball and weather vane were dismantled and put in storage, and for a few weeks there was nothing where the old cupola had been.[25] Soon the fiberglass replacement dome arrived and rested on the

---

25. When this second ball was replaced in 1992, it was discovered that one of the

ground nearby. Curiosity was piqued as people examined it and the new weather vane that would be attached to it.

Finally, on 31 October 1994, the new dome was installed. DeWayne Gray flew a Sundancer Helicopter from Las Vegas to St. George. A sizeable crowd watched as the helicopter lifted the replacement dome onto its base on the roof. Amanda Leigh Ballif wrote in the *Spectrum*:

"As the 'copter gingerly lifted the dome, the crowd collectively held its breath. The dome swayed in the air like an angel hovering over the temple grounds before reaching its destination. Once the top was secure, the crowd applauded. A hand popped up through the dome to grab the underneath of the vane. But the rope seemed to be caught. For a time Gray and the helicopter were tethered to the temple—attached by the weather vane—while the workers inside finished their task."[26]

One worker remembers vividly that as the dome neared their hands inside the tower, a breeze caught it and it swept past them. All four of the workers jumped down to the floor to escape being clipped by the swaying dome. This happened while the crowd of about 200 onlookers were clapping for what they thought was an easy conclusion to the risky undertaking.

Renovations continue in the temple today, not only by way of repairs but in a consistent effort to bring the appearance of the 1975 annex more in line with the lovely 1877 look of the original temple.

original workers, perhaps Christopher Riding himself, had left a cryptic message written on one of the small boards within the ball: "*Many men of many minds. Many firsts of many.*" The more one considers this, the more appropriate it seems. For instance, hundreds of men with almost unlimited variations in their thinking came together in the nineteenth century and became "of one heart and mind" as they built the temple. And there have occurred since then many ordinance "firsts" as well as an almost inexhaustible number of personal "firsts"—these as hearts and minds have been healed and uplifted through temple worship and service within these hallowed walls.

26. *Spectrum*, 1 November 1994.

Chapter 22

WHY COME TO THE TEMPLE TODAY?

Operating the St. George Temple requires approximately 2,300 or-dinance workers and other volunteers. Each week these volun-teers, as well as a few full-time and part-time employees, make it possible for the thousands of patrons to come to the temple and participate in the sacred ceremonies performed there.

Why do these people willingly and joyfully give such service? Here are some of the answers people gave recently when asked: "Why do you attend or serve in the temple?"

Some responded by stating that they felt it was their duty. They are responding to the doctrine that teaches that the temple ordinances are required for an individual to return to the presence of God. Having received their own "saving ordinances," these volunteers feel anxious to participate in this proxy work for those who for any reason did not have that opportunity while dwelling in mortality.

Similarly, many people feel their "hearts have been turned to their fathers," as prophesied by Malachi in the last chapter of the Old Testament (Malachi 4:5–6). Church members feel drawn to their ancestors and want to make temple blessings available to them by performing the temple ordinances in behalf of their deceased fathers or forebears.

Uniting a family for time and all eternity motivates many people. Such temple patrons may have a deceased spouse or child or parent who did not participate in the restored gospel during their mortal lifetime. Family members who remain in mortality often wish to perform these ordinances in behalf of a deceased relative, trusting that the individual will accept the covenants now that he or she has an eternal perspective. Nevertheless, they know their relatives are not bound by temple proxy work; receiving the ordinances performed in their behalf remains the choice of the deceased person.

Many come to the temple at a turning point in their lives—just prior to going on a mission, to be married, to send a child on a mission, or to see a son or daughter or grandchild be married for time and all eternity. Still others find the temple ceremonies to be a personal opportunity to learn and gain understanding. The teachings of the temple allow participants to draw closer to God as they reflect on the origins of the earth and the human race and the divine potential each of us possesses as spiritually begotten children of a loving Heavenly Father. Patrons are reminded of and reflect upon the redeeming sacrifice performed by Jesus Christ. Those who serve in the temple have an opportunity to renew their own sacred covenants and promise anew to honor the commitments they have made. Participation in the sacred ordinances is a type of worship that participants find spiritually refreshing and that provides encouragement to live a more exemplary life. Temple patrons and workers alike describe feeling the influence of the Holy Ghost while in that sacred building, which makes personal inspiration and revelation possible.

The temple is often described as a place of safety—a refuge from the turmoil of the world. Purity and peace are abundant there. So is silence. Seeking a blessing or searching for an answer to personal prayer is not uncommon among those who participate in temple worship. Comfort is to be found there. Patient consideration is taught and practiced. A warm feeling of brotherhood and sisterhood prevails in the temple, where each is equally welcomed and served, regardless of his or her station in life. Many speak of the joy it is to be where virtue is enjoined and thrives.

Young married couples often attend the temple as a type of date. These plan an activity together that is far more than just a social event. Serving together in the temple allows couples to review their own marriage vows and reflect on the importance of families—to bring back into focus what they hope to achieve in life.

There is no Church-specified frequency for temple attendance. Faithful Latter-day Saints individually determine how often they will participate in temple service. Some establish a pattern, choosing to attend weekly or monthly. Temple workers and the elderly often come more frequently than that. Attending the temple does not replace Sunday worship. In fact, the temple is not open on the Sabbath. Latter-day Saints participate as members of a congregation in their local wards or stakes on Sundays. Sometimes wards organize a temple excursion, but Church members most often attend the temple on their own initiative.

In the first few years of the history of the St. George Temple, there were only two sessions a day, on Tuesdays, Wednesdays, and Thursdays, and one session a month on Friday evenings. That has gradually increased over the past 135 years. Now the temple is also open on Monday mornings and all day every other weekday, including Saturdays. Instead of one shift of ordinance workers each day, it is necessary to have three shifts, except Mondays (in consideration of the Church's observance of family home evening), when the temple's last session is 11:20 A.M. As a result of this extended availability, annual temple activity now includes many thousands of ordinances. Clearly the motivation to attend the temple is substantial.

So we ask again: Why do people attend the temple? Consider this thought from the scriptures, part of an epistle from the Prophet Joseph Smith to the members of the Church:

"Behold, the great day of the Lord is at hand; and who can abide the day of his coming, and who can stand when he appeareth? For he is like a refiner's fire, and like a fuller's soap; and he shall sit as a refiner and purifier of silver, and he shall purify the sons of Levi, and purge them as gold and silver, that they may offer unto the Lord an offering in righteousness. Let us, therefore, as a church and a people, and as Latter-day Saints, offer unto the Lord an offering in righteousness; and let us present in his holy temple, when it is finished, a book containing the records of our dead, which shall be worthy of all acceptation."[1]

And from Ezekiel 37:26–27: "[And I] will set my sanctuary in the midst of them for evermore . . . : yea, I will be their God, and they shall be my people."

In each of God's holy sanctuaries scattered throughout the earth, Church members make covenants that, if kept, show to Him that they can be trusted with His knowledge and power. The covenants of the temple ordinances are, therefore, the keys that open the doors to the revelations of godliness—for those who desire them, ask for them in all sincerity, and are worthy. Without the temple covenants they do not receive this kind of knowledge; without the Melchizedek Priesthood and its proper use they will not be exalted. Why? Because the priesthood administers all ordinances pertaining to our full salvation or exaltation. "In fact, the ordinances, promises, and blessings of exaltation administered in the temple are called the fullness of the Melchizedek Priesthood, as President Ezra Taft Benson told us: 'To enter into the order of the Son of God is the equivalent today of entering into the fullness of the Melchizedek Priesthood, which is only received in the house of the Lord.'"[2]

"It cannot be emphasized too strongly that *only* in the temple can

---

1. Doctrine and Covenants 128:24.

2. Ezra Taft Benson, "What I Hope You Will Teach Your Children about the

men and women become entitled to the blessings of the fulness of the priesthood, as President Joseph Fielding Smith stated: 'I do not care what office you hold in this Church—you cannot receive the fulness of the priesthood unless you go into the temple of the Lord and receive these ordinances. . . . No one can get the fulness of the priesthood outside of the temple of the Lord. . . . No man or woman can receive the keys of exaltation in any other place.'"[3]

Whether as patrons, engineers, sealers, cafeteria staff, ordinance workers, grounds crews, recorders, security personnel, secretaries, the presidency, custodians, or whoever, in doing temple work of whatever nature, first for self and then for others who did not receive that opportunity, Church members become the servants of our Lord Jesus Christ and in time receive His keys of exaltation. Why, we may ask again? Because in His service they freely give of their time, talents, and all else with which they have been blessed, in behalf of their own ancestors or the ancestors of others they may never even know. Though rewards of inestimable wonder are promised those who enter into and keep temple covenants, temple patrons and workers serve without thought of reward. Such selfless service has come to be known as temple worship—which, in fact, it is, for they have not only entered into His service but at the same time have entered into His rest, His home, the literal House of the Lord, His peace-filled sanctuary upon the earth. There they are allowed to feel of His Holy Spirit during and often throughout their visits, and from time to time they may also experience a measure of the glory of His Holy Presence as they commune with Him in prayer and seek through personal revelation His divine guidance and counsel.

Just fifteen weeks before his passing, President Brigham Young reported to the Saints in Salt Lake City: "I am aware that you wish to hear something of our labors in the South. I will say that we have had

Temple," *Ensign*, August 1985, 8, as quoted in Andrew C. Skinner, *Temple Worship* (Salt Lake City: Deseret Book, 2007), 40.

3. Skinner, *Temple Worship*, 40.

a blessed time, such a time as no other people on the earth have enjoyed for many centuries that we have any knowledge of. We have been permitted to enjoy privileges for the possession of which we have been striving and laboring for many years. . . .

"The feeling experienced by those who participated in the blessings administered in the Temple is something which cannot be described to your understanding. Those only who shared with us in the Temple ordinances know for themselves the satisfaction in the work of salvation; that we have the privilege of receiving and obeying the truth, and securing ordinances for ourselves, [and] for doing the necessary work for our parents and forefathers, who have slept without the gospel, that they may partake also of the waters of life, and be judged according to men in the flesh. This is a privilege, a blessing, which no one can sense unless he is in possession of it. We are happy to know by our faith and feelings through the spirit of revelation within us that our labors have been accepted of the Lord. We have enjoyed ourselves exceedingly in the society of each other; the aged, the middle-aged and the youth have rejoiced and then made glad in this glorious work."[4]

And so in agreement with Brother Brigham, we say, Come to the temple. Come and be welcomed therein. Come and enter into Christ's holy service. Come ye, one and all, that thereby you may also enter into the joy and the rest of the Lord.

---

4. *Journal of Discourses*, 26 vols. (London: Latter-day Saints' Book Depot, 1854–86), 19:1–2, 29 April 1877.

Appendix

PIONEERS OF
ST. GEORGE, UTAH

The following lists of St. George's earliest settlers, which may be incomplete, were compiled by Dixie State College Encampment Mall Committee, Linda Huddleston, cochair, research being headed by Roberta Blake Barnum. It is alphabetical by surname (in all capital letters) of the man or husband; each wife is listed with her given names first and her maiden name last (in all capital letters).

Pioneers of 1861 to 1862

ALLEN, Orville Morgan
June WILSON
Susanna WARD
Elizabeth A BURKETT

ALLPHIN, Isreal Dodge
Burnetta COLLINS
Susan E. DAMRON
Christina RIDING

ALLPHIN, Joshua Horton
Alice HUNDLEY

ANDRUS, James
Laura Altha GIBSON
Manomas Luvina GIBSON

ANGUS, John Orson
Elizabeth PATRICK

ASHBY, Nathaniel (Jr.)
Mary V. GARR
Martha A TRUMAN

ASHBY, Richard Hammond
Esther Ann BUSBY

ATCHINSON, John Barton
Malinda E. STANTON

ATCHINSON, Lawson
Caroline A STANTON

ATCHINSON, William
Tabitha (Dicy) HAYES

ATWOOD, Samuel F.

BAKER, George
Mary Ann RANDALL

BALE, Joseph
Annie B CHAFFEE

BALLARD, John Harvey
Charlotte PINCOCK

BARLOW, Oswald
Catherine NIGHTINGALE
Mary Ann OLIVE

BARNES, William
Jane HOWARD

BARNEY, Danielson Buren
Laura MATHEWS
Sophia Arkansas HULSEY

BARNEY, Edson Marsh
Lillian Comstock BALLON
Louisa WALKER

BEACHAM, Jacob (Sr.)
Harriet RUNDEL

BIRCH, Joseph Flitcroft
Dorothy CHAMBERS
Mary SYLVESTER

BIRD, James
Jane M CARPENTER
Harriet CARPENTER

BIRD, Taylor Reeves
Alice STOKES

BLACK, George
Susannah JACKAWAY
Mary A DONNELLY

BLACK, William Valentine
Almira AYERS
Victoria AYERS

BLAIR, Seth Millington
Elizabeth FIFE
Sarah Jane FOSTER

BLAIR, Tarleton J.
Lydia ALLEN
Eliza Ann ALLEN
Elizabeth TERRY

BLAKE, Benjamin Frederick
Harriet HOLLIS
Mary A. Bowler ELLICOCK

BLAKE, Frederick
Emily GREEN
Eliza BARNETT

BLEAK, James Godson
Elizabeth MOOR
Caroline GOSNOLD
Jane THOMPSON
Matilda Irene THOMPSON

BLISS, Norman Ingles
Elizabeth Ann BIRD
Sarah LEWIS

BLISS, Orley Dwight
Harriet Josephine LEE

BOGGS, Francis
Eveline MARTIN

BONELLI, Daniel
Ann HAIGH

BOWN, William
Jane Ann METCALF

BOX, Thomas H.

BRACKEN, James Bennett
Sarah HEAD
Elizabeth FAWCETT

BRANCH, William Henry
Emily Cornelia ATWOOD
Ella COOMBS

BRENNICKE, Otto

BRINKERHOFF, James
Sally Ann SNYDER
Rebecca HAWK
Eliza J HENDERSON

BROOKS, George (Sr.)
Emily C BRANCH

BROOKS, George (Jr.)
Flora A TUFTS

BROWN, Edward M

BROWN, James Polly
Eunice REASOR
Petrea C PETERSON
Petrea K SORENSON
Ma[r]tha Ann MILLER

BROWN, Newman
  Lora A TAYLOR
  Jemima Bell PECTOL

BRUNDAGE, William Lane
  Huldah BARLOW
  Margaret B LANG

BRYCE, Ebenezer
  Mary Ann PARK

BRYNER, Casper
  Magdalena GUBLER
  Susanna STAHELI

BRYNER, Hans Ulrich (Sr.)
  Verena WINTCH

BRYNER, L Hans Ulrich (Jr.)
  Anna Marie D. MATHIS

BUNKER, Edward
  Emily ABBOTT
  Sarah Ann Lang BROWNING
  Mary Mathison MCQUARRIE

BURGESS, Harrison Joseph
  Sophia Minerva FOSTER
  Amanda Melvina HAMMOND

BURGESS, Hyrum W.

BURGESS, Melancthon
  Margaret Jane MCINTIRE

BURGESS, Samuel "I"
  Mahala J. MATHEWS

BURGESS, Thomas

BURGESS, William (Sr.)
  Vilate STOCKWELL
  Dorcas Keeling DYKES

BUTLER, William Franklin
  Sarah Ann DEWITT
  Katherine FUCHS

CALKINS, Asa Stanley
  Marietta Simmons BARNEY
  Agnes Eliz. PERKES

CAMERON, William
  Jane FLINT

CANFIELD, David
  Elizabeth Story DEPEW

CANNON, Angus Munn
  Sarah Maria MOUSLEY
  Ann Amanda MOUSLEY

CANNON, David Henry
  Wilhelmina MOUSLEY
  Josephine L CROSSGROVE
  Rhoda Ann KNELL

CANNON, Marsena
  Elizabeth Taylor BOUMAN

CARTER, William
  Ellen BENBOW
  Harriet T. UTLEY
  Sophronia E. TURNBOW

CHAFFIN, Louis Rice
  Sarah Marie Cossett (Cossit)
  MAYFIELD

CHESNEY, James A.
  Jane FINDLEY

CHURCH, Haden Wells
  Sarah Ann ARTERBURY
  Catherine GARDNER

CLARK, Lorenzo
  Beulah Ann ROGERS
  Mary HUNT

CLAYTON, Matthew
  Juliette C BADGER

COATES, Benjamin F. (Sr.)
  Rebecca ANGLIN

COLLINS, Fred

COPLAN, Willis
  Amelia A ANGIER

COTTAM, Thomas
  Caroline SMITH

COUCHER, William
Eliza THOMPSON

COX, Isaiah Sr.
Henrietta JANES
Elizabeth Ann STOUT
Martha CRAGUN

CRAIG, James S. (Sr.)
Sarah J. CHILDS

CROSBY, Jesse Wentworth
Hannah Elida BALDWIN
Minnie B KARL

CUNNINGHAM, Jacob

CUNNINGHAM, Samuel
Mary ELLIS

CUTLER, Royal James
Theadosia A. MORTON
Margaret ROSS

DAMERON, William

DAVIS, Edward H

DAVIS, Philetus Gould

DAYTON, Lysander
Matilda Ellen NAY

DE MILLE, Oliver (Sr.)
Emily Almira BEAL
Fidelia WINGET

DIX, Owen

DOCKSTADER, George
Louisa Myrel DAYTON

DODGE, Walter
Eleanor C MALONE

DORRITY, Dennis
Mary E BERRY

DUNCAN, Chapman
Lucky JONES
Rosannah TAYLOR

DUNCAN, Homer
Sarah TRIPPUS
America CLARK

DUZETTE, Edward Peas
Mary Adaline EWING

EARDLEY, John (Sr.)
Ann CROFFS
Ann JONES

EARL, James Calvin
Mary Eliz. PARSONS

EARL, Sylvester Henry
Lois Caroline OWENS
Margaret E JONES

EDDENS, J

ELDREDGE, Horace Sunderland

ELDREDGE, Joseph
Elizabeth Pearce RADBURN
Lavena Susannah EMMETT
Emily D EMMETT

ELMER, Ira Bartlett
Eveline E. Vashi WRIGHT

EVERETT, Addison
Orpha Marie REDFIELD

EYRING, Henry
Marie BONNELI
Deseret FAWCETT

FAWCETT, William
Jane Corner SMITH
Ida C WULFENSTIN

FINDLEY, Alexander F.
Elizabeth JACKSON

FORD, Charles

FORDHAM, Amos Pierre
Lydia A BRANDON

FORDHAM, Elijah (Sr.)
Anna Bibbins CHAFEE

FORSYTH, Thomas Robert (Sr.)
  Mary BROWETT
  Fredonia M GOHEEN

FOSTER, Solon (Sr.)
  Sarah DOWNING

FRAZER, Alexander G.

FROST, William

FULLERTON, Alexander
  Inezetta HARDY

GARDNER, George B.

GARDNER, Robert (Jr.)
  Jane McKEOWN
  Cynthia L. BERRY
  Mary Ann CARR
  Leonora CANNON

GATES, Jacob
  Mary Minerva SNOW
  Mary WARE
  Emma FORSBERRY
  Sarah Jane MEREDITH

GIBBONS, Richard Cornine
  Vilate BURGESS

GRAF, Jacob

GRANGE, Joseph
  Harriett L STANTON

GRANGE, Samuel

GRANGER, Walter
  Catherine GUTHRIE
  Christiana E KEIL

GREAVES, Robert

GREEN, Henry

GREEN, William
  Susannah LEGG

GROESBECK, Nicholas Harmon

GUBLER, Johann Heinrich
  Anna M. D. HESS
  Harriett L STANTON

HALL, John Charles
  Selena DE GRAY
  Keziah DE GRAY

HALLIDAY, William
  Lydia E. BLACKHURST
  Mary BLACKHURST

HAMMOND, Joseph
  Elizabeth EGBERT
  Delta Kelsey CHINN

HANCOCK, Cyrus Mortimer
  Martha A BRACKEN

HANCOCK, Mosiah Lyman
  Margaret McCLEVE
  Sarah TEW

HARDY, Augustus Poore
  Elizabeth Ann CAPNER

HARDY, Samuel Brocklebank
  Martha L. FOSTER
  Caroline Bacon ROGERS

HARDY, Samuel Prescott
  Almyra LAMB

HARMON, Appleton Milo
  Elmeda STRINGHAM
  Polly HENDRICKSON

HARMON, Jesse Perse
  Nancy CALKINS

HARMON, Joseph
  Maria MARKS
  Elizabeth EBERT
  Delta KELSEY
  Rebecca Dow Gale PEKO

HARPER, John
  Isabella (no surname available)

HARRIMAN, Henry
  Clarissa BOYNTON
  Eliza Elizabeth JONES

HARRIS, George

HASTINGS, William
Sarah SMITH

HAUPT, Charles V

HEATH, Henry
Sarah Ann BIRD

HENDRIX, Daniel
Lucy ALLEN

HEYWOOD, Joseph Leland
Martha SPENCE
Mary BELL

HIGBEE, Ezra

HIGGINS, (Dr.) Silus Gardner
Nancy Louisa CLARK
Clara Jane RIDING

HINDLEY, John

HILL, William Brown
Emma Maria MECHAM
Mary Jane PRICE

HILTON, Hugh
Isabella P. FROST

HOLBROOK, Chandler
Eunice DUNNING

HOLLY, James

HORNE, Joseph
Mary Isabella HALES

HORSLEY, Henry Harry
Mary MONTAQUE
Lois HOOK

HOUSTON, James
Margaret CRAWFORD

HOUTZ, Henry P.

HOUTZ, Jacob

HUBER, Edward

HULET, Sylvanius Cyrus
Catherine STOKER

HUNT, Amos (Sr.)
Nancy Garrett WELBOURN
Rebecca WIGGINS

HUNT, Isaac (Sr.)
Ann NEWLING
Partha Ann BARNEY

HUNT, William Bradford
Eleanor WIGGINS

HUNTINGTON, Oliver Boardman
Mary Melissa NEAL
Hannah M SANDERS

IVINS, Anthony

IVINS, (Dr.) Israel
Anna L. RIDGEWAY
Julia HILL

JACKSON, James (Jr.)
Annis BRADFORD

JARVIS, George
Ann PRIOR

JENSON, Anders

JOHNSON, (Dr.) Joseph Ellis
Harriet SNIDER
Hannah M GODDARD
Eliza SAUNDERS

JOHNSON, Joseph W.

JOLLEY, Peliqus Berry
Sarah KNIGHT

JONES, Frederick W. (Sr.)
Ellen MARSHALL
Eliza Jane BAKER

JONES, Nathaniel Vary

JONES, Robert

JUDD, Frederick
Emily ADAMS

JUDD, Samuel I
　Catherine HINES
　Mary J ASHWORTH
　Helen F. JONES

KEATE, James
　Verbena CHRISTOFFERSON
　Susanna SANGEOVANNI

KELSEY, Easton
　Abigail FINCH
　Mary Jane COX
　Janette MULLINER

KING, Charles

KLEINMAN, Conrad
　Elizabeth MALHOLM
　Anna BENZ
　Mary Ann GERMER

LAMB, Brigham Young
　Mary Foster HARDY

LAMB, Edwin Ruthben
　Elizabeth W. HARDY

LANG, John
　Mary Ann MICKELSON
　Martha MICKELSON
　Elizabeth STANDFIELD
　Elizabeth OGILVIE

LANG, Joseph

LANG, Nathan

LANG, William
　Mary PUGSLEY
　Mary Ann BAKER

LANEY, Isaac
　Sarah Ann HOWARD

LARSON, John
　Amelia Ann WEIGHT

LARSON, Lars
　Mary A BELLOWS

LAWRENCE, Henry W

LEE, Francis
　Jane Vail JOHNSON

LEE, George Washington
　Abigail Lucinda BUNKER
　Cynthia C. BUNKER

LEE, John N.

LEE, Samuel Francis
　Ann Dodd WHITE

LEE, William Henry

LEWIS, Phillip Beeson
　Maria Theressa BONNEY
　Emily LEWIS
　Mary SCOTT

LISTON, Commodore Perry
　Elizabeth REEVES
　Laura F SMITH
　Mary Bowers SNELUS
　Melissa WALLACE

LITTLE, James Amasy
　Mary H. LYTLE
　Anna M. BALDWIN
　Mary E. TULLEDGE

LOUGEE, Darius
　Alice Hulme THOMPSON
　Jane TUCKETT

LUFKIN, George Washington
　Martha Ann TOWNSEND
　Susan M. TOWNSEND

LUND, John

LYTLE, John
　Christina D. WITTNER

LYTLE, John Milton
　Lucinda Clarissa TUTTLE

LYTLE, William Perry
　Lucy C. ATCHINSON

MACE, Wandle
　Rebecca E. HOWELL

MANGUM, William

MANSFIELD, Mathew
  Johanna C. W. PETERSON
  Margaret HASLAM

MARVIN, Edward W.
  Nancy Bulford MORRIS

MATHIS, Hans Heinrich (Sr.)

MATHIS, Hans Heinrich (Jr.)
  Elizabeth HUBSCHMEID

MATHIS, John (Johannes)
  Anna Barbara BRYNER
  Maria Sophie REUSCH

McARTHUR, Daniel Duncan
  Matilda C. FULLER
  Mary Bice HILL
  Elizabeth BULLOCK
  Mary F CALLOWAY

McCARTHY, James Hardwick
  Lydia M CRAGUN
  Mary Ann M FRAZIER

McFATE, James
  Elizabeth WILLIAMS
  Lucy Thompson LISK
  Matilda BRACKEN

McINELLY, James
  Angeline V ELMER

McINTIRE, Robert

McINTIRE, William Patterson
  Anna PATTERSON

McMILLAN, William
  Harriet PERKINS

McQUARRIE, Hector
  Agnes GRAY
  Elizabeth MC MURTRIE

MEADS, Alexander

METCALF, John Edward (Sr.)

MILES, Orson P.

MINNERLY, Albert

MOODY, John Monroe
  Margaret A McINTIRE
  Elizabeth POOL
  Sarah M DAMRON
  Margaret L PACE

MOON, Hugh
  Marie Emeline MOTT
  Elizabeth KIMMISH
  Jannett NICOL

MORSE, Francis Young I
  Elizabeth THOMAS

MOSS, David A
  Julia Ann WHITTAKER
  Mary Ann KEY

MOUSLEY, Lewis Henry
  Mary CROSSGROVE
  Sarah T. CROSSGROVE

MUDD, John
  Esther BARNES

MUSTARD, David
  Margaret KAY

NEBEKER, Aaron Smith (Sr.)
  Jane Ann SMITH

NEBEKER, Ashton
  Lucy Delia PRATT

NEBEKER, John
  Mary WOODCOCK

NYE, John

OAKLEY, John DeGroot
  Louisa JONES

ORTON, Joseph
  Emma Webb HARRADENCE
  Rebecca H. WILKINSON

OXBORROW, Joseph
  Jannet POTTER

PACE, James
  Lucinda G. STRICKLAND
  Margaret CALHOUN
  Ann WEBB

PACE, William Byron
  Maria Empey GOULD

PARKER, Zadock
  Miriam PARKER

PATRICK, Rufus

PEARCE, Harrison
  Henrietta D CROMEENS
  Ann MEREDITH
  Magdalena SCHNEIDER

PEARCE, John David L.
  Martha Elmina PACE

PECK, Harrison Gray Otis
  Margaret Reed ANGIER

PENDLETON, Benjamin Franklin
  Lavina PATTEN
  Alice JEFFERY

PERKINS, William Gant
  Dicy RAY
  Hannah GOULD

PERKINS, William Job
  Martha P RANDALL
  Mary Jane WILLIS

PERKINS, Ute (Jr.)
  Amanda A WARREN

PERKINS, Ute Warren
  Sarah LAUB

PHILLIPS, Thomas

PICKETT, Horatio
  Harriet J. JOHNSON
  Philena HUNT

PILLING, John

PIXTON, Robert
  Elizabeth COOPER
  Martha SILCOCK

PLATT, Henry John
  Almeda Jane JOHNSON

PLAYER, Joseph (Jr.)
  Ann KEET

PLAYER, William (Sr.)

PLAYER, William (Jr.)

PRATT, Orson (Sr.) (Apostle)

PRATT, Orson (Jr.)
  Susan Lizette SNOW

PRISBREY, Miner Grant
  Mary Ann HERSHEY

PULSIPHER, Charles
  Ann BEERS
  Sarah Eliza ROBBINS
  Julia Abby JOHNSON

PULSIPHER, John
  Rozilla HUFFAKAER
  Esther M. Murry BARNUM

PULSIPHER, William
  Esther CHIDESTER

PYMM, John
  Sarah TABBERER
  Agnes DONALD
  Catherine Donald RANKIN

RANDALL, Alfred Jason
  Ruth CHAMPKIN
  Emerette DAVIS

RANSON, James
  Elizabeth ROWLEY

RICHEY, James
  Lucinda MANGUM

RIDING, Christopher Lister
  Mary Ann HALE
  Adelaide DOLBELL

ROBBINS, Lewis
  Martha JARVIS

ROGERS, David
  Mary Ann MEYER

ROMNEY, Miles
  Elizabeth G GASKALL
  Ann KING

RUSSELL, Alonzo Heventon
  Nancy Briggs POSTER
  Louisa Maria FOSTER
  Clarissa HARDY

RUSSELL, Henry

RUSSELL, James

RUSSELL, Thomas Wilson

SANDERS, Ellis Mendenhall (Sr.)
  Rachel Broom CONGER

SANGIOVANNI, Gyglielmo G.
  Rosette (no surname available)

SCHAERRER, Henry
  Anne GOETC

SCHLAPPI, Henry
  Margaret FUHRER
  Lena Schmutz WAGNER

SEVEY, George Washington
  Phoebe M BUTLER
  Margaret N IMLAY

SHIER, Jacob

SILL, Dan

SLAUGHTER, Charles M
  Fanny Piety KENNER

SMITH, Charles N.
  Mariah Brooks DE GREY

SMITH, Joseph
  Henrietta JAMES

SMITH, Samuel

SMITH, William G

SMITH, William White
  Jane TAYLOR
  Annie ELMER
  Maria HOLDEN

SNOW, Erastus Fairbanks (Apostle)
  Artimisia BEAMAN
  Minerva WHITE
  Elizabeth R. ASHBY

SPENCER, Claudius Victor
  Louisa KING
  Susanna F NELSON
  Matilda PRICE

SPENCER, George
  Emily Ann BUSH
  Mary Ann PAYNE
  Sarah M THOMPSON

STANTON, Daniel
  Angelina WATKINS

STARR, Edward William
  Amanda Ann K DUEL
  Mary OSTENSEN

STEVENS, James W.
  Lucinda MASSEY

STOKER, Michael

STOUT, Allen Joseph
  Amanda A FISK
  Elizabeth ANDERSON

STOUT, Hosea
  Alvira WILSON

STRATTON, Oliver
  Harriet Ann BROWN

STRINGHAM, Benjamin Joseph
  Emma Smith ASHBY

STRONG, Ezra

SULLIVAN, Archibald
  Julia A. MATHEWS

SWAPP, William
  Elizabeth HILL

TERRY, Charles Alphonso
Sarah L HAMMOND
Emeline WILSON

TERRY, Thomas Sirls (Sr.)
Mary Ann PULSIPHER
Eliza J. PULSIPHER

TERRY, William Renolds
Mary Allen PHILLIPS

THEOBALD, William
Martha LANE
Elizabeth OLDS
Elizabeth UREN

THOMAS, Charles John
Amy Hannah ADAMS
Mary Ann JONES

THOMPSON, Robert
Alice HULME

THOMPSON, William Henry
Matilda YOUNG
Emma COTTAM
Agnes E. P. CALKINS
Elizabeth J WRIGHT
Hannah M SELENDER

THURSTON, George Washington
Sarah Lucina SNOW

THURSTON, Smith Butler
Mary ISOM

THURSTON, Thomas Jefferson
Elizabeth J SMITH

TOWNSEND, James Foss
Elizabeth J DUNN

TROST, William

TRUMAN, Jacob Mica
Elizabeth BOYCE
Catherine MAXWELL

TURNER, William
Angeline P AVERETT

TYLER, Albert Peck
Celestia PRATT

TYLER, De Witt

UTLEY, Little John
Deborah WHITE

VANCE, John (Jr.)
Elizabeth CAMPBELL

WALKER, Charles Lowell
Abigail MIDDLEMASS

WALKER, Edwin

WALKER, William

WASHBURN, Daniel A

WELLS, Stephen Robert
Mary Ann LOWE
Ann T. GOLIGHTLY

WESTOVER, Charles
Eliza Ann HAVEN
Mary SHUMWAY

WHIPPLE, Eli
Patience FOSTER
Caroline LYTLE

WHITMORE, (Dr.) James M.
Eizabeth CARTER

WILKINS, James Wilson

WILSON, Charles

WILSON, Henry Hardy
Frances KELLEY

WILSON, Robert

WILTBANK, Spencer Watson
Annie SANDERS

WINDER, Thomas Harrison
Hannah SHREVE

WINSOR, Anson Perry (Sr.)
Emeline Zanette BROWER
Mary NELSON

WITTWER, Christian

WOODBURY, John Stillman
  Martha Alice PARKER

WOODBURY, Orin Nelson
  Ann CANNON
  Frances GODDARD

WOODBURY, Thomas Hobart (Sr.)
  Catherine R HASKELL
  Harriet MILLER

WOODS, Benjamin F

WOODS, Lyman Lafayette
  Marihah Ann BIRD

WOODWARD, George
  Thomazin DOWNING
  Mary Ann WALLACE

WOODWARD, Jabez
  Ann GRANGER

WORTHEN, Samuel
  Sarah HALLAM
  Maria L GROW
  Jane OSBORNE

YOUNG, Franklin Wheeler
  Nancy Lenora GREEN
  Anna Maria SABIN

YOUNG, John Ray
  Albina TERRY
  Lydia KNIGHT

YOUNG, Lorenzo Sobieski
  Amelia BLACK

Pioneers of 1862 to 1869

ADAMS, Samuel Lorenzo
  Emma JACKSON
  Mary Ann MORGAN
  Almira JACKSON

ALGER, John
  Sarah Ann PULSIPHER
  Jane Ann BURNETT
  Sarah Ann EDWARDS

ALLEN, Daniel (Jr.)

ALLEN, Rufus Chester
  Lavenia H. YEARSLEY
  Margaret MC CONNELL

ATKIN, William (Sr.)
  Rachel THOMPSON

AVERETT, Elisha
  Sarah Jane WITT

BAKER, Thomas
  Martha Ann LARSON

BECKSTROM, Peter Jeppson
  Christina LUND

BENTLEY, Richard
  Elizabeth PRICE
  Hannah C WEBSTER

BITTERS, Traugott
  Wilhelmina AUST

BRINGHURST, William
  Ann DILWORTH

BROWN, Lorenzo
  Frances CROSBY

BROWN, Robert H
  Elizabeth Ann TUTTLE
  Eunice PECTOL

BROWN, William

BURGEON, George

BURGESS, George Marin
  Rhoda Ann DYKES

BURGESS, William (Jr.)
  Mariah PULSIPHER
  Charlotte E. LIGETTE
  Catherine CHAMBERLAIN

BURT, William

CARPENTER, Joseph Wetherbee
  Annie RANDALL

CARPENTER, William H.
  Marmora SHEFFIELD

CHURCH, Abram
  Sarah ALGER

CLAYTON, Thomas
  Susanna Ellen HELM

CONGER, Leonard Smith (Sr.)
  Elizabeth SANDERS
  Artemish WESTOVER

COUSENS, Hugh Snap
  Lydia A GIBBS

COWLEY, William E.
  Sarah Ann ALGER

CRAGUN, James
  Eleanor LANE

CRAGUN, Thomas Calvin
  Amelia CHAMBERS

CRANE, Thomas Gibbs
  Elizabeth SMITH

CROFF, William Cowee
  Eliza Jane GREEN

DAGGETT, Francis
  Mary E CONGER

DAVIS, Edward Horace

DEANS, James
  Susannah HAMMOND

DODGE, Walter Erastus
  Eleanor C. MALONE

DORRITY, Dennis
  Mary E. BERRY

EARDLEY, John (Sr.)
  Ann CROFFS

EARL, James Calvin
  Mary Eliz. PARSONS

ELDREDGE, Horace Sunderlin

EMPEY, William Adam
  Martha FIELDING
  Mary H. PORTER

ENSIGN, John Calvin
  Emma GARN

EVERETT, Schuyler Alanson
  Rachel SANDERS

FARNSWORTH, Moses Franklin
  Clara CANFIELD

FAWCETT, Nephi Robert
  Ruth ORCHARD
  Morara CARPENTER

FOREMASTER, Frederick William
  Sophie C.M. LINDAU

FULLER, Cornelius
  Annie Elizabeth LEWIS

FULLER, Elijah Knapp
  Ellen C. WOODWARD
  Elizabeth VAUGHN
  Harriet A. WALKER

FULLER, Revilo
  Mary Davis EVERETT

FULLER, Wyllys Darwin
  Ann Bell CAMPKIN

GILLESPIE, Alexander
  Mary COOK

GODBE, William S.

GODDARD, Robert
  Margaret WOOLFENDEN

GOLDING, Robert Jackson
  Susan CHESHIRE

GOULD, George Washington
  Maria EMPEY

GOULD, Samuel William
  Sarah Ann LEWIS

GRAY, Benjamin Brown
Jerusha C. BURDICK

HALL, Thomas C.
Ann HUGHES

HAMMOND, Robert
Sarah Frances WILSON

HARDY, Josiah Guile
Sarah Clark PARKER
Ann DENSTON

HARDY, Warren
Carolyn Lucy BLAKE

HARRADENCE, Jeremiah
Mary Ann LINFORD

HARRIS, Moses
Fanny SMITH

HARRIS, Silas
Sariah ALDRICH

HEMENWAY, Luther S.
Harriet HODGSON
Sarah HODGSON

HORSLEY, Clarence
Catherine

IDE, James Monroe
Lydia Ann CRANSON
Mary JACKSON

JACKSON, Alden Appolos
Caroline A PERKINS

JEFFERY, Thomas A.
Elizabeth COWPER
Mary Ann HIBBERT

JEFFERY, Walter

JENSON, Anders

JONSON, Bengt
Anna HAKANSON

JONES, Thomas Jefferson
Emily MILLER

JUDD, Thomas

KEMP, William Button
Mary LOCKWOOD

LAUB, George W.
Mary J McGINNESS
Ann E. ERICKSON

LEWIS, Aaron
Sarah Ann WEEKS

LLOYD, James Elwood

LUND, Robert C.

LUND, Wilson
Eliza Ann BRACE
Ellen NIELSON

MACFARLANE, John Menzies
Ann CHATTERLY
Agnes E. HEYBOURNE
Elizabeth J. ADAMS

MAUDSLEY, Henry James
Mary S. FOREMASTER

MAXWELL, William B.
Lucretia C. BRACKEN
Martha Jane MATHIS
Maryetta M. HAMBLIN

McALLISTER, John Daniel T.
Ellen HANDLEY
Angeline GOFORTH
Cornelia A LENZI

McALLISTER, William James F
Eleanor J. ADAMS

McCLAIN, Marion

McCULLOUGH, James Dillard
Elizabeth M MOORE
Martha J LOWERY
Elizabeth M LOFTEN

McINTIRE, Wallace Marshall
Abba A HOVEY

McMILLAN, Wm.

McMILLIN, William
  Polly Ann COX

McNEIL, Archibald
  Agnes BROWN
  Helen HASWELL

MEEKS, William
  Mary E. RHODES

MERRICK, John A

MILES, Samuel (Sr.)
  Hannah M. COLBURN

MILLER, Henry William
  Elmira POND
  Fanny GUNN

MILNE, David
  Susan YOUNG
  Ann C. JARVIS
  Anna HESS

MOODY, William Cressfield
  Harriet HENSON
  Lola E. BESS
  Cynthia E. DAMRON

MORRIS, Richard
  Emma PACKER

NAY, John
  Thankful Lucy PINE

NEEDHAM, David Bennett
  Elizabeth A STAFFORD

NELSON, Aaron
  Mary STANDFORTH
  Selena C. PALFREYMAN

NELSON, William
  Mary Alice THOMPSON

NIXON, James
  Johannah M SCHULTZ
  Hannah I FAWCETT

OAKDEN, Phillip Louis
  Olivia ALGER

PARK, James Pollock
  Agnes FINDLAY
  Sarah Ann PYMM

PARRY, Edward Lloyd
  Elizabeth EVANS
  Ann PARRY

PATRICK, Rufus

PEARCE, Thomas Jefferson
  Angenetta ANGIER

PRINCE, George
  Sarah BOWMAN
  Frances WILKINS

PULSIPHER, Zera
  Mary Ann BROWN
  Prudence MACMAMARA
  Martha Ann HUGHES

RHONER, Johannes
  Barbara NEIDERSON

RICH, Joseph
  Dora (no surname available)

ROMNEY, Miles Park
  Hannah H HILL
  Caroline LAMBOURNE
  Catherine Jane COTTAM
  Millie Eyring SNOW

SAVAGE, Levi Mathers
  Ann BRUMMELL
  Adelaide COOPER
  Mary Ann COOPER

SCHMUTZ, Johannes (Sr.)
  Elizabeth LEHMANN

SEEGMILLER, Adam Frederick
  Laura QUAHM

SEEGMILLER, Charles William
  Marianne FORSYTH

SEEGMILLER, Daniel
  Ellen SMITH
  Artemissia S. WOOLEY

SEEGMILLER, Johann Adam
  Anna Eva KNECHTEL

SLAGOWSKI, Xceverius Francisus
  Maria M STEIBER

SMITH, Charles
  Sarah PRICE
  Eliza MATHEWS

SMITH, George Albert (Apostle)

SNELL, Richard Irvin
  Margaret EARL

SNOW, William
  Sally ADAMS
  Jane Marie SCHEARER
  Ann ROGERS

SQUIRE, William
  Maria MORREL
  Isabel WHITE

SUDWEEKS, Henry
  Sarah SWEET
  Emma SUDWEEKS

THOMAS, Daniel Monroe
  Ann CROSBY
  Jane M CARPENTER

THOMAS, Elijah
  Ann HAYWARD
  Harriet R JOHNSON

TITCOMB, John

TORONTO, Joseph

TUCKETT, Joseph
  Margaret Jane ISAACS

WARREN, Edward Eugene
  Saran (Ann) SMITH

WATTS, John

WEBB, William Badcock (Sr.)
  Amelia JARVIS

WESTOVER, Edwin Ruthben
  Sarah Jane BURWELL

WHITE, Thomas
  Bertha GILES

WHITEHEAD, Adolphus Rennie
  Mary Elizabeth GODDARD
  Myeza Jane ALEXANDER
  Mary Ester WELLS

WILSON, Ephraim
  Isabelle DEANS
  Margaret McNeil HOUSTON

WOOLLEY, Edwin Dilworth
  Mary Lovinia BENTLEY

WOOLLEY, Franklin Benjamin
  Olive Carl FOSS

WULFFENSTEIN, Bengt Pehr
  Olina GULBRANDSON

YOUNG, Joseph Watson
  Lurana ELDRIDGE
  Thankful ADAMS

YOUNG, William

INDEX

Accidents and injuries, 126, 187–88, 193n20, 223
Adair, Samuel, 54n26
Adams, John, 309n17
Adams, Samuel Lorenzo, 94, 102, 225, 228, 235
Address, terms of, 74
Adoption, law of, 294, 294–95n6
Ahlstrom, Mary Larsen, 128
Ahlstrom, Peter, 128
Allman, Emma Jane, 232
Allman, Jessie May, 232
Allman, Thomas, 230–37, 320
Allman, Verl, 234–36
Allred, Elizabeth Warren, 251
Anderson, Nels, 258, 317
Angell, Truman O., 83, 96, 233–34, 236
Angus, John O., 97
Animals, draft, 189. See also Ox(en)
Annex, 325–26, 329, 331, 339
Arches, 179n23, 215
Arthur, C. J., 106–107
Atkin, Eliza, 193n20
Atkin, Henry, 119
Atkin, Joseph, 53–54
Atkin, Rachel, 119, 211
Atkin, William, II, 119, 211
Atkin, William, III, 53–54, 119
Averett, Elisha, 31
Averett, Joseph A. F., 329

Bakery, 111
Ballif, Amanda Leigh, 342
Balls, sheet metal, 205–7, 207n28, 318–20, 341–42n25

Bankhead, John, 19
Baptism, of Indians, 194
Baptismal font, 125, 156, 156n7, 197–204
Baptism for the dead: Bruce R. McConkie on, 249; in St. George Temple, 279–80; revelation concerning, 288–90. See also Dead, salvation for
Barlow, Oswald, 44
Barnum, Roberta Blake, 187–88
Basement, 126
Benches, for patron seating, 227
Bennett, Charles, 111
Bennett, Martha, 211n36
Bennett, Richard E., 257, 259, 260–61
Bennett, Samuel, 201, 208, 210, 211nn35, 36
Benson, Ezra Taft, 346
Bents, 183–84, 195. See also Trusses
Bernhisel, John M., 305n6
Blackhawk Indian War, 84
Black Ridge, 18–19n6
Black Rock Road, 187–96
Blake, Benjamin, 180, 187–88
Blake, Eliza, 193n20
Blake, Frederick, 180, 187–88, 193, 193n20
Blake, Jane, 278, 281
Bleak, James G.: as record keeper, 25; on cornerstone box, 143; on Brigham Young's letter, 169–70; on placement of final bent, 195; on tithes, 243–44; on ordinances in St. George Temple, 280–81; and temple work for founding fathers, 309, 309–10n17; on lightning striking temple tower, 319
Bleak, Jane Thompson, 44–45

Booth, James, 221
Brooks, Juanita, 50, 71, 104n19, 246
Brown, John, 19
Brown, Lorenzo, 277–78
Brown, William Jr., 211
Bryce, Ebenezer, 180
Burgess, Harrison, 180
Burt, John, 223–24
Burt, William, 97, 222, 223
Buttresses, 125

Calkins, Asa, 44
Cane, of Brigham Young, 274, 277, 277nn15, 16
Cannon, iron, 102–5, 104n19
Cannon, Angus M., 44
Cannon, David H.: on land allotment, 48; as temple administrator, 87, 273n9, 298, 307, 309, 315; temple construction and, 107; as trustee, 136; on plastering of outside walls, 222; Brigham Young appears to, 321–22; on cleaning and repair work, 325–26
Cannon, David Henry Jr., 87, 98, 107
Cannon, George Q.: on temple construction, 126; inspects temple, 235, 264; and temple ceremony, 282; on completion of temple, 244; temple attendance of, 286–87
Carling, Isaac, 212–13
Carpenter, Annie Burdett Randall, 280n5
Carpenter, Joseph Weatherbee, 280n5
Carpentry work, 214–16
Carpets, 241–42, 266–68
Carson, Hannah Waggle, 54n26
Carson, Mary Ann, 54n26
Carson, Samuel Valentine, 54n26
Carson, Valentine, 54n26
Carter, Samuel Utley, 148
Carter, Sophronia, 43, 47, 55
Carter, William, 43, 47, 102
Ceilings, 82, 173, 225, 240n24
Chairs, 228–29
Chidester, John Peck, 67, 145, 193
Chidester, Susannah Foy, 67
Children, sealing and, 262
Christensen, Carl Christian Anthon, 156n8, 237–38
Christensen, C. L., 200–2, 203–4
Christian, Lewis Earl, 120n19

Christmas, 44–45, 58, 130, 163–65
Church, Clara Jane Randall, 280n5
Church, Haden Wells (Jr.), 280n5
Church, H. M., 108
Civic life, 74–75
Clayson, Lula Romney, 304n4
Cleaning and cleanup work, 325–26
Clock, 73
Clothes, temple, 251, 285, 316
Comfort, temple as place of, 344–45
Comish, Louise Larson, 315
Consecration, 138–40, 143–45, 154, 170, 176
Construction of St. George Temple: preparations for, 96–98; excavation and foundation, 98–105, 116–22, 124–26, 133–35, 339–41; provisions for, 106–116, 140–41, 154; workers for, 126–31, 144, 149–50; sacrifice for, 131–33, 143–45; cornerstone ceremony and, 141–43; walls, 145–49, 174–75; windows, 146–49, 147n25, 219nn1, 5, 239n22; floors, 147, 171–73; doors, 147–48; George Kirkham Jr. on, 152–62, 166, 178–80, 183–85; Alexander Spowart Izatt on, 158; reports on, 159–61; disagreements during, 161–62; George A. Smith on, 163; George A. Smith urges forward, 163–64; progress in, 167–68; Brigham Young on, 169–70; and lumber from Mt. Trumbull, 174–77, 179–82; Temple Trail and, 185–96; baptismal font, 197–204, 203n17; tower, 205–7; weather vane and sheet metal balls, 205–7; finish carpentry work, 215–19; plastering, 221–26; accidents and injuries in, 193n20, 223–25; Thomas Allman and, 230–36; painting, 236–39; William Henry Thompson and, 239–41; cleanup work, 241–42; grounds, 242–43; cost of, 243–44; completion of, 244–47
Cornerstones, 94, 141–43
Cornet, 28, 66
Cottam, Caroline Smith, 56, 304n4
Cottam, Thomas, 56, 58, 228–29
Cottam, Thomas Punter, 51n21, 56, 229, 304n4, 324
Cotton, 17, 22, 30–31, 57, 70

Courthouse, 72–73
Covenants, 346
Covington, Robert D., 38
Cowan, Richard, 252, 257, 263
Cox, Isaiah, 84
Cox, Martha Cragun, 68–69, 84
Cragun, Teresa, 152–53, 193
Crane, Thomas, 203, 203n17, 224
Crawl spaces, 125
Crosby, Elizabeth, 20
Crosby, Hannah Bunker, 33
Crosby, Hannah Elida Baldwin, 70n9, 112, 112n39
Crosby, Jesse W., 104–5, 111
Crosby, Oscar, 19–20
Crosby, William, 19–20
Crowds, accommodating, 285–87
Crowther, Thomas, 129
Cultural pursuits, in St. George, 62–63

Danish, Charles Pulsipher speaks in, 209–10
Davis, Kelly, 333–34
Davis, Nathan, 163, 197, 198n3, 200–1
Dead, salvation for: temples required for, 14; Joseph Smith on, 252–53; vicarious ordinances for, 261–62, 279–81; revelation concerning, 288–90; as reason for temple work, 343–44. *See also* Baptism for the dead; Temple work
Dean, Jim, 116
Deaths, during temple construction, 224
Declaration of Independence, signers of, 303–11, 303n2, 304n4, 309–10n17
Dedication(s): of temple site, 90–95; preparations for, 265–68; first, 269–78; full, 296–97
DeFriez, Charles, 203, 203n17
DeFriez, Ebenezer, 203, 203n17
Dodge, Walter E., 68–69
Dolls, 58, 58n36
Dome, 320, 341–42
Doors, 147–48
Dormitory, 106
Draft animals, 189. *See also* Ox(en)
Drains, 105
Dress, Wilford Woodruff said to have worn, 323
Drought, 58
Duyckinck, Evert, 306–7n11

Earthquake, 339–41
Elijah, 5, 7–8, 10–11, 260n34
Endowment House, 81
Endowment(s): Wilford Woodruff on, 10; Joseph Smith on, 13–15; given to Twelve, 250–52; in brick store, 251n6; administered to Saints, 253–56; Brigham Young on, 257–58n27, 262; in St. George Temple, 279–81
Enoch, order of, 137–39
Eternal families, 344
Eternal progression, 3–4
Evans, Jerry, 340
Everett, A. F., 238
Exaltation, eternal progression toward, 3–4
Excavation, for St. George Temple, 98–105, 116–22, 124–26, 134–35

Fackander, Margaret Ann, 264n45
Fackrell, Maria, 308n14
Fairbanks, John, 238
Families, eternal, 344
Farnsworth, Moses Franklin, 167, 292–93, 294n5
Faucett, George, 43
Fawcett, William, 30, 39
Felshaw, William, 251n6
Fetzer, Emil, 334–37
Films, 332, 335
Fire, 327–29, 333–34
Flake, Green, 19–20
Flooding, 45–47, 52–53
Floors, 147, 171–73
Folsom, William H., 163, 320
Font, baptismal, 125, 156, 156n7
Food production: in St. George, 57–62, 67–68, 71–72, 78–79; temple construction and, 106–111, 113–116, 148
Foremaster (Fuhrmeister), Albert, 83, 119–20
Foremaster (Fuhrmeister), Frederick William, 119–20
Foremaster (Fuhrmeister), Marta M., 210
Ft. Pearce, 84–85, 84–85n15, 186n7
Fort Harmony, 17, 18–19
Foster, Charles Franklin, 126
Foundation, temple, 98–105, 116, 124–26, 134–35, 340–41

Founding fathers, 303–11, 303n2, 304n4, 309–10n17
Foy, Susannah, 67
Freight, 111–112
Frye, Edna Rae Gardner, 329
Fuhrmeister (Foremaster), Albert, 119–20
Fuhrmeister (Foremaster), Frederick William, 119–20
Fuhrmeister (Foremaster), Marta M., 210–11
Fuller, Elijah, 111
Fuller, Rivelo, 111
Fullerton, Alex, 116

Gardner, Archibald, 32
Gardner, Celestia, 180
Gardner, Mary Ann, 180
Gardner, Robert: called to St. George, 32; on settling St. George, 36, 37–39; on storm and flooding, 46–47; temple location and, 87–88; temple construction and, 96; road construction and, 101; on temple foundation, 101; as trustee, 136; United Order and, 138–39; Mt. Trumbull lumber and, 176–77, 180–82, 185, 191n17; on quicksand, 188; on Temple Trail, 190–91
Garrett, Dean, 314
Gathering of Saints, 8
General conference, 295–98
Gift of tongues, 209–10
Glass, 147–48, 147n25
God, becoming like, 3–5
Goforth, Angeline Sophronia, 264n45
Government, 75, 136–37
Graining, 237, 237n10
Granger, Pete, 224
Grant, Ulysses S., 124
Grapes, 68
Grapevine Springs, 37–38
Grasshoppers, 148
Gray, Benjamin Browne, 213–14, 214nn42, 43
Gray, Benjamin Franklin, 214
Gray, DeWayne, 342
Greene, Evan F., 190
Groundbreaking, for St. George Temple, 93–95
Grounds, of St. George Temple, 242–43
Gubler, Alyce W. Gray, 214

Haight, Isaac, 185, 185n4
Hailstone, Ann Davis, 264n45
Hair, 132–33, 222
Hamblin, Jacob, 17, 21, 26–27, 47, 49
Hancock, John, 303n2
Hancock, Levi Ward, 303n2
Handley, Ellen, 264n45
Hardy, A. P., 17
Hardy, Josiah G., 196
Hardy, L. W., 114–15
Harmony, Fort, 17, 18
Haskell, Thales, 86n19
Heat, 121–22, 124
Hicks, George, 29, 37, 61
Highway, 332
Holmes, Bertha Gray, 213–14
Home construction, in St. George, 55–56
Honeymoon Trail, 312–16
Hopkinson, Art, 333–34
Horne, Joseph, 21
Hosanna Shout, 95
Howe, Amos, 197–98, 198n3
Hunt, Isaac, 111
Hunt, May, 314–15
Hunter, Edward W., 114–15
Huntington, Dimick B., 251n6
Huntsman, Orson Welcome, 114
Hyde, Orson, 11, 28, 203, 250

I-15 Highway, 332
Indians: George A. Smith Jr. killed by, 26–27; Charles Pulsipher and, 50–51; conflicts with, 84, 85–86; baptism of, 194
Industries, in St. George, 68–71
Injuries, during temple construction, 150, 193n20, 223–25
Interior work: progress in, 205; woodcarving, 217–21; plastering, 221–22; painting, 236–38; cleanup work, 241–42; renovation, 334–38
Interstate highway system, 332
Iron City, 198–99n5
Iron oxen, 197–200, 203
Itten, John R., 66
Ivins, Israel, 43, 108
Izatt, Alexander Spowart, 158, 158–59n11

Jackson, Caroline, 69–70
Jackson, Estella, 202

Jacobs, Norton, 195
Jarvis, Ann Prior, 59, 203n17
Jarvis, George: claims lot, 47; Cotton
    Mission and, 59n39; temple construc-
    tion and, 97, 118; scaffolding and,
    145–46; placement of final bent and,
    195; baptismal font and, 202–3; places
    temple front, 203n17
Jarvis, Heber, 227n17
Jarvis, Josephine, 203n17
Jarvis, Zora Smith, 175
Jefferson, Thomas, 309–10n17
Jennings, Annie McArthur, 304n4
Jepperson, Samuel, 156, 156n8, 237
Johnson, Joseph E., 78–79
Jones, Darrell E., 321n6
Jones, Emma Jane Allman, 232
Jones, Heber, 161–62
Jones, Josephine Cannon, 321–22
Jones, Samuel Steven, 232
Judd, Joseph, 155
Judd, Samuel, 83, 96, 120
Judd, Thomas, 155
Judd, Zadock K., 17

Kamp, Peter W., 238–39
Kanab, Utah, 85–86
Kane, Thomas L., 129
Kelsey, Easton, 111, 225
Kemp, Peter W., 329
Kimball, Heber C., 253–54
Kimball, J. Golden, 59
Kirkham, George Jr.: on temple construc-
    tion, 152–58, 160–62, 168–74, 178–80,
    183–84; on Christmas and New Year
    in St. George, 164–66; on placement
    of last stone, 191–192; on celebration
    in Tabernacle, 192–93; on baptism of
    Indians, 193–94; compared to Jacob,
    194–95n21
Kirkham, Joseph, 152–53, 157, 193
Kirkham, Mary, 153
Kirkham, Teresa Cragun, 153, 193
Kirtland Temple, 5–7, 89
Knight, Lydia, 69–70
Knight, Samuel, 23n13, 69
Knowledge, acquisition of, 248–49

Lang, Ann, 36
Lang, George, 224–25
Lang, William, 36
Larson, Alof, 314–15
Larson, Andrew Karl: on settlement
    preparations, 35; on Erastus Snow,
    40–41; on cannon, 104–5; on murals,
    237–38; on appearance and impact of
    temple, 246–47; on carpets, 268; on
    Brigham Young at temple dedication,
    274–75, 276–77
Larson, Ellen, 315
Larson, Emma, 314–15
Larson, May Hunt, 314–15
Larson, Mons, 315
Las Vegas Temple, 339
Lath-and-plaster walls, 240n24
Laub, George, 219–21
Laub, George Weydler, 219
Laub, John Franklin, 71, 220
Lava rock, 99–103, 100n9, 116–20, 125,
    133–35, 340
Law of adoption, 294–95, 294–95n6
Lay, Billy, 19, 133
Lay, Hark, 19–20
Lay, Sytha, 19, 20–21, 20–21n8
Lay, William Harvey (Billy), 19, 20–21n8
Leap Creek, 18–19n6
Legal knowledge, 137
Lenzi, Cornelia Agatha, 264n45
Lightning, strikes temple tower, 318–21,
    321n6
Lime, 120–21, 120–21n19
Little, James A., 114–15, 128
Logan Temple, 281
Logue, Larry, 74
Lumber: Robert Gardner and, 105–6,
    191n17; Charles Franklin Foster and,
    126; George Jarvis and, 145; from Mt.
    Trumbull, 174–77, 179–82; for finish
    work, 218–19
Luther, Martin, 309, 309–10n17
Lyman, Amasa M., 20

Macadamizing, 151, 151n34
Mace, Wandle, 32
Macfarlane, John M., 90
Mackley, Alvina, 264n45
Mackley, Jennifer, 310–11
Madsen, Truman, 7–8
Maintenance work, 341
Malaria, 18

Manti Temple, 208–10, 300
Markagunt Plateau, 40
Marriage. See Plural marriage; Sealing(s)
Martin, Glen E., 83n10
Mason, Ann, 307n11
McAdam, John Loudon, 151n34
McAllister, Ann, 308n14
McAllister, John Daniel Thompson: tours temple, 264; wives of, 264n45; temple dedication and, 265–66, 268, 270; as temple officiator, 298; and temple work for founding fathers, 307–9, 309n17; on damage from lightning, 319–20; Brigham Young appears to, 321–22
McAllister, Matilda Christina Nielsen, 264, 264n45
McArthur, D. D., 83–84
McArthur, Eldon, 324, 324–25n10, 327–29
McArthur, Emma Jarvis Cottam, 228–29, 269
McArthur, Jim, 328–29
McConkie, Bruce R., 249
McCullough, William Albert, 181–82
McDonald, Aaron, 221
McDonald, Alexander, 97, 111, 142, 190, 273n8
McNeil, Archibald, 97, 100, 116
McQuarrie, Robert, 221
Melchizedek Priesthood, 346
Miles, George, 161
Miles, John Horne, 161, 162n19, 203, 203n17
Miles, Josephine Jarvis, 203n17
Miles, Zaidee Walker, 73, 202
Miller, Albert E., 245–46
Milne, Alex, 237
Milne, Ann Catherine, 241–42
Milne, David, 97, 236
Moller, Ann, 264n45
Moody, John, 32–33
Moody, Margaret, 32–33
Morley, Phyllis, 320n5
Mormon settlements, 16–23. See also St. George
Motion pictures, 332, 335
Movies, 332
Mt. Trumbull, 174–77, 179–82, 184–96
Murals, 237–39, 238n20, 329
Music, 66–67

Musser, A. M., 189–90
Mustard, David, 193

Nagro, 86
Nails, 216n45
Nauvoo Temple, 24, 81, 89, 253–54
Navajos, 85–86
Nibley, Hugh, 2
Nielsen, Matilda Christina, 263–64, 264n45
Nielson, Rachel Violet Atkin, 211
Nielson, Swen O., 211
Nixon, Hannah, 43
Nuttall, L. John, 268

Old Iron Town, 198–99n5
"Old Mother Hubbard" dress, 323
"Once I Lived in Cottonwood" (Hicks), 29, 37
Order of Enoch, 137–39
Ordinances. See Temple ordinances
Orton, Joseph, 35–36, 54–55
"Our Temple" (Walker), 135
Oveson, Lars Peter, 129
Oxborrow, Joseph, 111
Ox(en), 35, 187–88. See also Draft animals; Iron oxen

Painting, 236–38, 238n20. See also Murals
Paiutes, 85
Parry, Edward L., 83, 96, 98–99, 117–18, 195
Peacock, George M., 26
Pearce, Fort, 84–85, 84–85n15, 186n7
Pearce, Jim, 111
Pearce, John David L., 84
Pearce, Tom, 111
Peart, Jacob Jr., 21–23
Peokon, 85–86, 86n19
Perkins, William A., 136
Perpetual Emigration Fund, 130
Persistence, 73
Peter's Leap, 18n6
Pickett, Horatio, 326
Pillars, 125–26, 171n9, 172
Pioneer Day, 122–24
Pipe Springs, 109–10
Plastering, 221–225
Plaster of paris, described, 225–26
Plural marriage, 69, 323–24
Population growth, 332

"Pounding Rock into the Temple
Foundation" (Walker), 103–4
Pratt, Orson, 11, 12n50, 27, 62
Pratt, Parley P., 11, 13–14n53, 30
Prayer: dedicating St. George Temple,
90–93; seeking answer to, 344–45
Priesthood: doctrine on, 4–5; fulness of,
347
Priesthood keys: restoration of, 8; conferred upon Twelve, 9–14, 250–51;
spirit of Elijah and, 10–11; sealing and,
12n50; Parley P. Pratt on, 13–14n53
Progression, eternal, 3–4
Provisions: for temple construction,
106–15, 140–41; George Kirkham on,
153–54; Brigham Young on, 175–76;
gathering of, 195; for Allman family,
234–35
Pulsipher, Charles: called to St. George,
31; travels to St. George, 34–35, 39;
surveys St. George, 43; on storm
and flooding, 45–46; interacts with
Indians, 50–51; provisions for temple
construction and, 107–9, 140–41,
195; on volunteer workers, 127–28; on
Manti Temple, 208–10; on death of
George A. Smith, 211–12; on contributions from poor, 212–13
Pulsipher, John, 31

Quicksand, 52, 188, 313

Raid, The, 323–24
Railroad, 41n1
Raleigh, Alonzo H., 267, 267n56, 283
Randall, Annie Burdett, 280n5
Randall, Clara Jane, 280n5
Records and record keeping, 155–56,
292–94, 324
Red Hill, 39, 43
Reid, H. Lorenzo, 247
Relief Society, 241
Renovation work, 325–37
Repair work, 325–26, 340
Restoration: of temple ordinances and
blessings, 1; of priesthood keys, 7;
comes line upon line, 248–49
Restroom facilities, 105, 105n22, 226n28
Revelation(s): concerning temple work,
259–61; concerning redemption of

dead, 288–90; regarding temple reno-
vation, 335–37. *See also* Vision(s)
Rich, Charles C., 20
Richie, Adam, 38
Riding, Christopher Lister, 205–7, 319,
320, 341–42n25
Riding, John Henry, 320
Roads: construction of, 101; repairing, 151,
151n34
Robbins, Lewis, 116
Rolfe, Samuel, 251n6
Romney, Miles: as construction superin-
tendent, 82–83, 96; involved in con-
struction accident, 150; obituary of,
150n31; and placement of final bent,
195; Thomas Allman replaces, 230–31
Roof, 193
Rooms, in St. George Temple, 225–28,
285–88
Russon, Mary, 153, 195n21
Russon, Sara, 195n21

Sacrifice: of St. George settlers, 30–31; for
temple construction, 81, 127–28, 132–
33, 143–44, 154–55; John W. Young
on, 143–44; blessings of, 212
Safety, temple as place of, 344–45
Salt Lake Temple, 1–2, 88n24
Sanders, Martin, 85
Santa Clara, Utah, 20, 27, 47, 54
Saunders, Ellis M., 95, 98
Savage, Charles R., 78
Scaffolding, 145
Scandinavian Saints, 28
Schmutz, John, 222
Schools, 51n21
Scoville, Lucius N., 251–52
Sealing(s): children and, 274; Orson Pratt
on, 12n50; in St. George Temple,
294n5
Seegmiller, Myrtle Gray, 213
Settlements, Mormon, 16–20. *See also*
St. George
Sheet metal balls, 205–7, 207n28, 318–21,
341–42n25
Sheets, Elijah, 200
Shirts, Peter, 18n6
Shoes, 49–50
Silk making, 69–70, 70n9
Smith, Emma Larson, 314–15

Smith, George A.: on Kirtland Temple construction, 6; on Black Ridge, 18n6; name of St. George and, 25–27; establishment of St. George and, 32, 36; on St. George and hell, 59; on St. George settlers, 64–65; votes for St. George Temple, 80; dedicates temple site, 90–93; temple groundbreaking and, 94; on temple foundation, 100–101; on food shortages, 114; United Order and, 138; on St. George, 144; calls for workers, 148–49; on St. George Temple, 156; surveys temple construction, 159; on temple construction, 163–64, 176–77; urges forward St. George Temple, 164; death of, 211–12

Smith, George A. Jr., 26–27, 86

Smith, Jesse N., 314–15

Smith, John L., 154, 209

Smith, Joseph: Brigham Young and, 2–3; priesthood ordinances and, 4–5; Kirtland Temple and, 5–7; teaches and prepares Twelve, 7–15, 250–53; charges Brigham Young with temple ceremonies, 14–15; cliff resembling, 83n10; on temple work for dead, 164; Restoration and, 248–49; on spirit of Elijah, 260n34

Smith, Joseph F., 163, 261–62

Smith, Joseph Fielding, 347

Smith, Lot, 313

Smoot, A. O., 114–15, 189

Snow, Edward H., 68

Snow, Erastus: establishment of St. George and, 27, 31, 40–41; as leader, 42, 43, 58–59; on St. George pioneers, 49; St. George Library Association and, 62; on progress in St. George, 67–68; on government, 75; votes for St. George Temple, 80; temple groundbreaking and, 94–95; on temple construction, 95; provisions for temple construction and, 106–9, 113–14, 140–41; disagreement with Brigham Young, 161; on contributions from poor, 212; temple dedication and, 272–73, 277; on temple attendance and ceremonies, 281–82

Snow, Harold S., 331

Snow, William, 139

Squire, Emma, 323

Staheli, George Johann, 28, 66–67, 90

Stake conference, 88–89

St. George: vision concerning, 23–24, 23n13; establishment of, 25–29; calls and journey to, 30–39, 18n6; challenges in, 39–41, 47–51, 84–86, 154–55; Erastus Snow and, 40–41; survey of, 42–43; first Christmas in, 44–45; storm and flooding in, 46–47; land allotment in, 47–48; building and land development in, 52–56; food production in, 57–62, 68; cultural pursuits in, 62–63; work and side occupations in, 63–64; George A. Smith on, 64–65, 144; specialized industries in, 68–70; progress in, 71–75, 77–79; weather in, 121–22, 124, 130; importance of, 317; population growth in, 332; pioneers of, 349–64

St. George Hall, 57–58

St. George Library Association, 62

St. George Stake, 73–74

St. George Tabernacle: construction of, 56, 57–58, 73; glass for, 147n25; Miles Romney injured at, 150; workers for, 168; celebration in, 192

St. George Temple: announcement and plans for, 80–84; impediments to, 83–86; site and location of, 87–90, 338–39; dedication of site, 90–93; groundbreaking of, 93–95; floors and rooms in, 226–28, 285–9; appearance and impact of, 244–47; purpose of, 263. *See also* Construction of St. George Temple

Stolensen, Soren, 182

Stone(s): for temple foundation, 100–103, 116–120, 125, 134–35; placement of last, 191; for windows, 219n5

Storm, 45–47, 269

Stout, Joseph Allen, 31

Stucki, John S., 23n13, 48–50, 59–60, 70

Stucki, Mary Ann, 60–61

Swiss immigrants, 27–28

Taylor, John: on St. George, 72; calls for workers, 148–49; on completion of temple, 245; on temple work, 261; on inspiration for St. George Temple, 263

Technology, 332
Telegraph line, 72
Temperatures, in St. George, 122, 124, 130
Temple Block, 242–43
Temple clothes, 251, 285, 316
Temple ordinances: restoration of, 1; importance of, 4–5, 249–50; St. George Saints and, 81; in St. George Temple, 226, 242; Joseph Smith and, 250–52; in Nauvoo Temple, 253–56; presentation of, 256–57; teachings on, 261–62; adjustments to, 284–85, 288–90; vision concerning, 321–22; motion pictures used in, 332, 335. *See also* Dead, salvation for
Temple records, 292–94, 324
Temples, gathering of Saints and, 7–8
Temple Trail, 183–96
Temple work: following Mormon exodus, 257–58; revelations concerning, 259–61; instructions for, 281–85; clarification on, 290n42; performed by Brigham Young, 291; recording, 292–94; performed by Wilford Woodruff, 294–95; for founding fathers, 303–10; reasons for participation in, 343–48
Terms of address, 74
Thayne, Will, 224
Thompson, Robert, 39
Thompson, William Henry, 195, 239–41
Timber. See Lumber
Tithes, 97–98, 106–7, 113, 130, 193, 243–44
Toilets, 105, 105n22, 226n28
Tonaquint, Utah, 46–47
Tongues, gift of, 209–10
Tower, of St. George Temple, 205–7, 318–21, 321n6
Trusses, 182–87, 184n2, 195
Trusteeship, 136–37
Tschang, Christian (Cristy), 330
Turner, Dave, 208, 210
Tutsegavit, Chief, 85, 85n17
Twelve Apostles, Joseph Smith teaches and prepares, 7–15, 250–53
Twiss, John Sanderson, 291, 294

Union Iron Company, 198, 198n5
United Order, 139, 154, 170, 175–77
Unity, 137–39, 297–98

Virgin River, 39–40, 52–54, 313
Vision(s): of St. George, 23; of temple construction worker, 131–33; of founding fathers, 303–11; of Brigham Young, 321–22. *See also* Revelation(s)
Visitors' center, 338–39
Volunteer workers, 126–28, 144, 149, 343

Waggle, Hannah, 54n26
Walker, Charles (Charlie): called to St. George, 33–34; on life in St. George, 62–64; on well, 71; on telegraph line, 72; faith of, 73; on government, 75; on St. George Temple announcement, 81–82; on temple site, 87; on stake conference, 89; on temple dedication, 90, 267–68; on Hosanna Shout, 95; on temple foundation, 103–4; on weather, 121–22; song written by, 122–24, 272; toasts given by, 124, 135; temple construction and, 130, 133, 150–51; on cornerstone ceremony, 142–43; on windows, 146; masonry work and, 204; on accident involving John Burt, 223–24; greets Brigham Young, 235; on temple grounds, 242–43; on Brigham Young, 258–59; on Brigham Young at temple dedication, 277
Walls: placement of, 145–49; problems with, 174; lath-and-plaster, 240n24
Washings and anointings, 6–7
Washington, George, 309–10n17
Water closets, 105, 105n22, 226n28
Water tower, 105
Weather, in St. George, 121, 124, 130
Weather vane, 205, 318–19, 341–42
Webb, Amelia Jarvis, 44, 59
Weeks, Shadrack, 111
Weggeland, Dan, 237–38
Welch, Thomas, 217–18, 227
Well, 71
Wells, Ann Eliza, 264n45
Wells, D. H., 296–97
Wesley, John, 309–10, 309–10n17
Weydler, George, 219–20
Whipple, Eli, 175
Whitehead, George F., 327
Whiting, Grandma, 315–16
Whitmore, Ann, 44
Wilson, Ephraim, 116

Wiltbank, Ett, 121

Wiltbank, Spencer, 111

Windows: construction and placement of, 146–48, 218n1, 219n5; glass for, 147n25; design and number of, 178–79; arches for, 215; swiveling, 239n22

Wine, 68–69, 192, 214–15n43

Winsor, Anson Parry, 110, 222–23

Winsor, Emeline Zanetta, 110

Winsor, Joseph, 110–11

Winter Home of Brigham Young, 267n53, 299, 299n22

Wittwer, Christian, 111

Women: sacrifice of, 132–33; as proxies, 289; temple work for eminent, 306, 306–7n11

Woodberry, Ann C., 70

Woodcarving, 217–19

Woodruff, Wilford: on endowment, 10; on Joseph Smith teaching Twelve, 13; inspects temple, 242, 264–65; on temple ceremonies, 256–57, 284–85; on ordinances for dead, 261–62; temple dedication and, 266, 268, 271, 297; on temple work for dead, 279–80; on temple attendance and ceremonies, 280–81; receives revelation of redemption of dead, 288–89; on Brigham Young and temple work, 291; calls Franklin Farnsworth as temple recorder, 292–93; performs temple work, 294–95; to preside over temple, 298; and temple work for founding fathers, 303–11, 309–10n17; and temple work for eminent women, 306–7n11; evades government deputies, 323

Word of Wisdom, 68

Young, Brigham: Salt Lake Temple and, 1–2, 88n24; Joseph Smith and, 2–3; on exaltation, 3–4; priesthood ordinances and, 4–5; Kirtland Temple and, 5–6; on temples and gathering of Saints, 8; priesthood authority conferred upon, 9, 13; on Joseph Smith teaching Twelve, 9–10; charged with temple ceremonies, 14; Mormon settlements and, 16–23; tours Southern Utah, 16–23; cliff

resembling, 21–22, 21n9; sees St. George in vision, 23, 23n13; urges forward St. George Temple, 25; sends settlers to St. George, 56; on St. George, 77–79; announces St. George Temple, 80–82; temple location and, 87–90; temple groundbreaking and, 93–94; on temple foundation, 99–100, 103; United Order and, 138–39; cornerstone ceremony and, 141–43; disagreement with Erastus Snow, 161; on temple construction, 169–70; on provisions for temple construction, 175–76; baptismal font and, 199–200, 156n7; George Laub and, 220; on deaths during temple construction, 224; Thomas Allman and, 230, 231–32, 234; involvement in temple construction, 233, 235–36; greeting for, 235; William Henry Thompson and, 240; inspects temple, 242; administers temple ordinances, 255–56; on endowment, 257–58n27; temple work and, 258–59, 347–48; and revelations concerning temple work, 259–60; on ordinances for dead, 262–63; calls John Daniel Thompson McAllister as temple worker, 263–64; tours temple, 264; office of, 267–68, 267n53; temple dedication and, 267, 272, 274–77; cane of, 276–77, 277nn16, 17; temple ceremonies and, 281–83; performs temple work, 291; improved health of, 295; on unity, 297–98; final trip to St. George of, 298–99; Winter Home of, 299, 299n22; death of, 300; ministry of, 317–18; and temple tower, 321n6; appears to John McAllister and David Cannon, 322

Young, Brigham Jr.: votes for St. George Temple, 80; inspects temple, 242, 264; temple dedication and, 271, 273–74; on temple attendance and ceremonies, 281–82; temple tower and, 321n6

Young, John W., 143–44, 185, 207–8, 279, 287

Young, Joseph T., 209

Young, Joseph W., 73, 94

Young, Lucy Bigelow, 129, 281, 285, 308